ADDISON WESLEY

Math
Makes Sense

6

Author Team

Peggy Morrow

Don Jones

Bryn Keyes

Steve Thomas

Nora Alexander

Cynthia Pratt Nicolson

Carole Saundry

Trevor Brown

Ralph Connelly

Michael Davis

Jason Johnston

Jeananne Thomas

Ray Appel

Linda Edwards

Ken Harper

Maggie Martin Connell

Sharon Jeroski

PEARSON
Addison
Wesley

Publishing Team
Enid Haley
Lesley Haynes
Lynne Gulliver
Susan Lishman
Sarah Mawson
Alison Rieger
Marg Bukta
Stephanie Cox
Kaari Turk
Judy Wilson
John Burnett

Publisher
Claire Burnett

Elementary Math Team Leader
Anne-Marie Scullion

Product Manager
Diane Wyman

Photo Research
Karen Hunter
Christina Beamish

Design
Word & Image Design Studio Inc.

ISBN 0-321-11823-5

Printed and bound in Canada.

11 12 13   16 15 14

The information and activities presented in this book have been carefully edited and reviewed. However, the publisher shall not be liable for any damages resulting, in whole or in part, from the reader's use of this material.

Brand names that appear in photographs of products in this textbook are intended to provide students with a sense of the real-world applications of mathematics and are in no way intended to endorse specific products.

The publisher wishes to thank the staff and students of
    Blake Street Junior Public School
    Pape Avenue Junior Public School
    Westwood Middle School
    Wilkinson Junior Public School
for their assisstance with photography.

PEARSON
Addison
Wesley

Program Consultants and Advisers

Program Consultants

Craig Featherstone
Maggie Martin Connell
Trevor Brown

Assessment Consultant
Sharon Jeroski

Elementary Mathematics Adviser
John A. Van de Walle

Program Advisers

Pearson Education thanks its Program Advisers, who helped shape the vision for *Addison Wesley Math Makes Sense* through discussions and reviews of prototype materials and manuscript.

Anthony Azzopardi
Sandra Ball
Victoria Barlow
Lorraine Baron
Bob Belcher
Judy Blake
Steve Cairns
Christina Chambers
Daryl M.J. Chichak
Lynda Colgan
Marg Craig
Jennifer Gardner
Florence Glanfield
Linden Gray
Pamela Hagen
Dennis Hamaguchi
Angie Harding
Andrea Helmer

Peggy Hill
Auriana Kowalchuk
Gordon Li
Werner Liedtke
Jodi Mackie
Lois Marchand
Betty Milne
Cathy Molinski
Bill Nimigon
Stephen Parks
Eileen Phillips
Evelyn Sawicki
Leyton Schnellert
Shannon Sharp
Michelle Skene
Lynn Strangway
Mignonne Wood

Program Reviewers

Field Testers

Pearson Education would like to thank the teachers and students who field-tested *Addison Wesley Math Makes Sense* prior to publication. Their feedback and constructive recommendations have been most valuable in helping us to develop a quality mathematics program.

Aboriginal Content Reviewers

Early Childhood and School Services Division
Department of Education, Culture, and Employment
Government of Northwest Territories:

Steven Daniel, Coordinator, Mathematics, Science, and Secondary Education
Liz Fowler, Coordinator, Culture Based Education
Margaret Erasmus, Coordinator, Aboriginal Languages

Grade 6 Reviewers

Emi Bakaic
Dufferin-Peel Catholic District
School Board, ON

L. Peggy Bergmann
St. Albert School District No. 6, AB

Richard Bridges
Calgary Board of Education, AB

Catherine Robinson Buyukozer
York Region District School Board,
ON

Margo Cahn
Edmonton Public Schools, AB

Mirella Cristello
Edmonton Catholic School Board,
AB

Mary Cuylle
Peel District School Board, ON

Betty Fancy
Durham District School Board, ON

Bev Ferner
Moose Jaw (Public) School Div. No. 1,
SK

Dennis Giesbrecht
School District 36 (Surrey), BC

Katherine L. Hunter
Peel District School Board, ON

Robert W. Kay
Limestone District School Board, ON

Carla Kozak
Edmonton Public Schools, AB

Karen Letwin
Edmonton Catholic Schools, AB

Anthony Levy
Toronto District School Board, ON

Catherine Lord
Peel Board of Education, ON

David MacLean
School District #43 (Coquitlam), BC

Rob Madunicky
Edmonton Catholic Schools, AB

Jason Mann
Greater Essex County District School
Board, ON

Kim Meyers
Thames Valley District School Board,
ON

Mary Middleton
Greater Essex County District School
Board, ON

James Moreau
Simcoe Muskoka Catholic District
School Board, ON

Carol Ann Myronuk
Vancouver School Board, BC

Denise Oliver
Toronto District School Board, ON

Jennifer Paziuk
Halton District School Board, ON

Alison Pikula
Brant Haldimand-Norfolk Catholic
District School Board, ON

Kathryn Scheurwater
Calgary Public School Board, AB

Ann Marie Slak
Dufferin-Peel Catholic District
School Board, ON

Debbie Sprentz
Hamilton-Wentworth District School
Board, ON

Nancy Stavert
Toronto District School Board, ON

Mariella Stradiotto
Wellington Catholic District School
Board, ON

Don Wood
Hamilton-Wentworth District School
Board, ON

Jonathan Young
Toronto District School Board, ON

Table of Contents

v

UNIT 6 Measurement

UNIT 7 Transformational Geometry

Welcome to
Addison Wesley Math Makes Sense 6

Math helps you to understand what you see and do every day.

You will use this book to learn about the math around you. Here's how.

In each Unit:

- A scene from the world around you reminds you of some of the math you already know.

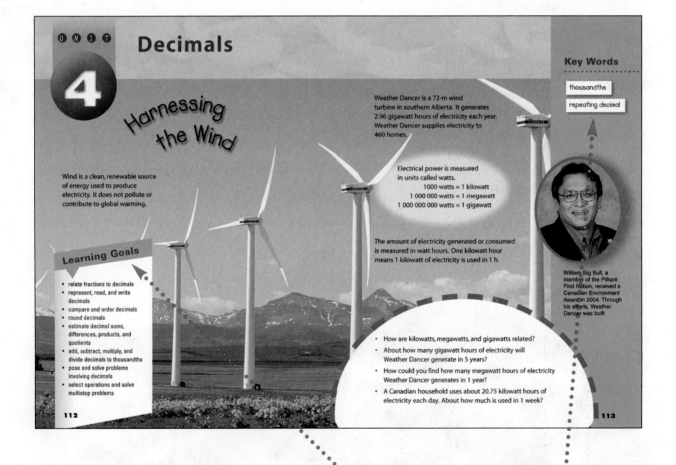

UNIT 4

Decimals

Harnessing the Wind

Wind is a clean, renewable source of energy used to produce electricity. It does not pollute or contribute to global warming.

Learning Goals

- relate fractions to decimals
- represent, read, and write decimals
- compare and order decimals
- round decimals
- estimate decimal sums, differences, products, and quotients
- add, subtract, multiply, and divide decimals to thousandths
- pose and solve problems involving decimals
- select operations and solve multistep problems

Weather Dancer is a 72-m wind turbine in southern Alberta. It generates 2.96 gigawatt hours of electricity each year. Weather Dancer supplies electricity to 460 homes.

Electrical power is measured in units called watts.

1000 watts = 1 kilowatt
1 000 000 watts = 1 megawatt
1 000 000 000 watts = 1 gigawatt

The amount of electricity generated or consumed is measured in watt hours. One kilowatt hour means 1 kilowatt of electricity is used in 1 h.

- How are kilowatts, megawatts, and gigawatts related?
- About how many gigawatt hours of electricity will Weather Dancer generate in 5 years?
- How could you find how many megawatt hours of electricity Weather Dancer generates in 1 year?
- A Canadian household uses about 20.75 kilowatt hours of electricity each day. About how much is used in 1 week?

Key Words

thousandths

repeating decimal

William Big Bull, a member of the Piikani First Nation, received a Canadian Environment Award in 2004. Through his efforts, Weather Dancer was built.

112   113

Find out what you will learn in the **Learning Goals** and important **Key Words**.

In each Lesson:

You **Explore** an idea or problem, usually with a partner. You often use materials.

Then you **Show and Share** your results with other students.

Practice questions help you to use and remember the math.

reminds you to use pictures, words, or numbers in your answers.

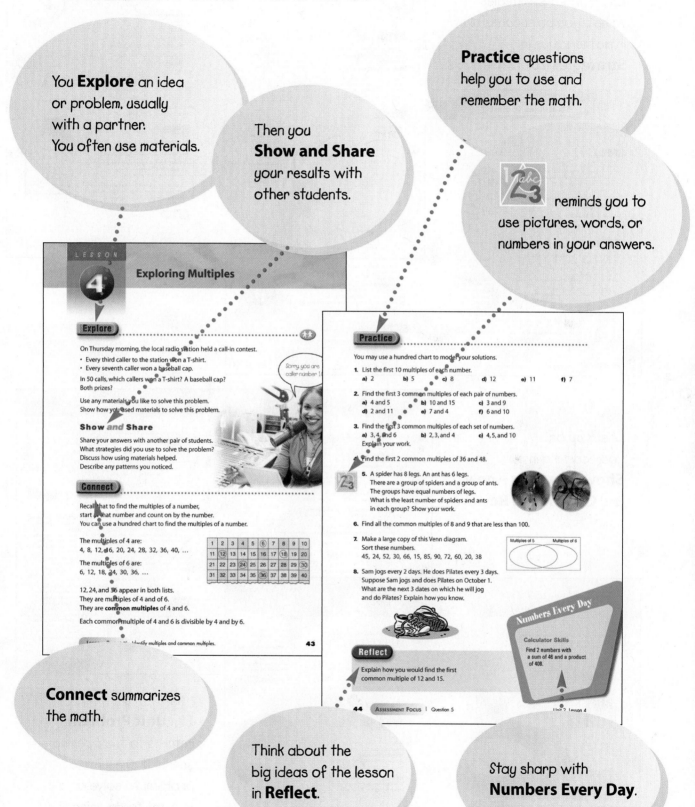

Connect summarizes the math.

Think about the big ideas of the lesson in **Reflect**.

Stay sharp with **Numbers Every Day**.

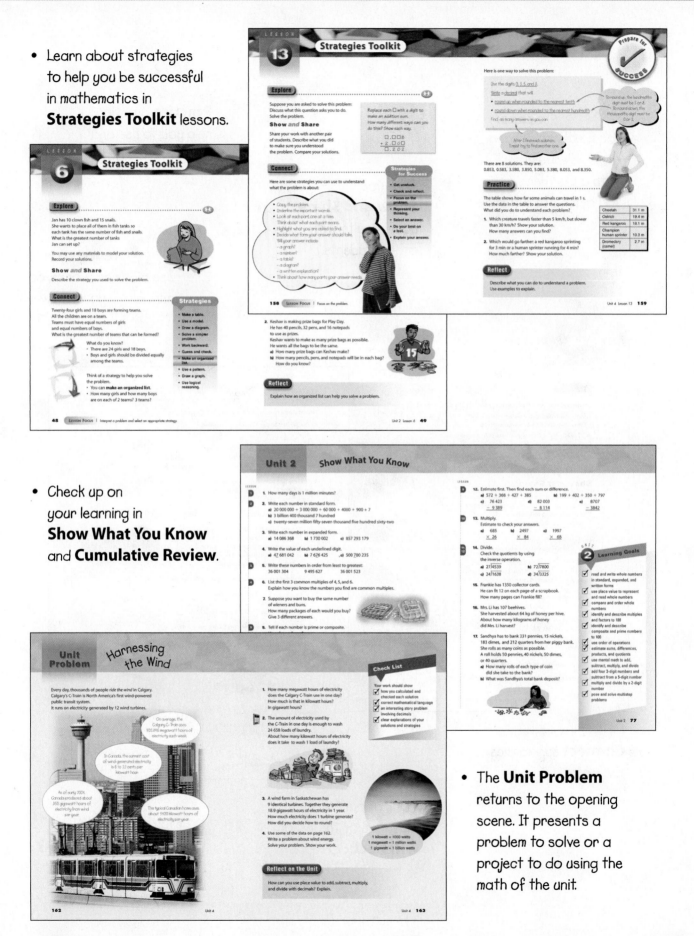

- Learn about strategies to help you be successful in mathematics in **Strategies Toolkit** lessons.

- Check up on your learning in **Show What You Know** and **Cumulative Review**.

- The **Unit Problem** returns to the opening scene. It presents a problem to solve or a project to do using the math of the unit.

Explore some interesting math when you do the **Investigations**.

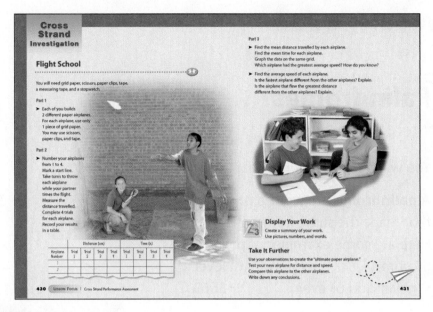

Use **Technology**.
Follow the step-by-step instructions for using a calculator or computer to do math.

Look for  and .

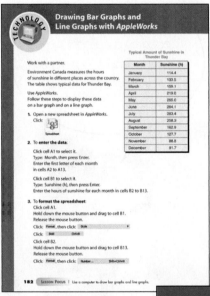

You will see **World of Work** and **Games** pages.

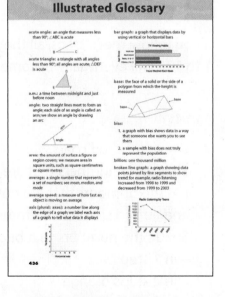

The **Glossary** is an illustrated dictionary of important math words.

Cross Strand Investigation

Palindromes

· ·

You will need a hundred chart and coloured pencils.

A **palindrome** is a word, a phrase, or a number
that reads the same from both directions.
Here are some examples of palindromes:
- mom
- never odd or even
- level
- 3663

Many numbers, such as 7, 11, and 232, are palindromes.
If a number is not a palindrome, follow these steps
to make it a palindrome:

Reverse the digits.   67
Add the reverse number to   + 76
the original number.   143

Continue to reverse and add   143
until the sum is a palindrome.   + 341
                                      484

Sixty-seven becomes a palindrome in 2 steps. I had to reverse the digits and add two times.

If you follow these steps, all the numbers from
1 to 100 will eventually become palindromes.

Part 1

➤ Use a hundred chart.
   Shade the numbers that are palindromes yellow.
   For the numbers that are not palindromes, reverse the digits
   and add to make palindromes.
   Shade the numbers that become palindromes:
   – in 1 step blue
   – in 2 steps orange
   – in 3 steps green
   – in 4 steps red
   – in more than 4 steps purple

➤ How are the numbers that became palindromes in 1 step related?
In 2 steps? In 3 steps? In 4 steps?
Describe any patterns you found.

Part 2

➤ A decimal such as 63.36 is a palindrome.
Why is a decimal such as 8.48 not a palindrome?

➤ Use the method from Part 1 to make palindrome decimals
from these decimals.
7.1   6.5   4.7   3.65   4.81
How do the results for 6.5 and 4.7 compare to the results
for 65 and 47?

Display Your Work

Create a summary of your work.
Use pictures, numbers, and words.

Take It Further

The years 1991 and 2002 are palindromes.
They are 11 years apart.
What is the next pair of palindrome years
that are 11 years apart? What was the previous pair?
How far apart are palindrome years usually?

Number Patterns

Crack the Code!

Learning Goals

- write a pattern rule for a number pattern
- identify, extend, and create patterns
- use patterns to pose and solve problems
- use patterns to explore divisibility rules

Guglielmo Marconi received the first transatlantic wireless communication on December 12, 1901.
Morse code for the letter "s" was sent from Poldhu, Cornwall to Signal Hill, St. John's Newfoundland

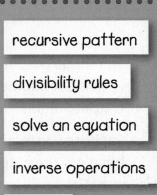

One early reason to code messages was to be able to communicate without using a spoken language.

Morse code was developed by Samuel Morse almost 175 years ago.
It uses dots and dashes to represent letters, numbers, and punctuation.

Number	International Morse Code
0	– – – – –
1	• – – – –
2	• • – – –
3	• • • – –
4	• • • • –
5	• • • • •
6	– • • • •
7	– – • • •
8	– – – • •
9	– – – – •

- What other reasons might there be to code a message?
- What patterns do you see in the Morse code for numbers?
- How would you write the number 503 in Morse code?

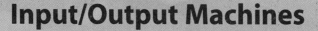

Input/Output Machines

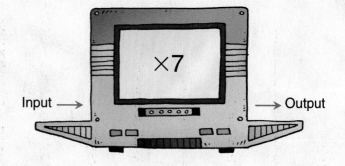

This Input/Output machine multiplies
each input number by 7.
Output numbers are multiples of 7.

Suppose you input 9.
What will the output be?

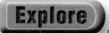

➤ Sketch an Input/Output machine like this one.

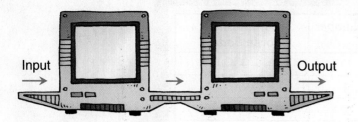

Choose a number and an operation
to go in the first part of the machine.
Choose a different number and a different
operation to go in the second part of the machine.

➤ Use the numbers 1 to 5 as input.
Find the output for each input number.
Record the input and output in a table.

➤ Write the pattern rule for the output numbers.
Describe how each output number is related to its input number.

Show *and* Share

Share your work with another pair of classmates.
Find the next 3 output numbers for
your classmates' Input/Output machine.

➤ This Input/Output machine doubles each input, then adds 6.
When the input is 1, the output is 8.
When the input is 4, the output is 14.

Input ×2 +6 Output

Input	Output
1	8
2	10
3	12
4	14

When each input goes up by 1, the output goes up by 2.

The pattern rule for the output is:

Start at 8. Add 2 each time.

➤ The table shows the input and output for this machine.
Identify the numbers and operations in the machine.

Input	Output
1	1
2	4
3	7
4	10
5	13

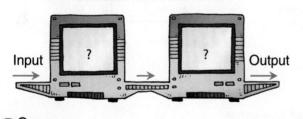

Input ? ? Output

Think:

The pattern rule for the output is:

Start at 1. Add 3 each time.
This suggests that the input numbers are multiplied by 3.

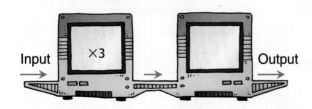

Input ×3 Output

The output goes up by 3. The inputs must be multiplied by 3.

Look at the input 2. Multiply by 3.

$2 \times 3 = 6$

But, the output is 4.

Think of the number and operation that would go into the second part of the machine. Try −2.

$6 - 2 = 4$

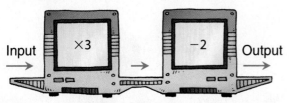

Input → ×3 → −2 Output →

This Input/Output machine multiplies each input by 3, then subtracts 2.

Practice

1. Copy and complete the table for each Input/Output machine.

   a)
   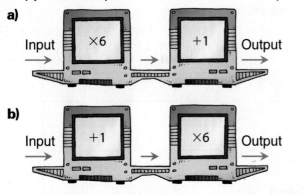

   Input → ×6 → +1 Output →

   b)

   Input → +1 → ×6 Output →

Input	Output
1	
2	
3	
4	
5	

2. Look at question 1 and your tables.
   a) How are the Input/Output machines the same? How are they different?
   b) How do the output numbers from the two machines compare?
   c) Is it possible to get more than one output number for each input? How do you know?

3. Copy and complete the table for this Input/Output machine.

   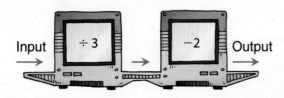

   Input → ÷3 → −2 Output →

Input	Output
30	
60	
90	
120	
150	

4. An Input/Output machine follows these steps:
Divide by 6, then add 5.
Check the data in the Input/Output table.
Identify any output numbers that are incorrect.
How do you know they are incorrect?
Show your work.

Input	Output
6	6
12	7
30	10
42	2
54	15

5. The table shows the input and output from a machine with two operations.
   a) Identify the numbers and the operations in the Input/Output machine.
   b) Choose four different input numbers. Find the output for each input.

Input	Output
1	5
2	9
3	13
4	17
5	21
6	25

6. Repeat question 5 for this Input/Output table.

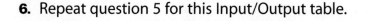

Input	Output
5	4
10	5
15	6
20	7
25	8
30	9

7. **a)** Draw an Input/Output machine with two operations.
   Choose two numbers and two operations for your machine.
   b) Choose five input numbers.
   Find the output numbers.
   c) Erase the input numbers.
   Trade tables with a classmate.
   Find your classmate's input numbers.

Reflect

When you look at an Input/Output table, what strategies do you use to identify the numbers and operations in the machine?

Numbers Every Day

Calculator Skills

Suppose the 5 key on your calculator is broken.
How can you find each result?

225×14

$10.5 - 3.2$

Number Patterns

Here are some number patterns.

- 99, 88, 77, 66, 55, …
- 10, 6, 11, 7, 12, …
- 1, 10, 12, 120, 122, 1220, 1222, …

How would you find each pattern rule?

Explore

➤ Write a pattern rule for each number pattern.
Write the next 3 terms. Use a calculator if it helps.
  - 1, 5, 13, 29, 61, …
  - 3, 10, 31, 94, 283, …
  - 300, 298, 296, 294, 292, …

➤ Make up a similar pattern.
Write the first 6 terms of your pattern. Write the pattern rule.

Show and Share

Trade patterns with another pair of classmates.
Identify your classmates' pattern rule.

Connect

Many number patterns you have explored are recursive.
In a **recursive pattern**, each term can be found by applying
the pattern rule to the previous term.

➤ Write the first 5 terms for a recursive pattern that starts at 7.

A pattern rule is:

Start at 7. Multiply by 2, then add 1 each time.

$7 \times 2 + 1 = 15$ $15 \times 2 + 1 = 31$ $31 \times 2 + 1 = 63$ $63 \times 2 + 1 = 127$

The first 5 terms of the pattern are: 7, 15, 31, 63, 127

LESSON FOCUS I Identify, extend, and create number patterns.

➤ Here is a recursive number pattern:
1, 6, 11, 16, 21, …

To find the pattern rule, find the difference between each pair of consecutive terms.

1 6 11 16 21
$6 - 1 = 5$ $11 - 6 = 5$ $16 - 11 = 5$ $21 - 16 = 5$

The difference between each term and the previous term is 5.

The pattern rule is:

Start at 1. Add 5 each time.

To extend the pattern, continue to add 5.
$21 + 5 = 26$ $26 + 5 = 31$
The next 2 terms are 26 and 31.

➤ Here is another recursive number pattern.
6, 13, 34, 97, 286, …

To find the pattern rule, find the difference between each pair of consecutive terms.

6 13 34 97 286
$13 - 6 = 7$ $34 - 13 = 21$ $97 - 34 = 63$ $286 - 97 = 189$

Each difference is triple the previous difference.
This suggests that $\times 3$ is part of the pattern rule.

Look at the first term, 6.
$3 \times 6 = 18$
The second term is 13.
Subtract 5 from 18 to get 13.
$18 - 5 = 13$

The pattern rule is:

Start at 6. Multiply by 3, then subtract 5 each time.

To extend the pattern, continue to multiply by 3, then subtract 5.
$286 \times 3 - 5 = 853$ $853 \times 3 - 5 = 2554$
The next 2 terms are 853 and 2554.

The difference between each pair of consecutive terms is 5. Add 5 to each term to find the next term.

I notice a pattern in the differences:
$7 \times 3 = 21$
$21 \times 3 = 63$
$63 \times 3 = 189$

I check that the rule works for each term.

Practice

You may use a calculator when it helps to find the pattern rule.

1. Write the first 6 terms of each pattern.
   Start at 10 each time.
   a) Multiply by 2, then subtract 5 each time.
   b) Multiply by 5, then subtract 2 each time.
   c) Subtract 5, then multiply by 2 each time.
   d) Subtract 2, then multiply by 5 each time.

2. Look at your patterns from question 1.
   How are the patterns the same? How are they different?

3. Identify each pattern rule.
   Then write the next 2 terms. Find the 10th term.
   a) 2, 4, 10, 28, 82, …   b) 250, 230, 210, 190, 170, …
   c) 3, 4, 6, 10, 18, …   d) 2, 5, 11, 23, 47, …

4. Which of these patterns are recursive?
   How do you know?
   a) 3, 6, 12, 24, 48, 96, …
   b) 1, 4, 9, 16, 25, 36, …
   c) 1, 3, 9, 27, 81, 243, …
   d) 4, 9, 19, 39, 79, 159, …

5. How many different recursive patterns
   can you find with 4 and 7 as the first 2 terms?
   Write the first 5 terms of each pattern,
   then write the pattern rule.

6. Copy and find the missing number.
   Find each pattern rule. Then find the 8th term.
   a) 5, 12, 26, □, 110, 222, …
   b) 300, 281, 262, □, 224, 205, …

Reflect

Describe how to identify the pattern rule for a recursive pattern.
Use examples to explain.

Your World

You can estimate how far away a thunderstorm is.
Count the seconds between seeing the lightning and hearing the thunder.
Divide the number of seconds by 3.
The result is the approximate distance in kilometres.

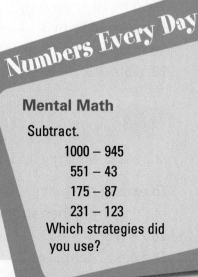

Numbers Every Day

Mental Math

Subtract.
    1000 − 945
    551 − 43
    175 − 87
    231 − 123
Which strategies did you use?

Patterns in Division

Which of these numbers are divisible by 2? How do you know?

- 64
- 309
- 8200
- 105
- 21
- 4164
- 72
- 9974

In this lesson, you will explore ways to tell if a whole number is divisible by different numbers.

 **Explore** •

You will need a calculator.

➤ Choose 15 consecutive 2-digit numbers.
Divide each number by 3.
Record a division sentence each time.
Repeat for 15 consecutive 3-digit numbers.

List the numbers that were divisible by 3.
Find the sum of the digits of each number.
What do you notice?

> The numbers that are divisible by 3 are multiples of 3.

Choose 4 different numbers you think are divisible by 3.
Divide each number by 3 to check.

➤ List the first 35 multiples of 4.
List all the multiples of 4 between 200 and 240.
List all the multiples of 4 between 500 and 540.
What do you notice about all the multiples of 4?

> Remember, every multiple of 4 is divisible by 4.

Choose 4 different numbers you think are divisible by 4.
Divide each number by 4 to check.

Show *and* Share

Share your work with another pair of students.
How did you choose 4 numbers that were divisible by 3? By 4?
Without dividing, how can you tell if a number is divisible by 3? By 4?

LESSON FOCUS | Use patterns to explore divisibility rules.

13

You can use patterns to find **divisibility rules** for different numbers.

➤ Here are some multiples of 5.
5, 10, 15, 20, 25, 30, 35, ..., 150, 155, 160, ...
The ones digits form a repeating pattern.
The core of the pattern is: 5, 0

> Every multiple of 5 has a ones digit of 0 or 5. A multiple of 5 is divisible by 5.

➤ This Venn diagram shows numbers that are divisible by 2 and by 3.

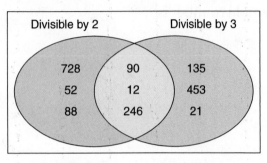

Divisible by 2   Divisible by 3

728   90   135
52   12   453
88   246   21

> A number that is divisible both by 2 and by 3 is also divisible by 6.

The numbers in the overlapping region are divisible both by 2 and by 3.
These numbers are also divisible by 6.

➤ One thousand is divisible by 8.
So multiples of 1000 are divisible by 8.

> $1000 \div 8 = 125$

For any whole number with 4 or more digits,
we only need to check the last 3 digits.
For 12 480: $480 \div 8 = 60$
The last 3 digits are divisible by 8, so 12 480 is divisible by 8.

Divisibility Rules
A whole number is divisible by:
2 if the number is even
3 if the sum of the digits is divisible by 3
4 if the number represented by the tens and ones digits is divisible by 4
5 if the ones digit is 0 or 5
6 if the number is divisible by 2 and by 3

8 if the number represented by the hundreds, tens, and ones digits is divisible by 8
9 if the sum of the digits is divisible by 9
10 if the ones digit is 0

1. Which numbers are divisible by 3? By 4?
   How do you know?
   a) 432   **b)** 2452   **c)** 3315
   d) 105   **e)** 228   **f)** 3138

2. Explain why a number with 0 in the ones place is divisible by 10.

3. List 20 multiples of 9.
   Use the multiples to justify the divisibility rule for 9.

4. Which numbers are divisible by 6? By 9?
   How do you know?
   a) 150   **b)** 1197   **c)** 23 598
   d) 498   **e)** 594   **f)** 568

5. Write 3 numbers that are divisible by 6.
   How did you choose the numbers?

6. Draw a Venn diagram with 3 loops.
   Label the loops: "Divisible by 2," "Divisible by 4," and "Divisible by 8"
   a) Explain why you drew the loops the way you did.
   b) Sort these numbers.

1046	322	460	1784	28
54	1088	224	382	3662

   How did you decide where to place each number?
   c) Find and insert 3 more 4-digit numbers in the Venn diagram.

7. A student uses this trick to check if a 3-digit number is divisible by 7:
   • Remove, then double, the last digit.
   • Subtract this number from the remaining digits.
   • If the difference is divisible by 7,
     the number is also.
   Does the trick work? Use examples to explain.

Reflect

Choose a 4-digit number.
Show how you find which numbers from 2 to 9
it is divisible by.

Numbers Every Day

Number Strategies
Find each product.
25×300
50×120
60×70
13×21

Solving Equations

An equation is a statement that two things are equal.
Which of these are equations?

$5 + 8 = 13$ $7 \times 3 = 21$ $4 + 9 - 7$

$19 = 25 - 6$ $42 - 21 + 18$ $63 \div 7 = 3 \times 3$

 ●● 🚶🚶 Game

What's My Number?

You will need a tetrahedron numbered 1 to 4
and 2 colours of counters.
Your teacher will give you a game board.

Each square on the game board has
an equation with one number missing.

➤ Take turns to roll the tetrahedron 2 times.
The first roll tells which row to look at
on your game board.
The second roll tells which column.

➤ On your turn, find the missing number
in the equation.
Record your work.
Your partner checks your answer.
If your answer is correct,
cover the square with a counter.
If your answer is not correct,
your partner can try.
If she is correct, she covers the square
with her counter.
If the square is already covered
with a counter, roll again.

The face the tetrahedron
lands on gives the number of
the row or column.

➤ The first player to cover the squares in one row,
column, or diagonal is the winner.

Show *and* Share

Compare answers with another pair of classmates.
Talk about the strategies you used to find the missing numbers.

Here are some different ways to find the missing number
in an equation.

➤ Use guess and check.
  Find the missing number.
  $163 = \square + 49$

  Guess 100: $100 + 49 = 149$
  This sum is too low.

  Guess 115: $115 + 49 = 164$
  This sum is 1 more than it should be.

  Guess 114: $114 + 49 = 163$

  The missing number is 114.

> When we find the value of a missing number in an equation, we **solve the equation.**

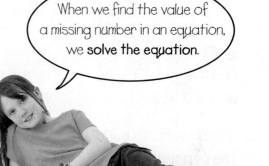

➤ Use the inverse operation.
  Solve this equation.
  $\square \div 6 = 144$

  Think multiplication.
  The number that is divided by 6 to get 144 is: $144 \times 6 = 864$

  So, $864 \div 6 = 144$

  The solution is 864.

> Multiplication and division are **inverse operations.** Addition and subtraction are also inverse operations.

1. Copy each equation.
   Find the missing number.
   a) $\square - 26 = 15$ b) $378 = 9 \times \square$ c) $74 + \square = 216$
   d) $354 \div \square = 6$ e) $16 = 37 - \square$ f) $\square + 87 = 142$

2. Copy this equation: $\square \times \triangle = 36$
   Replace each $\square$ and $\triangle$ with a number to make an equation.
   How many different ways can you do this?
   Record each way.

3. Solve each equation.
   a) $\square - 3 = 10 - 4$ b) $7 + 2 = 5 + \square$
   c) $10 + 4 = \square + 2$ d) $8 - \square = 6 - 2$
   e) $4 \times 3 = 2 \times \square$ f) $\square \times 10 = 8 \times 5$

4. Briana wants to build a rectangular pen with area 176 m^2.
   The pen must be 16 m long.
   a) What will the width of the pen be?
   b) Write an equation to model this problem.

5. Copy each equation.
   Find the missing numbers.
   How did you choose the numbers?
   Show your work.
   a) $\square - \triangle = 7 - 4$ b) $5 + 3 = \square + \triangle$
   c) $16 \times 3 = \square \times \triangle$ d) $8 - 6 = \square - \triangle$

6. Two sides of a triangle are 7 cm and 13 cm long.
   The perimeter of the triangle is 30 cm.
   a) Write an equation that models this problem.
   b) What is the length of the third side?

Reflect

What strategies can you use to find the value
of a missing number in an equation?
Use examples to explain.

Numbers Every Day

Mental Math

Add.
Which strategies did
you use?

$1289 + 2025$

$4104 + 5222$

Fraud Investigator

Hundreds of millions of financial transactions happen every day. Some dishonest people take advantage of those huge numbers to hide their theft. How do fraud investigators find the few thieves hiding among the millions of transactions?

In the 1920s and 1930s, Frank Benford, a scientist, studied the first four digits of thousands of numbers he came across in everyday life. He found that for every 100 numbers, 31 had a 1 as the first digit, 19 had a 2, and only 5 had a 9. His research led to the theory Benford's Law. Recently, investigators have been using Benford's Law to detect fraud.

When people commit fraud, they often change or invent numbers on cheques and other financial documents. Investigators looking for fraud examine all amounts on cheques. They use software to track how often the numbers in the first digits of the amounts appear on the cheques. When there is fraud, some numbers appear in the first-digit position more often than they should according to Benford's Law. That points investigators to transactions that should be examined in greater detail.

Those who cheat and steal using numbers can also get caught by those very same numbers!

Exploring Integers

Temperature is measured in degrees Celsius (°C).
Water freezes at 0°C.

On a typical summer day in Saskatoon, the temperature might be 24 degrees Celsius above zero.

On a typical winter day in Saskatoon, the temperature might be 18 degrees Celsius below zero.

A temperature greater than 0°C is positive.
We write: 24°C
We say: twenty-four degrees Celsius

A temperature less than 0°C is negative.
We write: −18°C
We say: minus eighteen degrees Celsius

Explore

Altitude is the vertical distance above sea level.
It is usually measured in metres.
For every 150 m above sea level, the temperature decreases about 1°C.

Kayla and Sydney are mountain climbing.
They begin climbing at an altitude of 1000 m.
The temperature is 6°C.
The table shows the altitude changes.

Altitude (m)	Temperature (°C)
1000	6
1300	
1600	

➤ Copy and continue the table for altitudes up to 2500 m. Find each temperature.

➤ Write a pattern rule for the altitudes.
Write a pattern rule for the temperatures.

Show *and* Share

Share your patterns with another pair of students. Estimate the altitude at which the temperature drops below 0°C.

Connect

Numbers such as 24 and −18 are **integers**.

➤ You can represent integers on a number line. The number line may be vertical or horizontal.

A thermometer is a vertical number line.

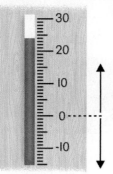

The thermometer shows 24°C.

You have used horizontal number lines to compare and order whole numbers. We extend the number line to the left of 0 to show negative numbers.

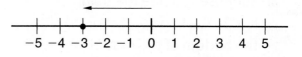

The arrow on the number line represents −3.

➤ We use integers to represent quantities that have both size and direction.
  • Mark spent $25.
    This can be represented as −$25.

  • Jane walked 5 steps forward.
    This can be represented as +5 steps, or 5 steps.

  • A scuba diver swam to a depth of 50 m.
    This can be represented as −50 m.

If no sign is written, the integer is positive.

1. Write an integer to represent each situation.
   a) Sascha dug a hole 1 m deep.
   b) Vincent deposited $50 in his bank account.
   c) A plane flies at an altitude of 11 000 m.
   d) A submarine travels at a depth of 400 m.

2. Describe a situation that could be represented by each integer.
   a) +125   b) −22   c) −900   d) +42 000   e) +4

3. The Brienzer-Rothorn Railway is in Brienz, Switzerland. It has a steam-powered cogwheel train. It takes passengers from an altitude of 566 m to an altitude of 2244 m on the Rothorn mountain.

   a) Suppose you ride the train. It is 23°C when you get on at the bottom of the mountain. Predict the temperature at the top of the mountain.
   b) Now suppose it is 9°C at the bottom of the mountain. Will the temperature be above or below 0°C at the top of the mountain? How do you know?

4. The speed with which a snowy tree cricket chirps depends on the temperature. To estimate the temperature in degrees Celsius:
   • Count the number of chirps in 15 s.
   • Multiply by 0.45.
   • Add 10.
   Estimate the temperature for each number of chirps in 15 s.
   a) 17 chirps   b) 12 chirps
   c) 30 chirps   d) 37 chirps

At Home

Reflect

How do integers help to describe quantities with size and direction? Use examples to explain.

Describe 2 situations in which you might use integers at home.

Equation Baseball

You will need a number cube, a set of Equation Baseball cards, one game board, and different coloured game pieces.

Each game card is marked with a circled number to indicate how many bases you move for a correct answer.
Each time a player crosses home plate on the way around the board, one run is awarded.

➤ Shuffle the equation cards.
  Place them face down in the middle of the game board.
  Each player places a game piece on home plate.
➤ Each player rolls the number cube.
  The player with the greatest number goes first.
  Play moves in a clockwise direction.
➤ The player turns over the top card for everyone to see.
  She solves the equation. The other players check the answer.
  If the answer is correct, she moves the number of bases
  indicated by the circled number on the card and places the card
  in the discard pile.
  If the answer is incorrect, the card is placed in the discard pile.
➤ The next player has a turn.
➤ The player with the most runs when all cards have been used wins.

Strategies Toolkit

Explore

Yulia started to solve this problem.
She looked at the first equation.
She knows $2 + 6 = 8$.
Yulia guessed that $\square = 2$
and $\triangle = 6$.
So, in the second equation, $\bigcirc = 12$.

$$\square + \triangle = 8$$
$$\triangle + \triangle = \bigcirc$$
$$\triangle + \square + \bigcirc = 14$$

When Yulia checked the numbers in the
third equation, the sum was 20, not 14.
Yulia was stuck.
Make some suggestions to help Yulia get unstuck.
Solve the problem.

Show *and* Share

Share your work with another pair of students.
Compare the strategies you used to solve the problem.

Connect

Here are some strategies you can use
if you are stuck on a math problem.

**Represent the information
in another way.**

For example:
• Rewrite the question in your own words.
• Reorganize the information.
• Draw a diagram or use a table.

Strategies for Success

• **Get unstuck.**

• **Check and reflect.**

• **Focus on the problem.**

• **Represent your thinking.**

• **Select an answer.**

• **Do your best on a test.**

• **Explain your answer.**

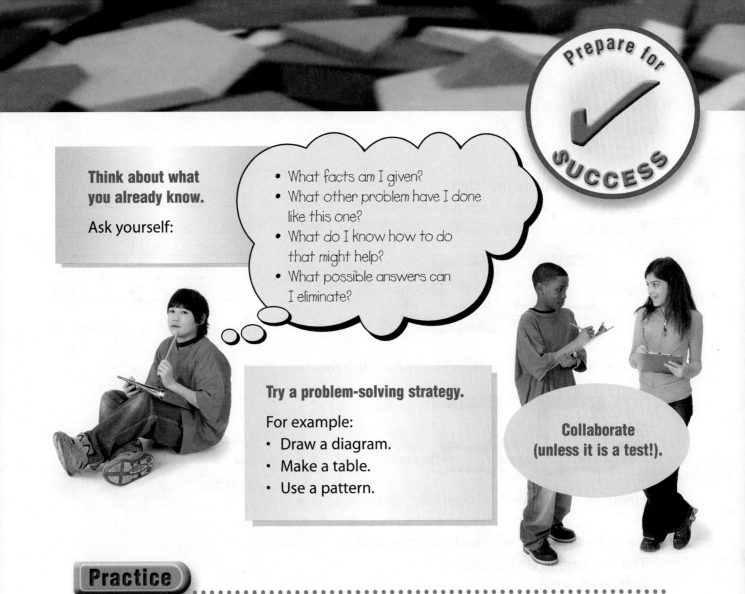

Think about what you already know.

Ask yourself:

- What facts am I given?
- What other problem have I done like this one?
- What do I know how to do that might help?
- What possible answers can I eliminate?

Try a problem-solving strategy.

For example:
- Draw a diagram.
- Make a table.
- Use a pattern.

Collaborate (unless it is a test!).

Prepare for SUCCESS

Practice

1. Write the next three terms in this number pattern.
   What is changing each time? Explain.
   1, 3, 5, 9, 15, 25, …

2. In these equations, each figure represents a different number.
   Find the number each figure represents.

   $\triangle - \bigcirc = 4$

   $\bigcirc + \bigcirc = \triangle$

   $\triangle + \square + \bigcirc = 17$

Reflect

Think of a math problem you had trouble solving.
Describe the strategies you used to get unstuck.

LESSON

1

1. Copy and complete the table
   for this Input/Output machine.
   Extend the table for 3 more rows.

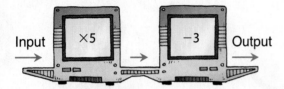

Input	Output
1	
2	
3	
4	
5	

2. The table shows the input and output for this machine.

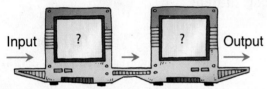

   Identify the numbers and operations in the machine.

Input	Output
2	2
3	5
4	8
5	11
6	14

2

3. Write the first 5 terms of each number pattern.
   The first term in each pattern is 7.
   a) Add 4 each time.
   b) Multiply by 3 each time.
   c) Multiply by 3, then subtract 2 each time.
   d) Multiply by 2, then add 1 each time.

4. Write the next 2 terms in each pattern.
   Write each pattern rule. Then write the 9th term.
   a) 5, 14, 22, 29, …   b) 470, 445, 420, 395, …
   c) 3, 5, 9, 17, …   d) 1, 2, 5, 14, …

5. Which of these patterns are recursive?
   Explain how you know.
   a) 1, 11, 111, 1111, 11 111, …   b) 1, 11, 21, 31, 41, …
   c) 1, 11, 20, 30, 39, …   d) 1, 11, 31, 71, 151, …

6. a) Write a recursive pattern that has 2 and 9 as the first 2 terms.
   b) Write the first 6 terms of the pattern, then write the pattern rule.

3

7. Which of these numbers are divisible by 5? By 8?
How do you know?
a) 12 680   b) 9185   c) 776
d) 9709   e) 67 200   f) 8210

8. Draw a Venn diagram with 2 loops.
Label the loops "Divisible by 6," and "Divisible by 9."
a) Should the loops overlap? Explain.
b) Write these numbers in the Venn diagram.

     330   639   5598   10 217
     2295   858   187   12 006

How did you know where to put each number?

9. For each question below:
If your answer is yes, write the number.
If your answer is no, explain why you cannot write a number.
a) Can you write a number that is divisible by 3 but not divisible by 6?
b) Can you write a number that is divisible by 6 but not divisible by 3?

4

10. Use guess and check to solve each equation.
Show your work.
a) $156 - \square = 27$ b) $529 = \square + 407$
c) $73 = 438 \div \square$ d) $108 = \square \times 27$

11. Copy each equation.
Find each missing number.
How did you find each number?
a) $7 + \square = 15$ b) $48 = 3 \times \square$
c) $\square - 12 = 5$ d) $\square - 9 = 4$
e) $14 + 3 = \square + 5$ f) $15 \times 2 = 5 \times \square$

12. The perimeter of a rectangle is 34 cm.
Its width is 5 cm.
How long is the rectangle?

5

13. Use an integer to represent each situation.
a) Sandha skated backward 100 m.
b) Karl earned $140 mowing lawns.

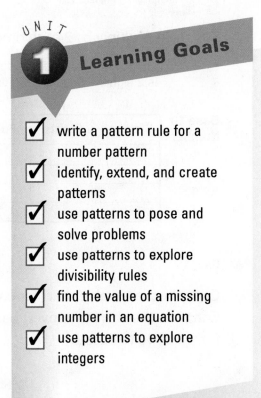

UNIT

1 Learning Goals

✓ write a pattern rule for a number pattern
✓ identify, extend, and create patterns
✓ use patterns to pose and solve problems
✓ use patterns to explore divisibility rules
✓ find the value of a missing number in an equation
✓ use patterns to explore integers

Our number system is base 10.
For the values of the places of whole numbers from right to left:

The pattern rule is:

Start at 1. Multiply by 10 each time.

1 ten thousand is 10 thousands.	1 thousand is 10 hundreds.	1 hundred is 10 tens.	1 ten is 10 ones.	
↓	↓	↓	↓	
Ten Thousands	**Thousands**	**Hundreds**	**Tens**	**Ones**

Computers use a binary, or base 2, number system.
The only digits used are 0 and 1.
For the values of the places from right to left:

The pattern rule is:

Start at 1. Multiply by 2 each time.

Base 10 Number	Sixteens	Eights	Fours	Twos	Ones	Base 2 Number
		1 sixteen is 2 eights. ↓	1 eight is 2 fours. ↓	1 four is 2 twos. ↓	1 two is 2 ones. ↓	
1					1	1
2				1	0	10
3				1	1	11
4			1	0	0	100

We say each digit of a base 2 number. So, we read 10 as "one zero."

Part 1

Copy the place-value chart for base 2.
Continue the chart to convert base 10 numbers
from 1 to 10 to base 2.

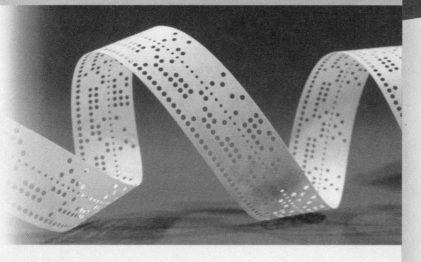

Check List

Your work should show
- ☑ the completed place-value chart
- ☑ the decoded messages
- ☑ how you used number patterns to solve and create binary code problems
- ☑ a clear explanation of your procedures and results

Part 2

This message was written using a binary code:

  10011   1101   1001   1100   101

Each letter of the alphabet was assigned a number, from A = 1 to Z = 26.
The base 10 numbers were then converted to base 2 numbers.
Decode the message.

Part 3

Use binary code.
Make up your own secret message.
Trade messages with a classmate.
Decode your classmate's message.

Reflect on the Unit

Describe the different ways you used patterns in this unit.

Whole Numbers

At the Apiary

Learning Goals

- read and write whole numbers in standard, expanded, and written forms
- use place value to represent and read whole numbers
- compare and order whole numbers
- identify and describe multiples and factors to 100
- identify and describe composite and prime numbers to 100
- use order of operations
- estimate sums, differences, products, and quotients
- use mental math to add, subtract, multiply, and divide
- add four 3-digit numbers and subtract from a 5-digit number
- multiply and divide by a 2-digit number
- pose and solve multistep problems

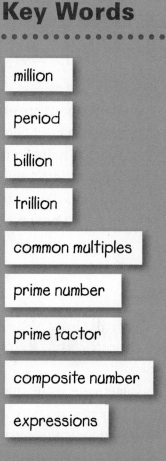

Key Words

- million
- period
- billion
- trillion
- common multiples
- prime number
- prime factor
- composite number
- expressions

Honeybees have been producing honey for more than 150 million years. Honeybees gather nectar from flowers. They convert the nectar to honey and store it as food in the beehive. A colony of honeybees produces more honey than it needs. For 6000 years, beekeepers have harvested honey for people to eat.

- Lesley Haynes has 20 hives.
  Each hive has about 75 000 honeybees.
  How could you find out how many honeybees Lesley has?

- A honeybee travels about 195 km in about 50 round trips to collect enough nectar to make 1 g of honey.
  About what distance does a honeybee travel in one round trip?
  How do you know?

- What else do you know about Lesley's honeybees?

1

Exploring One Million

Think about collecting 1 million of something.
Brown-haired people have about
100 000 hairs on their heads.
So, to collect 1 million hairs,
you would need the hair from
about 10 brown-haired people.

Explore

Here are some questions about 1 million.

How long do you think it would take to make a calculator count by ones to 1 million?

How many dictionary pages would it take to list 1 million words and their definitions?

How long would a line of 1 million children standing side by side be?

➤ Choose one of these questions to explore,
   or think of a question of your own.
➤ Gather any materials you will need.
➤ Estimate an answer to your question.
   Then develop and carry out a strategy to find the answer.

Show *and* Share

Share your question, estimate, and answer with another pair of students.
Describe the strategy you used to find your answer.
Is your answer exact or is it approximate? Explain.

One **million** is 1000 thousands. It is a very large number!
Here are some benchmarks to help you think about 1 million.

1 000 000 is equal to 1000 thousand cubes.

1 000 000 mm = 1 km

1 000 000 pennies = $10 000

$1 000 000 = ten thousand $100 bills

1 000 000 min is about 2 years.

Practice

1. **a)** How many small squares are there on this grid?

   b) How many small squares would be on 10 grids?
   On 100 grids?
   What strategy did you use to find your answers?

   c) Suppose you need 1 million small squares.
   Estimate the number of these grids you need.
   Find the number of grids needed to make 1 million.

2. How long would a line of 1 million centimetre cubes be?
   Give your answer in as many different standard units
   of measure as you can. Show your work.

3. **a)** Suppose you use a calculator to count by 100 000s to 1 000 000.
   How many times will you press ☐? Use a calculator to check.

   b) How many times would you have to press ☐
   to count by 10 000s to 1 000 000? Use a calculator to check.

4. How many days will it take you to spend $1 000 000,
   if each day you spend each amount?
   a) $100 000   **b)** $10 000   **c)** $1000
   d) $100   **e)** $10
   Show your work.

5. Estimate the length of 1 million straws arranged end to end.
   Find the answer. Show your work.
   Was your estimate high or low? Explain.

6. Write your own problem about 1 million.
   Trade problems with a classmate.
   Solve your classmate's problem.

7. Suppose your heart beats 70 times a minute.
   How long would it take to beat 1 million times?

Numbers Every Day

Mental Math

Write an equivalent
decimal for each number.

- 0.5
- 2.90
- 31.70
- 694.3

Reflect

Explain how you could figure out about
how many days there are in 1 million seconds.

LESSON

Understanding Large Numbers

The world's all-time best selling copyright book is *Guinness World Records*. From October 1955 to June 2002, 94 767 083 copies were sold.

You can extend the place-value chart to represent 94 767 083.

Hundred Millions	Ten Millions	Millions	Hundred Thousands	Ten Thousands	Thousands	Hundreds	Tens	Ones
	9	4	7	6	7	0	8	3

Explore

Here are some of the world records reported in the *Guinness World Records 2004*.

*   The largest bag of cookies was made in London, Ontario. It contained 100 152 chocolate chip cookies.
*   The greatest attendance at an Olympic Games was 5 797 923. The games took place in Los Angeles in 1984.
*   The most dominoes toppled by a group was 3 847 295, out of a possible 4 000 000. This took place at Domino Day "Expressions for Millions" in Leeuwarden, Netherlands.
*   The most common name in the world is Li. China alone has 87 000 000 people with this name.

➤ Take turns reading the records aloud.

➤ Each of you chooses 2 numbers from the records. Represent each number in as many ways as you can.

LESSON FOCUS | Read and write whole numbers up to and greater than one million.

35

Show *and* Share

Share your work with another pair of students.
Talk about the different ways you represented your numbers.

Connect ···

➤ These facts may help you read and write large whole numbers.

- From right to left, each group of 3 place values is called a **period**.

- Within each period, the digits of a number
  are read as hundreds, tens, and ones.

This place-value chart shows the number of items in the
world's largest collection of matchbook covers, 3 159 119.

Millions Period			Thousands Period			Units Period		
Hundreds	**Tens**	**Ones**	**Hundreds**	**Tens**	**Ones**	**Hundreds**	**Tens**	**Ones**
		3	1	5	9	1	1	9
		↑	↑	↑	↑	↑	↑	↑
		3 000 000	100 000	50 000	9000	100	10	9

We read this number as:
three *million* one hundred fifty-nine *thousand* one hundred nineteen

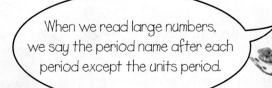

When we read large numbers,
we say the period name after each
period except the units period.

We leave a space between
the periods when we write a
number with 5 or more digits.

We can write this number in:

- standard form: 3 159 119

- expanded form: 3 000 000 + 100 000 + 50 000 + 9000 + 100 + 10 + 9

- number-word form: 3 million 159 thousand 119

One thousand million is one **billion**.
One thousand billion is one **trillion**.

➤ The place-value chart can be extended to the left to show greater whole numbers.
This place-value chart shows the approximate number of cells in the human body.

Trillions			Billions			Millions			Thousands			Units		
H	T	O	H	T	O	H	T	O	H	T	O	H	T	O
		5	0	0	0	0	1	0	0	0	0	0	0	0

We write: 50 000 100 000 000
We say: fifty trillion one hundred million

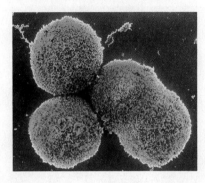

Practice

1. Write each number in standard form.
   a) 6 million 276 thousand 89
   b) 20 000 000 + 4 000 000 + 300 000 + 40 000 + 2000 + 500 + 80 + 4
   c) two billion four hundred sixty million sixty-nine thousand eighteen

2. How does a million compare to a thousand? To ten thousand?
   Use a calculator to check your answer.

3. Write each number in expanded form.
   a) 75 308 403   b) 64 308 470 204   c) 99 300 327

4. Write the value of each underlined digit.
   a) 6<u>2</u>7 384
   b) 5<u>4</u> 286 473
   c) 41 <u>9</u>62 014
   d) <u>25</u> 041 304 000

5. Write the number that is:
   a) 10 000 more than 881 462
   b) 100 000 less than 2 183 486
   c) 1 000 000 more than 746 000
   d) 1 000 000 less than 624 327 207
   Tell how you know.

Numbers Every Day

Number Strategies

Round each number to the nearest hundred, the nearest thousand, and the nearest ten thousand.

- 475 498
- 3 045 349
- 40 469
- 16 944 500

6. China is the most populated country in the world.
In 2001, it had an estimated population of one billion
two hundred seventy-four million nine hundred fifteen thousand.
Write this number in standard form and in expanded form.

7. The largest known prehistoric insect is a species of dragonfly.
It lived about 280 000 000 years ago.
Write this number in words.

8. The world's largest shopping centre is in Edmonton, Alberta.
It covers an area of 492 386 m² and cost
about $1 200 000 000 to build.
Write these numbers in a place-value chart.

9. A student read 3 000 146 as "three thousand one hundred forty-six."
How would you explain the student's error?

10. I am a number between 7 000 000 and 8 000 000.
All my digits are odd.
All the digits in my thousands period are the same.
All the digits in my units period are the same.
The sum of my digits is 31.
What number am I?
Give as many answers as you can.
What strategies did you use to find the
mystery number?

At Home

Reflect

Explain how you know the value of
each digit in the number 5 487 302.

Look through newspapers
and magazines.
Find large numbers.
How are the numbers written?

Comparing and Ordering Numbers

The area of Paraguay
is 406 752 km².
The area of Japan
is 377 835 km².
You can show
these numbers
on a number line.

Which country
has the greater area?
How do you know?

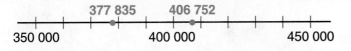

Explore

Use this table that shows the areas of 10 countries.
Draw a place-value chart you can use to record
each number.
➤ Partner A finds the greatest number
in the table and reads it aloud.
Partner B records the number in a
place-value chart.
➤ Partner B finds the next greatest number
and reads it aloud.
Partner A records the number in the
place-value chart.
➤ Continue until the numbers are in order
from greatest to least.
Order the countries from greatest area
to least area.

Country	Area (km²)
Argentina	2 766 890
Australia	7 686 850
Brazil	8 511 970
Canada	9 984 670
China	9 596 960
Egypt	1 001 450
Greenland	2 175 600
India	3 287 590
Russian Federation	17 075 200
United States	9 629 090

Show *and* Share

Share your results with another pair of students.
How did you know how many columns to put
in your place-value chart?
How did you label the columns?
What strategies did you use to choose the numbers?
Where would Paraguay's area fit in the ordered list?
Where would Japan's area fit?

Here is a table showing the areas of
3 more countries.

Country	Area (km²)
Colombia	1 138 910
South Africa	1 219 912
Thailand	514 000

You can use a place-value chart to order
the areas from greatest to least.

Country	Millions			Thousands			Units		
	Hundreds	Tens	Ones	Hundreds	Tens	Ones	Hundreds	Tens	Ones
Colombia			1	1	3	8	9	1	0
South Africa			1	2	1	9	9	1	2
Thailand				5	1	4	0	0	0

Both 1 219 912 and 1 138 910 have 1 million.
1 219 912 has 219 thousands.
1 138 910 has 138 thousands.
So, 1 219 912 is the greatest number.

514 000 has no millions.
It is the least number.

So, 1 219 912 > 1 138 910 > 514 000
The areas from greatest to least are:
1 219 912 km², 1 138 910 km², 514 000 km²

The order of the countries from greatest to least area is:
South Africa, Colombia, Thailand

Social Studies

Japan is one of Canada's trading partners. In 2001, the value of Japan's exports was US$403 496 million. That year, Canada's exports were worth US$259 858 million.

Practice

1. Copy and complete. Replace each □ with > or <.
   a) 11 208 464 □ 9 289 500
   b) 83 617 □ 1 327 090
   c) 50 985 362 □ 27 041
   d) 2 004 023 □ 385 008

2. Order these numbers from least to greatest.
   | 595 032 461 | 99 426 322 | 3 217 530 |
   | 84 620 | 1 300 124 | 685 428 |

3. The table shows estimates of the populations of some cities in 2015.

City	Expected Population in 2015
Dhaka (Bangladesh)	22 766 000
Mumbai (India)	22 577 000
Tokyo (Japan)	27 190 000

   a) Why do you think the expected population numbers are rounded?
   b) Which of these cities is expected to have the greatest population in 2015? The least? How do you know?

4. Use the digits 1, 2, 4, 6, 7, 8, and 9 once in each number.
   Write five 7-digit numbers between 8 000 000 and 9 000 000.
   Order the numbers from least to greatest.
   What strategies did you use to form the numbers?
   Could you write more than 5 numbers? Explain.

5. This table shows the approximate areas of the oceans of the world.

Ocean	Area (km²)
Arctic	9 485 000
Atlantic	86 557 000
Indian	73 427 000
Pacific	166 241 000

Order the oceans from greatest to least area.

6. Clayton and Olivia played a computer game.
Olivia's final score was 2 306 421 and Clayton's was 2 302 972.
Show these numbers on a number line.
Whose score was greater? How do you know?

7. The table shows the approximate populations of some Canadian provinces in 2002.
   a) Which of these provinces had the least population? The greatest population?
   b) Which of these provinces had a population greater than 1 million? Less than 1 million?
   c) Which province had a population of about 4 million? About half a million?
   d) Saskatchewan's population in 2002 was 1 011 800.
   Which province's population was about 3 times that of Saskatchewan?

Province	Population
Alberta	3 113 600
British Columbia	4 141 300
Manitoba	1 150 000
New Brunswick	756 700
Newfoundland and Labrador	531 600
Nova Scotia	944 800
Ontario	12 068 300

8. How many different ways can you replace ☐ with a digit so each statement is true?
Show your work.
   a) 3 267 001 < 3 ☐34 379
   b) 6 481 736 > 6 ☐82 159

Reflect

Manitoba's population was 1 123 900 in 1994, and 1 119 583 in 2001.
Did the population increase or decrease between these years? How do you know?

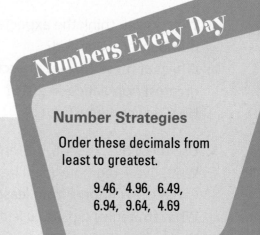

Numbers Every Day

Number Strategies

Order these decimals from least to greatest.

9.46, 4.96, 6.49,
6.94, 9.64, 4.69

Exploring Multiples

Explore

On Thursday morning, the local radio station held a call-in contest.

- Every third caller to the station won a T-shirt.
- Every seventh caller won a baseball cap.

In 50 calls, which callers won a T-shirt? A baseball cap? Both prizes?

Use any materials you like to solve this problem.
Show how you used materials to solve this problem.

Sorry, you are caller number 10.

Show *and* Share

Share your answers with another pair of students.
What strategies did you use to solve the problem?
Discuss how using materials helped.
Describe any patterns you noticed.

Connect

Recall that to find the multiples of a number,
start at that number and count on by the number.
You can use a hundred chart to find the multiples of a number.

The multiples of 4 are:
4, 8, 12, 16, 20, 24, 28, 32, 36, 40, …

The multiples of 6 are:
6, 12, 18, 24, 30, 36, …

1	2	3	4	5	6	7	8	9	10
11	12	13	14	15	16	17	18	19	20
21	22	23	24	25	26	27	28	29	30
31	32	33	34	35	36	37	38	39	40

12, 24, and 36 appear in both lists.
They are multiples of 4 and of 6.
They are **common multiples** of 4 and 6.

Each common multiple of 4 and 6 is divisible by 4 and by 6.

Practice

You may use a hundred chart to model your solutions.

1. List the first 10 multiples of each number.

    a) 2   **b)** 5   **c)** 8   **d)** 12   **e)** 11   **f)** 7

2. Find the first 3 common multiples of each pair of numbers.

    a) 4 and 5   **b)** 10 and 15   **c)** 3 and 9

    d) 2 and 11   **e)** 7 and 4   **f)** 6 and 10

3. Find the first 3 common multiples of each set of numbers.

    a) 3, 4, and 6   **b)** 2, 3, and 4   **c)** 4, 5, and 10

    Explain your work.

4. Find the first 2 common multiples of 36 and 48.

5. A spider has 8 legs. An ant has 6 legs.
There are a group of spiders and a group of ants.
The groups have equal numbers of legs.
What is the least number of spiders and ants
in each group? Show your work.

6. Find all the common multiples of 8 and 9 that are less than 100.

7. Make a large copy of this Venn diagram.
Sort these numbers.
45, 24, 52, 30, 66, 15, 85, 90, 72, 60, 20, 38

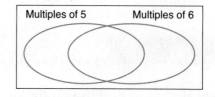

8. Sam jogs every 2 days. He does Pilates every 3 days.
Suppose Sam jogs and does Pilates on October 1.
What are the next 3 dates on which he will jog
and do Pilates? Explain how you know.

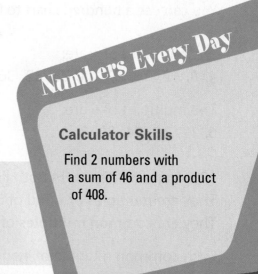

Numbers Every Day

Calculator Skills

Find 2 numbers with
a sum of 46 and a product
of 408.

Reflect

Explain how you would find the first
common multiple of 12 and 15.

Prime and Composite Numbers

Numbers multiplied to form a product are factors of the product.

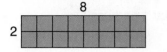

8
2

$2 \times 8 = 16$

factor factor product

2 and 8 are factors of 16.
What other factors of 16 can you name?

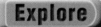

You will need Colour Tiles or
congruent squares and grid paper.

➤ Find all the different rectangles you
can make using each number
of tiles from 2 to 20.
Record each rectangle on grid paper.
Write a multiplication sentence that
describes the number of tiles in
each rectangle.

➤ For which numbers of tiles could
you make only 1 rectangle?
For which numbers of tiles could
you make more than 1 rectangle?

A 2 by 1 rectangle
is the same as
a 1 by 2 rectangle.

Show and Share

Share your work with another group of students.
What are the factors of 2? Of 3?
What are the factors of 16? Of 20?
How could you find the factors of a number without making rectangles?

Connect

➤ Suppose you have 23 Colour Tiles.
You can make only 1 rectangle with all 23 tiles.

23 has 2 factors: 1 and 23.
A number with exactly 2 factors,
1 and itself, is a **prime number**.
23 is a prime number.

> A prime number is a number greater than 1 that is divisible only by 1 and itself.

➤ Suppose you have 24 Colour Tiles.
You can make 4 different rectangles with 24 tiles.

$1 \times 24 = 24$

$2 \times 12 = 24$

$3 \times 8 = 24$

$4 \times 6 = 24$

> A composite number can be written as a product of prime factors:
> $24 = 2 \times 2 \times 2 \times 3$

24 has 8 factors: 1, 2, 3, 4, 6, 8, 12, and 24.
The **prime factors** of 24 are 2 and 3.
A number with more than 2 factors is a **composite number**.

Practice

You may use Colour Tiles or counters to model your solutions.

1. List all the factors of each number. Which factors are prime factors?
   a) 25   b) 30   c) 12   d) 50
   e) 28   f) 100   g) 20   h) 63

2. Write 3 numbers between 30 and 50 that have:
   a) exactly 2 factors each   b) more than 2 factors each

3. Write 3 numbers less than 100 that have exactly 4 factors each.

4. Tell if each number is prime or composite. How do you know?
   Write each composite number as a product of prime factors.
   a) 59   b) 93   c) 97   d) 87   e) 73   f) 45

5. Between 20 and 28 students signed up for the chess club.
The students could not be divided exactly
into groups of 2, 3, 4, or 5.
How many students signed up for the chess club?
Show your work.

6. Three numbers between 70 and 80 are prime numbers.
What numbers are they?
Explain how you know they are prime numbers.

7. How many days in September
have a prime number date?
How many have a composite
number date?
Show how you know.

September					2006	
Su	M	Tu	W	Th	F	Sa
					1	2
3	4	5	6	7	8	9
10	11	12	13	14	15	16
17	18	19	20	21	22	23
24	25	26	27	28	29	30

8. How can you tell that 32 and 95 are not
prime numbers without finding their factors?

9. Carmine and Nasra play a game with this spinner.
Carmine gets a point if the pointer lands on a prime number.
Nasra gets a point if the pointer lands on a composite number.
Is this a fair game? How do you know?

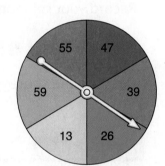

10. Alexis said, "All prime numbers except for
the number 2 are odd. So, all odd numbers
must be prime numbers."
Do you agree with Alexis? Explain.

11. Copy this table.

	Prime	Composite
Even		
Odd		

Sort the numbers from 2 to 30 in the table.

Reflect

Jamie thinks that 1 is neither prime
nor composite.
Show why you agree or disagree with him.

Numbers Every Day

Number Strategies

Round each number to the nearest
hundred thousand, and to the
nearest million.

- 46 201 988
- 9 998 765
- 10 040 678
- 52 061 215

Strategies Toolkit

Explore

Jan has 10 clown fish and 15 snails.
She wants to place all of them in fish tanks so
each tank has the same number of fish and snails.
What is the greatest number of tanks
Jan can set up?

You may use any materials to model your solution.
Record your solutions.

Show **and** Share

Describe the strategy you used to solve the problem.

Connect

Twenty-four girls and 18 boys are forming teams.
All the children are on a team.
Teams must have equal numbers of girls
and equal numbers of boys.
What is the greatest number of teams that can be formed?

Understand

What do you know?
- There are 24 girls and 18 boys.
- Boys and girls should be divided equally
  among the teams.

Plan

Think of a strategy to help you solve
the problem.
- You can **make an organized list**.
- How many girls and how many boys
  are on each of 2 teams? 3 teams?

Strategies

- **Make a table.**
- **Use a model.**
- **Draw a diagram.**
- **Solve a simpler problem.**
- **Work backward.**
- **Guess and check.**
- **Make an organized list.**
- **Use a pattern.**
- **Draw a graph.**
- **Use logical reasoning.**

Solve

Can you make 4 teams? 5 teams? 6 teams?
Explain.
What is the greatest possible number of teams?
How many girls and how many boys
will be on each team?

Look Back

Check your work.
Did you find the greatest number of teams?
Does each team have the same number of girls
and the same number of boys?
How could you have used common factors
to solve this problem?

Practice · Choose one of the **Strategies**

1. Projecta has 36 photos of her favourite rock star.
   She wants to arrange the photos in groups that have
   equal numbers of rows and columns.
   How many different arrangements can Projecta make?
   Show your work.

2. Keshav is making prize bags for Play Day.
   He has 40 pencils, 32 pens, and 16 notepads
   to use as prizes.
   Keshav wants to make as many prize bags as possible.
   He wants all the bags to be the same.
   a) How many prize bags can Keshav make?
   b) How many pencils, pens, and notepads will be in each bag?
      How do you know?

Reflect

Explain how an organized list can help you solve a problem.

7

Using Mental Math

Explore

On a bike trip, Marta and Sulyn
rode 39 km a day for 7 days.
How far did they travel in 7 days?
Use mental math to find out.
Record your answer.

Show *and* Share

Share your solution with a classmate.
Compare the mental math strategies you used.

Connect

➤ Use mental math to add: 60 + 35 + 40
Rearrange and use compatible numbers.
Compatible numbers are pairs of numbers that are easy to compute.

$$60 + 35 + 40 = (60 + 40) + 35$$
$$= 100 + 35$$
$$= 135$$

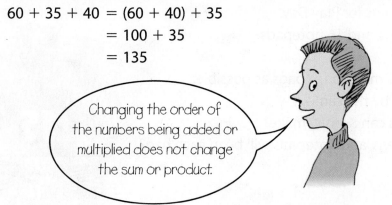

> Changing the order of
> the numbers being added or
> multiplied does not change
> the sum or product.

➤ Use mental math to subtract: 687 − 464
When no regrouping is needed, start subtracting from the left.

$$687 − 464 = 223$$

Think:
$600 − 400 = 200$
$80 − 60 = 20$
$7 − 4 = 3$

➤ Use mental math to multiply: $4 \times 19 \times 25$

Rearrange and use compatible numbers.

$$4 \times 19 \times 25 = 19 \times (4 \times 25)$$
$$= 19 \times 100$$
$$= 1900$$

25 and 4 are compatible numbers. Their product, 100, is easy to multiply with any other factor.

➤ Use mental math to multiply: 6×27
Break one of the numbers apart to make numbers that are simple to work with.

$$6 \times 27 = 6 \times (20 + 7)$$
$$= (6 \times 20) + (6 \times 7)$$
$$= 120 + 42$$
$$= 162$$

Twenty-seven breaks apart to 20 + 7. It's easy to multiply 20 by 6 and 7 by 6.

Think of the area of a rectangle.

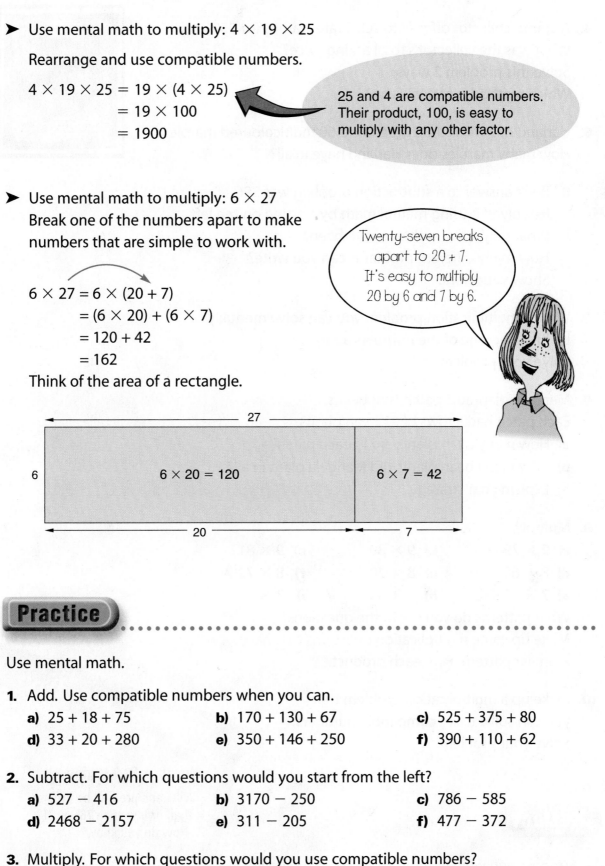

	27	
6	$6 \times 20 = 120$	$6 \times 7 = 42$
	20	7

Practice

Use mental math.

1. Add. Use compatible numbers when you can.
   a) $25 + 18 + 75$ b) $170 + 130 + 67$ c) $525 + 375 + 80$
   d) $33 + 20 + 280$ e) $350 + 146 + 250$ f) $390 + 110 + 62$

2. Subtract. For which questions would you start from the left?
   a) $527 - 416$ b) $3170 - 250$ c) $786 - 585$
   d) $2468 - 2157$ e) $311 - 205$ f) $477 - 372$

3. Multiply. For which questions would you use compatible numbers?
   a) $5 \times 36 \times 20$ b) $65 \times 50 \times 10$ c) 27×4
   d) 7×59 e) 17×5 f) $250 \times 18 \times 4$

4. A stamp collector offered to sell 6 rare stamps for $59 each.
What was the collector's total asking price?
Solve this problem 2 ways.
Which method is easier? Why?

5. Harland has 140 red, 86 green, and 60 multicoloured marbles.
How many marbles does Harland have in all?

6. Ben's answer to a subtraction problem was 396.
He solved it using mental math by starting on the left.
What might the problem have been?
How many different problems can you write?
Show your work.

7. Write a multiplication problem you can solve mentally
by breaking one of the numbers apart.
Solve your problem.

8. Manuela planted 5 patches of beans.
Each patch had 8 rows of 27 bean plants.
a) How many bean plants are in each patch?
b) How many bean plants did Manuela plant in all?
Explain your strategy.

9. Multiply.
a) 9×79 **b)** 9×80 **c)** 9×81
d) 8×68 **e)** 8×70 **f)** 8×72
g) 7×57 **h)** 7×60 **i)** 7×63
What patterns do you see in the questions?
Make up some multiplication questions that have
a similar pattern. Find each product.

10. Make up a multiplication problem that
you can solve using compatible numbers.
Solve your problem.

Reflect

Suppose you were to multiply 86 by 30 mentally.
Which number would you break apart? Explain.

Numbers Every Day

Number Strategies

Will each product be greater
than or less than 765×21?
How do you know?

800×20
750×20
770×25

Buzz!

You will need a watch or a clock with a second hand.

The last player to remain in the game is the winner.
As a group, decide how many seconds to allow between
the numbers as they are counted.
Decide who will be Player A, Player B, and Player C.

➤ Player B selects a target number from 2 to 9.
➤ Player C will monitor the pace and make sure
  Player A's response is correct.
  A player is eliminated for:
  • saying "buzz!" at the wrong time
  • not saying "buzz!" at the right time
➤ Player B starts to count by 1s from 1 at the agreed speed.
  Player A must say "buzz!" whenever a multiple
  of the target number is reached.
  For example, if the target number is 5, play should go as follows:
  1, 2, 3, 4, "buzz!," 6, 7, 8, 9, "buzz!," ...
  Player B stops counting at 120 if Player A has been correct
  to that point.
➤ Change roles and play again. An eliminated player becomes Player C.
  The new Player B selects the target number for the new Player A.
  Play until only one player remains in the game.

Order of Operations

You have added, subtracted, multiplied, or divided with whole numbers.
Add, subtract, multiply, and divide are operations.

In this lesson, you will perform calculations using more than one operation.

 Explore

To win a contest, Harry's dad must answer this skill-testing question:

$$9 + 3 \times 6 - 4 = \underline{\qquad}$$

➤ Find the answer in as many ways as you can.
➤ Record the strategy you use for each method.
➤ The correct answer is 23.
  Which strategy gives this answer?

Show *and* Share

Share your work with another student.
Discuss how to rewrite the question so the only possible answer is 23.

Connect

When you solve a problem that uses more than one operation,
the answer depends on the order in which you perform the operations.

Solve the expression: $3 + 6 \times 4$
If you add first, you get: $9 \times 4 = 36$
If you multiply first, you get: $3 + 24 = 27$

An **expression** is a
mathematical statement
with numbers and operations.
When we calculate the answer,
we solve the expression.

To avoid getting two answers, there is a rule
that multiplication is done before addition.

So, $3 + 6 \times 4 = 3 + 24 = 27$, which is the correct answer

We use brackets if we want certain operations carried out first.
To make sure everyone gets the same answer when solving
an expression, we use this order of operations:

> • Do the operations in brackets.
> • Multiply and divide, in order, from left to right.
> • Then add and subtract, in order, from left to right.

➤ Solve: $16 - 14 \div 2$

$16 - 14 \div 2$

$= 16 - 7$

$= 9$

Divide first: $14 \div 2 = 7$
Then subtract: $16 - 7 = 9$

➤ Solve: $18 - 10 + 6$

$18 - 10 + 6$

$= 8 + 6$

$= 14$

Subtract first: $18 - 10 = 8$
Then add: $8 + 6 = 14$

➤ Solve: $7 \times (4 + 8)$

$7 \times (4 + 8)$

$= 7 \times 12$

$= 84$

Do the operation
in brackets first:
$4 + 8 = 12$
Then multiply:
$7 \times 12 = 84$

The order of operations is :
Brackets
Multiply and Divide
Add and Subtract

Practice

1. Solve each expression.
Use the order of operations.

a) $18 + 4 \times 2$ **b)** $25 - 12 \div 3$ **c)** $24 + 36 \div 9$

d) $12 - 8 - 4$ **e)** $50 - 7 \times 6$ **f)** $7 \times (2 + 9)$

g) $81 \div 9 - 6$ **h)** $25 \div (9 - 4)$ **i)** $13 - 6 + 8$

2. Some calculators follow the order of operations.
Others do not.
Press: $9 \boxed{+} 6 \boxed{\times} 3 \boxed{=}$
Does your calculator follow the order of operations?
Explain how you know.

3. Bianca entered $52 \boxed{+} 8 \boxed{\times} 2 \boxed{=}$ in her calculator.
She got the answer 120.
In what order did Bianca's calculator perform the operations?
How do you know?

4. Use mental math to solve.

a) $20\,000 - 4000 \times 2$ **b)** $6 + 125 \div 25$

c) $(1000 + 6000) \times 3$ **d)** $60 \times 3 \div 9$

e) $5 \times (4 + 11)$ **f)** $50 + 50 \div 50$

g) $(50 + 50) \div 50$ **h)** $(9 \times 10) - (30 + 30)$

i) $16 \div 2 \times 9$ **j)** $200 - (200 \div 20)$

5. Use mental math to solve.

a) $4 \times 7 - 2 + 1$ **b)** $4 \times (7 - 2) + 1$

c) $4 \times 7 - (2 - 1)$ **d)** $4 \times (7 - 2 + 1)$

e) $(4 \times 7 - 2) + 1$ **f)** $4 \times 7 - (2 + 1)$

Which expression gives the greatest answer?
The least answer?

6. Use the numbers 2, 3, and 4 and any operations or brackets.
Write an expression that equals each number.

a) 9   **b)** 10   **c)** 14   **d)** 20   **e)** 6

Try to do this more than one way.

7. How many different answers can you get by inserting
one pair of brackets in this expression?
$10 + 6 - 4 \div 2 \times 3$
Write each expression, then solve it.

8. Alexi bought 5 T-shirts for $12 each
and 3 pairs of socks for $2 a pair.
Which expression shows how much Alexi spent in dollars?
Explain.
a) $5 \times 12 \times 3 \times 2$
b) $5 \times 12 + 3 \times 2$
c) $(5 + 3) \times (12 + 2)$

9. Choose mental math, a calculator, or paper and pencil
to solve.
For each question, how did you decide which method to use?
a) $238 - (2 \times 73)$ b) $47 \times (16 \times 18)$
c) $(36 + 14) \div 10$ d) $36 \times (48 \times 8)$
e) $60 \times (4 \div 2)$ f) $(200 + 50) \times (9 \div 3)$

10. Mr. Bradshaw bought 2 boxes of fruit bars for his 3 children.
Each box has 6 fruit bars.
The children shared the fruit bars equally.
How many fruit bars did each child get?
Write a number sentence to show the order of operations you used.

11. Copy each number sentence.
Use brackets to make each number sentence true.
a) $36 \div 4 \times 3 = 3$
b) $20 \div 5 \times 2 + 3 = 5$
c) $10 - 4 \div 2 - 1 = 6$

Reflect

Why do we need rules for the order in which we
perform operations?
Give examples to support your answer.

Numbers Every Day

Number Strategies

Write each number in
expanded form, and in words.

• 26 408 579
• 103 568 904
• 400 017
• 9 872 003
• 89 000 200

OoOps Bingo!

You will need:
- a set of game cards
- counters
- a set of expression cards
- a paper bag
- a record sheet

The object of the game is to be the first player
to correctly cover the whole game card.

Cut out the expression cards and put them in the paper bag.
Decide who will be the Game Keeper.

➤ The Game Keeper draws an expression card and shows it
to the players.
Everyone solves the expression and records his work.
The Game Keeper uses a counter to cover the answer
on the record sheet.
If possible, each player uses a counter to cover the answer
on her game card.

➤ The game ends when one player has correctly covered
a game card.

➤ Switch roles.
Play the game again.

Environmentalist

Environmentalists the world over are working hard to track species' populations. They want to understand the reasons for changes in their numbers, and to reverse the trend, when necessary.

Environmentalists cannot count all the animals and plants. Instead, they do smaller counts for a limited area, and then multiply to estimate regional and even worldwide populations. For example, when exploring the impact of factory fishing, they may count a sample and then estimate the total number of fish caught, and subtract this number from an estimate of the population.

The health of both the local environment and the food chain are crucial to species' survival. Every piece of data environmentalists collect helps in the effort to turn back the tide of extinctions.

Adding and Subtracting Whole Numbers

Explore

The table shows the number of cell phones sold
at We Sell Cells in each of the first 4 months of the year.

- How many cell phones were sold altogether
  in the 4 months?
- By the end of the year, 12 854 cell phones
  had been sold.
  How many phones were sold from May to December?

Cell Phone Sales

Month	Number of Phones
January	765
February	847
March	939
April	808

Show *and* Share

Share your work with another pair of students.
How did you decide which operations to use to solve the problems?
Did you use the same methods? Explain.
How can you check your answers?

Connect

➤ Maha's cell phone plan gives her 300 min of air time each month.
  She used 298 min in June, 276 min in July,
  287 min in August, and 248 min in September.
  How many minutes did Maha use in the 4 months?

Add: 298 + 276 + 287 + 248
Use place value to add.

Add the ones: 29 ones Regroup as 2 tens 9 ones.	Add the tens: 30 tens Regroup as 3 hundreds 0 tens.	Add the hundreds: 11 hundreds
 ² 298 276 287 + 248 9	 ³² 298 276 287 + 248 09	 ³² 298 276 287 + 248 1109

Estimate to check your answer is reasonable.
Round each number to the nearest 100.
298, 276, and 287 each round to 300.
248 rounds to 200.
300 + 300 + 300 + 200 = 1100
1109 is a reasonable answer.

Maha used 1109 min.

➤ Here is another way to find the sum 298 + 276 + 287 + 248.

Add: 298 + 276	Add: 574 + 287	Then add: 861 + 248
298 + 276 ───── 574	574 + 287 ───── 861	861 + 248 ───── 1109

➤ Maha's 3-year plan gives her a total of 10 800 min.
Suppose she used 9586 min in 3 years.
How many unused minutes does Maha have?

Subtract: 10 800 − 9586
Use place value to subtract.

You cannot take 6 ones from 0 ones.
There are no tens to regroup.
Regroup 8 hundreds as 7 hundreds 10 tens.
Regroup 10 tens as 9 tens 10 ones.

$$\begin{array}{r} {\scriptstyle 9} \\ {\scriptstyle 7\ 10\ 10} \\ 1\,0\,8\,0\,0 \\ -\ \ 9\,5\,8\,6 \\ \hline \end{array}$$

Subtract the ones.
Subtract the tens.
Subtract the hundreds.
To subtract the thousands,
regroup 1 ten thousand as 10 thousands.

$$\begin{array}{r} {\scriptstyle 9} \\ {\scriptstyle 10\ 7\ 10\ 10} \\ 1\,0\,8\,0\,0 \\ -\ \ 9\,5\,8\,6 \\ \hline 1\,2\,1\,4 \end{array}$$

Add to check your answer is correct.
The total number of used and unused minutes
should equal the total number of minutes in the plan.
Add: 9586 + 1214
The sum should be 10 800.
9586 + 1214 = 10 800

So, the answer is correct.
Maha has 1214 unused minutes.

> Recall that adding to check a subtraction is using the inverse operation. Addition is the inverse of subtraction.

1. Add. Estimate to check.

   a) 469
      308
      529
      + 637

   b) 832
      759
      621
      + 500

   c) 567
      720
      863
      + 144

   d) 944
      140
      229
      + 687

   e) 543
      691
      107
      + 420

   f) 312
      477
      210
      + 390

2. Subtract. Use the inverse operation to check.

   a) 5326
      − 1417

   b) 8004
      − 5361

   c) 4094
      − 2397

   d) 36 187
      − 3 829

   e) 52 109
      − 763

   f) 23 000
      − 422

3. Derek emptied his 4 jars of pennies.
   He counted 587 pennies from the first jar, 724 from the second,
   611 from the third, and 801 from the fourth.
   a) How many pennies does Derek have?
   b) How much is that in dollars?

4. The table shows the numbers of 4 books in stock
   at a book depository.

Books	Number
Woodworking Wisdom	425
Butterflies	631
The Monarchy	214
Casserole Creations	523

   a) Find the total number of these books.
   b) The depository has a total of 10 402 books in stock.
      How many other books are in stock?
      Show how you know.

5. Write a story problem that could be solved by subtracting 4285 from 11 000. Trade problems with a classmate. Solve your classmate's problem.

6. This table shows the daily attendance at this year's Multicultural Festival. How many people attended the festival in total?

Multicultural Festival Attendance

Day	Attendance
Thursday	428
Friday	637
Saturday	958
Sunday	994

7. Jillian subtracted 9387 from a number. The difference was 3447. What was the number? Explain how you got your answer.

8. The sum of four 3-digit numbers is 3615. What might the four numbers be?

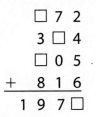

9. The sum of four consecutive 3-digit numbers is 866. What are the four numbers? Explain your strategy.

> Consecutive numbers are numbers such as 100, 101, 102, 103.

10. Find the missing digits. How many different ways can you do this?

```
   □ 7 2
   3 □ 4
   □ 0 5
 +   8 1 6
 ─────────
   1 9 7 □
```

Reflect

Use mental math to find 12 000 − 5001. Explain why it is easier to do this subtraction mentally than with paper and pencil.

Numbers Every Day

Mental Math

Find each product.

60×80

301×6

49×30

298×5

10

Multiplying Whole Numbers

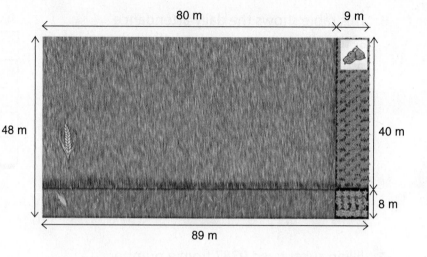

Reza's field is 89 m long
and 48 m wide.
She has divided the field
into 4 sections.

How can you find the area
of each section of the field?
The whole field?

Explore

Patrick's orchard is rectangular. It measures 198 m by 82 m.
Find the area of Patrick's orchard.
Estimate to check your answer.

Show and Share

Share your solution with another student.
How is multiplying a 3-digit number by a 2-digit number
the same as multiplying a 2-digit number by a 2-digit number?
How is it different?

Connect

Yolanda packed 68 cartons of DVDs. She put 197 DVDs in each carton.
How many DVDs did Yolanda pack?

The total number of DVDs is 68 × 197.

➤ You can use an
area model to multiply.
Sketch a rectangle.
Label the length
and the width.

197

68

Divide the rectangle to show hundreds, tens, and ones.
Label the dimensions of the sections.
Find the area of each section.

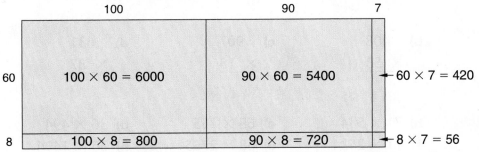

Add the areas: 6000 + 5400 + 420 + 800 + 720 + 56 = 13 396

68 × 197 = 13 396
Yolanda packed 13 396 DVDs.

➤ You can break the numbers apart to multiply.

$$
\begin{array}{r}
197 \quad (100 + 90 + 7)\\
\times \quad 68 \quad (60 + 8)
\end{array}
$$

Multiply: 8 × 7   56
         8 × 90   720
         8 × 100   800
         60 × 7   420
         60 × 90   5400
         60 × 100   + 6000
Add: 13396

➤ You can use a short way to multiply.

$$
\begin{array}{r}
197\\
\times \quad 68
\end{array}
$$

Multiply: 197 × 8   1576
Multiply: 197 × 60   + 11820
Add: 13396

 ➤ You can check by dividing.
The total number of DVDs divided by
the number put in each carton should
equal the number of cartons.

Divide: 13 396 ÷ 197 = 68
So, 13 396 is the correct answer.

Multiplication and division
are inverse operations.
You can use one to check
the other.

Practice

Use a calculator or estimate to check your answers.

1. Multiply.

   a)   576
          × 28

   b)   408
          × 53

   c)   907
          × 18

   d)   631
          × 87

2. Multiply.

   a) 46 × 522

   b) 71 × 534

   c) 68 × 755

   d) 36 × 494

   e) 46 × 1522

   f) 71 × 2534

   g) 68 × 2755

   h) 36 × 1494

3. One bottle holds 750 mL of lemonade.
   How much lemonade will 24 bottles hold?
   Give your answer in 2 different standard units of measurement.

4. Write a story problem that can be solved by
   multiplying a 3-digit number by a 2-digit number.
   Solve your problem. Show your work.

5. Param needs 375 g of chocolate chips for
   one batch of cookies.
   He has two 2-kg bags of chocolate chips.
   Does Param have enough chocolate chips to make
   12 batches of cookies? Explain.

6. Find each product.

   a)   825
          × 52

   b)   837
          × 29

   c)   66
          × 77

   d)   744
          × 32

   e)   397
          × 17

   f)   45
          × 92

   g)   807
          × 28

   h)   583
          × 23

7. Choose the most appropriate method to find each product.
   Describe how you decided which method to use.

   a)   1146
         × 83

   b)   2500
         × 25

   c)   1346
         × 85

   d)   5400
         × 60

   e)   2868
         × 57

   f)   2843
         × 41

   g)   1954
         × 15

   h)   9250
         × 18

8. Tanya and Adeola multiplied 399 by 25.
   Tanya's answer was 2793. Adeola's answer was 9975.
   a) Whose answer is reasonable? Explain.
   b) Explain the other student's error.

9. The ticket agent sold 357 adult tickets
   and 662 student tickets for a concert.
   How much money did the ticket agent take in?

10. Estimate the product 47 × 294.
    Will the product be closer to 12 000 or to 15 000?
    Explain.

11. The Fairview Secondary School community
    of 1854 students and 58 teachers attended
    a special performance of a play at the local theatre.
    The theatre has 49 rows of 48 seats each.
    a) Were any seats empty? How do you know?
    b) If your answer to part a is yes, find the number
       of empty seats.

12. Use the digits 2, 3, 4, 5, 6, 7 to form a 4-digit number
    and a 2-digit number that result in:
    a) the greatest product
    b) the least product
    Show your work.

Reflect

Suppose you multiply a 4-digit number
by a 2-digit number.
Will the product ever be a 7-digit number?
Use numbers and words to explain.

Numbers Every Day

Mental Math
Multiply.

    37 × 50

  146 × 80

  197 × 60

  235 × 90

Dividing by a 2-Digit Number

In this division sentence, which is the divisor?
The dividend? The quotient?

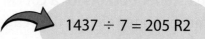

$$1437 \div 7 = 205 \text{ R}2$$

Explore

Use any materials you wish.

Gilbert has 15 sets of collector sports cards.
All the sets have equal numbers of cards.
Gilbert has 375 sports cards.
How many cards are in each set?
Show your work.

Show *and* Share

Share your solution with another pair
of students.
What strategies did you use to solve
the problem?

Connect

Melody has 2421 marbles to share equally
among her 13 cousins.
How many marbles will each cousin get?

Divide: $13\overline{)2421}$

➤ You can use Base Ten Blocks
   and place value to divide $2421 \div 13$.

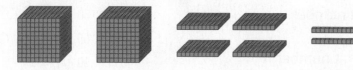

LESSON FOCUS | Use different strategies to divide a 4-digit number by a 2-digit number.

You cannot divide 2 thousands into 13 groups.
Trade 2 thousands for 20 hundreds.

20 hundreds + 4 hundreds = 24 hundreds

Divide 24 hundreds into 13 groups.
Each group gets 1 hundred.
There are 11 hundreds left over.

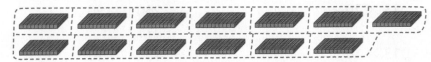

Trade 11 hundreds for 110 tens.

110 tens + 2 tens = 112 tens

Divide 112 tens into 13 groups.
Each group gets 8 tens.
There are 8 tens left over.

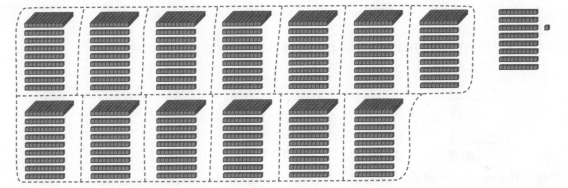

Trade 8 tens for 80 ones.

80 ones + 1 one = 81 ones

Divide 81 ones into 13 groups.
Each group gets 6 ones.
There are 3 ones left over.

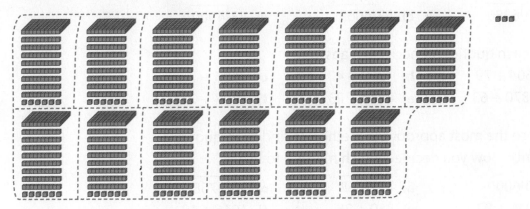

So, 2421 ÷ 13 = 186 R3

➤ Here is another way to divide 2421 marbles into 13 equal groups.

Put each listed amount into each group, then subtract: 13)2421

• 100 marbles	13 × 100	− 1300 | 100
		1121
• 50 marbles	13 × 50	− 650 | 50
		471
• 20 marbles	13 × 20	− 260 | 20
		211
• 10 marbles	13 × 10	− 130 | 10
		81
• 5 marbles	13 × 5	− 65 | 5
		16
• 1 marble	13 × 1	− 13 | + 1
		3 | 186

2421 ÷ 13 = 186 R3

Each cousin gets 186 marbles and there are 3 marbles left over.

To check the answer, multiply 186 by 13 and then add the leftover 3:

```
      186
  ×    13
      558
  + 1860
     2418        2418 + 3 = 2421
```

This is the number of marbles at the beginning, so the answer is correct.

Practice

1. Divide. Multiply to check each answer.

    a) 14)2487   b) 36)8543   c) 43)2623

    d) 29)6480   e) 57)6069   f) 43)4900

2. Find each quotient. Check each answer.

    a) 5604 ÷ 79   b) 1368 ÷ 42   c) 7603 ÷ 73

    d) 6870 ÷ 63   e) 6914 ÷ 23   f) 7727 ÷ 25

3. Choose the most appropriate method to find each quotient.
   Describe how you decided which method to use.

    a) 20)6000   b) 45)9068   c) 38)9768

    d) 4045 ÷ 92   e) 250 ÷ 25   f) 1936 ÷ 12

4. Mr. Talby's hens laid 1098 eggs this past month. How many dozen is that?

5. The attendance at today's baseball game is 4344. Each row of bleachers holds 48 people. How many rows of bleachers could be filled?

6. A hockey team sold 1246 raffle tickets in 45 days. About how many raffle tickets per day is that?

7. Copy each table.
Complete each table. What patterns do you see?

a)

Dividend	Divisor	Quotient
1955	23	
	23	86
2001	23	

b)

Dividend	Divisor	Quotient
2193	43	
2244	44	
2295		51

8. Copy each division sentence.
Replace each □ with a number from the tables so the division sentence is true.
Show your work.

Dividends	Divisors
2536	58
1851	42
3654	25

a) □ ÷ □ = 44 R3
b) □ ÷ □ = 63
c) □ ÷ □ = 101 R11
d) □ ÷ □ = 31 R53

9. The food bank received 30 cases of 24 cans of soup, and 20 cases of 48 cans of soup.
How many packages of 14 cans of soup can be made?

10. Write a problem that can be solved by dividing a 4-digit number by a 2-digit number.
Solve your problem. Show your work.

Numbers Every Day

Number Strategies

Order these numbers from least to greatest.

7 048 963, 71 048 963, 704 896, 7 408 963, 74 018 963, 7 840 369

Reflect

Suppose you divide a 4-digit whole number by a 2-digit whole number.
Will the quotient ever be a 4-digit whole number?
Use words and numbers to explain.

Another Method for Dividing

When the weather turns cold and the days get shorter, many aquatic animals move to warmer waters.
Finback whales migrate about 8000 km from the Bering Sea and the Arctic Ocean to the warmer Indian Ocean.
The journey takes a month or more.

Explore

Suppose a finback whale travels 8055 km in 34 days.
About how far does it travel each day?
Estimate first. Then use any strategy you like to solve this problem.
Show your work.

Show *and* Share

Compare your work with that of another pair of students.
Which strategies did you use?
How did you decide what to do with the remainder?

Connect

Some beluga whales took 58 days to travel 4840 km along the Arctic coast from the Beaufort Sea to the waters around Baffin Island.
About how far did the whales travel each day?

Divide: $58\overline{)4840}$

➤ Estimate first:
   Round 58 to 60.
   Round 4840 to 4800.
   Since $48 \div 6 = 8$, $4800 \div 60$ is 80.
   So, $4840 \div 58$ is about 80.

> You can also estimate by thinking multiplication.
> $60 \times \mathbf{80} = 4800$
> So, $4840 \div 58$ is about 80.

➤ Use place value to divide.

Step 1

We cannot divide 4 thousands into 58 groups.
Trade 4 thousands for 40 hundreds.
40 hundreds + 8 hundreds = 48 hundreds
We cannot divide 48 hundreds into 58 groups.
Trade 48 hundreds for 480 tens.

480 tens + 4 tens = 484 tens

Round to estimate.
58 is close to 60. 484 tens is close to 480 tens.

480 tens ÷ 60 = 8 tens

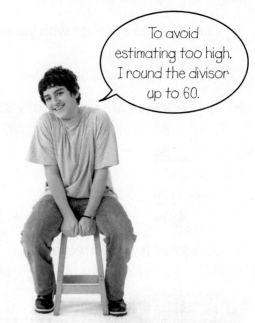

To avoid estimating too high, I round the divisor up to 60.

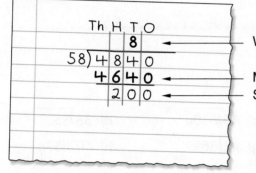

Write 8 tens.

Multiply 58 by 8 tens: 58 × 80 = 4640
Subtract. There are 200 ones left.

Step 2

Divide 200 ones into 58 equal groups.
Round to estimate. 200 is between 180 and 240.

180 ÷ 60 = 3   240 ÷ 60 = 4

So, 200 ÷ 60 is between 3 and 4.

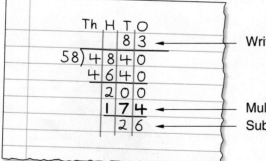

Write 3 ones.

Multiply 58 by 3 ones: 58 × 3 = 174
Subtract. There are 26 ones left.

4840 ÷ 58 = 83 R26

We write 83 R26 as $83\frac{26}{58}$.

We do not want to report the distance using a remainder or a fraction.

The fraction $\frac{26}{58}$ is about $\frac{30}{60}$, which is $\frac{1}{2}$ or 0.5.

So, we write $83\frac{26}{58}$ as about 83.5.

The whales travelled about 83.5 km each day.

➤ Compare the quotient with your estimate:

83.5 is close to 80.

So, 83.5 is a reasonable answer.

➤ To check your answer, multiply 83 by 58 and then add the remainder, 26:

$$\begin{array}{r} 83 \\ \times\ \ 58 \\ \hline 664 \\ +\ 4150 \\ \hline 4814 \end{array} \qquad 4814 + 26 = 4840$$

So, 83 R26 is the correct answer.

Practice

Use remainders where appropriate.

1. Divide, then check.

a) 73)8541 b) 62)9347 c) 45)6300 d) 38)3521

e) 58)6076 f) 97)1047 g) 42)8694 h) 60)6534

2. Estimate each quotient. Then divide.

a) 93 ÷ 21 b) 208 ÷ 73 c) 3550 ÷ 50

d) 9243 ÷ 46 e) 6843 ÷ 15 f) 7812 ÷ 93

3. In the fall, Monarch butterflies migrate to central Mexico.
The trip is about 4000 km. Suppose they fly 75 km each day.
About how long does it take the butterflies to reach Mexico?

4. Lucinda's great-grandfather is 1074 months old.
How old is he in years?

5. The Festival of the Midnight Sun Theatre
has 7875 seats arranged in 75 equal rows.
How many seats are in each row?

6. A DVD player costs $81, including tax.
How many DVD players can be bought for $3000?

7. Without dividing, predict which division question
has the greatest quotient. The least quotient.
Explain your prediction. Divide to check.

a) 43)7638 b) 19)8614 c) 85)7689

8. Use mental math, paper and pencil, or a calculator to find each quotient.
   How did you decide which method to use?

   a) $68\overline{)4735}$ b) $12\overline{)6000}$ c) $5679\overline{)85\,185}$

9. A lunar probe took 4316 photographs
   of the moon's surface.
   Thirty-two photographs had to be discarded.
   The remainder were divided among 42 scientists
   to be studied.
   How many photographs did each scientist study?

10. The owners of a building renovated 18 apartments.
    Painting cost $5580 and new lights cost $3186.
    What was the cost for each apartment?

11. a) Write a division question with a divisor of 73,
       a quotient of 105, and a remainder of 34.
    b) Write a story problem using your division question.
       Solve your problem.

12. A rectangular sheet of cardboard measures 64 cm by 15 cm.
    Suppose the width is changed to 16 cm.
    What would the length have to be for the rectangle
    to have the same area?

13. A newspaper prints 8762 papers.
    Each paper has 16 pages.
    A roll of newsprint can be used to print 6150 pages.
    How many rolls of newsprint are required?

14. A radio station received 3815 phone calls in 35 min.
    How many calls would it expect to receive in 1 h?

15. A 22-m by 14-m rectangular yard is to be seeded.
    Each bag of seed covers 18 m².
    How many bags of seed are needed?

Numbers Every Day

Calculator Skills

Find 3 prime numbers that
have a product of 12 121
and a sum of 71.

Reflect

Without dividing, how can you tell the quotient
3534 ÷ 57 has 2 digits? Explain.

LESSON

1 1. How many days is 1 million minutes?

2 2. Write each number in standard form.
   a) 20 000 000 + 3 000 000 + 60 000 + 4000 + 900 + 7
   b) 3 billion 400 thousand 7 hundred
   c) twenty-seven million fifty-seven thousand five hundred sixty-two

3. Write each number in expanded form.
   a) 14 086 368   b) 1 730 002   c) 857 293 179

4. Write the value of each underlined digit.
   a) 4<u>7</u> 681 042   b) 7 6<u>7</u>6 425   c) 500 <u>7</u>00 235

3 5. Write these numbers in order from least to greatest:
   36 001 304   9 495 627   36 001 523

4 6. List the first 3 common multiples of 4, 5, and 6.
   Explain how you know the numbers you find are common multiples.

7. Suppose you want to buy the same number
   of wieners and buns.
   How many packages of each would you buy?
   Give 3 different answers.

5 8. Tell if each number is prime or composite.
   How do you know?
   Write each composite number as a product of prime factors.
   a) 13   b) 21   c) 46   d) 36

9. Only one prime number is even.
   Which number is it?
   How do you know it is a prime number?

7 10. Use mental math to solve.
   a) 150 × 16 × 2   b) 240 + 83 + 160   c) 28 × 4

8 11. Use the order of operations to solve.
   a) 35 − 16 ÷ 4   b) 8 × (6 + 4)   c) 86 − 9 × 9

9

12. Estimate first. Then find each sum or difference.

    a) 572 + 368 + 427 + 385   **b)** 199 + 402 + 350 + 797

    c)   76 423   **d)**   82 003   **e)**   8707
          − 9 389   − 8 114   − 3842

10

13. Multiply.
Estimate to check your answers.

    a)   685   **b)**   2497   **c)**   1997
        $\times$ 26 $\times$ 84 $\times$ 68

11
12

14. Divide.
Check the quotients by using
the inverse operation.

    a) $27\overline{)4539}$ **b)** $72\overline{)7800}$

    c) $24\overline{)1638}$ **d)** $34\overline{)3325}$

15. Frankie has 1350 collector cards.
He can fit 12 on each page of a scrapbook.
How many pages can Frankie fill?

16. Mrs. Li has 107 beehives.
She harvested about 64 kg of honey per hive.
About how many kilograms of honey
did Mrs. Li harvest?

17. Sandhya has to bank 331 pennies, 15 nickels,
183 dimes, and 212 quarters from her piggy bank.
She rolls as many coins as possible.
A roll holds 50 pennies, 40 nickels, 50 dimes,
or 40 quarters.

    a) How many rolls of each type of coin
        did she take to the bank?

    b) What was Sandhya's total bank deposit?

U N I T

2 Learning Goals

☑ read and write whole numbers
in standard, expanded, and
written forms

☑ use place value to represent
and read whole numbers

☑ compare and order whole
numbers

☑ identify and describe multiples
and factors to 100

☑ identify and describe
composite and prime numbers
to 100

☑ use order of operations

☑ estimate sums, differences,
products, and quotients

☑ use mental math to add,
subtract, multiply, and divide

☑ add four 3-digit numbers and
subtract from a 5-digit number

☑ multiply and divide by a 2-digit
number

☑ pose and solve multistep
problems

Honeybees have 4 wings that beat about 11 400 times per minute.

A honeybee flies an average of 22 km each hour.

A honeybee visits about 4400 flowers to gather enough nectar to make 10 g of honey.

During her busy season, the queen bee lays about 1500 eggs in 24 h.

In 2000, there were 603 828 hives in Canada. The average number of hives per beekeeper was 61, and the average yield of honey per hive was 52 kg.

Your work should show
- ✓ that you can choose the correct operation
- ✓ how you calculated and checked your solutions
- ✓ an interesting story problem involving whole numbers
- ✓ clear explanations of your solutions and strategies

Solve each of questions 1 to 3.
Check your solutions. Show all your work.

1. During her busy season, about how many eggs does the queen bee lay each hour? Each minute?

2. Each day, the queen bee eats 80 times her mass in food.
   Suppose you needed to eat 80 times your mass each day.
   How many kilograms of food would you eat each day? Each month?

3. The typical Canadian eats about 880 g of honey each year.
   Millicent is 12 years old.
   She estimates she has eaten about 10.5 kg of honey in her lifetime.
   Is Millicent a typical Canadian honey eater? Explain.

4. Use some of the honeybee data on page 78 or use data you can find about honeybees.
   Write a story problem.
   Solve the problem.
   Describe your solution strategy.

Reflect on the Unit

Explain how you decide which computation method (mental math, paper and pencil, estimation, or calculator) to use when calculating with whole numbers.

3

Angle Hunt

Geometry

Learning Goals

- estimate, measure, and construct angles to 360°
- classify figures by side and by angle properties
- construct figures
- identify, sketch, and draw nets of solids
- build and draw objects

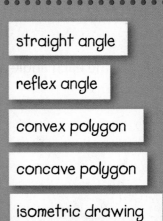

straight angle

reflex angle

convex polygon

concave polygon

isometric drawing

Angles and geometric figures
are everywhere!

- Which figures do you see?

- How are the figures different? The same?

- What types of angles do you see?

- How are the angles different? The same?

1 Investigating Angles

Name each angle as acute, obtuse, or right.

Explore

Your teacher will give you a large copy of these angles.

➤ Estimate the measure of each angle.
Then find each angle measure. Use any materials that help.
Record your estimates and the angle measures.

➤ Find the sum of the angles in each pair:
A and B   C and D   E and F
What do you notice about the angles in each pair?

Show **and** Share

Share your work with a classmate.
How did you estimate the measure of each angle?
Were your estimates reasonable? Explain.
Describe the method you used to find each angle measure.
What is the sum of the two angles formed by one pair of arms?

Numbers Every Day

Number Strategies

Order the numbers in each set from least to greatest.

- 123 321, 121 232,
  123 231, 113 321

- 4 432 344, 4 344 342,
  4 242 444, 4 432 413

➤ Some angles are greater than or equal to 180°.

A **straight angle** measures 180°.

The measure of a **reflex angle** is between 180° and 360°.

The measure of an angle in one complete turn is 360°.

➤ You can use a 360° protractor to measure a reflex angle.

Step 1
Place the protractor on the angle with the vertex at the centre of the protractor. Align one arm of the angle with the base line of the protractor through 0°.

Step 2
Start at 0° on the arm along the base line. Read the measure at the point where the other arm of the angle meets the protractor. This angle measures 225°.

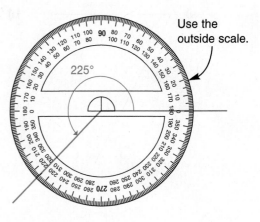

Use the outside scale.

225°

➤ You can use a 360° protractor to construct a 300° angle.

Step 1
Use a ruler to draw one arm of the angle.

Step 2
Place the protractor on the arm with one end at the centre of the protractor. The arm lines up with the base line of the protractor.
Start at 0° on the arm along the base line.
Make a mark at 300°.

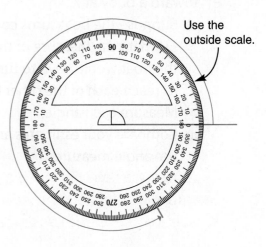

Use the outside scale.

Step 3

Remove the protractor.
Draw the second arm.
Label the angle with its measure.

300°

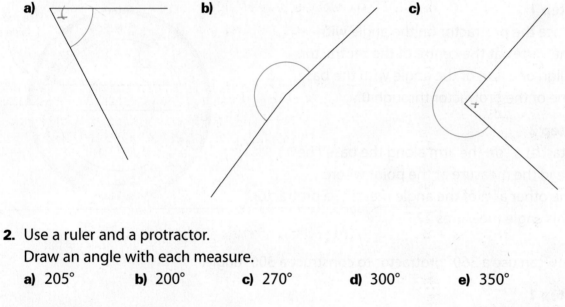

Practice

1. For each angle:
   • Tell whether it is acute, right, obtuse, straight, or reflex.
   • Estimate its measure.
   • Measure to check.

   a)   **b)**   **c)**

2. Use a ruler and a protractor.
   Draw an angle with each measure.
   a) 205°   **b)** 200°   **c)** 270°   **d)** 300°   **e)** 350°

3. The sailboat is headed due east
   toward a buoy at X.
   a) Suppose the boat turns counterclockwise.
   Estimate the measure of the angle
   the boat would have to turn through
   to reach each of the other buoys.
   b) Measure each angle.
   c) Compare your estimates and
   the angle measures.

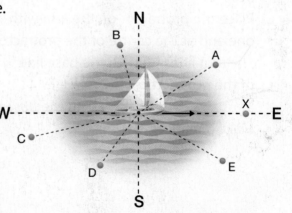

4. The moon orbits Earth in a counterclockwise direction.
The picture shows the phases of the moon as it orbits Earth.

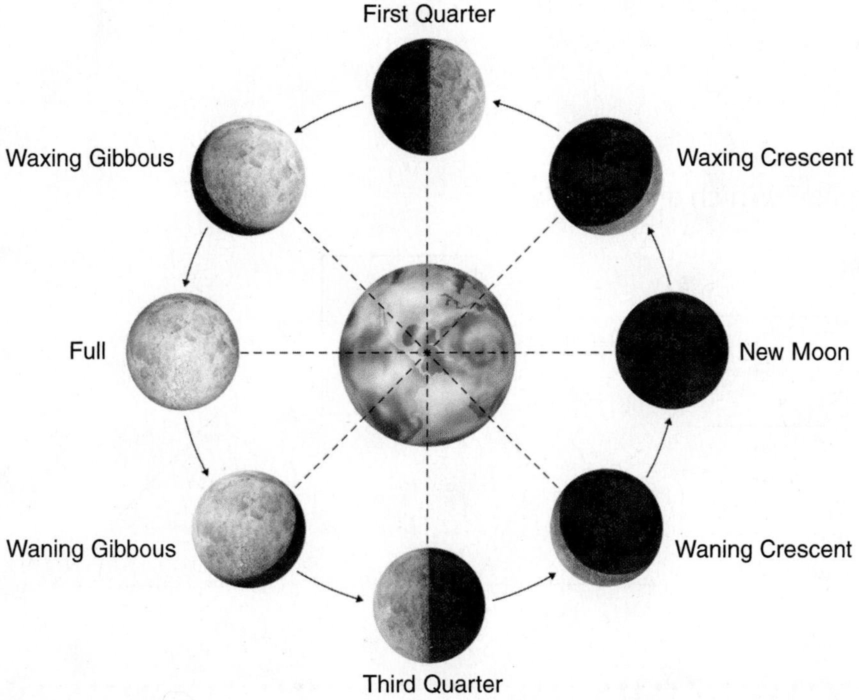

First Quarter

Waxing Gibbous

Waxing Crescent

Full

New Moon

Waning Gibbous

Waning Crescent

Third Quarter

a) Estimate the angle through which the moon revolves from
the new moon to each other phase of the moon.
How did you estimate each angle?

b) Find each angle measure.
How do the angle measures compare to your estimates?

5. Is it possible to draw a reflex angle so
the other angle formed by the arms is:
a) acute? **b)** obtuse? **c)** straight?
Use examples to explain.

6. Suppose you have a 180° protractor.
a) Describe how you would measure a reflex angle.
b) Describe how you would draw a reflex angle
that measures 245°.

Reflect

How is a reflex angle related to the
other angle formed by the same
arms? Use examples to explain.

At Home

Look around your home for
examples of angles with
different sizes.
Sketch each angle and estimate
its measure.

Classifying Figures

Which figures are regular? Which are irregular?
How do you know?

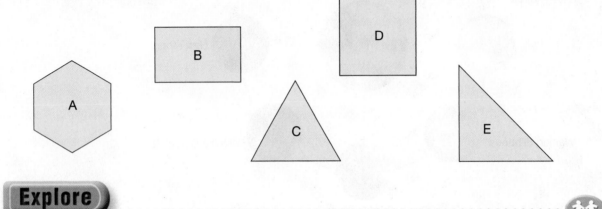

Explore

You will need scissors, chart paper, and a large copy of these figures.

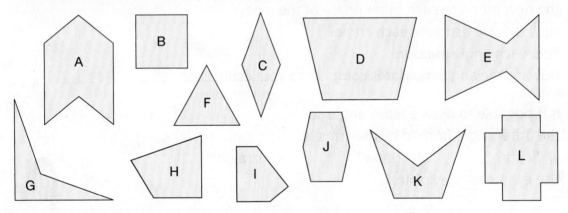

➤ Cut out the figures.
On chart paper, draw a large Venn diagram with 2 loops.
Decide how you will label each loop. Choose from these attributes.

Regular	Irregular	Triangle	Acute Angle
Quadrilateral	Pentagon	Hexagon	Right Angle
Parallel Sides	Equal Sides	Reflex Angle	Obtuse Angle

Take turns choosing a figure and placing it on the Venn diagram.
Record your work.

➤ Repeat the activity.
This time, choose attributes that allow you to place
as many figures in the loops as possible.

Show *and* Share

Share your sorting with another pair of students.
Which figure had the most attributes? The fewest?
Which attribute described the most figures? Why?

Connect ....

There are many ways to sort and classify figures.

➤ We can sort triangles by the number of equal sides and by angle measure.

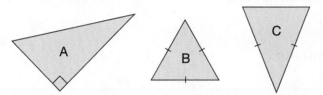 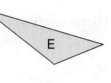

	Acute	Obtuse	Right
Scalene		E	A
Isosceles	C		D
Equilateral	B		

➤ We can sort quadrilaterals in a Venn diagram.

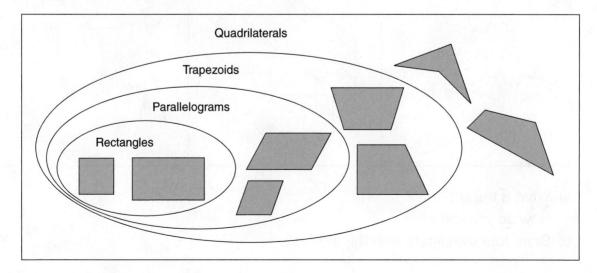

➤ Each of these polygons has all angles less than 180°.
These are **convex polygons**.

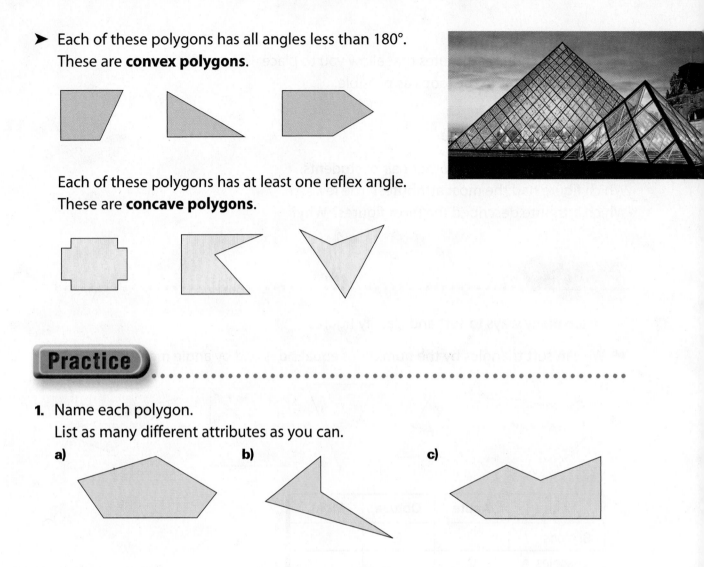

Each of these polygons has at least one reflex angle.
These are **concave polygons**.

Practice

1. Name each polygon.
   List as many different attributes as you can.

   a)

   b)

   c)

2. Find the mystery attribute.

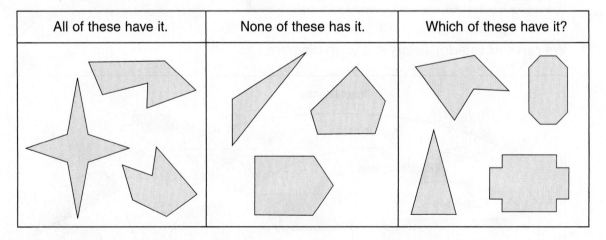

All of these have it.	None of these has it.	Which of these have it?

   a) What is the attribute?
   How do you know?
   b) Draw your own figure with this attribute.

You will need a large copy of these figures for questions 3 to 5.

3. Sort these figures using a Venn diagram with 2 loops.
How did you choose the attributes?

4. a) Sort the figures using a Venn diagram with 3 loops.
Record your work.
   b) Do any of the loops overlap?
How do you know?

5. a) Identify the figures that are quadrilaterals.
   b) Use a protractor to measure the angles of each quadrilateral.
Then, add the measures for each quadrilateral.
What do you notice?

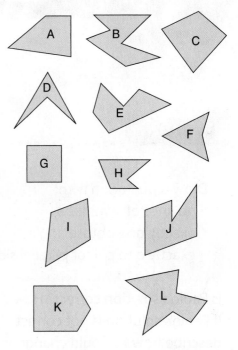

6. Use dot paper.
Sketch 3 different figures for each set of clues.
Name each figure.
   a) I do not have any right angles; all my sides have the same length.
   b) I have a reflex angle and four sides.
   c) I have exactly two parallel sides.

7. Use dot paper.
   a) Draw a polygon. Label it A.
List the attributes of polygon A.
   b) Draw a different polygon. Label it B.
List the attributes of polygon B.
   c) Compare polygons A and B.
How are they the same?
How are they different?

Reflect

Describe some different ways you can sort and classify figures.
Use pictures and words to explain.

Numbers Every Day

Mental Math

Estimate each quotient.

2343 ÷ 99

5456 ÷ 50

3620 ÷ 60

8405 ÷ 12

Strategies Toolkit

Explore

Draw a pentagon with:
• no lines of symmetry
• exactly one obtuse angle
• exactly one pair of parallel sides

Is Paolo's solution correct? How do you know?
If Paolo's solution is not correct,
describe how he could change the figure
so his solution is correct.

Show and Share

Share your work with a classmate.
Is it possible to draw more than one figure to solve
this problem? Explain.

Connect

➤ Marg drew this figure to solve the problem below.

Draw a concave pentagon with:
• at least one right angle
• no parallel sides

Marg checked that the figure
she drew meets all the criteria.

• The figure is a pentagon.   Yes
• The figure is concave.   Yes
• The figure has at least one right angle.   No
• The figure does not have any parallel sides.   Yes

Strategies for Success

• **Get unstuck.**
• **Check and reflect.**
• **Focus on the problem.**
• **Represent your thinking.**
• **Select an answer.**
• **Do your best on a test.**
• **Explain your answer.**

LESSON FOCUS | Check and reflect.

Marg's figure is a concave pentagon with no right angles and no sides parallel.
She must change the figure
to include at least one right angle.

➤ When you solve problems, always check your solution.

✔ What was I asked to find? Did I answer the question?
✔ Did I include all the parts I needed?
✔ Is my answer reasonable?
✔ Are the calculations correct?
✔ How well did my strategy work?

Practice

1. Find the mystery attribute.
   Show how you checked your answer.

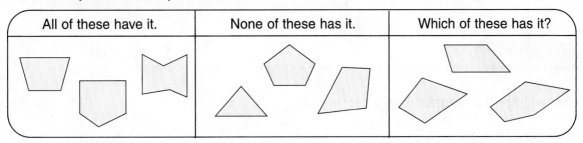

All of these have it.	None of these has it.	Which of these has it?

2. A student found the quotient 2046 ÷ 13 this way:
   a) Is the answer reasonable? How do you know?
   b) Is the answer correct?
   If it is not correct, find the error.
   Show your work.

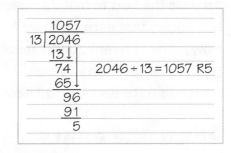

```
       1057
  13 ) 2046
       13↓
       74↓        2046 ÷ 13 = 1057 R5
       65↓
        96
        91
         5
```

Reflect

Why is it important to always check your solution?

Constructing Figures

Figures can be combined to make another figure.

Explore

You will need a tangram and a protractor.

Choose 2 or more tans.
Arrange the tans to make a quadrilateral with
two angles that each measure 135°.
How many different quadrilaterals with
two 135° angles can you make?
Sketch or trace each quadrilateral.

Show *and* Share

Share your quadrilaterals with another pair of students.
Describe the quadrilaterals.
How did you decide which tans to use?

Another way to construct a figure is to use a ruler and a compass or a protractor.

➤ Construct △ABC with sides AB = 6 cm,
AC = 5 cm, and BC = 4 cm.

The △ symbol means triangle.

Step 1
Use the ruler to draw segment AB 6 cm long.

Step 2
Set the compass so the pencil and
the compass point are 5 cm apart.
Place the compass point on A.
Draw an arc.
Set the compass so the pencil and
the compass point are 4 cm apart.
Place the compass point on B.
Draw an arc so the two arcs intersect.
Label the point C where the arcs intersect.

Step 3
Draw segments AC and BC to complete
the triangle.
Label each segment with its length.

When an angle is identified
by three letters, the middle letter
indicates the vertex of the angle.
For example, ∠A is also ∠CAB.

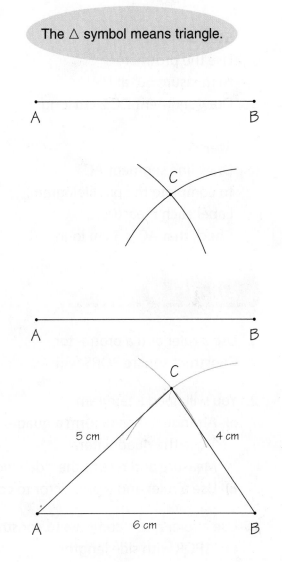

➤ Use a ruler and a protractor to construct parallelogram BACD, with
AC = BD = 5 cm, BA = DC = 2 cm,
∠ABD = 120°, and ∠BDC = 60°.

Step 1
Use a ruler to draw
segment BD 5 cm long.

Since I know the measures
of the angles at B and at D,
I draw BD first.

B   D

Step 2

At B, use the protractor
to measure 120°.
Draw segment BA 2 cm long.

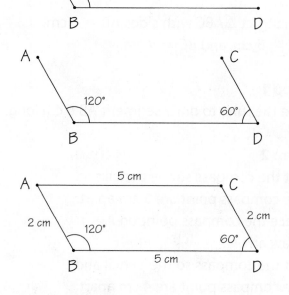

Step 3

Use the protractor
to measure 60° at D.
Draw segment DC 2 cm long.

Step 4

Draw line segment AC
to complete the parallelogram.
Label each measure.
Check that AC is 5 cm long.

Practice

1. Use a ruler and a protractor.
   Construct square PQRS with side length 8 cm.

2. You will need a tangram.
   a) Arrange 3 tans to form a quadrilateral.
   Trace the quadrilateral.
   Measure and record the side lengths and the angles.
   b) Use a ruler and a protractor to construct the quadrilateral from part a.

3. Use a ruler and a compass to construct each triangle:
   a) △PQR with side lengths
   PQ = 6 cm, QR = 8 cm, and PR = 10 cm
   b) △CDE with all sides 65 mm long
   c) △LMN with two sides 7 cm long
   and one side 4 cm long
   In each case, how many different triangles are possible?
   How do you know?
   Classify each triangle by sides and by angles.

4. Construct △FGH with ∠HFG = 50°,
   ∠FGH = 60°, and ∠GHF = 70°.
   Compare your triangle with that of another student.
   Are the triangles congruent? How do you know?

5. Use a ruler and a compass to construct △BCD.
The side lengths are:
BD = 85 mm
CD = 80 mm
BC = 43 mm
Measure the angles.

6. Use triangular dot paper.
   a) Construct a concave hexagon.
   The hexagon must have at least one angle
   with each measure: 60°, 240°
   Three or more sides must be 3 units long.
   How many different hexagons can you draw?
   b) Choose one of your hexagons.
   Explain how you decided each side length and angle measure.

7. Construct quadrilateral CDEF with these angle measures:
   ∠C = 110°
   ∠D = 130°
   ∠F = 50°
   a) What is the measure of ∠E?
   b) Can you draw a different quadrilateral CDEF? Explain.

8. Use a ruler and a protractor.
   Construct trapezoid STUV with sides TU = 8 cm,
   TS = VU = 3 cm, and with ∠STU = ∠TUV= 70°.
   What is the length of SV?

9. Construct two different pentagons MNPQR with these measures:
   RQ = QP = PN = 6 cm; RM = MN = 4 cm; ∠RQP = ∠QPN = 90°
   a) In each pentagon, find the measures of ∠QRM, ∠RMN, and ∠MNP.
   b) Why is it possible to draw two different pentagons?

Reflect

Describe how you could construct a concave
pentagon with 3 equal sides and one angle that
measures 240°.
Use diagrams to explain.

Numbers Every Day

Number Strategies

Find each quotient.

1530 ÷ 9

8575 ÷ 25

6344 ÷ 52

2136 ÷ 12

Work with a partner.

Use *The Geometer's Sketchpad*.

Follow these steps to construct polygons and to measure angles.

1. Open a new sketch in *The Geometer's Sketchpad*.
   Click: File , then click: New Sketch   Ctrl+N

2. To **draw a polygon**, select the Straightedge Tool, ╱.
   Click, hold down the mouse button, and drag
   until the segment is as long as you want it.
   Release the mouse button.
   Place the cursor on one endpoint of the segment, then
   click and drag to construct the next side of the polygon.
   Continue to draw segments until your polygon is complete.

3. To **label the polygon**, select the Text Tool, A .
   The cursor will look like this: ☝

   Click each vertex.
   Each vertex will be labelled with a letter.

   To change a label, double-click the label.
   A dialogue box will appear.
   Type the new label, then click: OK
   Click anywhere outside the figure to deselect everything.

4. To **measure the side lengths** of the polygon,
   select the Selection Arrow Tool, ↖.
   Click to select one side of the polygon.
   Click: Measure , then click: Length
   The length of the side appears in the top left of the screen.
   Click anywhere outside the polygon to deselect the segment.

   Repeat to measure each side of the polygon.

5. To **measure the angles** in the polygon,
   select the Selection Arrow Tool, ![arrow].
   Click to select 3 vertices in clockwise order.
   Click: Measure , then click: Angle
   The measure of the angle appears in the top left of the screen.
   Click anywhere outside the polygon to deselect the angle measure.

   Repeat to measure each angle in the polygon.

6. To **change the shape** of the polygon,
   select the Selection Arrow Tool, ![arrow].
   Click a line segment or a vertex.
   Hold down the mouse button.
   Drag the line segment or vertex until it is where you want it.
   Watch what happens to the side lengths and angle measures
   as you move the line segment or vertex.
   Release the mouse button.

7. Save your polygon.
   Click: File , then click: Save As...
   Give your file a name.
   Click: Save

8. Print your polygon.
   Click: File , then click: Print...
   Click: OK

9. Repeat Steps 1 to 8 to construct and
   measure polygons with different numbers
   of sides.

Reflect

What is the advantage of using a computer to draw
a polygon?
Use diagrams and words to explain.

5 Nets of Objects

You will need scissors and tape.
Your teacher will give you a large copy of these diagrams.

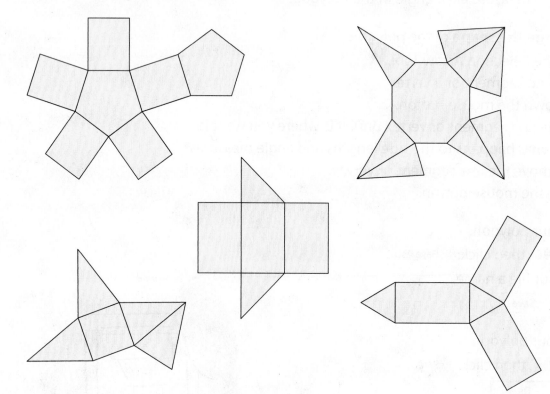

Is each diagram the net of an object?
If your answer is yes, identify the object.
If your answer is no, what changes could you make
so it could be a net?

Show *and* Share

Share your work with another pair of students.
How can you tell if a diagram is a net for an object?
How do you identify the object?

A net shows all the faces of an object.
Each face is joined to another face along one edge.
The net can be folded to make the object.

To identify if a diagram is a net for an object,
look at each figure and at how the figures are arranged.

➤ This is *not* a net for a rectangular prism.

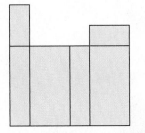

The rectangles for the end faces of the prism are along
the same side of the net.
If this diagram were folded, it would be a box that is open at one end.
At the opposite end, two rectangles would overlap.

➤ This is a net for a pentagonal pyramid.
The diagram has 1 regular pentagon
and 5 congruent isosceles triangles.
If this diagram were folded, it would be
a pentagonal pyramid.
Pairs of sides that align to form an edge
of the pyramid have the same length.

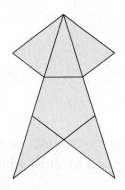

Practice •

You will need a variety of objects.

1. Identify the object that has each net.

   a) 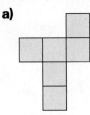   b)    c)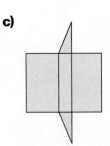

2. A pyramid has a regular octagon for its base.
The other faces are isosceles triangles.
Sketch a net for a regular octagonal pyramid.
Use hatch marks to show which sides have the same length.
How do you know how many congruent faces to draw?

3. Which diagrams are nets? How do you know?
For each net, identify the object.

a) 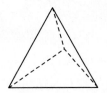   b) 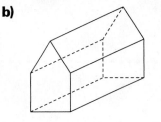   c) 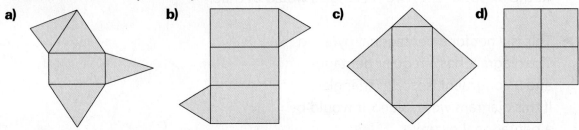   d)

4. Sketch two different nets for each object.
Use hatch marks to show which sides have the same length.

a)   b)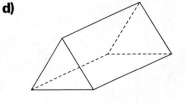

c) 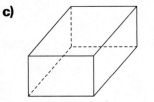   d)

5. Identify the object that has each set of faces.
Sketch the faces to form a net.
How do you know that your arrangement is a net?
a) four equilateral triangles and one square
b) two squares and four rectangles
c) one rectangle and two pairs
of congruent triangles
d) five triangles and one pentagon
e) four equilateral triangles

6. You will need triangular dot paper.
a) A triangular pyramid with all faces congruent
is a regular tetrahedron.
Draw all the possible nets for a regular tetrahedron.
b) Draw all the possible nets for a pyramid with an equilateral
triangular base and three isosceles triangular faces.
c) Compare your nets in parts a and b.
Explain any differences.

7. The sums of the numbers on opposite faces of a number cube are equal.
Copy each net onto grid paper.
Label each face with a number from 1 to 6.

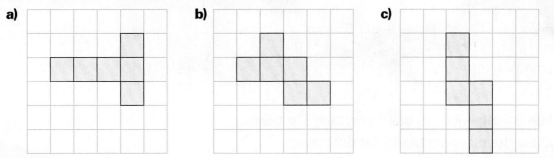

a)　　　　　**b)**　　　　　**c)**

Reflect

When you see a diagram that may be a net of an object, how do you find out if it is a net?
Use an example to explain.

Numbers Every Day

Number Strategies

Round each number to the nearest thousand and to the nearest hundred thousand.

- 4 682 364
- 803 091 531
- 9 989 899

Illustrating Objects

Explore

You will need linking cubes, triangular dot paper, and square grid paper.

➤ Use linking cubes to build a rectangular prism.
Draw the prism on triangular dot paper.
The length, width, and height of the prism
must be visible.
➤ Use grid paper.
Draw the top, front, and side views of your prism.

Show and Share

Trade drawings with another pair of students.
Use the dot paper drawing or the views to make
your classmates' prism.
Compare your prism with theirs.

Numbers Every Day

Number Strategies

Write 4 different numbers
that have a remainder of 3
when divided by 5.
How did you find the
numbers?

Here is a prism made with linking cubes.

➤ We can draw the prism on triangular dot paper.

First, join 3 dots for 1 vertical edge.	

Join 4 dots to draw the edges of cubes that appear to go up to the right. Join 5 dots to draw the edges of cubes that appear to go up to the left.	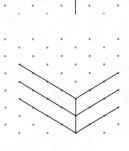

Join the dots to represent the other vertical edges of cubes.	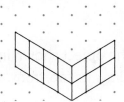

Join dots to complete the prism.	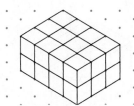

➤ We can build the prism given its top, front, and side views.
Join cubes to match the top view.
Add another layer to make the front view.
Check that the side view matches.

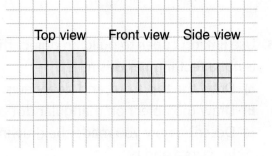

1. Build each object.
   Then, draw the object on triangular dot paper.

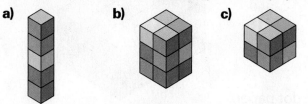

   a)   **b)**   **c)**

2. Draw the top, front, and side views for each object in question 1.

3. For each set of views:
   • Use linking cubes to build the object.
   • Draw the object on triangular dot paper.

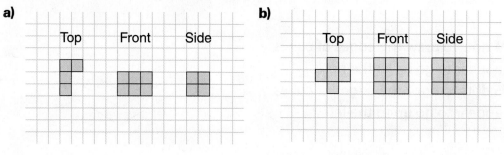

   a)   Top   Front   Side

   b)   Top   Front   Side

4. **a)** Build the object shown in the drawing.
   b) Then, draw its top, front, and side views.

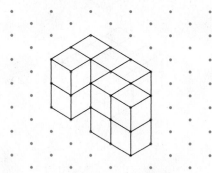

A drawing on triangular dot paper is called an **isometric drawing**.

5. Use linking cubes to build an object that is *not* a rectangular prism.
   a) Draw the top, front, and side views.
   b) Draw the object on triangular dot paper.
   c) Describe how you made the drawings in parts a and b.

6. For each object:
- Draw its front and side views.
- Draw it on triangular dot paper.

a)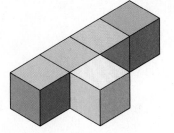

b)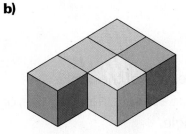

7. Here is the net for an object.

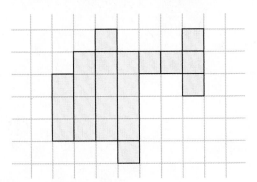

a) Build the object.
b) Draw the object on triangular dot paper.

Reflect

When you see an object made with linking cubes, how do you draw it?

LESSON

1

1. For each angle:
    *   Estimate the measure of the angle.
    *   Classify the angle as acute, right, obtuse, or reflex.
    *   Measure the angle.

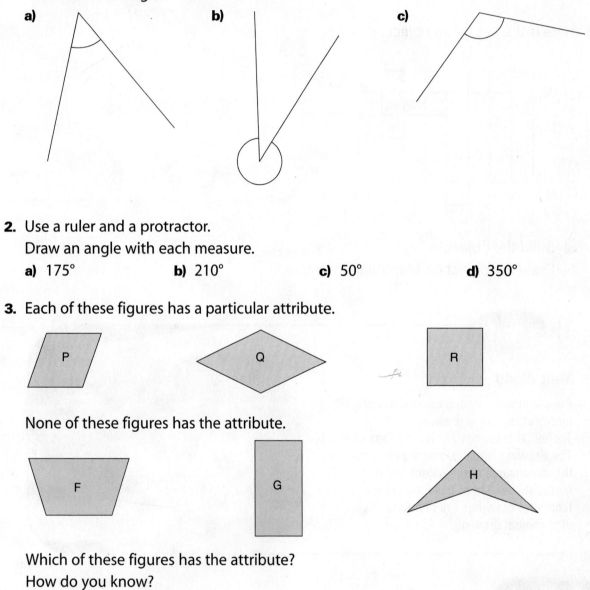

    a)   b)   c)

2. Use a ruler and a protractor.
    Draw an angle with each measure.
    a) 175°   **b)** 210°   **c)** 50°   **d)** 350°

2

3. Each of these figures has a particular attribute.

    P   Q   R

    None of these figures has the attribute.

    F   G   H

    Which of these figures has the attribute?
    How do you know?

    A   B   C   D

4

4. Use a ruler, a protractor, and a compass.
Construct rectangle KLMN with these side lengths:
KL = 8 cm, NK = 4 cm

5. Use a ruler and a protractor.
  a) Construct a parallelogram with two angles that measure 70° and 110°.
  Two side lengths are 9 cm and 5 cm.
  b) Find the measures of the other 2 angles and 2 sides.

5

6. Which diagrams are nets?
For each net, identify the object.

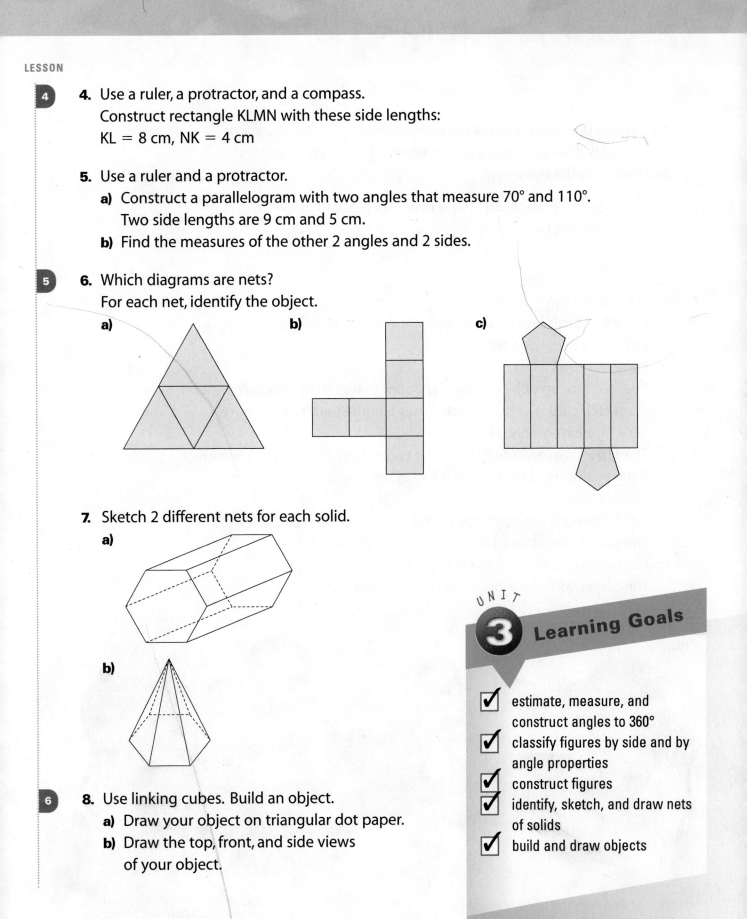

a)

b)

c)

7. Sketch 2 different nets for each solid.
  a)

  b)

6

8. Use linking cubes. Build an object.
  a) Draw your object on triangular dot paper.
  b) Draw the top, front, and side views
  of your object.

Angle Hunt

Angles and geometric figures are everywhere.
You will play, then design, a game in which you search for angles
and figures in the classroom.

You will need a protractor, a ruler, a pencil, paper, and game cards.
Work in a group of 4.

Part 1

➤ Shuffle the game cards.
Place the cards face down in the centre of the table.
Decide who will go first.

➤ Player 1 draws a card.
She looks for an object in the classroom that matches the description.
If a sketch card is drawn, she sketches a figure with the attribute.
Each figure may only be used once.
The other players identify the object and check that Player 1 is correct.
If the answer is correct, Player 1 keeps the card and it is the next
player's turn.
If the answer is incorrect, the card is passed to the next player to try.
The card is passed until it is answered correctly.

➤ Players take turns until all cards have been drawn.
The player with the most cards is the winner.

Part 2

Play the game again.

➤ This time, Player 1 takes the top 2 cards.
  He hunts for one figure that has both attributes.
  If 2 sketch cards are drawn, he sketches a figure
  with both attributes.

➤ If the answer is correct, Player 1 keeps both cards.
  If the combination is impossible, one card
  is returned to the bottom of the pile and
  the next card is selected.

➤ If the answer is incorrect, the next player
  may choose either one or both cards.
  Additional cards are returned to the pile.

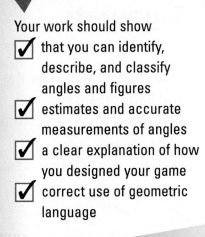

Check List

Your work should show
- ✓ that you can identify, describe, and classify angles and figures
- ✓ estimates and accurate measurements of angles
- ✓ a clear explanation of how you designed your game
- ✓ correct use of geometric language

Part 3

Design your own Angle Hunt game.
Include a set of game cards and instructions on how to play the game.

Reflect on the Unit

What have you learned about angles, polygons, and objects?
Use diagrams and words to explain.

Cross Strand Investigation

Ziggurats

Ziggurats were built by the ancient Assyrians and Babylonians.
A ziggurat is a tiered pyramid that was used as a temple.
Each tier of a ziggurat is smaller than the one below it.

> Tiers are layers arranged one on top of another.

You will need linking cubes and triangular dot paper.

Part 1

➤ Use linking cubes.
Build a ziggurat with each number of tiers:
1 tier   2 tiers   3 tiers
Each tier is centred on the tier below it.

Each block covers the block below it.

You can do this.

You cannot do this.

➤ Draw each ziggurat on triangular dot paper.

➤ Predict the number of cubes required to build a 4-tier ziggurat.
Build it to check your prediction.

Part 2

➤ Find the volume of each ziggurat in Part 1.
Record the numbers of tiers and the volumes in a table.
Write a pattern rule for the volumes.

➤ Use the pattern rule.
What is the volume of a 6-tier ziggurat? Explain.

Display Your Work

Create a summary of your work.
Describe all the patterns you used.
Use pictures, numbers, and words.

Take It Further

Suppose you built staircases like this one.
Predict a pattern rule for the volumes of staircases
with different numbers of tiers.
Build the staircases to check your prediction.
Draw each staircase on triangular dot paper.

UNIT

4

Decimals

Harnessing the Wind

Wind is a clean, renewable source of energy used to produce electricity. It does not pollute or contribute to global warming.

Learning Goals

- relate fractions to decimals
- represent, read, and write decimals
- compare and order decimals
- round decimals
- estimate decimal sums, differences, products, and quotients
- add, subtract, multiply, and divide decimals to thousandths
- pose and solve problems involving decimals
- select operations and solve multistep problems

112

Weather Dancer is a 72-m wind turbine in southern Alberta. It generates 2.96 gigawatt hours of electricity each year. Weather Dancer supplies electricity to 460 homes.

Electrical power is measured in units called watts.

1000 watts = 1 kilowatt
1 000 000 watts = 1 megawatt
1 000 000 000 watts = 1 gigawatt

The amount of electricity generated or consumed is measured in watt hours. One kilowatt hour means 1 kilowatt of electricity is used in 1 h.

William Big Bull, a member of the Piikani First Nation, received a Canadian Environment Award in 2004. Through his efforts, Weather Dancer was built.

- How are kilowatts, megawatts, and gigawatts related?

- About how many gigawatt hours of electricity will Weather Dancer generate in 5 years?

- How could you find how many megawatt hours of electricity Weather Dancer generates in 1 year?

- A Canadian household uses about 20.75 kilowatt hours of electricity each day. About how much is used in 1 week?

Numbers in the Media

Scientists Find Fossil 2.1 Billion Years Old

Reports in the media
often contain large numbers.

Montreal Group Builds Millipede
Using 3 Million LEGO Bricks

Dutch Team Topples
3.8 Million Dominoes

You have represented large numbers in standard form,
expanded form, word form, and place-value charts.
In this lesson, you will explore another way to represent large numbers.

Explore

You will need newspapers and magazines.

Find examples of large numbers represented in different ways.
Record the numbers you find.
Rewrite each number as many different ways as you can.

Show *and* Share

Share your work with another pair of students.
Which of the numbers do you think are estimates? Explain.

Numbers in the media are often rounded and reported using decimals or fractions.

➤ **2.25 Million Cast Votes for World's Funniest Joke**

Write 2.25 million in standard form.
2.25 million is 2 million plus 0.25 million.
0.25 million is $\frac{1}{4}$ million.

Think: There are 1000 thousands in 1 million.
So, there are 250 thousands,
or 250 000, in 0.25 million.

2.25 million is 2 250 000.

> 2.25 million is the number of votes rounded to the nearest hundredth of a million.

➤ **World Population to Reach $7\frac{1}{2}$ Billion by 2020**

Write $7\frac{1}{2}$ billion in standard form.
$7\frac{1}{2}$ billion is 7 billion plus $\frac{1}{2}$ billion.

Think: There are 1000 millions in 1 billion.
So, there are 500 millions,
or 500 000 000, in $\frac{1}{2}$ billion.

$7\frac{1}{2}$ billion is 7 500 000 000.

> $7\frac{1}{2}$ billion is 7.5 billion.
> So, $7\frac{1}{2}$ billion represents the world population rounded to the nearest tenth of a billion.

➤ In 1961, the population of Canada
was 18 238 247.
You can write a headline using this number
rounded to the nearest tenth of a million.

18 238 247 rounded to the nearest
hundred thousand is 18 200 000.
You can write this as 18.2 million.

> $\frac{1}{10}$ of a million is 100 000.

Canada's Population Reached 18.2 Million in 1961

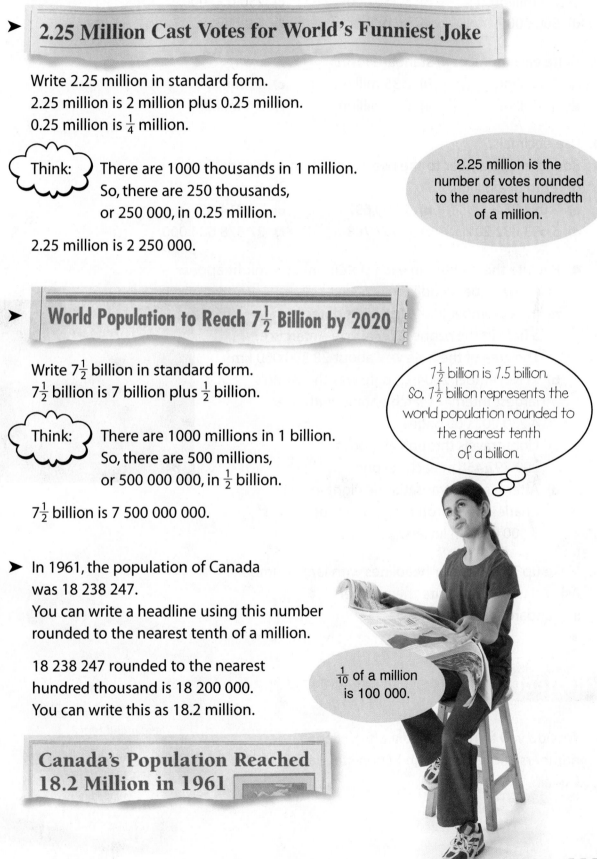

1. Rewrite each number as many different ways as you can.
   a) 2.5 million
   b) 3 750 000
   c) 250 000 000
   d) 500 000
   e) $9\frac{1}{4}$ million
   f) 4.9 billion

2. Write each number in standard form.
   a) 7.8 billion
   b) 2.35 million
   c) $4\frac{1}{4}$ million
   d) 5.1 billion
   e) 6.15 billion
   f) 3.6 million

3. Use decimals.
   Round each number to the nearest tenth of a million
   or tenth of a billion.
   a) 7 097 284
   b) 2 500 697
   c) 17 914 351
   d) 5 693 482 201
   e) 6 497 708
   f) 27 578 684 000

4. Rewrite the number in each statement as it might appear
   in a newspaper headline.
   a) In September 2000, scientists detected
   a hole in the ozone layer above Antarctica.
   The area of the hole was about 28 300 000 km².
   b) In November 2004, Google was the world's
   largest Internet search engine, with over
   4 280 000 000 pages.
   c) Light travels through air about
   299 792 458 m each second.
   d) After his solo transatlantic flight in 1927,
   Charles Lindbergh received about
   3 500 000 fan letters.

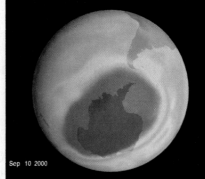
Sep 10 2000

5. Make up 3 newspaper headlines with large numbers.
   Ask a classmate to write the numbers
   in standard form.

Numbers Every Day

Number Strategies

Write each number in
expanded form.

947 503

20 807 476

2 458 289

Reflect

Why do you think the media often round large
numbers and record them in non-standard forms?
Explain.

2 Exploring Thousandths

This design contains 100 small square tiles.
Each tile represents one-hundredth ($\frac{1}{100}$) of the design.
What fraction of the design is each colour?

 **Explore** ·

You will need Base Ten Blocks and coloured pencils.
Your teacher will give you a set of grids like this one.

Each grid has 1000 congruent squares.

➤ Suppose ▨ represents 1 whole.
What does 1 flat represent? 1 rod?
1 unit cube?

➤ Use Base Ten Blocks to model
each number.
Each time, use the fewest
blocks possible.

$\frac{700}{1000}$ $\frac{3}{10}$ $1\frac{41}{1000}$ $\frac{70}{100}$ $\frac{732}{1000}$ $\frac{1062}{1000}$ $\frac{300}{1000}$

➤ Colour grids to show each number.
Write each number in words.

Show and Share

Share your work with another pair of students.
How did you decide what each type of Base Ten Block represents? Explain.
For which pairs of numbers did you use the same blocks? Why?
For which numbers did you use more than one grid? Why?

LESSON FOCUS | Explore mixed numbers, fractions, and decimals with thousandths.   **117**

➤ Numbers with tenths and hundredths can be written as decimals.

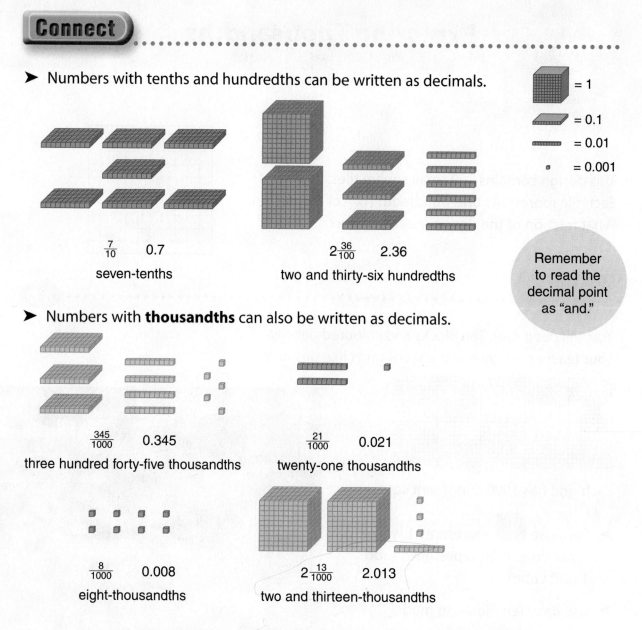

= 1
= 0.1
= 0.01
= 0.001

$\frac{7}{10}$ 0.7

seven-tenths

$2\frac{36}{100}$ 2.36

two and thirty-six hundredths

Remember to read the decimal point as "and."

➤ Numbers with **thousandths** can also be written as decimals.

$\frac{345}{1000}$ 0.345

three hundred forty-five thousandths

$\frac{21}{1000}$ 0.021

twenty-one thousandths

$\frac{8}{1000}$ 0.008

eight-thousandths

$2\frac{13}{1000}$ 2.013

two and thirteen-thousandths

➤ You can extend the place-value chart to show decimals with thousandths.
Write 3.248 in a place-value chart.

Tens	Ones •	Tenths	Hundredths	Thousandths	Ten Thousandths	Hundred Thousandths
	3 •	2	4	8		

The place-value chart can be extended to more places to the right to show smaller fractional parts.

➤ You can write decimals in expanded form.
3.248 = 3 ones + 2 tenths + 4 hundredths + 8 thousandths
= 3 + 0.2 + 0.04 + 0.008

➤ Equivalent decimals name the same amount.
This is a thousandths grid. It represents 1 whole.
It contains 1000 congruent squares.

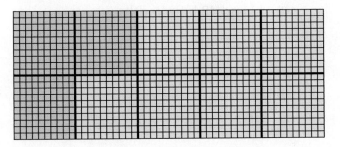

300 small squares are $\frac{300}{1000}$, or 0.300.

3 large squares are $\frac{3}{10}$, or 0.3.

300 small squares = 3 large squares

So, 0.300 = 0.3

Practice

You may use Base Ten Blocks or thousandths grids to model numbers.

1. Write a fraction or mixed number and a decimal for each picture.

   a)
   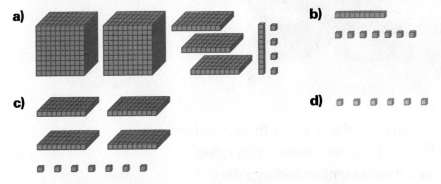

   b)

   c)

   d)

2. Colour thousandths grids to show each decimal.
   Then write the decimal as a fraction or a mixed number.
   a) 0.358   b) 0.209   c) 0.001   d) 2.048

3. Use the data in the table.
   Write the number that has:
   a) a 5 in the tenths place
   b) a 2 in the thousandths place
   c) a 6 in the hundredths place
   d) a 6 in the ones place
   e) a 5 in the thousandths place
   f) a 0 in the tenths place

Creature	Length (cm)
Praying Mantis	7.620
Garden Spider	2.412
Dust Mite	0.015
Walking Stick	7.564
Desert Tarantula	6.943

4. Write each number in standard form.
Then record the number in a place-value chart.
   a) 85 thousandths
   b) 425 and 32 thousandths
   c) 2 and 408 thousandths
   d) 48 and 48 hundredths

5. Record each number in expanded form.
   a) 573 thousandths
   b) 86.093
   c) 6 and 240 thousandths
   d) 29 273
   e) 0.124
   f) 0.107

6. Write each number as a decimal.
   a) $\frac{341}{1000}$
   b) $25\frac{16}{1000}$
   c) $2\frac{3}{1000}$
   d) $964\frac{24}{1000}$

7. Write each number in question 6 in words.

8. The fastest-moving insect on land clocked a record speed of 5.407 km/h.
Write this number as many ways as you can.

> At an average speed of 5.407 km/h, the insect would travel 5.407 km in 1 h.

9. Earth revolves around the sun about every three hundred sixty-five and two hundred fifty-six thousandths days.
Write this number as a mixed number and as a decimal.

10. Use the digits 0, 2, 5, and 8.
Make a number that is less than 5 but greater than 1.
Find as many numbers as you can.
Explain the strategies you used.

Reflect

Explain why 0.2, 0.20, and 0.200 are equivalent decimals.

Comparing and Ordering Decimals

Mount Logan in the Yukon is the highest mountain in Canada.
It is 5.959 km high!

Explore

This table shows the heights
of the highest mountains
in some other Canadian provinces
and a territory.

Use any materials or strategies
you wish.
Order the heights from least
to greatest.

Province/Territory	Mountain	Height (km)
Alberta	Columbia	3.747
British Columbia	Fairweather	4.663
Manitoba	Baldy	0.832
New Brunswick	Carleton	0.817
Newfoundland and Labrador	Caubvick	1.652
Nunavut	Barbeau Peak	2.616

Show *and* Share

Share your results with another pair of students.
Explain the strategies you used to order the heights.
An unnamed peak in the Northwest Territories is 2.773 km high.
Where does this height fit in your ordered list?
Explain why it fits there.

The table shows
the lengths of
4 micro-organisms
in a laboratory.

Micro-organism	Length (mm)
Tardigrade	0.15
Euglena	0.139
Vorticella	0.11
Paramecium	0.125

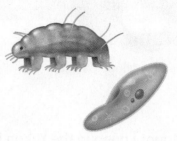

Here are 3 ways to order the lengths from longest to shortest.

➤ Use Base Ten Blocks to model each number, then put the numbers in order.

	Ones	•	Tenths	Hundredths	Thousandths	
Tardigrade		•	▦	▭ ▭		0.15
Euglena		•	▦	▭ ▭	▫ ▫ ▫ ▫ ▫ ▫ ▫ ▫ ▫	0.139
Vorticella		•	▦	▭		0.11
Paramecium		•	▦	▭ ▭	▫ ▫ ▫ ▫ ▫	0.125

The numbers from greatest to least are: 0.15, 0.139, 0.125, 0.11

➤ Write each decimal in a place-value chart.

Use equivalent decimals.

	Ones	•	Tenths	Hundredths	Thousandths
Tardigrade	0	•	1	5	0
Euglena	0	•	1	3	9
Vorticella	0	•	1	1	0
Paramecium	0	•	1	2	5

15 hundredths is
150 thousandths.

11 hundredths is
110 thousandths.

Compare the ones. All four numbers have 0 ones.

Compare the tenths. All four numbers have 1 tenth.

Compare the hundredths. 5 hundredths is the greatest number
of hundredths, then 3 hundredths, 2 hundredths, and 1 hundredth.

The numbers in order from greatest to least are: 0.15, 0.139, 0.125, 0.11

➤ Use a number line.
0.15, 0.139, 0.11, and 0.125 are between 0.1 and 0.2.
So, label the endpoints of the number line 0.1 and 0.2.
Divide the interval between 0.1 and 0.2 to show hundredths.

```
|----+----+----+----+----+----+----+----+----+----+----|
0.1  0.11 0.12 0.13 0.14 0.15 0.16 0.17 0.18 0.19  0.2
```

Divide the hundredths to show thousandths.
Mark a dot for each number.

The farther to the right on the number line, the greater a number is.
So, reading the numbers from right to left gives the lengths
from longest to shortest.

The lengths from longest to shortest are: 0.15 mm, 0.139 mm, 0.125 mm, 0.11 mm

Practice

You may use Base Ten Blocks, a place-value chart, or a number line
to model your solutions.

1. Copy and complete. Use >, <, or =.
   a) 0.237 ☐ 0.209   b) 3.069 ☐ 3.068
   c) 5.69 ☐ 5.690   d) 1.9 ☐ 1.931

2. Order the numbers from least to greatest.
   a) 24.351, 24.762, 24.109   b) 0.59, 0.598, 0.5
   c) 1.7, 1.639, 1.78   d) 0.4, 2.968, 2.84

3. Order the numbers from greatest to least.
   a) 0.571, 3.53 , 0.538   b) 1.002, 1.35, 1.267
   c) 15.2, 15.012, 16   d) 2.041, 2.3, 2.76

4. Write a number between 6.73 and 6.741.
   How did you choose the number?

5. Lian's paper airplane flew 4.247 m and Maude's flew 4.25 m.
   Whose plane flew farther? Show how you know.

6. Write two numbers between 1.51 and 1.52.
   How did you choose the numbers?

7. This table shows the results of a watermelon
   seed-spitting contest.
   a) Whose seed went the greatest distance?
   b) Whose seed went the least distance?
   c) Whose seed went farther than Poppy's
      but not as far as Luis'?
   d) Order the distances from greatest to least.

Name	Distance (m)
Vladimir	2.357
Abu	2.4
Poppy	2.35
Suki	1.943
Cy	1.7
Luis	2.438

8. Use the graph.
The masses in grams of the hummingbird eggs, in no specific order, are:
0.482, 0.44, 0.32, 0.56, 0.374
What is the mass of the egg of:
a) the Costa's hummingbird?
b) the bee hummingbird?
c) the black-chinned hummingbird?

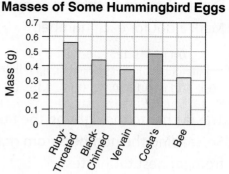

Masses of Some Hummingbird Eggs

9. Which number is closest to 6?
Explain how you know.
5.014, 6.4, 6.002, or 5.91

10. Copy.
Write a decimal with thousandths to make each statement true.
a) 0.43 > □   **b)** 5.7 < □   **c)** 32.002 > □
d) 2.31 < □   **e)** 21.24 > □   **f)** 0.1 > □

11. Use the data in the table.
a) Which frog jumped the greatest distance?
b) Which frog jumped the least distance?
c) Look at the number line.
Match each letter with the frog that jumped that distance.

Frog Olympics

Name	Distance (m)
Ajax	1.393
Hoppy	1.362
Goliath	1.304
Zeus	1.351
Cleo	1.38

```
    A                    B   C      D    E
├┼┼┼┼┼┼┼┼┼┼┼┼┼┼┼┼┼┼┼┼┼┼┼┼┼┼┼┼┼┼┼┼┼┤
1.3  1.31  1.32  1.33  1.34  1.35  1.36  1.37  1.38  1.39  1.4
```

12. You will need a number line.
Order these numbers on the number line:
1.27, 1.284, 1.236, 1.2, 1.279

Reflect

A student says that 7.52 is to the left of 7.516 on a number line because 52 is less than 516. Is the student correct? Explain.

Numbers Every Day

Number Strategies

Find 6 numbers each with exactly 3 factors, including 1.
What do all the numbers have in common?

Canadian exports are usually priced in United States (US) dollars. When an exporter is paid, those US dollars are exchanged for Canadian dollars. When importers buy goods from abroad, the price is usually given in US dollars. And when Canadians holiday abroad, they take some other country's money, or currency. Companies and individuals get their foreign currency from banks.

It is the currency traders' job to buy and sell foreign currency. Currency traders have to know which countries have decimal currencies (like the Canadian and US dollars) and which do not (like the Japanese currency, called yen). There is no fraction of a yen.

One yen (¥) is worth less than one Canadian dollar (C$). For example, in December 2004, ¥1 was worth C$0.01198. To convert ¥1 million to Canadian dollars:

$1\ 000\ 000 \times 0.01198 = 11\ 980$

So, ¥1 million are equivalent to C$11 980.

Suppose you had C$10. How could you find its equivalent in yen?

Rounding Decimals

The longest eyelashes ever measured on a dog were 11.94 cm long.
What is this length to the nearest centimetre?

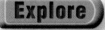 **Explore** •••

This table, based on data from *Guinness World Records 2005*, shows the lengths of features of some pets.

Use any materials or strategies you wish.
Round each length to:
• the nearest centimetre
• the nearest tenth of a centimetre

Pet Records

Animal	Feature	Length (cm)
Cat	Whiskers	17.37
Cat	Length	121.92
Dog	Ears	33.19
Rabbit	Ears	79.06
Goat	Horns	132.08

Show *and* Share

Share your rounded numbers with another pair of classmates.
What strategies did you use to round?
How is rounding to the nearest tenth like rounding to the nearest whole number?

Connect •••

You can round numbers when you estimate an answer, or when you do not need as precise a measurement as you are given.

The smallest bone in the human body is the stapes, or stirrup bone, in the middle ear.
A stapes bone is about 2.84 mm long.

actual size

➤ You can use a number line to round 2.84 mm to the nearest millimetre and to the nearest tenth of a millimetre.

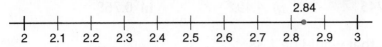

2.84 is between 2 and 3, but closer to 3.
So, 2.84 mm rounded to the nearest millimetre is 3 mm.

2.84 is between 2.8 and 2.9, but closer to 2.8.
So, 2.84 mm rounded to the nearest tenth of a millimetre is 2.8 mm.

2.84 mm is more precise than 2.8 mm or 3 mm because it is measured to one-hundredth of a millimetre.

The smallest muscle in the human body is the stapedius, the muscle that controls the stapes. It is about 0.125 cm long.
➤ You can use a number line to round 0.125 cm to the nearest centimetre.

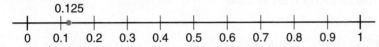

0.125 is between 0 and 1, but closer to 0.
So, 0.125 cm rounded to the nearest centimetre is 0 cm.

➤ You can also use a number line to round 0.125 cm to the nearest tenth of a centimetre, and to the nearest hundredth of a centimetre.

```
       0.125
+---+--+--+---+---+---+---+---+---+---+
0.1 0.11 0.12 0.13 0.14 0.15 0.16 0.17 0.18 0.19 0.2
```

When a length is rounded to the nearest tenth of a centimetre, it is rounded to the nearest millimetre.

0.125 is between 0.1 and 0.2, but closer to 0.1.
So, 0.125 rounded to the nearest tenth of a centimetre is 0.1 cm.

0.125 cm is halfway between 0.12 and 0.13.
So, 0.125 cm rounded to the nearest hundredth of a centimetre is 0.13 cm.

When a number is halfway between, we round up.

Practice

1. Round to the nearest whole number.
    a) 2.09   b) 8.6   c) 5.318   d) 28.532
    e) 2.845   f) 7.345   g) 9.508   h) 0.786

2. Round to the nearest tenth.
    a) 6.25   b) 8.62   c) 0.081   d) 1.98
    e) 2.468   f) 38.097   g) 16.72   h) 4.685

3. Round to the nearest hundredth.
   a) 5.637   **b)** 100.584   **c)** 45.515   **d)** 5.555
   e) 8.371   **f)** 0.745   **g)** 4.492   **h)** 0.768

4. Write 2 different decimals that would be 1.38
   when rounded to the nearest hundredth.

5. A stapes bone has a mass of about 4.276 mg.
   Round this number to the nearest hundredth of a milligram,
   to the nearest tenth of a milligram, and to the nearest milligram.

6. The tongue of a boxer dog named Brandy
   has been measured at 43.18 cm.
   Round this number to the nearest tenth
   of a centimetre, and to the nearest centimetre.

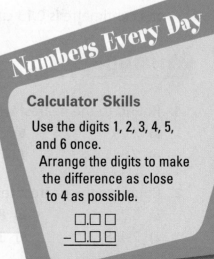

7. Write two decimals with thousandths that would
   give 0.2 when rounded to the nearest tenth
   and 0.20 when rounded to the nearest hundredth.

8. Marley and Hassan rounded the number 7.483.
   Marley's answer was greater than 7.483,
   and Hassan's answer was less.
   To what place might the number have been
   rounded by Marley? By Hassan? Explain.

9. This table shows the lengths of three spiders.
   Which measurement do you think is the
   most precise? Explain.

Spider	Length (cm)
Patu Marplesi	0.4
Turret	1.715
Orb Weaver	1.89

10. Use the digits 1, 3, 5, and 7.
   Write a decimal that will round up
   if rounded to the nearest tenth
   but round down if rounded to the nearest hundredth.
   Find as many answers as you can.

Reflect

Explain how you round 6.247 to the nearest
whole number, to the nearest tenth,
and to the nearest hundredth.

Numbers Every Day

Calculator Skills

Use the digits 1, 2, 3, 4, 5,
and 6 once.
Arrange the digits to make
the difference as close
to 4 as possible.

☐.☐☐
−☐.☐☐

Estimating Sums and Differences

Explore •

Use the data in the table, taken from *Guinness World Records 2005*.

➤ Take turns to choose 2 fruits and estimate their
combined mass. Tell your partner your estimate.
Have your partner guess which 2 fruits you chose.
If your partner guesses incorrectly, try to provide
a closer estimate. Continue with different pairs of fruit.

➤ Repeat the activity.
This time, estimate the difference in masses of 2 fruits.

**Most Massive Fruits
on Record**

Fruit	Mass (kg)
Apple	1.673
Grapefruit	3.065
Lemon	5.265
Mango	1.940
Peach	0.725
Strawberry	0.231

Show *and* Share

Discuss the strategies you used to estimate the sums
and differences. Which strategies gave the closest estimate?

Connect •

According to *Guinness World Records 2005*, the most massive
head of garlic had a mass of 1.191 kg.
The most massive potato had a mass of 3.487 kg.

➤ Here are 3 ways to estimate the combined mass of these vegetables:
Estimate: 1.191 + 3.487

* Round each decimal to the nearest whole number.
1 + 3 = 4
So, 1.191 kg + 3.487 kg is about 4 kg.

* Round only 1 decimal to the nearest whole number.
1 + 3.487 = 4.487
So, 1.191 kg + 3.487 kg is about 4.487 kg.

* Round each decimal to the nearest tenth or hundredth.
1.2 + 3.5 = 4.7   or   1.19 + 3.49 = 4.68
So, 1.191 kg + 3.487 kg is about 4.7 kg or 4.68 kg.

> 1.191 + 3.487 = 4.678
> So, rounding both decimals
> to the nearest hundredth
> gave the estimate closest
> to the actual sum.

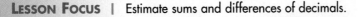

LESSON FOCUS | Estimate sums and differences of decimals.

129

➤ Here are two ways to estimate the difference in the masses of the potato and the garlic.
Estimate: 3.487 − 1.191

- Round the decimal being subtracted, to the nearest whole number.
  3.487 − 1 = 2.487
  So, 3.487 kg − 1.191 kg is about 2.487 kg.

- Round both decimals to the nearest tenth or hundredth.
  3.5 − 1.2 = 2.3   or   3.49 − 1.19 = 2.30
  So, 3.487 kg − 1.191 kg is about 2.3 kg.

3.487 − 1.191 = 2.296
In this case, rounding both decimals to the nearest hundredth and rounding both decimals to the nearest tenth gave the estimates closest to the actual difference.

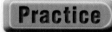

Practice

1. Estimate each sum. Explain your strategies.
   a) 7.36 + 2.23   **b)** 1.689 + 3.128
   c) 2.014 + 3.213   **d)** 4.405 + 2.167
   e) 3.8 + 2.67   **f)** 5.278 + 0.732
   g) 6.112 + 7.351   **h)** 6.204 + 3.009
   i) 5.641 + 1.318   **j)** 4.219 + 8.604

2. Estimate each difference. Explain your strategies.
   a) 4.255 − 1.386   **b)** 6.593 − 4.991
   c) 8.737 − 5.837   **d)** 0.456 − 0.214
   e) 4.32 − 1.245   **f)** 3.104 − 0.892

3. The tallest woman on record was 2.483 m tall.
   The shortest woman on record was 0.61 m tall.
   Estimate the difference in their heights.
   Show your work.

4. Choose the better estimate. Explain your choice.
   a) 2.225 + 6.95   8 or 9   **b)** 83.1 − 34.016   50 or 60
   c) 58.37 − 22.845   35 or 36   **d)** 19.531 + 16.8   35 or 36

Numbers Every Day

Number Strategies

Arrange the numbers from 17 to 25 so the sums of the numbers in each row, column, and diagonal are the same.

5. A grand piano has a mass of 396.696 kg.
An upright piano has a mass of 267.728 kg.

   a) Could both pianos be put in a freight elevator
   with a mass limit of 650 kg? Explain how you know.

   b) About how much over or under the 650-kg limit
   is the combined mass of the two pianos?

6. Mount Everest is 8.850 km high.
Mount Logan is 5.959 km high.
What is the approximate difference in their heights?

7. The reticulated python is the world's longest snake.
The thread snake is the world's shortest snake.
A reptile centre has a 6.248-m reticulated python
and a 0.108-m thread snake.
Estimate the difference in the lengths of these snakes.

8. A toy store has a sale.
It will pay the tax if your purchase totals $25 or more.
Jessica buys a computer game for $14.95
and some batteries for $7.99.
About how much more would she need to spend
and not pay the tax?

9. Tyrel and Jordana estimated the sum of 2.853 + 0.986.
Tyrel's estimate was 3.8 and Jordana's was 3.853.

   a) Explain how Tyrel and Jordana may have estimated.

   b) Whose estimate was closer to the actual sum?
   How do you know?

At Home

Reflect

Describe a situation when you might
estimate the sum or difference of
two decimals.

Talk with family members.
When do they estimate sums
or differences?
What strategies do they use?
Write about what you find out.

Adding and Subtracting Decimals

When you go to the theatre to see a movie, your attendance and how much you paid to see the movie are entered in a database. Data are collected from theatres all across Canada and the United States.

Movie studios use these data to help predict how much money the movie will earn.

Explore

Shrek 2 was one of the highest-earning movies of 2004.

The table shows how much money *Shrek 2* earned in Canada and the United States for the first week it played in theatres. Studios record the earnings in millions of US dollars.

Date	Earnings (US$ millions)
Wednesday, May 19	11.786
Thursday, May 20	9.159
Friday, May 21	28.340
Saturday, May 22	44.797
Sunday, May 23	34.901
Monday, May 24	11.512
Tuesday, May 25	8.023

➤ Estimate first.
  Then find the combined earnings on:
  • the first 2 days
  • Saturday and Sunday
  • all 7 days

➤ Estimate first.
  Then find the difference in earnings on:
  • Thursday and Friday
  • Saturday and Sunday
  • Sunday and Monday
  • the days with the greatest and the least earnings

Show *and* Share

Share your results with another pair of classmates.
Discuss the strategies you used to estimate and to find the sums and differences.

Yu-Gi-Oh! is an animated movie that played in theatres in 2004.
It was first shown on Friday, August 13.
That Friday, it earned US$4.328 million in Canadian and American theatres.
It earned US$3.019 million the next day.

➤ To find the combined earnings on Friday and Saturday,
add: 4.328 + 3.019
Here are two ways to find the sum.

- Use Base Ten Blocks.
  Model 4.328 and 3.019 on a place-value mat.

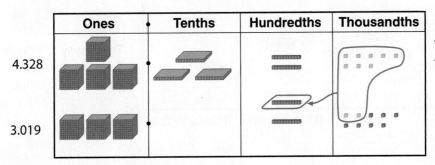

Trade 10 thousandths for 1 hundredth.

4.328 + 3.019 = 7.347

- Use place value.
  Step 1: Estimate.
  Round 3.019 to 3.
  Add: 4.328 + 3 = 7.328

  Step 2: Record the numbers.
  Align the numbers as you aligned the blocks.
  Add as you would with whole numbers.

$$\begin{array}{r} \overset{1}{4.328} \\ + 3.019 \\ \hline 7.347 \end{array}$$

7.347 is close to the estimate 7.328,
so the answer is reasonable.

The combined earnings were US$7.347 million.

> Add the thousandths.
> Regroup as 1 hundredth
> and 7 thousandths.
> Add the hundredths.
> Add the tenths.
> Add the ones.

➤ To find the difference in the earnings on Friday and Saturday, subtract: 4.328 − 3.019
Here are two ways to find the difference.

• Use Base Ten Blocks.
  Model 4.328 on a place-value mat.

You cannot take
9 thousandths from
8 thousandths.
Trade 1 hundredth
for 10 thousandths.

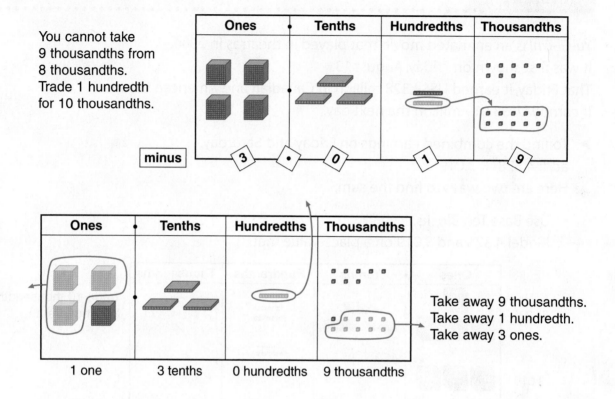

Take away 9 thousandths.
Take away 1 hundredth.
Take away 3 ones.

1 one   3 tenths   0 hundredths   9 thousandths

• Use place value.

    Step 1: Estimate.
    Round 3.019 to 3.
    Subtract: 4.328 − 3 = 1.328

    Step 2: Record the numbers.
    Align the numbers as you aligned the blocks.
    Subtract as you would with whole numbers.

$$
\begin{array}{r}
4.3\overset{1\,18}{\cancel{2}\cancel{8}} \\
-\ 3.019 \\
\hline
1.309
\end{array}
$$

1.309 is close to the estimate 1.328,
so the answer is reasonable.

The movie earned US$1.309 million
more on Friday than on Saturday.

Regroup 1 hundredth
as 10 thousandths.
Subtract the thousandths.
Subtract the hundredths.
Subtract the tenths.
Subtract the ones.

134

Use the inverse operation to check.

Add: 3.019 + 1.309

The sum should be 4.328.

$$
\begin{array}{r}
\overset{1}{3.019} \\
+\ 1.309 \\
\hline
4.328
\end{array}
$$

So, the answer is correct.

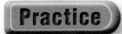

Practice

1. Add or subtract. Use the inverse operation to check your answers.

   a)   3.251
       + 8.960

   b)   17.324
       − 9.166

   c)   84.032
       − 8.263

   d)   4.629
       + 0.576

   e)   28.63
       + 14.97

   f)   10.003
       − 6.897

   g)   0.124
       + 0.986

   h)   7.285
       − 5.019

   i)   15.194
       − 8.017

2. Estimate first. Then find each sum or difference.

   a) 2.876 − 0.975

   b) 71.382 + 9

   c) 0.58 + 0.736

   d) 0.14 + 4.038

   e) 7 − 0.187

   f) 0.999 − 0.99

3. Use each of the digits 0 to 7 once.
   Make 2 decimals with thousandths whose sum is close to 2
   and whose difference is close to 1.
   Explain your choices. Show your work.

4. I am a decimal.
   • If you double me, my double is between 0.6 and 0.7,
     but closer to 0.6.
   • My thousandths digit is not a 2,
     but the thousandths digit of my double is.
   What decimal might I be?

5. Mirko is making fruit punch.
   Will the contents of these 3 containers
   fit in a 3-L punch bowl?
   Explain.

6. Use the data in the table. For each type of pet, find the difference in the masses of the largest and smallest animals.

| Animal | Mass (kg) | |
	Smallest	Largest
Rabbit	0.397	11.991
Dog	0.113	155.582
Cat	1.361	44.452

7. Winsome is being trained as a guide dog for a blind person. At birth, she had a mass of 0.475 kg. At 6 weeks, her mass was 4.06 kg. At 12 weeks, her mass was 9.25 kg.
   a) By how much did her mass change from birth to 6 weeks?
   b) By how much did her mass change from 6 weeks to 12 weeks?

8. Write a story problem that can be solved by subtracting two decimals with thousandths. Solve your problem. Show your work.

9. Use each of the digits from 0 to 7 once to make this addition true. Find as many different answers as you can.

    ☐.☐☐☐
  + ☐.☐☐☐
  ─────────
    5 . 7 8 8

10. A student added 0.523 and 2.36 and got the sum 0.759.
    a) What mistake did the student make?
    b) What is the correct answer?

11. The difference in the capacities of 2 containers is 0.653 L. What might the capacity of each container be?

12. Could 5.3 be the difference of 2 numbers with thousandths other than zero? Explain.

Reflect

When Mahala subtracted 2.768 from 5.9, she wrote 5.9 as 5.900. Why might she have done this?

Numbers Every Day

Mental Math

Six coins have a total value of 38¢.

Which coins are they?

Multiplying Decimals by 10, 100, 1000, 10 000

Margaret DeCiman has played for both
the Junior and Senior Canadian Women's
National Basketball Teams.
She is 2.007 m tall.
How tall is she in decimetres? In centimetres?

Explore

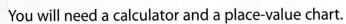

You will need a calculator and a place-value chart.
➤ Use a calculator to find each product.
  Record the products in a place-value chart.

Ten Thousands	Thousands	Hundreds	Tens	Ones	Tenths	Hundredths	Thousandths

Look for patterns in the products.
How can you find similar products without using a calculator?

38 × 10	16.2 × 10	9.04 × 10	0.023 × 10
38 × 100	16.2 × 100	9.04 × 100	0.023 × 100
38 × 1000	16.2 × 1000	9.04 × 1000	0.023 × 1000

➤ Use mental math to find each product. Then check with a calculator.

2.134 × 10	0.246 × 1000	7.028 × 100
25.489 × 1000	7.89 × 100	6 × 1000

Show *and* Share

Share the patterns you found with another pair of students.
What happens to the digits in a decimal when you multiply by 10?
By 100? By 1000?
What do you think happens to the digits in a decimal when you multiply by 10 000?
Use a calculator to check your ideas.

The tallest man on record, Robert Wadlow,
was 2.721 m tall.
What was his height in decimetres?
In centimetres? In millimetres?

> 1 m = 10 dm
> 1 m = 100 cm
> 1 m = 1000 mm

To change metres to decimetres, multiply by 10: 2.721×10
To change metres to centimetres, multiply by 100: 2.721×100
To change metres to millimetres, multiply by 1000: 2.721×1000

➤ You can use mental math to multiply a decimal by 10,
   by 100, and by 1000. Think about place value.

	Thousands	Hundreds	Tens	Ones	Tenths	Hundredths	Thousandths
				2	7	2	1
2.721×10 →			2	7	2	1	
2.721×100 →		2	7	2	1		
2.721×1000 →	2	7	2	1			

➤ When you multiply a decimal by 10, the digits shift
   1 place to the left.
   You can show this by moving the decimal point
   1 place to the right.

   $2.721 \times 10 = 27.21$

So, Wadlow's height was 27.21 dm.

➤ When you multiply a decimal by 100, the digits shift 2 places to the left.
   You can show this by moving the decimal point 2 places to the right.

   $2.721 \times 100 = 272.1$

So, Wadlow's height was 272.1 cm.

➤ When you multiply a decimal by 1000, the digits shift 3 places to the left.
   You can show this by moving the decimal point 3 places to the right.

   $2.721 \times 1000 = 2721$

So, Wadlow's height was 2721 mm.

> You do not have to put a
> decimal point after a whole number.

1. Record each product in a place-value chart.

   a) 2.8 × 10   **b)** 0.7 × 100   **c)** 6 × 1000

   d) 7.86 × 100   **e)** 12.46 × 10 000   **f)** 3.08 × 10

   g) 0.893 × 10 000   **h)** 5.109 × 100   **i)** 6.372 × 1000

   > When you multiply a decimal by 10 000, the digits shift 4 places to the left.

2. Use mental math to find each product.

   a) 17.6 × 10   **b)** 485.37 × 10   **c)** 9.048 × 100
       17.6 × 100   485.37 × 100   9.048 × 1000
       17.6 × 1000   485.37 × 1000   9.048 × 10 000

Use mental math to answer each question.

3. Each of 10 members of the Science Club paid $9.50 to go to the Science Centre. How much did they pay altogether?

4. The bus stop is 0.325 km from Galeria's front door. Write this distance in metres.

5. When water drips in a cave it leaves minerals on the ceiling. Over many years, the minerals form a column of rock called a stalactite. Some stalactites grow only 0.212 mm a year. How much would they grow in 10 years? 100 years? 1000 years? 10 000 years?

Math Link

Science

Speleology is the study of stalactites and other mineral deposits found in caves. Stalactites give us information about climate conditions thousands of years ago. This may help us understand changes in our climate today.

6. A dime has a mass of 1.75 g.
   a) What is the total mass of 1000 dimes?
   b) What is the total value of 1000 dimes?
   Explain your mental math strategies.

7. A bumblebee bat has a mass of 1.875 g. What is the combined mass of 10 of these bats? 100 of them? 1000 of them? 10 000 of them?

Reflect

Explain how to use mental math to multiply 7.63 by 10, by 100, by 1000, and by 10 000.

Numbers Every Day

Number Strategies

Order the numbers from least to greatest.

32.23, 30.323, 32.303, 32.033

Dividing Decimals by 10, 100, 1000, 10 000

Explore

You will need a calculator and a place-value chart.

➤ Use a calculator to find each quotient.
Record the quotients in a place-value chart.
Label a 7-column place-value chart from tens
to hundred thousandths.
Look for patterns in the quotients.
How can you predict similar quotients?

7 ÷ 10	2.4 ÷ 10	15.63 ÷ 10
7 ÷ 100	2.4 ÷ 100	15.63 ÷ 100
7 ÷ 1000	2.4 ÷ 1000	15.63 ÷ 1000

➤ Use mental math to find each quotient.
Then check with a calculator.

0.23 ÷ 10	9 ÷ 100	1.16 ÷ 1000
17 ÷ 1000	8.57 ÷ 10	3.854 ÷ 100

Show *and* Share

Share your work with another pair of students.
What happens to the digits in a decimal when you divide by 10? By 100? By 1000?
What do you think happens to the digits in a decimal when you divide by 10 000?
Use a calculator to check your ideas.

Connect

You can use mental math to divide a decimal by 10, 100, 1000, and 10 000
by thinking about place value.

➤ Divide: 2.8 ÷ 10   2.8 ÷ 1000
             2.8 ÷ 100   2.8 ÷ 10 000

	Ones	Tenths	Hundredths	Thousandths	Ten Thousandths	Hundred Thousandths
	2	8				
2.8 ÷ 10	0	2	8			
2.8 ÷ 100	0	0	2	8		
2.8 ÷ 1000	0	0	0	2	8	
2.8 ÷ 10 000	0	0	0	0	2	8

➤ Divide: 9 ÷ 10   9 ÷ 100   9 ÷ 1000   9 ÷ 10 000

> 9 is a decimal, too.
> You can write 9 as 9. or 9.0.

	Ones	Tenths	Hundredths	Thousandths	Ten Thousandths	Hundred Thousandths
	9					
9 ÷ 10	0	9				
9 ÷ 100	0	0	9			
9 ÷ 1000	0	0	0	9		
9 ÷ 10 000	0	0	0	0	9	

When you divide a decimal by 10, the digits shift 1 place to the right.
You can show this by moving the decimal point 1 place to the left.

$$2.8 ÷ 10 = 0.28 \qquad\qquad 9 ÷ 10 = 0.9$$

When you divide a decimal by 100, the digits shift 2 places to the right.
You can show this by moving the decimal point 2 places to the left.

$$2.8 ÷ 100 = 0.028 \qquad\qquad 9 ÷ 100 = 0.09$$

When you divide a decimal by 1000, the digits shift 3 places to the right.
You can show this by moving the decimal point 3 places to the left.

$$2.8 ÷ 1000 = 0.0028 \qquad\qquad 9 ÷ 1000 = 0.009$$

When you divide a decimal by 10 000, the digits shift 4 places to the right.
You can show this by moving the decimal point 4 places to the left.

$$2.8 ÷ 10\ 000 = 0.000\ 28 \qquad\qquad 9 ÷ 10\ 000 = 0.0009$$

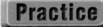

Practice

1. Use mental math to divide.
   a) 297.25 ÷ 100
   b) 12 ÷ 10 000
   c) 2.32 ÷ 1000
   d) 5 ÷ 10 000
   e) 63.48 ÷ 1000
   f) 6.24 ÷ 10
   g) 54.1 ÷ 1000
   h) 0.43 ÷ 10

Use mental math to answer each question.

2. One hundred new toonies have a mass of 730 g.
What is the mass of one toonie?

3. The world's largest living thing is a Giant Sequoia
named the General Sherman Tree.
In 2002, the distance around its trunk
at ground level was about 3124.2 cm.
What is this measurement in decimetres? In metres?

4. A bullfrog travelled 9.32 m in 10 jumps.
About how far did the bullfrog jump each time?

5. The CN Tower in Toronto is 553.33 m tall.
Write this height in kilometres.

6. Belinda's Great Dane is 74.9 cm tall and 225 cm long.
Write these lengths in metres.

7. A pile of 10 000 sheets of paper is 89 cm thick.
How thick is 1 sheet of paper?

8. The distance around a go-cart track is 575 m.
Ravi drove around the track 10 times.
Write how far Ravi drove as many different ways as possible.
Show your work.

9. The Confederation Bridge joins New Brunswick and Prince Edward Island.
It is the world's longest bridge over ice-covered water.
The bridge is about 12 900 m long. How many kilometres is that?

Numbers Every Day

Number Strategies

Find a 2-digit number that
is 3 times the product of
its digits.

Reflect

Explain how to use mental math to divide
7.3 by 10, 100, 1000, and 10 000.

Multiplying Whole Numbers by 0.1, 0.01, 0.001

In Lesson 8, you divided decimals by 10, 100, and 1000.
In this lesson, you will multiply numbers by 0.1, 0.01, and 0.001.
These operations are related.

 Explore

You will need a calculator and place-value charts.

➤ Choose a 1-digit whole number.
Use a calculator.
Multiply the number by 0.1, 0.01, and 0.001.
Record the products in a place-value chart.
Repeat with a 2-digit whole number and
a 3-digit whole number.

Look for patterns in the place-value charts.
How can you use mental math to multiply
a whole number by 0.1, 0.01, and 0.001?

➤ Use mental math to predict each product.
Then check with a calculator.

8 × 0.1	1 × 0.01	5 × 0.001
76 × 0.1	85 × 0.01	99 × 0.001
424 × 0.1	280 × 0.01	708 × 0.001

Show *and* Share

Share your patterns with another pair of students.
When you multiply a whole number by 0.1, 0.01, or 0.001,
is the product greater than or less than the whole number?

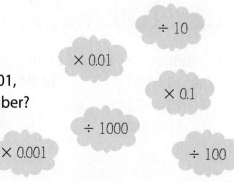

➤ You can use mental math to multiply
   a whole number by 0.1, 0.01, and 0.001.

Multiply: 48 × 0.1
         48 × 0.01
         48 × 0.001

When you multiply
a whole number by 0.1, 0.01,
and 0.001, the products
are less than the
whole number.

	Tens	Ones	Tenths	Hundredths	Thousandths
	4	8			
48 × 0.1		4	8		
48 × 0.01		0	4	8	
48 × 0.001			0	0	4	8

- When you multiply by 0.1, the digits shift 1 place to the right.
  To show this, move the decimal point 1 place to the left.

  48 × 0.1 = 4.8

- When you multiply by 0.01, the digits shift 2 places to the right.
  To show this, move the decimal point 2 places to the left.

  48 × 0.01 = 0.48

- When you multiply by 0.001, the digits shift 3 places to the right.
  To show this, move the decimal point 3 places to the left.

  48 × 0.001 = 0.048

Practice •

1. Multiply. Use mental math.
   a) 13 × 0.1   b) 50 × 0.1   c) 1 × 0.1
      13 × 0.01   50 × 0.01   1 × 0.01
      13 × 0.001   50 × 0.001   1 × 0.001

2. Multiply. Use mental math. Describe your strategies.

    a) 15×0.1 **b)** 3×0.001 **c)** 485×0.01

    d) 4×0.01 **e)** 173×0.1 **f)** 14×0.001

3. Use mental math to multiply or divide.

    a) 7×0.1 **b)** 16×0.01 **c)** 42×0.001

        $7 \div 10$ $16 \div 100$ $42 \div 1000$

    d) 28×0.1 **e)** 3×0.01 **f)** 33×0.001

        $28 \div 10$ $3 \div 100$ $33 \div 1000$

4. a) What do you notice about your answers in question 3?

    b) How are multiplication and division related?

Use mental math to solve each problem.

5. A typical house spider has a mass of 0.1 g.

    a) What is the combined mass of 50 house spiders?

    b) How many house spiders would it take to make 1 kg?

    Describe the mental math strategies you used.

6. Erica cut a ribbon into 15 equal pieces.

    Each piece was 0.1 m long.

    a) How long was the ribbon before Erica cut it?

    b) How many cuts did she make?

7. Each side of a regular octagon is 0.001 km long.

    What is the perimeter of the octagon?

    Give your answer in as many different units as you can.

8. One marshmallow cookie contains
0.1 g of polyunsaturated fat.
How many grams of
polyunsaturated fat are in
6 cookies?

Reflect

Jorge said that multiplying 9 by 0.01 is the same
as dividing 9 by 100. Do you agree? Explain.

Place-Value Concentration

Work with a partner in the group.

You will need 1 set of Expression Cards and 1 set of Answer Cards.

The object of the game is to match each expression with its answer.

One point is awarded for each correct match.

➤ Shuffle each set of cards.
  Arrange each set, face down, in an array.
➤ One student in Pair 1 turns over a card
  from the Expressions Array.
  All students in the group solve the expression.
  The second student in Pair 1 turns over a card
  from the Answers Array.
  If everyone agrees that this card shows the correct answer,
  Pair 1 removes both cards from the arrays.
  If the card does not show the correct answer,
  turn both cards face down again.
➤ Pair 2 has a turn.
➤ Pairs of students continue to take turns until
  all expressions have been matched with their answers.
➤ Each pair counts the number of pairs of matching cards it has.
  The pair of students with more points wins.

Multiplying Decimals by a 1-Digit Whole Number

Most Canadians love the thrill of riding a roller coaster. There are at least 54 roller coasters in Canada.

 **Explore**

This table shows the lengths of some of the world's top roller coasters.
Choose 3 roller coasters you would like to ride.
Suppose you rode each of them 8 times.
Estimate how far you would travel on each roller coaster.
Then calculate the actual distance.

Roller Coaster	Country	Length (km)
The Beast	USA	2.256
The Steel Dragon	Japan	2.479
The Corkscrew	Canada	0.732
The Dragon Khan	Spain	1.269
The Mighty Canadian Minebuster	Canada	1.167
The Ultimate	England	2.271

Show *and* Share

Share your results with another pair of students.
Discuss the strategies you used to estimate and to calculate.
How do you know your answers are reasonable?

The Superman Ride of Steel roller coaster is 1.646 km long.
Beth and Ujjal rode this roller coaster 3 times.
How far did Beth and Ujjal travel on the Superman Ride of Steel?

Multiply: 1.646 × 3
Here are two ways to find 1.646 × 3.

➤ Use Base Ten Blocks.
   Model 3 groups of 1.646.

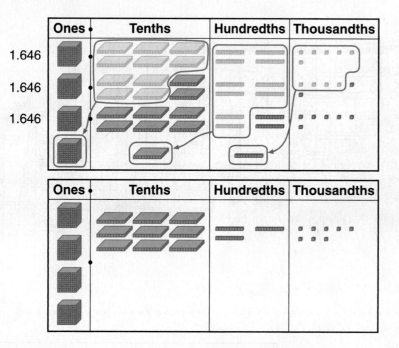

Regroup 10 thousandths
as 1 hundredth.
Regroup 10 hundredths
as 1 tenth.
Regroup 10 tenths as 1 one.

4 ones + 9 tenths + 3 hundredths + 8 thousandths = 4.938
So, 1.646 × 3 = 4.938

➤ Use what you know about multiplying whole numbers.

• First estimate.
  Round 1.646 to 2.
  2 × 3 = 6
  So, 1.646 × 3 is about 6.

1.646 is less than 2.
So, the product will be
less than 6.

- Record the numbers
  without the decimal point.
  Multiply as you would
  with whole numbers.

$$\begin{array}{r} 1646 \\ \times \quad 3 \\ \hline 18 \\ 120 \\ 1800 \\ 3000 \\ \hline 4938 \end{array}$$

- Use the estimate to place the decimal point in the product.
  The estimate is 6, so place the decimal point after 4.
  $1.646 \times 3 = 4.938$

Beth and Ujjal travelled 4.938 km on the Superman Ride of Steel.

Practice

1. Estimate. Then multiply.

   a) $\begin{array}{r} 4.3 \\ \times \ 6 \end{array}$

   b) $\begin{array}{r} 1.8 \\ \times \ 9 \end{array}$

   c) $\begin{array}{r} 7.27 \\ \times \ 5 \end{array}$

   d) $\begin{array}{r} 0.42 \\ \times \ 7 \end{array}$

   e) $\begin{array}{r} \$26.47 \\ \times \quad 2 \end{array}$

   f) $\begin{array}{r} 2.009 \\ \times \quad 4 \end{array}$

   g) $\begin{array}{r} 2.362 \\ \times \quad 3 \end{array}$

   h) $\begin{array}{r} 0.12 \\ \times \quad 8 \end{array}$

2. Multiply.

   a) 8.2×4
   b) 1.02×6
   c) 5.9×2
   d) $\$1.95 \times 8$
   e) 6.112×3
   f) 0.525×7
   g) 5.351×6
   h) 0.607×5

3. Elisa works in a hospital lab.
   This morning, she tested 7 tubes of blood.
   Each tube contained 12.25 mL of blood.
   How much blood did Elisa test?

4. Naja saved $14.75 each week for 9 weeks.
   She had just enough money to buy a DVD player.
   What was the cost of the DVD player?

5. Julian has six 2.54-L bottles of fruit juice.
   He needs 20 L of juice for a party.
   a) Does Julian have enough juice?
   b) How much more or less than 20 L does Julian have?

6. Tianna has saved $9.25 each week for 7 weeks.
She wants to buy a skateboard that costs $80.45, including tax.
a) Does Tianna have enough money?
b) If your answer to part a is no, how much more does Tianna need?

7. Michael needs 4 m of fabric to upholster a sofa.
He sees two fabrics he likes.
One costs $8.59 per metre.
The other costs $5.98 per metre.
How much money will Michael save
if he buys the less-expensive fabric?

8. a) Ammar bought three 0.375-L bottles of maple syrup.
Did Ammar buy more or less than 1 L of syrup?
How much more or less? Explain how you know.
b) Ammar paid $4.79 for each bottle of syrup.
How much did he spend?

9. The Kitti's hog-nosed bat lives in limestone caves in Thailand.
It has a mass of 1.812 g.
What is the combined mass of 5 of these tiny bats?

10. Write a problem that can be solved by multiplying 4.026 by 7.
Solve your problem.

11. You can estimate how tall a child will be as an adult
by doubling her height at 2 years of age.
Serena is 2 years old and 81.4 cm tall.
About how tall will Serena be as an adult?

12. A bakery sells multigrain bread for $1.79 per loaf.
Saima buys 3 loaves.
a) Saima gives the cashier $6.
How much change should she receive?
b) Each loaf has a mass of 0.675 kg.
Does Saima have more or less than 2 kg
of bread altogether? How do you know?

Reflect

Explain how you decide where to place the
decimal point in the product 7.146×7.

Dividing Decimals by a 1-Digit Whole Number

The Paralympic Games are an international sports competition for athletes with disabilities. They are held in the same year and city as the Olympic Games.

For most paralympic sports, the athletes are grouped into classes according to their balance, coordination, range of motion, and skills required for the sport.

Explore

One event in the Paralympics is the men's 1-km time trial cycling. Each competitor completes 4 laps of a 250-m track. In 2004, the winner of the gold medal in the CP3/4 class was Darren Kenny of Great Britain. He completed the 4 laps in 74.472 s.

The Canadian competitor in this event was Jean Quevillon. He finished in 10th place, with a time of 83.848 s.

What was the mean time for each cyclist to complete one lap? Use any materials you think may help. Estimate first. Then find the answers.

Show and Share

Share your solutions with another pair of students. Discuss the strategies you used to estimate and to solve the problems. How can you verify your answers? In a race, do you think the time to complete each lap would be the same? Explain.

➤ At the annual Frog Derby, Jendayi's frog travelled 3 m in 4 jumps.
What was the mean distance for each jump?

Divide: 3 ÷ 4

• Estimate first. 3 is less than 4.
So, each jump is a little less than 1 m.

• Use Base Ten Blocks. Model 3.

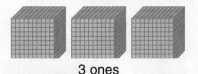

3 ones

Trade each 1 for 10 tenths.

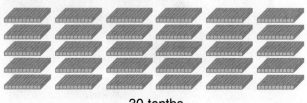

30 tenths

Divide 30 tenths into 4 equal groups.

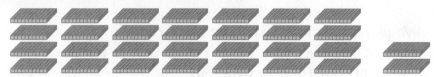

There are 4 groups of 7 tenths, with 2 tenths left over.

Trade 2 tenths for 20 hundredths.
Divide 20 hundredths among the 4 groups.

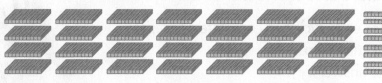

There are 7 tenths and 5 hundredths in each group.
7 tenths and 5 hundredths = 75 hundredths
75 hundredths = 0.75

The mean distance for each jump was 0.75 m.

> 0.75 m is a
> little less than 1 m,
> so the answer is
> reasonable.

➤ Here is another way to find 3 ÷ 4.
Since the divisor, 4, is greater than the dividend, 3,
the quotient will be less than 1.
So, write 3 as a decimal: 3.0

To divide 3.0 by 4:

Divide the ones.
There are 3 ones left over.
This is 30 tenths.

$4\overline{|3.^30}$
0.

Divide the tenths.
There are 2 tenths left over.
This is 20 hundredths.

$4\overline{|3.^30^2}$
0. 7

Write a zero in the hundredths place.
Divide the hundredths.

$4\overline{|3.^30^20}$
0. 7 5

The mean distance for each jump was 0.75 m.

Another way to find this quotient is to remember that $3 \div 4 = \frac{3}{4}$ and $\frac{3}{4} = 0.75$.

➤ Marcie's frog travelled 2.232 m in 3 jumps.
What was the mean distance for each jump?

Divide: $2.232 \div 3$

Here is another way to divide.

- Record the numbers without the decimal point.
  Divide as you would with whole numbers.

$3\overline{|22^13^12}$
7 4 4 $2232 \div 3 = 744$

- Estimate to place the decimal point.
  2.232 rounds to 2.
  $2 \div 3$ is a little less than 1.
  The answer must be 744 thousandths.
  744 thousandths = 0.744
  So, $2.232 \div 3 = 0.744$

You write a zero in the ones place when there is no digit there.

- Check by multiplying:
  $0.744 \times 3 = 2.232$
  So, the answer is correct.

The mean distance for each jump was 0.744 m.

Practice

1. Estimate. Then divide.
   a) $2.4 \div 4$ b) $8.5 \div 5$ c) $0.9 \div 9$
   d) $6 \div 8$ e) $0.639 \div 3$ f) $7 \div 2$

2. Divide. Multiply to check your answers.
   a) $27.02 \div 5$ b) $3.42 \div 6$ c) $0.735 \div 7$
   d) $0.072 \div 8$ e) $50 \div 8$ f) $3.438 \div 6$

3. Raj in-line skated 2.644 km in 4 min.
What was the mean distance Raj travelled each minute?

4. Eric cycled 2.25 km in 5 min.
Josie cycled 2.76 km in 8 min.
Who travelled faster? Show your work.

5. Winnie paid $6.99 for 3 tennis balls.
    a) How much did each tennis ball cost?
    b) How much would Winnie pay for 12 tennis balls?

6. Sharma paid $58.50 to board her cat at a kennel for 5 days.
Her friend Miles paid $12.50 each day to board his cat
at a different kennel.
Who got the better deal? Explain how you know.

7. Write a story problem that can be solved by dividing 3 by 8.
Solve the problem.

8. A square park has a perimeter of 14.984 km.
How long is each side of the square?

9. Rolf paid $1.44 for half a dozen eggs.
    a) How much did Rolf pay per egg?
    b) How much change did Rolf get from a $5 bill?

10. A student divided 1.374 by 4 and got 3.435.
    a) Without dividing, how do you know if the answer is correct?
    b) If the answer is not correct, what do you think the student did wrong?

11. In good weather, Hannah rides her bike to school
and back each day.
One week, Hannah rode her bike on 4 days.
That week Hannah rode 10.8 km in total.
The following week, she rode her bike all 5 days.
How far did Hannah ride the second week?

Numbers Every Day

Calculator Skills

Arrange the digits 3, 4, and 6 to make a 3-digit prime number.
How many different prime numbers can you make?

Reflect

How would you find the quotient of 4 ÷ 5?
Use words, diagrams, or numbers to explain.

Dividing Decimals

Explore

A group on a 4-day hiking trip travelled
96.575 km on the Trans Canada Trail.
What was the mean distance travelled each day?

To pay for the trip, each group of 3 hikers
had to raise at least $125.
How much did each hiker have to raise?

Use any materials you want.
Solve the problems. Show your work.

Show *and* Share

Share your work with another pair of students.
What strategies did you use to estimate? To calculate?
Are your answers exact? How do you know?
What strategies can you use to check your answers?

Connect

➤ Four hikers want to share a 0.945-L bottle of water equally.
How much water will each hiker get?

Divide: $0.945 \div 4$

Estimate first.
0.945 is a little less than 1.
$1 \div 4 = \frac{1}{4}$
$\qquad = 0.25$
So, $0.945 \div 4$ is about 0.25.

Divide.

$4\overline{)0.9^14^25^10^20}$
$\quad 0.2\ 3\ 6\ 2\ 5$

> Remember: sometimes, you
> need to write zeros in the dividend
> so you can continue to divide.

There were only 3 decimal places in the dividend 0.945.
So, round the quotient to the nearest thousandth.
0.236 25 rounds to 0.236.
So, each hiker gets about 0.236 L of water.

> 0.236 is close to the estimate 0.25.
> So, the answer is reasonable.

> You can change litres to millilitres by multiplying by 1000:
> $0.236 \times 1000 = 236$
> So, each hiker gets about 236 mL of water.

➤ One morning, the hikers travelled 11 km in 3 h.
What was the mean distance the hikers travelled each hour?

Estimate first:
Round 11 to 12.
$12 \div 3 = 4$
So, $11 \div 3$ is a little less than 4.

Divide: $11 \div 3$

$3\overline{\smash{)}11.^20^20^20^20^2}$
    $3.\ 6\ 6\ 6\ 6$

> Sometimes you may never stop dividing, no matter how many zeros you write in the dividend.

This is called a **repeating decimal**.

> 3.7 is a little less than 4, so the answer is reasonable.

Round the quotient to the nearest tenth:
3.6666… rounds to 3.7.
So, the hikers travelled about 3.7 km each hour.

Check the answer by multiplying
the quotient by the divisor:
$3.7 \times 3 = 11.1$
11.1 is close to the dividend, 11.
So, the answer is reasonable.

Practice

1. Estimate first. Then divide.
   a) $8.235 \div 6$
   b) $12 \div 5$
   c) $39.77 \div 2$
   d) $88.2 \div 5$
   e) $2.367 \div 4$
   f) $4.573 \div 5$

2. Divide. Round each quotient to the same number of decimal places as there are in the dividend.
   a) 3.05 ÷ 2
   b) $49.67 ÷ 4
   c) 6.1 ÷ 9
   d) 1.189 ÷ 4
   e) 25 ÷ 3
   f) $26.52 ÷ 5

3. Use Base Ten Blocks to show why the quotient of 1 ÷ 9 is a repeating decimal. The large cube represents 1.

4. Use a calculator to divide. Round each quotient to the nearest hundredth.
   a) 11 ÷ 9
   b) 1.216 ÷ 7
   c) 17.5 ÷ 9

5. A group of students goes camping. Each tent holds 5 students. How many tents are needed for 38 students? Show your work.

6. Six students share 16 energy bars equally. How many energy bars does each student get?

7. Richard divided a 0.954-L bottle of spicy tomato juice equally among 5 glasses. How much juice is in each glass? Give your answer in 2 different units.

8. Marina packed eight 2.54-L bottles of lemon-lime fruit punch for a 3-day camping trip. About how many litres of fruit punch does that allow for each day? Show your work.

9. Three friends buy a box of cereal for $3.49 and a carton of milk for $1.89. They want to share the cost. How much should each person pay?

10. In a snail-racing contest, Noba's snail crawled 1.677 m in 5 min. What is the mean distance the snail travelled each minute? Give your answer in as many different units as you can.

11. Write a story problem you can solve by dividing 4.738 by 5. Solve your problem. Multiply to check your answer.

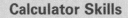

Numbers Every Day

Calculator Skills

Find six consecutive even numbers with a sum of 390.

Reflect

Explain how you can multiply to check the quotient of 2.768 ÷ 3.

Strategies Toolkit

Explore •

Suppose you are asked to solve this problem:
Discuss what this question asks you to do.
Solve the problem.

Show *and* Share

Share your work with another pair
of students. Describe what you did
to make sure you understood
the problem. Compare your solutions.

> Replace each □ with a digit to
> make an addition sum.
> How many different ways can you
> do this? Show each way.
>
> ```
>     □ . □ □ 8
> + 2 . □ 0 □
> ─────────────
>     □ . 2 0 2
> ```

Connect •

Here are some strategies you can use to understand
what the problem is about:

- Copy the problem.
- Underline the important words.
- Look at each part, one at a time.
  Think about what each part means.
- Highlight what you are asked to find.
- Decide what form your answer should take.
  Will your answer include:
  - a graph?
  - a number?
  - a table?
  - a diagram?
  - a written explanation?
- Think about how many parts your answer needs.

Strategies for Success

- **Get unstuck.**
- **Check and reflect.**
- **Focus on the problem.**
- **Represent your thinking.**
- **Select an answer.**
- **Do your best on a test.**
- **Explain your answer.**

Here is one way to solve this problem:

Use the digits 0, 3, 5, and 8.

Write a decimal that will:

- round up when rounded to the nearest tenth

- round down when rounded to the nearest hundredth

Find as many answers as you can.

To round up, the hundredths digit must be 5 or 8. To round down, the thousandths digit must be 0 or 3.

After I find each solution, I must try to find another one.

There are 8 solutions. They are:
0.853, 0.583, 3.580, 3.850, 5.083, 5.380, 8.053, and 8.350.

Practice

The table shows how far some animals can travel in 1 s.
Use the data in the table to answer the questions.
What did you do to understand each problem?

Cheetah	31.1 m
Ostrich	19.4 m
Red kangaroo	18.1 m
Champion human sprinter	10.3 m
Dromedary (camel)	2.7 m

1. Which creature travels faster than 5 km/h, but slower than 30 km/h? Show your solution.
   How many answers can you find?

2. Which would go farther: a red kangaroo sprinting for 3 min or a human sprinter running for 4 min? How much farther? Show your solution.

Reflect

Describe what you can do to understand a problem.
Use examples to explain.

LESSON

1

1. Write each number in standard form.

   a) 5.9 million   **b)** 1.45 billion   **c)** $8\frac{3}{4}$ million

2

2. Write each decimal as a fraction or a mixed number.

   a) 0.005   **b)** 7.104   **c)** 26.3

3. Write each number as a decimal.

   a) $1\frac{172}{1000}$ **b)** $2\frac{6}{100}$ **c)** $9\frac{41}{1000}$

4. Record each number in a place-value chart.

   a) 217 thousandths   **b)** 40.209   **c)** 1.468

3

5. Copy and complete. Use >, <, or =.

   a) 1.467 ☐ 1.47   **b)** 4.905 ☐ 4.9   **c)** 76.853 ☐ 7.19

6. Order the decimals from least to greatest.

   a) 6.318, 6.394, 6.095   **b)** 9.9, 9.49, 9.362

7. Write 2 numbers between 8.43 and 8.437.
   How did you choose the numbers?

4

8. Round each number to the nearest hundredth and to the nearest tenth.

   a) 0.693   **b)** 6.245   **c)** 17.068

5

9. Estimate each sum or difference.
   Explain your strategies.

   a) 2.793 + 4.012   **b)** 17.276 − 8.357   **c)** 0.947 − 0.063

6

10. Add or subtract.
   Use the inverse operation to check each answer.

   a) 2.689 + 7.385   **b)** 9.085 − 2.378   **c)** 0.862 + 1.297

7
8

11. Multiply or divide.

   a) 0.7 × 100   **b)** 1.385 ÷ 10   **c)** 6.389 × 10 000

   d) 18.62 ÷ 100   **e)** 2 ÷ 10 000   **f)** 3.5 ÷ 100

12. Shandra's cat is 23.4 cm tall and 38 cm long.
   Express these lengths in metres and in millimetres.

9

13. Multiply. Use mental math.

    a) 17×0.1 **b)** 8×0.001 **c)** 37×0.01 **d)** 519×0.001

10
11

14. Multiply or divide. Give each answer to the nearest thousandth.
Use the inverse operation to check your answers.

    a) 3.09×7 **b)** 8.3×9 **c)** 4.951×6

    d) $1.484 \div 4$ **e)** $5 \div 8$ **f)** $0.09 \div 9$

10

15. The Giant Fan Palm produces the world's largest seed.
A seed has a mass of about 9.075 kg.
What is the combined mass of 5 of these seeds?

16. The recipe Sebastian wants to make requires
1.5 L of evaporated milk.
He has four 0.385-L cans.
Does he have enough milk? Show your work.

6
11

17. Glitz Decorations packages glitter for resale.
The masses of four sample packages are
1.195 g, 1.24 g, 1.249 g, and 1.208 g.
Find the mean mass.

12

18. Gerard, Akbar, and Oga find a $10 bill
on the way to school. They share the money.
How much will each person get? Explain.

19. The Coulter Pine produces the world's
most massive pine cones. The combined mass
of 8 of these cones is 25.259 kg.
Find the mean mass of one
Coulter Pine cone to the nearest hundredth
of a kilogram.

UNIT

4 **Learning Goals**

☑ relate fractions to decimals
☑ represent, read, and write
decimals
☑ compare and order decimals
☑ round decimals
☑ estimate decimal sums,
differences, products, and
quotients
☑ add, subtract, multiply, and
divide decimals to
thousandths
☑ pose and solve problems
involving decimals
☑ select operations and solve
multistep problems

Unit Problem

Harnessing the Wind

Every day, thousands of people *ride the wind* in Calgary.
Calgary's C-Train is North America's first wind-powered
public transit system.
It runs on electricity generated by 12 wind turbines.

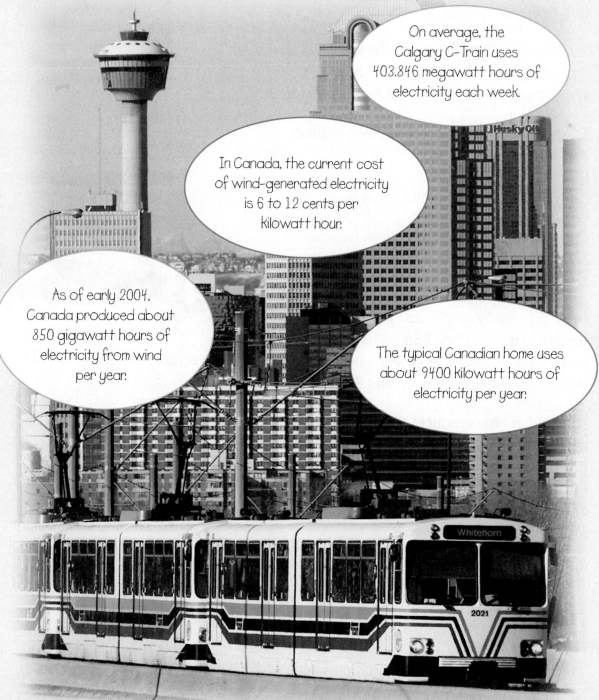

On average, the Calgary C-Train uses 403.846 megawatt hours of electricity each week.

In Canada, the current cost of wind-generated electricity is 6 to 12 cents per kilowatt hour.

As of early 2004, Canada produced about 850 gigawatt hours of electricity from wind per year.

The typical Canadian home uses about 9400 kilowatt hours of electricity per year.

Check List

Your work should show
☑ how you calculated and
   checked each solution
☑ correct mathematical language
☑ an interesting story problem
   involving decimals
☑ clear explanations of your
   solutions and strategies

1. How many megawatt hours of electricity
   does the Calgary C-Train use in one day?
   How much is that in kilowatt hours?
   In gigawatt hours?

2. The amount of electricity used by
   the C-Train in one day is enough to wash
   24 658 loads of laundry.
   About how many kilowatt hours of electricity
   does it take to wash 1 load of laundry?

3. A wind farm in Saskatchewan has
   9 identical turbines. Together they generate
   18.9 gigawatt hours of electricity in 1 year.
   How much electricity does 1 turbine generate?
   How did you decide how to round?

4. Use some of the data on page 162.
   Write a problem about wind energy.
   Solve your problem. Show your work.

1 kilowatt = 1000 watts
1 megawatt = 1 million watts
1 gigawatt = 1 billion watts

Reflect on the Unit

How can you use place value to add, subtract, multiply,
and divide with decimals? Explain.

Unit

1

1. The table shows the input and output
   for this machine.

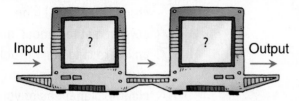

Input →   ? →   ? → Output →

Input	Output
1	1
2	6
3	11
4	16
5	21

   Identify the numbers and operations in the machine.

2. Copy this Venn diagram.
   Sort these numbers.

320	264	762	4926
2660	1293	488	504

   How did you know where to put each number?

   Divisible by 4   Divisible by 6

3. Solve each equation.
   a) $6 \times \square = 432$ **b)** $483 = 3 \times \square$ **c)** $\square \div 12 = 54$

2

4. Find all the common multiples of 4 and 3 between 10 and 100.

5. Draw a Venn diagram with two loops.
   Label the loops "Prime Number" and "Composite Number."
   a) How did you decide how to draw the loops?
   b) Sort the numbers from 15 to 40.
       Explain how you knew where to put each number.

6. Copy this number sentence.
   Insert brackets to make the number sentence an equation.
   $16 \div 4 \times 2 + 6 = 8$

7. The difference between two 4-digit numbers is 217.
   What might the two numbers be?
   Give three different answers.

8 Find each product or quotient.
   a) 476×21 **b)** $840 \div 21$ **c)** $2816 \div 32$
   d) 622×45 **e)** 292×93 **f)** $3496 \div 46$

9. Use a ruler and a protractor. Draw an angle with each measure.

    a) 185°   **b)** 100°   **c)** 290°

10. Sketch each polygon.

    a) a convex quadrilateral   **b)** a concave pentagon

11. Use a ruler, a compass, and a protractor.
Construct △ABC with sides AB = 5 cm, AC = 7 cm, and BC = 6 cm.
Find the measure of each angle in △ABC.

12. You will need linking cubes, triangular dot paper, and grid paper.

    a) Build an object with linking cubes.

    b) Draw the object on triangular dot paper.

    c) Draw the front, top, and side views of the object.

13. Write each number as many different ways as you can.

    a) 76 thousandths   **b)** $5\frac{1}{4}$ million   **c)** 4 651 000   **d)** 3 750 000 000

14. Add or subtract. Estimate to check.

    a) 3.864 − 1.905   **b)** 12.064 − 8.445   **c)** 9.681 + 7.021

15. Write each mass in tonnes.

    a) an elephant has a mass of 3630 kg.   1 t = 1000 kg

    b) The mass of a skid of books is 119 kg.

16. Use mental math to multiply.

    a) 426 × 0.01   **b)** 37 × 0.001   **c)** 8 × 0.01

17. Multiply or divide.

    a) 1.763 × 4   **b)** 3.898 ÷ 4   **c)** 23.62 ÷ 5

    d) 45.9 ÷ 3   **e)** 2.033 × 7   **f)** 6.841 × 6

18. Each day Ryan earns $18.00 walking dogs.
He is saving to buy inline skating equipment.
The skates cost $59.95. A helmet costs $22.90.
A set of elbow, knee, and wrist guards costs $24.95.
How long will it take Ryan to save enough money
to buy the equipment?

Data Management

Playing with Letters

Learning Goals

- analyse data to make inferences and convincing arguments
- find the mean, median, and mode
- plot and describe the location of points on a Cartesian plane
- choose an appropriate graph to display data
- compare different displays of the same data
- draw bar graphs, line graphs, and scatter plots by hand and with a computer
- design and conduct surveys
- evaluate collected data and explain how the data represent the population

In a paragraph of text, some letters appear more often than others. This bar graph shows the most common letters in the English language. Each bar represents the number of times you could expect to find the letter in a sample of English writing containing 1000 letters.

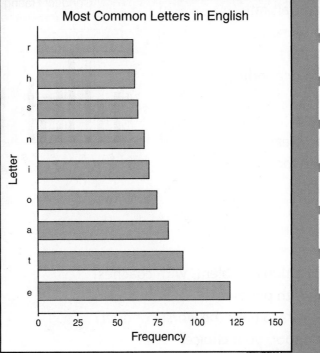

Most Common Letters in English

- Which vowel is not among the 9 most common letters in English?

- Which 4 letters are each used about one-half as often as "e"? How can you tell this from the graph?

- Suppose you had a sample of writing in English containing 2000 letters.
  About how many times could you expect each of these letters to appear?

  i   t   e

167

Interpreting Data

In recent years, people have been concerned about poor conduct in organized sports.
Elaine Raakman of Ontario has developed a program, called JustPlay, for tracking conduct at sporting events.
JustPlay displays the data it collects in graphs.

Explore

After each game, officials rate the behaviour of players, coaches, and spectators on a scale from 1 (very good) to 5 (very poor).
This graph shows the conduct ratings for 7 teams in a hockey program for 13- and 14-year-olds.

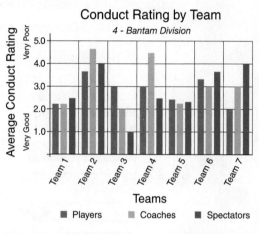

Conduct Rating by Team
4 - Bantam Division

Players   Coaches   Spectators

- Any bar over 3.5 represents a serious problem.
  Which teams had serious problems with coaches?
  With spectators? With players?
- Which group appears to have the worst conduct?
  Use the data to support your choice.

A rating of 4 or 5 is called a critical incident.
The circle graph shows the source of critical incidents in a minor hockey association over a two-year period.

- Rank the groups from worst to best conduct.
- A statement with the graph says that coaches and spectators were the source of almost $\frac{3}{4}$ of the critical incidents.
  Is this correct? Explain.

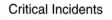

Critical Incidents

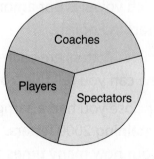

Coaches

Players   Spectators

Show *and* Share

Write two questions that can be answered from the graphs.
Trade questions with another pair of classmates.
Answer your classmates' questions.

Connect

A topic often studied is how Canadians spend their leisure time.

➤ This graph shows how much time people spend watching TV each week.

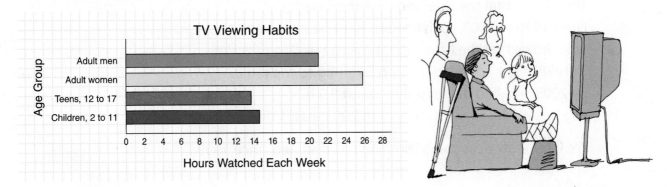

From the graph:
- Adult women watch about 26 h of television each week.
- Teens watch about 14 h.
- Adult men watch about 21 h of TV.

We **infer** that adult women watch almost twice as much TV each week as teens.
Adult men watch about 7 h more TV than teens.

> An **inference** is a conclusion we reach by reasoning.

➤ In a circle graph, data are shown as parts of a whole.
This graph shows the types of radio stations people listen to.

Adult Contemporary is about $\frac{1}{4}$ of the circle.
We infer that about $\frac{1}{4}$ of people 12 years of age and older who listen to the radio are tuned to adult contemporary stations.
Each of CBC, Country, and Talk has about the same share of the listening audience, about $\frac{1}{10}$.

We infer that about $\frac{1}{2}$ of the listening audience listen to CBC, country, talk, or rock radio stations.

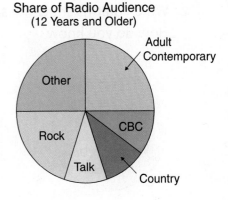

Share of Radio Audience
(12 Years and Older)

➤ A line graph shows data that change over time. This graph shows how the number of hours teens spent listening to the radio each week changed from 1998 to 2003.

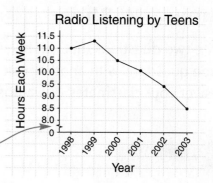

Radio Listening by Teens

The symbol on the vertical axis means that the numbers between 0 and 8.0 are not shown.

From 1998 to 1999, the line segment goes up to the right.
This shows that the listening time increased.
From 1999 to 2003, each line segment goes down to the right.
This shows that the listening time decreased.
In 1998, teens spent about 11 h listening to the radio.
By 2003, this had decreased to about 8.5 h.
The overall decrease from 1998 to 2003 was: 11 h − 8.5 h = 2.5 h

We infer that teens' radio listening has declined since 1999.

Practice

1. Use the circle graph to answer these questions.
   a) Which province made up about $\frac{1}{3}$ of the population of the region?
   b) Which province had a population almost twice as great as that of Newfoundland and Labrador?
   How does the circle graph help you find this quickly?

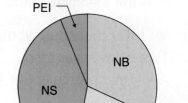

Population of Atlantic Provinces, 2001

2. Which graphs show the same information? How do you know?

Means of Transportation to School

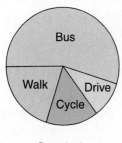

Graph A

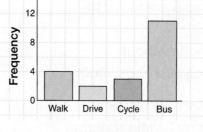

Graph B

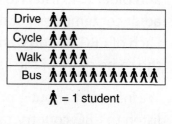

🕯 = 1 student

Graph C

3. What can you infer from this graph?

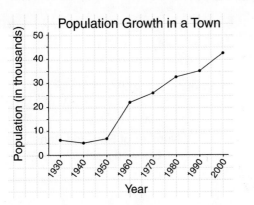

Population Growth in a Town

4. Both graphs in questions 1 and 3 show population data. Explain why a circle graph was used in question 1 but a line graph was used in question 3.

5. In *Explore*, you investigated the conduct rating of teams in a hockey league. This graph shows the conduct rating of the same teams the following season.

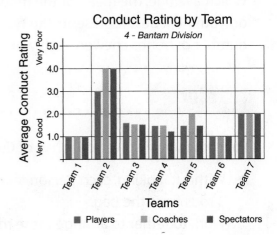

Conduct Rating by Team

4 - Bantam Division

■ Players   ■ Coaches   ■ Spectators

   a) Any bar over 3.5 represents a serious problem.
   Which teams had serious problems with coaches? With spectators? With players?

   b) Which team showed the greatest improvement from the first season to the second? Explain how you know.

   c) Did the conduct of any team worsen from the first season to the second? How do you know?

   d) The JustPlay ratings range from 1 to 5, but the vertical axes on the bar graphs start at 0. Could any team have received a rating less than 1? Explain.

   e) What else can you infer from this graph?

Reflect

How do you interpret data on a graph?
Include examples in your explanation.

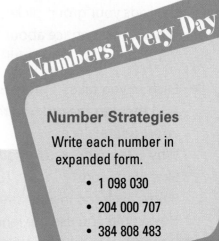

Numbers Every Day

Number Strategies

Write each number in expanded form.

- 1 098 030
- 204 000 707
- 384 808 483

Finding the Median

The graph shows the number of rawhide bones some dogs chew each week.

How many bones does each dog chew each week?
What is the mean number of bones chewed each week? The mode number?
How did you find the mean and the mode?
Which average, the mean or the mode, do you think best represents the typical number of bones chewed each week? Why?

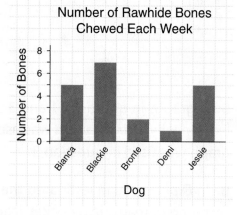

Number of Rawhide Bones
Chewed Each Week

Explore

Your teacher will give you a bag of Cuisenaire rods. You will need a ruler.

➤ Without looking, each person takes 3 rods from the bag.
Work together to arrange these rods from shortest to longest.
Find the middle rod.
How many rods are to its right? To its left?
In what way is the middle rod typical of the rods your group picked?
What do you notice about the rods to the left and right of the middle rod?

➤ Each of you takes 1 more rod from the bag.
Add them to the ordered rods in the appropriate places.
Why is there no middle rod now?
Sketch the rods.
Below each rod in your sketch, write its length.
How could you use the lengths to find a "middle" length?
How is the middle length typical of the rods in your sketch?

Show *and* Share

Share your results with another group.
Compare the methods you used to find a "middle" length.

The **median** of a data set is the middle number when the data
are arranged in order.

➤ There are 11 Grade 6 students in Ms. Shim's
combined Grades 6 and 7 class.
To find the median, she listed their marks
on the last science test from greatest to least:

95, 92, 87, 85, 80, 78, 76, 73, 70, 66, 54

The middle number is 78.
There are 5 marks greater than 78, and 5 marks less than 78.
The median mark is 78.

> When there is an odd number of data, the median is the middle number.

➤ Another grade 6 student transfers to Ms. Shim's class.
He writes the same test and receives a mark of 72.

To find the new median, the teacher adds his mark
to the ordered list:

95, 92, 87, 85, 80, 78, 76, 73, 72, 70, 66, 54

There are two middle numbers, 78 and 76.
There are 5 marks greater than 78 and 5 marks less than 76.
The median is the mean of the 2 middle numbers:
(78 + 76) ÷ 2 = 77
The median mark is 77.

> When there is an even number of data, the median is the mean of the two middle numbers.

> When there is an even number of data, the median might **not** be one of the numbers in the data set.

Numbers Every Day

Number Strategies

Find two 2-digit numbers
with a product of 900.
How many different pairs
can you find?

➤ The hourly wages in dollars of 10 workers are: 8, 8, 8, 8, 9, 9, 9, 11, 12, 20
Which measure of the average best represents these numbers?

To find the mean wage:
- Add: 8 + 8 + 8 + 8 + 9 + 9 + 9 + 11 + 12 + 20 = 102
- Divide by the number of data, 10: 102 ÷ 10 = 10.2

Only 3 workers have an hourly wage greater than the mean wage, $10.20.
The mode wage is $8. This is the least number.
The median wage is $9.

The median best represents these hourly wages.

Practice

1. Find the median of each set of data.
   a) 85, 80, 100, 90, 85, 95, 90
   b) 12 kg, 61 kg, 85 kg, 52 kg, 19 kg, 15 kg, 21 kg, 30 kg

2. Ammar applied for a clerical job with
   2 different companies.
   The table shows the salaries of people
   with clerical jobs at each company.
   a) Find the mean, the median, and
      the mode salary at each company.
   b) Suppose both companies offer Ammar a job.
      Based on these salary data, which job
      would you tell him to take?
      Explain your reasons.

Annual Salary ($)	
Company A	23 000, 24 000, 25 000, 26 500, 27 000, 29 200, 34 000, 36 500
Company B	24 500, 25 000, 27 500, 28 000, 30 000, 30 000, 31 000

3. Mary is a real estate agent.
   One month she sold 7 houses at these prices:
   $171 000, $165 000, $178 000, $161 000, $174 000, $168 000, $240 000
   a) What is the median price of the houses she sold?
   b) Do you think the mean price is greater than or less than the
      median price? Explain. Calculate to check.
   c) Which average do you think better represents a typical price
      of the houses she sold that month? Why?

4. Each time, write two different data sets with 6 numbers.
   a) The mode is 100. The median and the mean are equal.
   b) The mode is 100. The mean is less than the median.

5. A company is looking at employee salaries to make sure employees with the same job receive the same pay. The salaries, in dollars, of employees in one job class are:

34 750, 27 800, 41 900, 36 000, 34 750, 34 900, 38 500

What salary should all these employees receive?
Use the mean, the median, or the mode to explain your answer.

6. In 2004, the Six Nations Arrows represented Ontario in the Minto Cup Junior A Lacrosse Championship.
Here are the 2004 season statistics for 10 players on the team.

Player	Games	Goals	Assists	Points	Penalty Minutes
Stewart Monture	19	31	25	56	44
Cody Jamieson	18	31	25	56	28
Craig Point	20	26	30	56	20
Mitch Nanticoke	19	19	26	45	14
Ben Powless	19	15	20	35	56
Rayce Vyse	17	7	24	31	22
Matt Myke	20	11	19	30	18
Mike Abrams	18	7	9	16	6
Sid Smith	19	2	14	16	6
Brett Bucktooth	4	8	6	14	10

a) Calculate the mean, the median, and the mode of each set of numbers in the table.
b) Which average would you use as the typical number for each set? Explain your choice.
c) Make up a question about the mean, the median, and the mode that can be answered using these data. Answer your question.

Reflect

A median is the strip of land or concrete barrier separating lanes of highway traffic travelling in opposite directions. How is this meaning similar to its meaning in math?

Strategies Toolkit

Explore •••

Sarah put 2 pennies in one box,
1 penny and 1 nickel in another box,
and 2 nickels in a third box.
Sarah then labelled the boxes incorrectly
with labels of 2¢, 6¢, and 10¢.
How can you identify the contents of
each box by taking 1 coin from 1 box?

Show *and* Share

Describe the strategy you used
to solve the problem.

Connect ••

How many ways can you make $1.00 without using pennies?

Understand

What do you know?
• You want a combination of coins that
  total $1.00.
• You cannot use pennies.
• You will not use toonies.
  Their value is too great.

Plan

Think of strategies to help you solve
the problem.
• You can **make a table** or **make an
  organized list.**
• You can **use logical reasoning**
  to complete the table or list.

Strategies

• **Make a table.**
• **Use a model.**
• **Draw a diagram.**
• **Solve a simpler
  problem.**
• **Work backward.**
• **Guess and check.**
• **Make an organized
  list.**
• **Use a pattern.**
• **Draw a graph.**
• **Use logical reasoning.**

Solve

Think of the coins you can use (loonies, quarters, dimes, nickels). Start with the greatest number of the highest-valued coin.

Loonies	Quarters	Dimes	Nickels	Total Value
1	0	0	0	$1.00
0	4	0	0	$1.00
0	3	2	1	75¢ + 20¢ + 5¢ = 100¢, or $1.00
0	3	1	3	75¢ + 10¢ + 15¢ = 100¢, or $1.00

Complete the table with combinations using 3 quarters, then 2 quarters, then 1 quarter, then 0 quarters.

Look Back

How can you be sure you have found all the possible combinations?

Practice

Choose one of the

Strategies

1. Hatif bought 5 books, each with a whole-number price.
   The mean price of the books was $20.
   The median price was $18.
   The most expensive book cost $25 and the cheapest cost $17.
   What are the possible prices of the other 3 books?

2. a) How many three-digit numbers can be made using the digits 2, 4, and 6 once each?
   b) Find the median and the mean of the numbers in part a. What do you notice?
   c) Suppose you repeat this activity using the digits 1, 3, and 5. What do you predict would happen? Check your prediction.

Reflect

Choose one of the *Practice* questions.
Describe how you solved the problem.

Constructing and Interpreting Graphs

Different types of graphs can show the same data.

Number of Pets

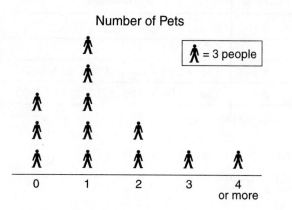

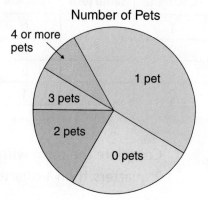

How are the graphs alike? How are they different?
The type of graph you draw depends on the data,
what you want to show, and who will be using your graph.
What might affect the appearance of a graph?

Explore

You will need a ruler and grid paper.

Measure each other's hand span to
the nearest centimetre.
Record the measurements on the board.
Are the results reasonable?
Draw a graph to display the data
for the whole class.

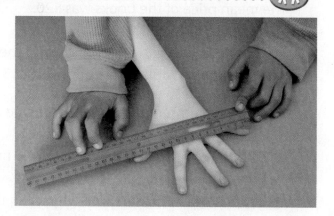

Show and Share

Share your graph with another pair of students.
Justify your choice of graph.
Could you have drawn a different graph? Explain.

Mr. Salvati's Grade 6 class used data from the Internet to investigate new car sales.

The data are given in categories, so Emily and Carla decided to draw a bar graph.

The length of each bar in a bar graph represents the total for that category.

New Car Sales in Canada

Year	Imports
1995	118 000
1996	89 000
1997	110 000
1998	151 000
1999	187 000
2000	209 000
2001	249 000
2002	283 000

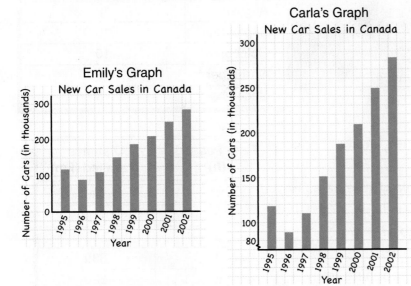

The numbers on the vertical axis show the scale.

Each girl chose a different vertical scale for her graph. On Carla's graph, the year-to-year changes appear greater than those on Emily's graph.

The data show change over time.
So Herman and Jake drew line graphs.

Jake's graph suggests that from 1996 to 2002 sales increased steadily. Herman's graph suggests the same, but the increase appears to be more rapid over the same period.

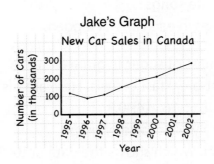

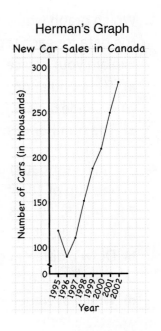

1. This table shows the mean monthly
   temperatures in Vancouver in 2003.
   a) Draw a graph.
      Explain your choice
      of graph.
   b) What inferences
      can you make
      from the graph?

Month	Mean Temperature (°C)
January	3
February	5
March	7
April	9
May	12
June	15
July	18
August	18
September	15
October	10
November	6
December	3

2. The table shows how far René's family
   travelled on a car trip.
   a) Draw a line graph to display these data.
   b) What was the distance travelled
      each hour from hours 2 to 4?
      From hours 6 to 8?
   c) What do you think was happening from
      hour 4 to hour 5 on the trip?
   d) What other inferences can you make
      from the graph?

Time Passed (h)	Distance Travelled (km)
1	80
2	180
3	280
4	380
5	380
6	480
7	530
8	580

3. Which graph would you use to display
   the data for each topic below?
   Explain your choice.
   a) The population of Canada from 1901 to 2001
   b) A Grade 6 class' favourite songs
   c) The number of syllables in each line of a poem

4. Pascal investigated the mass of sugar, in grams,
   in one cup of 10 different breakfast cereals. Here are his data:
   7.8, 14, 15, 10, 7.8, 0.2, 8.5, 16, 14, 0.3
   a) Graph the data. Justify your choice of graph.
   b) Draw a different graph. Which shows the data better? Explain.
   c) Calculate the mean, the median, and the mode of the data.
   d) Which average best represents the data? Explain.

Rebecca's Height

Age (years)	Height (cm)
7	120
8	125
9	130
10	138
11	143
12	150
13	155
14	158
15	158
16	159
17	160

5. The table shows Rebecca's height
in centimetres each year from age 7 to 17.
  a) Draw a graph to display these data.
  b) How did you decide on the type of graph
  to draw?
  c) How did you choose the scale?
  d) Draw a different graph.
  e) Which graph represents the data better?
  Explain.
  f) What do you think Rebecca's height
  will be at age 20? Age 30?
  Give reasons for your predictions.

6. The table shows the medal totals for
3 countries for 5 Summer Olympic Games.

	1988	1992	1996	2000	2004
Australia	20	27	41	58	49
Canada	24	23	22	14	12
China	28	54	56	59	63

  a) Display each country's data
  on a line graph on the same grid.
  Use a different colour for each country.
  b) Write a statement about what the graph
  shows for each country.
  c) In 2008, Beijing, China, will host the Summer
  Olympic Games.
  For each country, predict if it will win
  more medals in the 2008 Games than in 2004,
  fewer medals, or the same number of medals.
  Explain your predictions.
  d) Write a question that can be answered using
  either your graph or the data in the table.

Reflect

How do you decide which type of graph best displays
a set of data? Use examples in your explanation.

Numbers Every Day

Mental Math

Find each quotient. Write a
related multiplication sentence
for each division sentence.

$45 \div 3 = \square$

$96 \div 6 = \square$

$144 \div 24 = \square$

Drawing Bar Graphs and Line Graphs with *AppleWorks*

Work with a partner.

Environment Canada measures the hours of sunshine in different places across the country. The table shows typical data for Thunder Bay.

Use *AppleWorks*.
Follow these steps to display these data on a bar graph and on a line graph.

1. Open a new spreadsheet in *AppleWorks*.
Click:

Spreadsheet

2. To **enter the data**:

Click cell A1 to select it.
Type: Month, then press Enter.
Enter the first letter of each month
in cells A2 to A13.

Click cell B1 to select it.
Type: Sunshine (h), then press Enter.
Enter the hours of sunshine for each month in cells B2 to B13.

3. To **format the spreadsheet**:
Click cell A1.
Hold down the mouse button and drag to cell B1.
Release the mouse button.

Click: Format , then click: Style   ▶

Click: Bold   Ctrl+B

Click cell B2.
Hold down the mouse button and drag to cell B13.
Release the mouse button.

Click: Format , then click: Number...   Shft+Ctrl+N

Typical Amount of Sunshine in Thunder Bay

Month	Sunshine (h)
January	114.4
February	133.5
March	159.1
April	219.0
May	265.0
June	264.1
July	283.4
August	258.3
September	162.9
October	127.7
November	88.8
December	91.7

From the dropdown menu showing
the number options, select Fixed.
For decimal precision, enter 1.

Click: OK

Format Number, Date, and Time

Options

⦿ Number: Fixed   ▼

☐ Show Separators for Thousands

☐ Show Negatives in Parentheses

Decimal Precision: 1

4. To **create a bar graph**:
Click cell A2.
Hold down the mouse button and drag to cell B13.
Release the mouse button.

Click: Options , then click: Make Chart...   Ctrl+M

Click the Gallery tab, then click:
Bar

Ensure no options are selected.

To **give the graph a title**:
Click the Labels tab.
Select Show Title.
Make sure Show Legend
is not selected.
Type: Sunshine in Thunder Bay

Chart Options

Gallery | Axes | Series | Labels | General

☑ Show Title

Title: Sunshine in Thunder Bay

☑ Horizontal
☐ Shadow

☐ Show Legend

To **label the axes**:
Click the Axes tab.

Click: ⦿ X axis

Type the Axis label: Month

Click: ⦿ Y axis

Type the Axis label: Sunshine (h)
Enter these settings:

Minimum:	Maximum:	Step size:	☐ Log:
0	300	50	

Click: OK

5. To **move the graph**:

Click the graph to select it.
Click and hold down the mouse button.
Drag the graph until it is where you want it.
Release the mouse button.

6. To **print the graph**:

Click: File , then click: Print...   Ctrl+P

Click: OK

7. To **save your spreadsheet and graph**:

Click: File , then click: Save As...   Shft+Ctrl+S

Name your file, then click: Save

8. Repeat Step 4 to draw 3 different bar graphs.
Each time, use different step sizes for the Y-axis.
Print each graph.
Compare the graphs. How are they the same?
How are they different?

> Try different values of
> Maximum greater than 300.

9. To **create a line graph**:

Ensure cells A2 to B13 are selected.

Click: Options , then click: Make Chart...   Ctrl+M

Click the Gallery tab, then click:
Line

Ensure no options are selected.

To **give the graph a title**:

Click the Labels tab. Select Show Title.
Make sure Show Legend is not selected.
Type: Sunshine in Thunder Bay

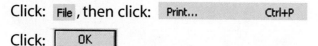

To **label the axes**:

Click the Axes tab.

Click: ⦿ X axis

Type the Axis label: Month

Click: ⦿ Y axis

Type the Axis label: Sunshine (h)

Enter these settings:

Minimum:	Maximum:	Step size:	☐ Log:
0	300	50	

Click: [OK]

Save and print the graph.

10. Repeat Step 9 to draw 3 different line graphs.
    Each time, use different step sizes for the Y-axis.
    Print each graph.
    Compare the graphs.
    How are they the same?
    How are they different?

11. Compare the line graphs from
    Steps 9 and 10 to the bar graphs
    from Steps 4 to 8.
    Which graph do you think best
    represents the data? Why?

 **Reflect**

When might you display data in a bar graph? In a line graph? Explain.

5 Graphing on a Coordinate Grid

How could Hannah describe where her great-grandmother is in this family photo?

In math, we need a way to describe the position of a point on a grid.

Explore

You need 2 sets of numeral cards from 0 to 10, a grid with axes labelled from 0 to 10, and a ruler.

➤ Shuffle the numeral cards and place them in a pile.
➤ Draw a card. Record the number and keep the card. Start at 0. Move that many squares along the horizontal axis.
➤ Draw another card.
  Record the number and keep the card.
  Move that many squares vertically from the point you reached on the horizontal axis.
  Mark a point where you end up.
➤ Repeat until you have plotted 3 points.
➤ Use a ruler to join pairs of points.
  You will probably have drawn a triangle.
  Label the triangle ABC.
➤ Find a way to describe the position of each vertex of △ABC.

Show *and* Share

Share your work with another classmate.
Trade descriptions of the positions of the vertices of each triangle.
Draw the triangle your classmate described.
Compare your drawings.
Was your classmate able to follow your description? Explain.
If not, how could you improve your description?

Connect

René Descartes was a French mathematician
who lived from 1596 to 1650.
He developed the coordinate grid system we use today.
In his honour, it is called the **Cartesian plane**.

➤ We use an **ordered pair**
to describe the coordinates
of a point.
The coordinates of point B
are (6, 2).

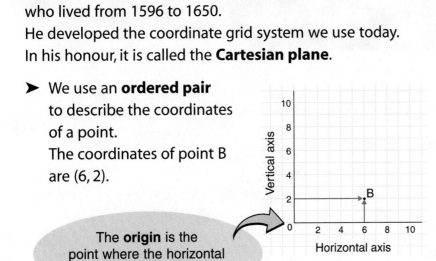

The **origin** is the
point where the horizontal
and vertical axes meet.

In an ordered pair:

• The first number tells the horizontal distance from the origin.

• The second number tells the vertical distance from the origin.

(6, 2)

➤ We use an ordered pair to locate
or **plot** a point.
The coordinates of point A are (4, 3).
To draw point A on the coordinate grid:
Start at the origin, move to 4 on the
horizontal axis, then move up 3 units.

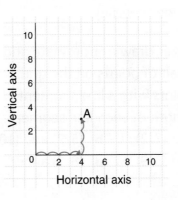

Agriculture

To maximize crop yield, farmers test the soil in their fields for nutrients. The results help farmers to decide on the amount and type of fertilizer to use. Grid soil sampling is one method of collecting samples. The field is divided into a grid. A soil sample is taken from the centre of each grid cell.

Numbers Every Day

Mental Math

Is 62×230 greater than 10 000?
How do you know without finding the product?

Practice

1. Find the letter on the grid represented by each ordered pair.
   Record the letters in order.
   What is the message?
   $(1, 4)$, $(9, 9)$, $(6, 2)$, $(0, 5)$, $(8, 1)$, $(3, 3)$, $(10, 5)$, $(2, 8)$, $(7, 10)$

2. Make up a word or phrase using the letters on the grid in question 1.
   Write the corresponding ordered pairs in order.
   Give your list of ordered pairs to a classmate.
   Have your classmate use the grid to decode your message.

3. On grid paper, draw a coordinate grid with axes labelled from 0 to 10.
   Plot each pair of points on the grid.
   Join the points with a line segment.
   Find the length of each line segment.
   a) $(4, 2)$ and $(7, 2)$ **b)** $(5, 7)$ and $(10, 7)$
   c) $(3, 4)$ and $(3, 9)$ **d)** $(8, 1)$ and $(8, 7)$

4. On grid paper, draw a coordinate grid with axes labelled from 1 to 10.
Plot each set of points on the grid.
Join the points in order. Join the last point to the first point.
Name the figure you have drawn. Find its perimeter and area.

   a) A(4, 3), B(8, 3), C(8, 9), D(4, 9)   **b)** E(3, 4), F(7, 4), G(7, 8), H(3, 8)

5. Use grid paper. Draw and label a coordinate grid.

   a) Plot each point on the grid.
      A(2, 1), B(1, 3), C(2, 5), D(4, 5), E(5, 3), F(4, 1)

   b) Join the points in order. Then join F to A.
      What figure have you drawn?
      Is it a regular figure? How do you know?

6. On grid paper, draw a coordinate grid.

   a) Plot a point at P(3, 5).
      This is one vertex of rectangle PQRS.
      Finish the drawing so that PQRS has area 20 square units.

   b) What are the coordinates of the other vertices?

   c) What is the perimeter of the rectangle?

7. On grid paper, draw and label a grid.

   a) Plot the points A(5, 1) and B(5, 5). Join the points.

   b) Find point C so that △ABC is isosceles.
      How many different ways can you do this?
      Draw each way you find. Write the coordinates of C.
      How do you know each triangle is isosceles?

   c) Find point D so that △ABD is scalene.
      Show 3 different scalene triangles.
      Write the coordinates of D each time.
      How do you know each triangle is scalene?

   d) Can you find point E on a grid point
      so that △ABE is equilateral?
      If so, draw △ABE. Write the coordinates of E.
      If not, explain why △ABE cannot be drawn.

Reflect

Explain how to use ordered pairs to
describe and locate points on a grid.
Use words, numbers, and pictures.

At Home

Most town and city maps use a grid
system. Find one you can study.
How is the map grid similar to the
Cartesian grid? How is it different?
How does the street index describe
where to look for a particular road?

Scatter Plots

You can use your knowledge of the coordinate grid to compare two sets of data.

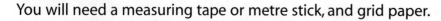

Explore

You will need a measuring tape or metre stick, and grid paper.

➤ Measure and record your arm spans, in centimetres.
Measure and record the length of your shoe.
➤ Record your results in two columns of a table on the board.
Each row in the table is an ordered pair of numbers.
➤ Plot each ordered pair of the class data on a coordinate grid.

> Your arm span is the length from fingertip to fingertip, when your arms are fully outstretched.

Show *and* Share

Share your graph with another pair of students.
How are your graphs alike? How are they different?
Describe your graphs.

Connect

A **scatter plot** is a graph of ordered pairs on a coordinate grid.
Each point on the grid represents two quantities.
The horizontal axis shows one quantity.
The vertical axis shows a second quantity.

This table shows the arm spans and the heights for a group of students.

Height (cm)	Arm Span (cm)
157	150
172	168
160	162
168	160
174	174
152	150
170	166

We can draw a scatter plot to find out if a person's height and arm span are related.

Plot each row as an ordered pair on a coordinate grid. Plot the heights on the horizontal axis and the arm spans on the vertical axis.
The range of the heights is: $174 - 152 = 22$
The range of the arm spans is: $174 - 150 = 24$
Start each axis at 150 and count by 2s.
Plot a point for each row of the table.

Each point on the graph represents both the height and arm span for one student.

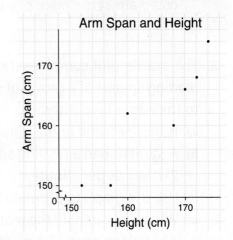

Arm Span and Height

As you move to the right along the horizontal axis, the points go up to the right.
The graph has an **upward trend**.
There appears to be a relationship between a person's height and arm span:
the taller a person is, the longer her or his arm span.

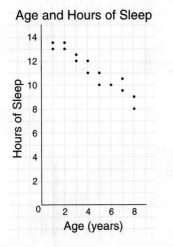

Age and Hours of Sleep

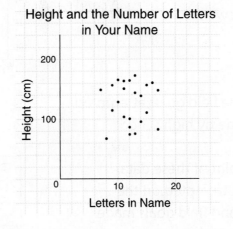

Height and the Number of Letters in Your Name

In this scatter plot, the points go down to the right. We say the graph has a **downward trend**.
The older you are, the less sleep you need.

In this scatter plot, there does not appear to be any trend. There is no relationship between people's heights and the numbers of letters in their names.

1. The scatter plot shows the prices
   for some used cars.

   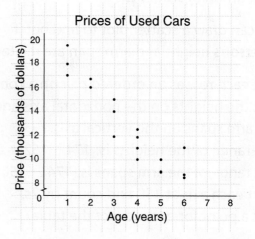

   Prices of Used Cars

   a) Is there a trend in the graph?
   If your answer is yes, explain what
   the trend shows.

   b) Are all the cars that are the same age
   the same price? How can you tell?

   c) What things, other than its age,
   could affect the price of a used car?

2. This scatter plot compares the
   reading speeds of a group of students
   to their ages in months.

   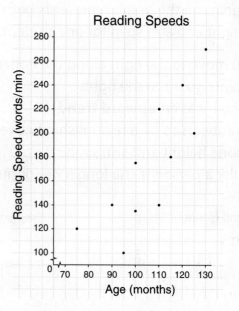

   Reading Speeds

   a) Is there a trend in the graph? Explain.

   b) A student had a reading speed of
   210 words per minute.
   Use the graph to estimate her age.

   c) What do you think the reading speed
   of a person aged 500 months might be?
   Explain your answer.

3. This table shows the field goals attempted
   and field goals made by high school
   basketball players.

   a) Draw a scatter plot of these data.
   Plot field goals attempted on the
   horizontal axis and field goals made
   on the vertical axis.

   b) Is there a trend in the graph? Explain.

   Field Goals

Attempted	Made
19	8
6	4
11	6
14	8
14	5
11	11
13	6
7	4
3	3
1	0

   A field goal is any
   basket other than
   a free throw.

4. This scatter plot shows the masses in grams
   of protein and fat in one serving
   of three types of foods.
   - A blue dot represents a dessert.
   - A red dot represents meat and fish.
   - A green dot represents a grain product.
   a) An English muffin, a wiener, and a slice of
      lemon meringue pie each have 5 g of
      protein. Use the scatter plot to find
      the mass of fat in each food.
   b) Which type of food has the most protein
      in each serving? How do you know?
   c) Which type of food has the least fat in each serving?
      How do you know?
   d) Is there a trend in the graph? Explain.

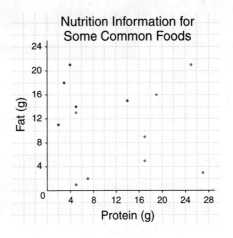

Nutrition Information for
Some Common Foods

Fat (g) / Protein (g)

5. This table shows the ages and heights of a group of students.

Age (months)	76	68	78	81	90	101	145	144	108
Height (cm)	126	112	123	117	127	127	172	158	135
Age (months)	113	120	132	132	149	148	73	105	140
Height (cm)	138	146	147	155	157	164	117	147	152

   a) Draw a scatter plot of the data.
   b) Can you tell from your scatter plot if the youngest student
      is also the shortest? Explain.
   c) Is there a relationship between a person's age and height?
      Explain.
   d) People stop growing as they get older.
      Suppose data for several adults
      were added.
      How would this affect the graph?

Numbers Every Day

Number Strategies

Order the numbers in each set
from greatest to least.

- 0.95, 95, 955.5, 9.55, 95.5
- 1 200 000, 12 000, 125 000, 25 000 000, 25 000
- $\frac{1}{8}$, $\frac{2}{4}$, $\frac{3}{2}$, $\frac{3}{8}$, $\frac{4}{4}$, $\frac{7}{8}$
- 0.25, 0.075, 1.00, 0.01, 0.10, 0.15

Reflect

Give an example of two quantities you would
expect to show a trend and two quantities you
would not expect to show a trend if you were to
draw scatter plots.
Use words, pictures, or numbers to explain.

Drawing a Scatter Plot with *AppleWorks*

For his science fair project, Muneeb explored if age affects
how long it takes a person to react to a sudden flash of light.
He developed a computer program to measure the reaction times.
Here are some of his results.

Age (years)	23	34	38	47	40	56	64	75	71	27
Reaction time (s)	0.3	0.23	0.25	0.34	0.31	0.31	0.38	0.44	0.43	0.24

Age (years)	31	45	53	41	24	49	72	68	56	34
Reaction time (s)	0.26	0.26	0.35	0.3	0.25	0.28	0.44	0.42	0.36	0.22

Work with a partner. Use *AppleWorks*.
Follow these steps to display these data on a scatter plot.

1. Open a new spreadsheet in *AppleWorks*. Click:

   Spreadsheet

2. To **change the width of the columns**:
   Click cell A1.
   Hold down the mouse button and drag to cell B1.
   Release the mouse button.
   Click: Format , then click: Column Width...
   Enter 104 pt for the column width.
   Click: OK

   Column Width

   Column Width: 104 pt
   ☐ Use default
   ⑦   OK   Cancel

3. To **enter the data**:
   Click cell A1 to select it.
   Type: Age
   Press Enter.
   Enter the ages in cells A2 to A21.

   Click cell B1 to select it.
   Type: Reaction time (s)
   Press Enter.
   Enter the reaction time for each age in cells B2 to B21.

4. To **create a scatter plot**:
   Click cell A2.
   Hold down the mouse button and drag to cell B21.
   Release the mouse button.

   Click: Options , then click: Make Chart...   Ctrl+M

   Click the Gallery tab, then click:
   X-Y
   Scatter

   Ensure no options are selected.

   To **give the graph a title**:
   Click the Labels tab.
   Select Show Title.
   Make sure Show Legend is not selected.
   Type: Reaction Times to Light

   To **label the axes**:
   Click the Axes tab.
   Click: ⦿ X axis

   Type the Axis label: Age (years)
   Enter these settings:

Minimum:	Maximum:	Step size:	☐ Log:
20	80	5	

   Click: ⦿ Y axis
   Type the Axis label: Reaction time (s)
   Enter these settings:

Minimum:	Maximum:	Step size:	☐ Log:
0	0.5	0.1	

   Click: OK

5. To **move the graph**:
   Click the graph to select it.
   Click and hold down the mouse button.
   Drag the graph until it is where you want it.
   Release the mouse button.

6. To **print the graph**:
   Click: File , then click: Print...   Ctrl+P
   Click: OK

7. To **save your spreadsheet and graph**:
   Click: File , then click: Save As...   Shft+Ctrl+S

   Name your file. Then click: Save

8. Repeat Step 4 to draw a different scatter plot.
   This time, use these settings for the Y-axis:

Minimum:	Maximum:	Step size:	Log:
0.2	0.5	0.1	

   Print the graph.
   Compare the graphs
   from Step 4 and Step 8.
   How are they the same?
   How are they different?

 Reflect

Suppose you want to convince someone that there is a
relationship between age and reaction time.
Which of the two scatter plots you made would you use?
Give reasons for your choice.

Conducting a Survey

The students in Ms. Siu's class want to support the local children's hospital.
To raise money, they will sell snack foods at recess.
To find out which snacks to sell, they conduct a survey.
Who should they ask?

Explore

Your class has been assigned a project on after-school activities.
As part of your project, you must collect data.
Choose one of these topics:
- The hours of TV students watch each week
- The number of books students read each month
- The favourite kind of music listened to
- A topic of your choice approved by your teacher

➤ Plan a survey. Write a survey question.
➤ Collect the data from students in your class.
  Record the results in a tally chart.
➤ Graph the data. Justify your choice of graph.
  What do you infer from your data?

Show *and* Share

Share your results with another group.
Suppose you collected the same data from students in all classes
in your school. Would your results change? Explain.
Would your inferences change? Explain.

Connect

When you write a survey question:
- The question should be understood in the same way by all people.
- All possible answers to the question should be provided.
- The question should not lead people to answer a certain way.

To ensure your survey results are not biased:
- Survey people who are typical of the group of people you are interested in.
- If you cannot ask everyone in the population, try to ask as many people as you can.

When conducting a survey, the **population** is the entire group being discussed.

One group of students investigated the sports played most often by students.

Here is their survey question:

What sport do you play most?
- ☐ Baseball   ☐ Hockey
- ☐ Soccer   ☐ Tennis
- ☐ None
- ☐ Other (please specify) _____

The students surveyed all the members of their Grade 6 class. Here are their results.

Sport	Tally
Baseball	IIII
Hockey	HHT HHT
Soccer	HHT I
Tennis	II
None	
Other	IIII

The students displayed the results on a bar graph.

The students decided that their Grade 6 class is typical of the Grade 6 students in their school. So, the results represented the school's Grade 6 population.
The students inferred that hockey was the most popular sport played.
Their report said that students in other grades might prefer to play different sports.

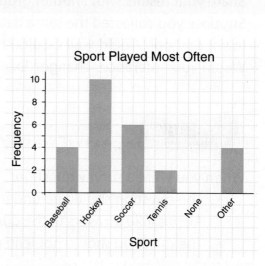

Sport Played Most Often

1. The bar graph shows the results of
   a class survey.
   a) Write what the survey question
      might have been.
   b) Write 2 things you learned from
      this graph.
   c) Do you think the results would change
      if students in all classes were surveyed?
      Explain.

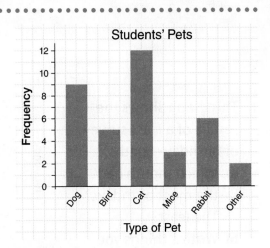

Students' Pets

Frequency / Type of Pet

Dog, Bird, Cat, Mice, Rabbit, Other

2. Each survey question (written in italics) can be improved.
   Write a better question for each. Explain why you think it is better.
   a) To discover how much time each person spends
      doing homework each day:
      Do you spend a lot of time each day doing homework?
   b) To find out how students get to school:
      Do you usually walk to school or ride your bike?
   c) To find out the favourite type of TV programs:
      Do you prefer to watch mindless comedies or exciting dramas?

3. Work with a partner.
   Choose one of the improved survey questions from question 2.
   Survey all the students in your class.
   Organize your results in a table or a graph.
   What can you infer?

4. Do the results of your survey in question 3 represent
   each of the following populations? Explain.
   a) Grade 6s in your school
   b) Grade 2s in your school
   c) Grade 6s in Canada
   d) Grade 6s in another country

Reflect

How do you decide how well data represent
a population?
Use examples to explain.

Numbers Every Day

Mental Math

List all the factors of
each number.

8, 16, 24, 28, 32, 36

LESSON

1

1. This graph shows the results of a class survey of birthday months.

   Birthday Months

   a) Which month had the most birthdays? The least?
   b) Write 2 things you learned from the graph.

2. Use the circle graph to answer these questions.

   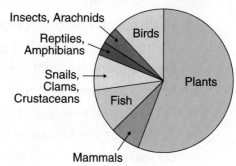

   Endangered Species in North America

   a) Which category has the most endangered species?
   b) Which two groups have about the same numbers of endangered species? Explain.
   c) What else can you infer from the graph?

2

3. Fuller Realty sold houses last week for these prices in dollars:
   85 890, 156 000, 124 500, 349 995, 128 750, 85 900
   What was the median price?

4. The mean of 5 numbers is 20. The median is 23. What might the numbers be? Find 2 different answers.

2
4

5. In 2004, when Rahul bought gas, he recorded the price he paid for 1 L. He calculated the mean price he paid each month, rounded to the nearest cent.

   a) What is the difference between the highest and lowest prices?
   b) Find the mean, the median, and the mode prices. Which do you think best represents the average price? Explain your choice.
   c) Draw a graph to display the data. Explain how you chose which type of graph to draw.
   d) When did the price increase? Decrease? Stay the same? How can you tell this from the graph?
   e) What else can you infer from the graph?

Month	Mean Price for 1 L (¢)
January	75
February	85
March	88
April	84
May	80
June	80
July	80
August	90
September	80
October	77
November	77
December	75

6. Use grid paper. Draw a coordinate grid.
Plot these points and join them in order.
Join the last point to the first point.
Describe the figure you have drawn.
A(2, 2), B(5, 3), C(8, 2), D(7, 5), E(9, 8), F(6, 7), G(5, 10), H(4, 7), I(1, 8), J(3, 5)

7. The table shows the foot lengths and heights
in centimetres for 20 students.

Foot length (cm)	17	20	21	23	21	18	21	22	22	15
Height (cm)	112	116	122	124	126	136	135	135	160	129

Foot length (cm)	20	22	23	25	30	27	28	26	27	32
Height (cm)	140	146	146	150	168	158	162	164	164	172

a) Draw a scatter plot of these data.
What inferences can you make from the graph?
b) Measure your height and foot length.
Add them to your scatter plot.
Do they fit the pattern? Explain.

8. The students in a Grade 6 class want to find out
how many students at their school have
computers at home.
For those students who do, the class wants
to know how they use them.
Write two survey questions students could use
to collect the data.

9. A group asked this survey question:
*Do you agree that all countries should sign
the Kyoto Accord?*
a) Describe any problems with this question.
b) How would you improve the question?

UNIT

5 Learning Goals

☑ analyse data to make inferences and convincing arguments
☑ find the mean, median, and mode
☑ plot and describe the location of points on a Cartesian plane
☑ choose an appropriate graph to display data
☑ compare different displays of the same data
☑ draw bar graphs, line graphs, and scatter plots by hand and with a computer
☑ design and conduct surveys
☑ evaluate collected data and explain how the data represent the population

Playing with Letters

Fox on the Ice is a picture book written by Tomson Highway. It tells the story of two brothers who spend a winter day ice fishing with their parents. The words in the book are shown in both Cree and English.

Work with a partner.
You will need grid paper.
Your teacher will give you a copy of the sample text from *Fox on the Ice*.

Part 1

- Count the number of times these letters appear in the English text: e, t, a, o, i, n, s, h, r
- Graph your data.
- Compare your graph to the graph on page 167. Do your data support the data on page 167? Explain.

Part 2

- Look at the Cree text. Which letters do you think will be most common?
- The letters u, b, d, f, q, g, j, u, v, x, and z are not used in Cree. The letters r and l are rarely used. Count the number of times each other letter appears in this Cree text.
- Why does d appear in the sample even though it is not used in Cree?

Ignore the accents when you count. So, "á" will count as an "a."

- Draw a graph to show the 10 most common letters in this sample of Cree.
- Compare your graph to the graph you drew in Part 1.
  Which letters appear on both graphs?
  Which letters appear only on the Cree graph?
- Suppose you are given a sample of writing in an unknown language.
  What clues could help you decide if it is Cree?
- Native North American languages were used in World War I and World War II to create codes. A code based on the Navajo language was the only code never broken in WWII.
  Why do you think these languages can be used to make such efficient codes?

Part 3

- Suppose you were asked to find the most common letters in French.
  Do you think the results would be more similar to English or to Cree? Explain.
- Get a children's book written in French from your school library. Choose a paragraph.
  Choose about 10 letters that appear often.
  Count these letters.
  Draw a graph to show how often the 5 most common letters were used.
  Was your prediction correct?

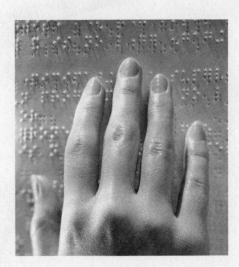

Reflect on the Unit

Why do we use different types of graphs to display different data?
Give examples to explain.

UNIT

6

Measurement

Travelling Time

9:33
17:20   1   On Time
21   19:10   2   Delayed
08   21:30   2   Arrived
18:23   2   On Tim
4   On

Learning Goals

- use time zone maps
- relate 12-h and 24-h clocks
- find elapsed times
- estimate and count money to $10 000
- estimate, calculate, and develop formulas for surface area and volume of a rectangular prism
- relate cubic centimetres and cubic metres
- relate linear, square, and cubic units
- estimate, measure, and compare volume and capacity
- relate units of mass

- In an airport, when might you use each measure?

  time   mass   cost   volume   capacity

  Think of as many examples as you can.

- Why would airport staff need accurate measurements?

1

Time Zones

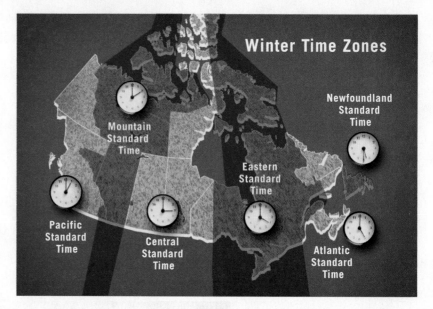

Winter Time Zones

Mountain Standard Time

Pacific Standard Time

Central Standard Time

Eastern Standard Time

Newfoundland Standard Time

Atlantic Standard Time

In the late 1800s, Sir Sanford Fleming created a plan for standard time zones to be used around the world.

This map shows the time zones used in Canada in the winter. The clocks show the time in each zone when it is 1:00 a.m. in the Pacific zone.

Explore

Heidi lives in Regina, Saskatchewan.
Her cousin Filip lives in Victoria, British Columbia.
Filip has a birthday in November.
Heidi wants to call Filip on his birthday.

There are 4 times that Heidi could call.
Each time shown is the time in Regina.

- before school   8:00 a.m.
- when she comes home for lunch   12:30 p.m.
- after school   4:30 p.m.
- in the evening   9:00 p.m.

Which would be the best time for Heidi to phone?
Why should she not call at the other times?
Suppose Filip wanted to call Heidi.
What time should he call? Why?

Show *and* Share

Share your answers with other students.
Did you choose the same times?
If not, explain your choice to your classmates.

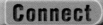

This map shows the time zones used in Canada in the summer.
Saskatchewan does not use daylight saving time. So, Saskatchewan
is considered part of the Mountain zone from April to October.

From the first Sunday in April until the last Sunday in October, most Canadians use daylight savings time. We move our clocks ahead 1 h.

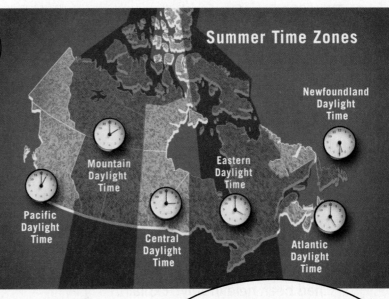

If one of the places is in Saskatchewan or another area that changes zones, we need to know the season as well.

We can use the maps to find the time in any place
in Canada if we know the time in another place.

➤ It is 11:00 p.m. in Whitehorse, Yukon.
  What time is it in Saint John, New Brunswick?

  Whitehorse is in the Pacific zone.
  Saint John is in the Atlantic zone.
  Use the clocks on either map.
  When it is 1:00 a.m. in the Pacific zone,
  it is 5:00 a.m. in the Atlantic zone.
  The time in the Atlantic zone is 4 h later
  than in the Pacific.
  So, when it is 11:00 p.m. in Whitehorse,
  it is 3:00 a.m. in Saint John, the next day.

1. In *Explore*, you found the best times for Heidi and Filip
   to phone each other in November.
   Heidi's birthday is in May. What is the best time
   for Filip to phone Heidi on a school day in May?

2. The 2004 Grey Cup football game was played in
   Ottawa, Ontario. The game began at 6:00 p.m.
   It was shown live on television across Canada.
   The BC Lions were one of the teams playing.
   What time did fans in Nanaimo, British Columbia,
   have to turn on their TVs to watch the game?

3. In January 2005, a concert was held in Vancouver,
   British Columbia, to raise money for tsunami relief
   in South Asia. The concert began at 7:00 p.m.
   It was shown live on television across Canada.
   a) What time did the show begin in each time zone?
   b) Would your answers be different if the concert
   had been held in July? Explain.

4. It is just after midnight on January 1.
   Trey lives in Saskatoon, Saskatchewan.
   He phones his cousin Kyla to wish her a Happy New Year.
   Kyla says Trey has phoned too early.
   Where might Kyla live? How do you know?

5. Harunn is flying from St. John's, Newfoundland, to Toronto, Ontario.
   His flight leaves at 7:00 a.m. It arrives at 9:15 a.m.
   There are no stops on the way.
   Does this mean Harunn will be travelling
   for 2 h 15 min? Explain.

Reflect

Tori lives in Alberta. She wants to phone a
campground in Nova Scotia.
Explain how she could use a time zone map to
choose a good time of day to call.

Numbers Every Day

Number Strategies

Round each amount to the
nearest ten dollars, the
nearest fifty dollars, and the
nearest hundred dollars.
- $2378
- $421
- $1642
- $9896
- $965
- $59 732

2

The 24-Hour Clock

What time is shown
on the watch?
Can you tell from the watch
if it is morning or afternoon?
How do we show morning
and afternoon when we write times?

Explore

Both Kaylin and Tasha
live in Toronto, Ontario.
Each girl is taking
a train to visit
her grandparents.
Kaylin will travel north
to Cochrane, Ontario.
Tasha will travel south
to New York City,
New York.
The schedules for their
trains are shown.

Toronto • Cochrane	
DP **Toronto, ON**	18:20
Washago	20:20
Gravenhurst	20:38
Bracebridge	20:52
Huntsville	21:20
South River	22:12
AR	23:15
North Bay	
DP	23:35
Temagami	01:05
Cobalt	01:50
New Liskeard	02:10
Englehart	02:40
Swastika	03:20
Matheson	04:05
AR **Cochrane, ON**	05:00

Toronto • Niagara Falls • New York	
DP **Toronto, ON**	09:40
Oakville	10:20
Aldershot	10:37
Grimsby	10:51
St. Catharines	11:09
AR	11:34
Niagara Falls, ON	
DP	11:40
Niagara Falls, NY	
DP	13:10
Buffalo (Exchange St. Stn.)	13:45
Buffalo (Depew Stn.)	14:00
Rochester	14:57
Syracuse	16:20
Rome	16:58
Utica	17:16
Amsterdam	18:12
Schenectady	18:31
Albany-Rensselaer	19:15
Hudson	19:40
Rhinecliff	20:01
Poughkeepsie	20:16
Croton-Harmon	20:53
Yonkers	21:12
AR **New York, NY**	21:45

- Is it morning, afternoon, or evening
  when each girl leaves Toronto?
- Both girls leave on a Monday.
  What day is it when each girl arrives?
- What meals, if any, might each girl eat on the train?
- Who spends more time on the train? Explain how you know.

Show *and* Share

Share your results with another pair of students.
Compare the methods you used to find the time each girl spent travelling.

LESSON FOCUS | Relate 12-h and 24-h clocks and calculate elapsed time.

209

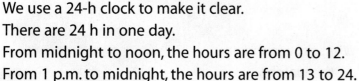
A friend says his flight will arrive at 9 o'clock.

Does he mean 9 a.m. or 9 p.m.?

We use a 24-h clock to make it clear.

There are 24 h in one day.

From midnight to noon, the hours are from 0 to 12.

From 1 p.m. to midnight, the hours are from 13 to 24.

When we use the 24-h clock, we use 4 digits to write the time.

7:45 a.m. is written 07:45.   3:15 p.m. is written 15:15.

Before 10:00 a.m., I write 0 in front of the hour. After noon, I add 12 to the hour. So, 2 o'clock in the afternoon is 12:00 + 2:00 = 14:00

We use a similar notation for time in seconds.

10:19:28 is 19 min and 28 s after 10 a.m.

19:43:21 is 43 min and 21 s after 7 p.m.

➤ Spencer arrived at the library at 09:15 and left at 13:10. How long did he spend in the library?

Here is one strategy.

Count on to find the time.

09:15 to 10:00 is 45 min.   10:00 to 13:00 is 3 h.   13:00 to 13:10 is 10 min.

Total time: 45 min + 3 h + 10 min = 3 h 55 min

Spencer spent 3 h 55 min at the library.

1. Which clocks show the same time?

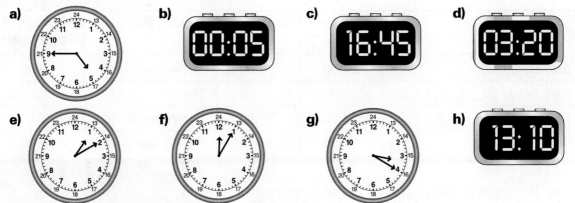

a)   b) 00:05   c) 16:45   d) 03:20

e)   f)   g)   h) 13:10

2. Each time is given in 24-h notation.
Write each time in 12-h notation. Use a.m. or p.m.

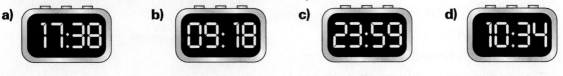

a) 17:38   b) 09:18   c) 23:59   d) 10:34

3. Write each time using a 24-h clock.

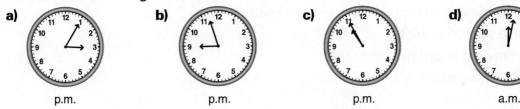

a) p.m.   b) p.m.   c) p.m.   d) a.m.

4. Sandeep picked up his cousin at the airport.
Her flight was supposed to arrive at 19:40.
It arrived at 20:13. How many minutes late was the flight?

5. A bus leaves Halifax, Nova Scotia, at 09:50.
It arrives in Sydney, Nova Scotia, at 16:20. How long is the trip?

6. Michel is flying from Montreal, Quebec, to Fort Lauderdale, Florida.
The flight leaves at 16:15.
  a) Passengers to the United States should check in
     at least 1 h 30 min before their flights leave.
     Michel's watch shows the time he arrived at the airport.
     Is he on time?
  b) The plane is scheduled to land at 19:30.
     Florida is in the same time zone as Montreal.
     How long is the flight?

7. Many cruise ships stop in Prince Rupert, British Columbia, on the way to or from Alaska.
   The table shows the cruise ship schedule for August 2005.

Dates	Arrival	Departure	Ship Name	Number of Passengers
Tuesday 09, 30	07:00	16:00	Norwegian Dream	1800
Wednesday 03, 10, 17, 24, 31	20:00	24:00	Mercury	2000
Thursday 04, 11, 18, 25	14:00	21:00	Norwegian Spirit	2000
Saturday 20	10:00	18:00	Norwegian Dream	1800

a) Which ship always arrived in the morning?
   In the afternoon?
   In the evening?

b) Did any of the ships stay
   in Prince Rupert overnight?
   How can you tell?

c) How much time did each ship
   spend in Prince Rupert on each trip?

8. Bryan and Shannon's time in the sailing regatta was 5:17:23.
   The race started at 10:30.
   What time did they finish the race?
   Write the time two ways.

9. A plane leaves Calgary, Alberta, at 09:20 Mountain Time.
   It arrives in Halifax, Nova Scotia, at 16:34
   Atlantic Time. How long is the flight?

Reflect

When is it better to use the 24-h clock instead
of the 12-h clock?
Include examples in your explanation.

Clock Concentration

Your teacher will give you a set of
Clock Concentration cards.
The cards come in pairs.
One card in each pair shows a time on a clock face.
The other card shows the same time
written in 24-h notation.

The object of the game is to collect pairs
of matching cards.

➤ Look through the cards and practise recognizing matching pairs.
➤ Shuffle the cards.
  Spread them out face down on a table.
➤ The first player turns over two cards.
  If they match, the player keeps them and takes another turn.
  If they do not match, the player turns the cards over.
  The second player takes a turn.
➤ Players continue to take turns until all the cards are paired.
➤ The player with more pairs wins.

Money to $10 000

Explore

At Splash Camp, 10- to 15-year-olds take swimming and water safety lessons and play water sports.

The camp director has $10 000 to buy equipment. Help her decide what to buy.

Equipment	Price (to nearest $)
Lifejacket (PFD)	65
Inflatable kayak	198
Plastic kayak	799
Inflatable dinghy	325
Canoe	1970
6-passenger banana sled	1199
Wind surfer	2060
Water bike	2468
Water trampoline	3599
Inflatable floating island with slide	3996

➤ Use estimation. Which items could you buy to spend as much of the $10 000 as you can without going over? Use a calculator to check your estimate. How did you choose what to buy?

➤ How much money would be left? Which bills and coins equal this amount?

Show and Share

Compare and discuss your choices with another group of students. What is the least number of items that you could buy? The greatest number?

You can round to "friendly numbers" to estimate
the sum of large amounts of money.
How you round depends on:

- the numbers you like working with
- how you will use the rounded numbers
- how close to the actual amount you need your final answer to be

Friendly numbers
are numbers that are
easy to work with.

Seven schools raised this money for a guide-dog charity:
$492.50, $681.10, $732.75, $614.80, $697.25, $563.40, $750.75
About how much money was raised altogether?

➤ Here is one way to estimate the sum.

$500	$1 \times \$500 = \$500$
$700	$3 \times \$700 = \$2100$
$700	$2 \times \$600 = \$1200$
$600	$1 \times \$800 = \$800$
$700	
$600	$\$500 + \$2100 + \$1200 + \$800 = \$4600$
+ $800	

I rounded each
amount to the nearest $100.
Then, I counted how many of
each rounded number I had.
I multiplied, and added
the products.

About $4600 was raised.

➤ Here is another way to estimate the sum.

$500	$\$750 + \$750 = \$1500$
$700	$\$700 + \$700 + \$600 = \$2000$
$750	$\$500 + \$550 = \$1050$
$600	
$700	
$550	$\$1500 + \$2000 + \$1050 = \$4550$
+ $750	

I rounded each
amount to the nearest
$50. Then, I arranged
the rounded numbers into
groups whose sums
are easy to find.
Then I added.

About $4550 was raised.

These two methods produced different estimates.
The actual total amount raised was $4532.55.
Both estimates are close to the actual total
so both are reasonable.

1. Write each amount using numbers.
   a) eight hundred ninety-two dollars
   b) one thousand two hundred seventy-five dollars
   c) four thousand forty-seven dollars
   d) nine thousand nine hundred dollars and fifty cents
   e) seven thousand four hundred twenty-six dollars and eighty-nine cents

2. Write each price in words.

   a) $235.00
   b) $1392.00
   c) $479.00
   d) $3249.97

3. Suppose you have won a $5000 shopping spree at an electronics store.
   a) Estimate to find out if you could choose 1 of each item in question 2.
   b) If the total is too great, which item would you put back? Why?
   c) How could you round the numbers to make sure you do not go over $5000?

4. Use friendly numbers. Estimate each sum or difference. Show your work.
   a) $899.50 + $228.85
   b) $3566.25 + $994.68
   c) $7142.49 + $1863.38
   d) $3333.33 + $6666.66
   e) $680.90 − $298.00
   f) $2850.10 − $705.98
   g) $5925.76 − $3889.99
   h) $9898.98 − $8989.89

5. For $8000, a charity can build a village school in Nepal. The table shows how much money students have raised for the charity.
   a) Find the amount raised.
   b) Find the amount needed to reach $8000. Estimate to check that your answers are reasonable.

Event	Amount Raised ($)
Car wash	248.25
Fashion show	2681.50
Lines of pennies	226.11
Pancake breakfast	190.06
Silent auction	735.00
Dance-a-thon	3117.85

6. Two cashiers sorted money for counting.

Cashier A

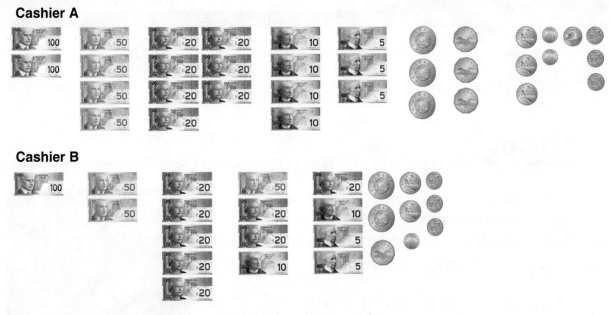

Cashier B

a) Describe the strategy you think each cashier used
to organize the money.
How much money does each cashier have altogether?

b) Which strategy do you prefer? Why?

7. Aidan is going to Greece.
The money used in Greece is called the euro.
Aidan needs to change Canadian dollars into euros.

a) Aidan buys 100 euros.
How much is that in Canadian dollars?

b) About how many euros could Aidan buy for $400?

Reflect

Describe some strategies you find useful
when working with large sums of money.
Use examples to explain.

Numbers Every Day

Calculator Skills

Find each product.

2.3 × 7.1

5.9 × 4.5

7.2 × 8.4

1.8 × 6.6

LESSON 4

Strategies Toolkit

Explore

Aislinn bought two tickets for "Spectacle on Ice."
Aislinn gave the cashier two $50 bills.
She got the fewest possible bills and coins as change.
What bills and coins did Aislinn get?

Show *and* Share

Describe the strategy or strategies you used
to solve this problem.

Tickets: $38.90

Connect

Yazan returned a CD player for a refund of $94.27.
The cashier gave Yazan three $20 bills, three $10 bills,
4 loonies, 2 dimes, 1 nickel, and 2 pennies.
Did the cashier use the fewest possible bills and coins?
Explain using numbers and words.

Understand

What do you know?
- The price of the CD player was $94.27.
- The cashier gave Yazan three $20 bills,
  three $10 bills, 4 loonies, 2 dimes,
  1 nickel, and 2 pennies.

Plan

Think of a strategy to help you solve
the problem.
- You could **use logical reasoning**.

Strategies

- **Make a table.**
- **Use a model.**
- **Draw a diagram.**
- **Solve a simpler problem.**
- **Work backward.**
- **Guess and check.**
- **Make an organized list.**
- **Use a pattern.**
- **Draw a graph.**
- **Use logical reasoning.**

LESSON FOCUS | Interpret a problem and select an appropriate strategy.

Check if any combination of bills or coins can be traded for one bill or coin with the same value.

- Two $10 bills can be traded for one $20 bill.
- Four loonies can be traded for 2 toonies.
- Two dimes and 1 nickel can be traded for 1 quarter. Can any other bills or coins can be traded? Explain.

Did you find the fewest bills and coins? How could you solve this problem another way?

Practice •

Choose one of the

Strategies

1. Keltie bought ice skates with a $50 bill. The cashier gave her one $10 bill, 2 toonies, 1 loonie, 1 quarter, 5 dimes, and 1 penny as change. How much did Keltie pay for her skates?

2. Rick buys a magazine for $5.35. He has 3 toonies, 2 quarters, 2 dimes, 1 nickel, and 2 pennies. When Rick pays, he gets 1 loonie as change. Which coins did Rick give the cashier?

Reflect

Choose one of the *Practice* questions. Describe how you solved the problem.

Surface Area of a Rectangular Prism

In 2003, chefs in Aleppo, Syria, created
a marzipan sweet with a mass of about 4200 kg.
This is greater than 4 t!
The sweet was 16.4 m long, 12.2 m wide, and 1.6 cm thick.
Do you think the sweet could be wrapped? Explain.

Explore

You will need an empty cardboard box, scissors, and a ruler.

➤ Estimate the surface area of your box.
  Record your estimate.
➤ Find the surface area of your box.
  Record your work.
➤ Was your estimate reasonable? Explain.

> The **surface area** of an object is the sum of the areas of its faces.

Show **and** Share

Share your work with another pair of students.
Did you use the same strategies? Explain.
Did you find any shortcuts? Explain.

Here is a rectangular prism.
Each face is a rectangle.

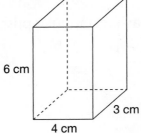

To find the surface area of the prism,
we find the areas of its faces, then add.
This net shows each face.

To find the area
of a rectangle,
multiply the length
by the width.

Face	Length (cm)	Width (cm)	Area (cm²)
A	4	6	24
B	4	6	24
C	3	6	18
D	3	6	18
E	4	3	12
F	4	3	12

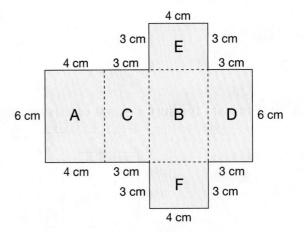

$24 \text{ cm}^2 + 24 \text{ cm}^2 + 18 \text{ cm}^2 + 18 \text{ cm}^2 + 12 \text{ cm}^2 + 12 \text{ cm}^2 = 108 \text{ cm}^2$

The surface area of the prism is 108 cm².

➤ Opposite faces of a rectangular prism are congruent.
So, you can find the surface area of a rectangular prism
by calculating the areas of the front, side, and top faces.
Then, add these areas. Multiply the sum by 2.

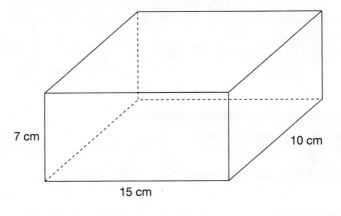

Area of front face = 15 cm × 7 cm
= 105 cm²

Area of side face = 10 cm × 7 cm
= 70 cm²

Area of top face = 15 cm × 10 cm
= 150 cm²

$(105 \text{ cm}^2 + 70 \text{ cm}^2 + 150 \text{ cm}^2) \times 2 = 325 \text{ cm}^2 \times 2$
$= 650 \text{ cm}^2$

The surface area of the prism is 650 cm².

1. Find the surface area of each rectangular prism.

a)

10 cm, 10 cm, 10 cm

b)

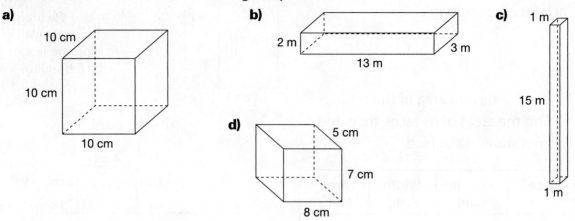

2 m, 13 m, 3 m

c)

1 m, 15 m, 1 m

d)

5 cm, 7 cm, 8 cm

2. a) Estimate the surface area of this rectangular prism.

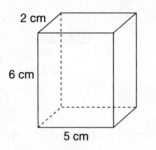

2 cm, 6 cm, 5 cm

b) Calculate the surface area of the prism.

3. a) Predict the order of the rectangular prisms from greatest to least surface area.

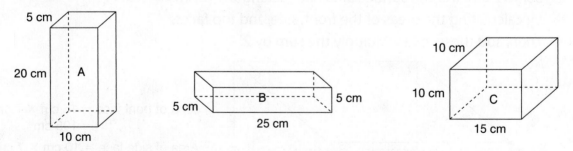

A: 5 cm, 20 cm, 10 cm

B: 5 cm, 5 cm, 25 cm

C: 10 cm, 10 cm, 15 cm

b) Order the rectangular prisms from greatest to least surface area.

c) How does the order compare with your prediction?

4. Emma needs to wrap a rectangular box with dimensions 24 cm by 54 cm by 4 cm.
   a) Find the surface area of the box.
   b) Estimate the area of wrapping paper Emma needs. Explain your estimate.

5. Sketch a net of this rectangular prism.

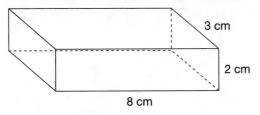

3 cm

2 cm

8 cm

What is its surface area?

6. Four faces of a rectangular prism are congruent rectangles.
Each rectangle has length 10 m and width 8 m.
Sketch the prism and find its surface area.

7. Three faces of a rectangular prism have areas 32 cm^2,
40 cm^2, and 20 cm^2.
a) Find the surface area of the prism.
b) What are possible dimensions of the prism?
How do you know?
c) Sketch and label the prism.

8. Jeremy's bedroom is 5.2 m long, 3.0 m wide, and 2.4 m high.
It has a doorway 0.8 m by 2.0 m and
two small windows each 1.75 m by 0.75 m.
How much wallpaper is needed to cover
the walls? Show your work.

9. A cube has surface area 384 cm^2.
What is the edge length of the cube?
Explain how you know.

10. A packaging company makes boxes that are
rectangular prisms.
The company charges $0.22 for 1000 cm^2 of cardboard.
What would a box with dimensions
1.2 m by 0.9 m by 0.7 m cost?

Reflect

Suppose you have a large sheet of wrapping paper.
How can you use what you know about surface area
to find the dimensions of the largest rectangular prism
you can wrap?
Use pictures, numbers, and words to explain.

Numbers Every Day

Number Strategies

Find each sum.

237 + 893

9820 + 1023

8923 + 329 + 553

2663 + 7310 + 4799

6 Volume of a Rectangular Prism

A centimetre cube has a length, width, and height of 1 cm.
It has a volume of one cubic centimetre, or 1 cm^3.

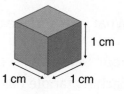

1 cm

1 cm   1 cm

You will need 2 empty boxes and centimetre cubes.

➤ Choose one box.
   Estimate how many centimetre cubes
   the box can hold.

➤ Fill the bottom of the box with one layer
   of cubes.
   How many cubes are in that layer?
   How many layers can fit in the box?
   How do you know?

➤ How many cubes can the box
   hold altogether?
   Describe how you found your answer.
   Record your answer on the box.

➤ Use the first box as a reference.
   Estimate how many cubes the
   second box can hold. Then find out
   how many cubes it can hold.
   Record your answer on the box.

Show and Share

Share the boxes you used with the class.
For each box, tell how many cubes were in each layer,
how many layers in the box, and the total number of cubes that fit in the box.
How can you use centimetre cubes to find the volume of a box?
Will your answer be exact? Explain.
Work together to order all the boxes from least to greatest volume.

A rectangular prism is 10 cm long, 5 cm wide, and 6 cm high.

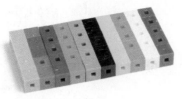
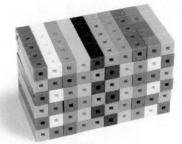

The length is 10 cm.
It is 1 row of 10 cubes.

The width is 5 cm.
Five rows of 10 cubes
make 1 layer of 50 cubes.

The height is 6 cm.
Six layers of 50 cubes make
a volume of 300 cubes.

The volume is 50 cm³ × 6 = 300 cm³.

It is not always practical to count centimetre cubes to find the volume
of a rectangular prism.
We can develop a formula for the volume of a rectangular prism.

Volume = Number of cubes in each layer × Number of layers

The number of cubes in each layer is
the area of the base of the prism.
It is the length times the width.

The number of layers in
the prism is its height.

So,
Volume = Base area × Height

Another way to write the formula is:
Volume = Length × Width × Height

 ➤ You can use the formula to find the volume of
a rectangular prism 10.5 cm long, 4.2 cm wide,
and 5.0 cm high.

Volume = Length × Width × Height
    = 10.5 cm × 4.2 cm × 5.0 cm
    = 44.1 cm² × 5.0 cm
    = 220.5 cm³

The volume of the prism is 220.5 cm³.

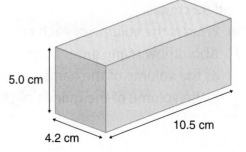

5.0 cm

10.5 cm

4.2 cm

Practice

1. Find the volume of each rectangular prism.

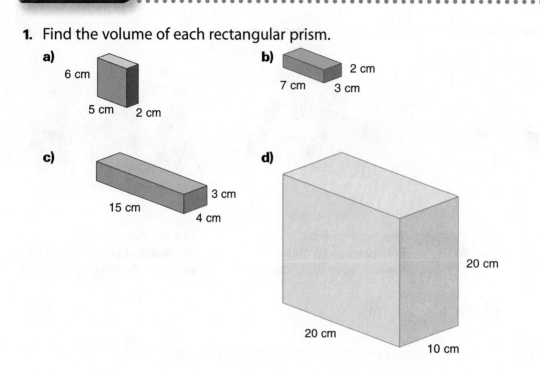

a)

6 cm
5 cm   2 cm

b)

2 cm
7 cm   3 cm

c)

3 cm
15 cm
4 cm

d)

20 cm
20 cm
10 cm

2. Estimate, then calculate, the volume of a rectangular prism with these dimensions. Use a calculator when you need to.

	Length (cm)	Width (cm)	Height (cm)
a)	18	9	12
b)	30	15	6
c)	5.7	1.9	2.2
d)	9.1	3.5	7.0

3. Two friends are comparing the sizes of their pets' cages.
   Atul has a hamster.
   Its cage is 58 cm long, 30 cm wide, and 25 cm tall.
   Nicole has a guinea pig.
   Its cage is 82 cm long, 59 cm wide, and 92 cm tall.

   a) What is the volume of each cage?

   b) About how many times as great as the volume of the hamster cage is the volume of the guinea pig cage?

226

4. A rectangular prism has volume 90 cm³.
The area of its base is 45 cm². What is its height?
How do you know?

5. A rectangular prism has volume 186.0 cm³.
It is 1.6 cm high. What is the area of its base?
How do you know?

6. How many different rectangular prisms can you make
with volume 24 cm³?
Sketch each prism you find.
Label each sketch with the dimensions.
How do you know the prisms are different?

7. Canada's food guide recommends that we eat
2 to 4 servings of dairy products every day.
A cube of cheese with edge length 2.5 cm is
1 serving of dairy products.
   a) What is the volume of a cube with edge length 2.5 cm?
   b) Is the piece of cheese at the right more or less than
   1 serving? How do you know?

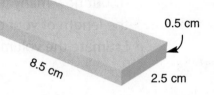

0.5 cm
8.5 cm
2.5 cm

8. Each block in a set is 15 cm long, 10 cm wide, and 5 cm high.
Suppose you are to put the blocks in a box
that is 50 cm long, 35 cm wide, and 30 cm high.
   a) What is the volume of the box? Of each block?
   b) Suppose you only consider the volume.
   How many blocks would you expect to fit in the box?
   c) Suppose you arrange the blocks neatly in layers.
   How many different ways can you layer the blocks?
   How many blocks fit in the box each way?
   d) Compare your answers to parts b and c.
   Explain any differences.
   e) Which is the best way to pack the blocks? Why?

Numbers Every Day

Number Strategies

The product of 3 numbers
is 120.
One number is 4.
What might the other
2 numbers be?

Reflect

When you know the volume and the height of a
rectangular prism, how can you find the area of its base?
Use an example to explain.

The Cubic Metre

Explore

You will need metre sticks, newspaper, and tape.

➤ Create 12 lengths of rolled up newspapers, each 1 m long.
Arrange 4 lengths to show a square metre.
Connect the remaining lengths to show a cubic metre.

➤ Compare the size of the cube to the size of your classroom.
About how many times would your cubic metre fit along
the length of your classroom? The width? The height?
Estimate the volume of your classroom.

Show *and* Share

Share your estimates for the volume of your classroom
with another group of students.
Work together. Use metre sticks to find the length, the width,
and the height of the room to the nearest tenth of a metre.
Calculate the volume. How close were your estimates?

A line segment and a distance have only one dimension.
They can be measured using **linear units** such
as centimetres, metres, and kilometres.

A flat surface has two dimensions.
The area it covers can be measured using **square units**
such as square centimetres or square metres.

An object has three dimensions.
The space it occupies can be measured using **cubic units**
such as cubic centimetres or cubic metres.

A cube with edge length 1 m has volume one cubic metre, or 1 m^3.

Here is a way to construct a cubic metre using centimetre cubes.

Make a row 100 cubes long.
The row measures 1 m, or 100 cm.

Add 99 more rows, each with 100 cubes.
This makes a layer 100 cm by 100 cm.
The layer has: 100 × 100, or 10 000 cubes
The layer covers an area of one square metre,
or 1 m^2.

Add 99 more layers, each with 10 000 cubes.
This makes a cube 100 cm by 100 cm
by 100 cm.
The volume of the cube is one cubic metre,
or 1 m^3.

$$1 \text{ m}^3 = 100 \text{ cm} \times 100 \text{ cm} \times 100 \text{ cm}$$
$$= 1\,000\,000 \text{ cm}^3$$

➤ Would you use a linear, square, or cubic unit of measure?
Explain your choice and suggest an appropriate unit.

- the space occupied by a school portable

> A portable is an object. It has three dimensions.
>
> I would use a cubic unit to describe the space it occupies.
>
> I would use cubic metres.

- the distance from your home to the school

> The distance from my home to the school has only one dimension.
>
> I would use a linear unit to describe it. I would use kilometres.
>
> If I lived very close to the school, I might use metres.

- the area of the schoolyard

> The schoolyard is a region. It has two dimensions.
>
> I would use a square unit to describe its area.
>
> I would use square metres.

Practice

1. Suppose you have to measure each item below.
Would you use a linear, square, or cubic unit of measure?
Explain your choice and suggest an appropriate unit.
   a) a campsite
   b) wall-to-wall carpet
   c) a pool cover
   d) the cargo space in a truck
   e) a tent
   f) a track and field race

2. How many cubic centimetres are in 1 m³?
Explain how you know using pictures, numbers, and words.

3. The measurements of some boxes are given.
Each box is a rectangular prism.
Is the volume of each box less than, greater than, or equal to 1 m³?
How do you know?
   a) length 20 cm, width 10 cm, height 50 cm
   b) length 200 cm, width 100 cm, height 50 cm
   c) area of base 1000 cm², height 1000 cm
   d) area of base 2000 cm², height 500 cm

4. A container has volume 1 m³.
It is a rectangular prism.
The length of the container is 200 cm.
List all the possible dimensions of the container.
Each dimension is a whole number of centimetres.

5. a) Measure and record the length and width of one sheet
of letter-size photocopy paper.

b) Measure and record the thickness of a package
of 500 sheets of photocopy paper.

c) About how many sheets of photocopy paper are there in 1 m³?
Use numbers and words to explain your thinking.

6. An exhaust fan should change all the air in a room
about 10 times each hour.
The Leungs' bathroom is 3.7 m long, 1.8 m wide, and 2.5 m high.
They are installing a fan in the room.
They have 4 fans to choose from.
The fans are described by the amount of air they can move
each minute: 1.7 m³, 2.5 m³, 3.1 m³, 4.2 m³
Which fan should the Leungs buy for their bathroom? Why?

7. Estimate how long it would take to construct a cubic metre
by placing one centimetre cube at a time.
Show all calculations.

Reflect

Explain the relationships among linear, square,
and cubic units.
Use numbers, pictures, and words.

Numbers Every Day

Mental Math

Find each quotient.

73.1 ÷ 100
2.83 ÷ 100
195.4 ÷ 1000
38.75 ÷ 1000

8 Capacity and Volume

Take a deep breath. Hold it for a moment.
Then breathe out.

The amount of air you are able to take in
each time you breathe is called your lung capacity.

Explore

You will use displacement to measure your lung capacity.

You will need:
* an empty plastic bottle, capacity 3 L or more, with lid
* a waterproof marker
* a measuring cup
* a funnel
* a large plastic bowl
* water
* masking tape
* 6 flexible straws

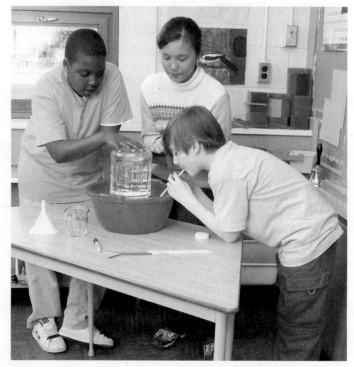

➤ Fill the plastic bowl about half full
  of water.
  Measure 250 mL of water.
  Pour it into the bottle and draw a line
  to show the water level.
  Repeat until the bottle is almost full.
  Then fill it to the top and put on
  the lid.

➤ Join 2 straws to form one long straw.

➤ Turn the bottle upside down.
  Hold the lid and neck under the water in the bowl.

➤ With the lid and neck under water, remove the lid.
   Place one end of the straw inside the bottle.
   Take a deep breath and breathe out as much air as you can into the straw.
   What happens to the water in the bottle? Why?

➤ With the neck still under water, replace the lid.
   Lift the bottle from the water.

➤ Keep the bottle upside down.
   Use the marks you drew to estimate how many millilitres of air
   are in the bottle. Record your estimates.
   This is your approximate lung capacity.

➤ Repeat the experiment for each member of your group.

Show *and* Share

Share the results of your experiment with the class.
Find the average lung capacity of the students in your class.
What was the greatest lung capacity?

Connect

Units of both volume and capacity are used to measure
the "size" of three-dimensional objects.

$1\ L = 1000\ mL$

Units of capacity, such as millilitres
(mL) or litres (L), are used to measure
liquids or gases and the containers
that hold them.

Units of volume, such as cubic centimetres
(cm^3) or cubic metres (m^3), are used to
measure the space an object occupies.

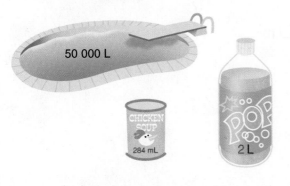

You can use these relationships to convert between volume
and capacity measures.

$1\ cm^3 = 1\ mL$ $1\ m^3 = 1000\ L$ $1000\ cm^3 = 1\ L$

➤ You can write 132 cm³ as a capacity measured in millilitres or litres.

$$1 \text{ cm}^3 = 1 \text{ mL} \qquad\qquad 1000 \text{ cm}^3 = 1 \text{ L}$$
$$132 \text{ cm}^3 = 132 \times 1 \text{ mL} \qquad 132 \text{ cm}^3 = \frac{132}{1000} \text{ L}$$
$$= 132 \text{ mL} \qquad\qquad\qquad = 0.132 \text{ L}$$

$\frac{132}{1000}$ is another way to write:

$132 \div 1000$

➤ You can write 3.5 m³ as a capacity in litres.

$$1 \text{ m}^3 = 1000 \text{ L}$$
$$3.5 \text{ m}^3 = 3.5 \times 1000 \text{ L}$$
$$= 3500 \text{ L}$$

➤ You can write 6250 L as a volume in cubic metres.

$$1000 \text{ L} = 1 \text{ m}^3$$
$$6250 \text{ L} = \frac{6250}{1000} \text{ m}^3$$
$$= 6.25 \text{ m}^3$$

Practice

1. Select the most appropriate measure of volume or capacity.
   Explain your choice.
a) a hot air balloon	10 cm³	1000 L	100 m³	10 000 mL
b) a car's gas tank	50 cm³	50 m³	50 mL	50 L
c) a brick	15 cm³	1000 mL	2000 cm³	0.5 m³
d) a cup of soup	0.25 L	10 mL	2 L	25 cm³
e) a bathtub of water	0.5 m³	150 L	2000 mL	100 cm³
f) a can of paint	20 mL	2 m³	3.8 L	380 cm³

2. Copy and complete.
   a) 2400 mL = □ L
   b) 6.2 L = □ mL
   c) 5 m³ = □ cm³
   d) 500 000 cm³ = □ m³

3. Copy and complete.
   a) 10 mL = □ cm³
   b) 79 cm³ = □ mL
   c) 2 L = □ cm³
   d) 250 cm³ = □ L
   e) 3 m³ = □ L
   f) 4500 L = □ m³

4. a) How many cubic centimetres are in 1 m³?
   b) How many cubic centimetres are in 1 L?
   c) How can you use the results of parts a and b
   to verify that 1 m³ = 1000 L?

5. An empty swimming pool has capacity 14 400 L.
A garden hose adds 20 L of water to the pool every minute.
How long will it take to fill the pool?

6. Many houses use natural gas to heat rooms and water.
The amount of gas used is measured in cubic metres.
The Kovacs used about 13.9 m³ of gas each day in February.
They pay 30¢ per cubic metre.
How much did the Kovacs pay for gas in February?

7. The aquarium in Shippagan, New Brunswick,
has 31 exhibit tanks. They contain a total of
90 000 L of saltwater and 50 000 L of freshwater.
a) Find the total volume of water in cubic metres.
b) Suppose the water in part a fills a rectangular
swimming pool to a depth of 2 m.
List as many possible dimensions as you can
for its length and width. Each dimension
should be a whole number of metres.
c) Which of the dimensions in part b would be
the most practical for a pool? Explain.

8. In *Explore*, you found your lung capacity in millilitres.
a) What is your lung capacity in cubic centimetres?
b) Would a rectangular prism with this volume
be larger or smaller than a typical shoe box? Explain.

9. Two stones are in a 500-mL container half full of water.
When one stone is removed, the water level decreases
to 225 mL.
The second stone has volume 50 cm³.
How much water is in the container? Explain.

Reflect

How do you know when to use millilitres, litres,
cubic centimetres, or cubic metres?
List some things you would measure using each unit.

Numbers Every Day

Mental Math

Find each product.

9.4 × 100
28.13 × 100
4.75 × 1000
71.6 × 1000

Almost two-thirds of the world's trade is shipped in containers. They are loaded onto ships, trains, trucks, and airplanes. A shipping manager decides how to use the container space to keep shipping costs to a minimum.

Containers are very large, strong boxes in different sizes. A standard container measures 6.1 m by 2.4 m by 2.6 m. The dimensions of other containers are multiples of these dimensions. A cargo ship is described according to the number of standard containers it can carry.

A standard container has a rating of 24 000 kg—the maximum mass of the container plus its cargo. The maximum mass of the cargo is called the payload. It is usually about 17 500 kg. The space available for cargo in a standard container is usually about 33 m^3.

Containers can be filled with many types of cargo, from fruit to television sets. How much will fit in a container depends on many things, including the type of cargo and size of cartons it is packed in.

Go for a Million!

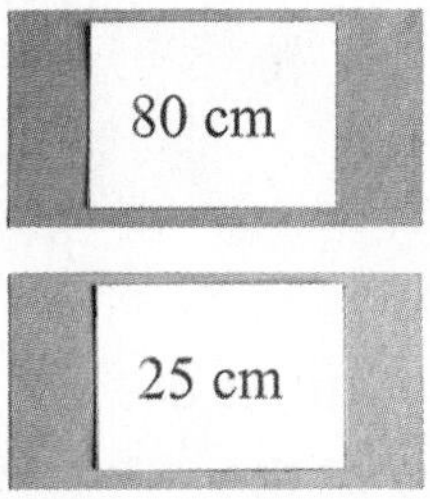

You will need a calculator and a set of game cards.
A length is printed on each card.

80 cm

25 cm

Play as a group.
You will calculate the volumes of rectangular
prisms and add the volumes.
Your goal is to reach a total volume of 1 000 000 cm^3, or 1 m^3.

➤ Shuffle the cards. Spread them out face down on a table.
➤ Each player turns over one card.
   Record the lengths from the cards.
   Use the lengths as the dimensions of a rectangular prism.
   Calculate and record the volume of the prism.
   Put the three cards in a discard pile.
➤ Repeat the previous step.
   Once you have recorded the volume, add it to the
   previous volume. This is your new total.
➤ Repeat the process until your total volume is at least 1 000 000 cm^3.
   How many prisms did it take to reach this goal?

Play the game several times.
What was the fewest prisms it took
to reach the goal?
Did you ever run out of cards
before you could reach the goal?

Relating Units of Mass

Coins for many countries are
made in Winnipeg at the
Royal Canadian Mint.

Explore

Explore the masses of some common Canadian coins.

➤ Suppose someone offers you 1 kg of coins.
Which of these 4 coins do you think would be
the best to choose? The worst? Why?

➤ Estimate how many of each coin it would take
to make 1 kg.
What is the value of the coins?

➤ Calculate the number of each coin it takes to make 1 kg.
Then calculate the value of the coins.
Were your estimates close? Explain.

**Some Canadian Coins
and their Masses**

Coin	Mass (mg)
Dime	1750
Quarter	4400
Loonie	7000
Toonie	7300

Show and Share

Compare your results with those of another pair
of students.
Is it better to have 1 kg of dimes or 1 kg of quarters?
Is it better to have 1 kg of loonies or 1 kg of toonies?
Justify your answers.

Numbers Every Day

Calculator Skills

• A million dollars is how
many $100 bills?
• A million hours is about
how many weeks?
• A million days is about
how many decades?

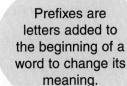

Connect

The gram is the basic unit of mass in the metric system.
The other units are named by adding prefixes to the word "gram."

For example, the prefix "milli" means thousandths.
So, one milligram is one-thousandth of a gram.

Prefixes are letters added to the beginning of a word to change its meaning.

$$1 \text{ mg} = 0.001 \text{ g}$$

$$1000 \text{ mg} = 1000 \times 0.001 \text{ g}$$
$$= 1 \text{ g}$$

The prefix "kilo" means thousands.
So, one kilogram is one thousand grams.

$$1 \text{ kg} = 1000 \text{ g}$$

1 g is one-thousandth of 1 kg.
$$1 \text{ g} = 0.001 \text{ kg}$$

The only unit of mass that is not named using a prefix is the tonne.
One tonne is one thousand kilograms.

$$1 \text{ t} = 1000 \text{ kg}$$

1 kg is one-thousandth of 1 t.
$$1 \text{ kg} = 0.001 \text{ t}$$

➤ The original design of the toonie shows an adult polar bear.
Polar bears are the world's largest carnivores that live on land.
A male polar bear can have a mass of about 725 kg.
How many tonnes is this?

$$725 \text{ kg} = 725 \times 0.001 \text{ t}$$
$$= 0.725 \text{ t}$$

A male polar bear can have a mass of about 0.725 t.

Math Link

Your World

The toonie was introduced in 1996.
The coin should last about 20 times as long as the paper $2 bill it replaced.
The Royal Canadian Mint has a patent on the process it uses to hold together the two metals that make up the coin.

➤ The loonie shows a common loon.
This bird's call can be heard on lakes across Canada.
A typical mass for an adult loon is about 4.1 kg.
How many grams is this?

$$1 \text{ kg} = 1000 \text{ g}$$
$$4.1 \text{ kg} = 4.1 \times 1000 \text{ g}$$
$$= 4100 \text{ g}$$

A typical mass for an adult loon is about 4100 g.

Practice

1. Select the most appropriate unit for measuring the mass of each object.
   a) an apple   **b)** a dog   **c)** a truck   **d)** a grain of sand

2. Copy and complete.
   a) $100 \text{ g} = \square \text{ mg}$ **b)** $5500 \text{ mg} = \square \text{ g}$ **c)** $88 \text{ g} = \square \text{ mg}$
   d) $50 \text{ mg} = \square \text{ g}$ **e)** $6 \text{ g} = \square \text{ mg}$ **f)** $0.5 \text{ g} = \square \text{ mg}$

3. Copy and complete.
   a) $76 \text{ kg} = \square \text{ g}$ **b)** $432 \text{ g} = \square \text{ kg}$ **c)** $2500 \text{ g} = \square \text{ kg}$
   d) $0.65 \text{ kg} = \square \text{ g}$ **e)** $12\,535 \text{ kg} = \square \text{ t}$ **f)** $7.62 \text{ t} = \square \text{ kg}$

4. What is the most likely mass?

a) a minivan	1800 kg	18 t	180 kg	1800 g
b) a dictionary	1.2 kg	0.12 t	1200 mg	120 g
c) a hockey puck	1.7 kg	170 g	1700 mg	170 mg
d) a dalmatian	3 kg	30 kg	300 g	3000 mg

5. Use balance scales and a set of standard masses.
   Find an object in your classroom with each mass.
   a) less than 10 g   **b)** between 50 g and 100 g
   c) about 500 g   **d)** about 1 kg

6. Write each mass using two different units.
   a) 500 kg   **b)** 850 g   **c)** 4300 g   **d)** 2.1 t

7. Use metric bathroom scales.
   Choose a heavy object and measure its mass to the nearest kilogram.
   About how many of these objects would you need to have a total mass of 1 t?

8. Which is the greater mass:
$\frac{1}{5}$ of 5 kg or $\frac{1}{4}$ of 5000 g?
Use words or numbers to explain your thinking.

9. An elevator has a mass limit of 0.9 t.
Two people are waiting to enter it.
The elevator arrives.
It is already carrying four people and
their belongings.
a) Is it safe for the two people to get on
the elevator? Explain.
b) Other than the total mass, what factors
might influence whether the two people
get on the elevator?

10. Every year at the Royal Winter Fair, art students
from Toronto compete in a butter-sculpting contest.
Each contestant has a block of butter with mass 22.7 kg.
a) Butter is sold in 454-g packages.
How many packages could be made from a 22.7-kg block?
b) A 454-g package of butter is a rectangular prism
with length 11.3 cm, width 6.5 cm, and height 6.5 cm.
What is the total volume of all the packages in part a?

11. A large jar contains 500 identical marbles.
Suppose you have an identical empty jar, a set of
standard masses, and balance scales.
How would you find the mass of one marble
without opening or breaking the jar? Explain.

At Home

Reflect

When you convert units of mass,
how do you know whether to
multiply or divide?
Use examples to explain.

Which metric measuring tools
that measure length, mass, or
capacity can you find at home?
Describe several things that can
be measured with each tool.

1

1. Use the time zone maps in Lesson 1.

The 2010 Winter Olympics will be held in Vancouver, British Columbia.
Fadumo lives in Halifax, Nova Scotia.
She wants to watch the women's downhill skiing competition live.
It begins at 9:00 a.m. Pacific Time.
What time should Fadumo turn on her TV?

2

2. Which pairs of clocks could show times that differ by 2 h 30 min?

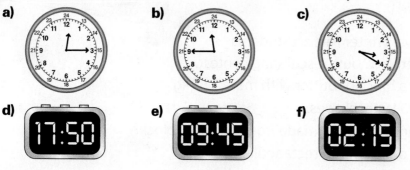

a)   b)   c)

d) **17:50**   e) **09:45**   f) **02:15**

3. Churchill, Manitoba, is known as the Polar Bear Capital of the World.
Tourists travel almost 1700 km from Winnipeg, Manitoba, to see the bears.

  a) Nick left Winnipeg by train on Tuesday at 20:45.
  He arrived in Churchill on Thursday at 08:30.
  How long did the trip take?

  b) Cheryl left Winnipeg by airplane at 08:45.
  She arrived in Churchill at 11:25 the same day.
  How long did the flight take?

3

4. A school received a $10 000 grant for
new musical instruments.
The music teacher wants to buy
2 clarinets, 2 flutes, 2 trumpets, 2 saxophones,
1 tuba, 4 acoustic guitars, and 1 drum set.

  a) What is the total cost of the instruments
  the teacher wants?

  b) If the total in part a is greater than $10 000,
  suggest an item to delete.
  If it is less, suggest an item or items to add.
  Explain your choice.

Instrument	Cost ($)
Clarinet, flute, or trumpet	599
Saxophone or tuba	1295
Acoustic guitar	349
Drum set	399

3
4

5. How much change would you receive for each purchase?
You are given the fewest possible numbers of coins and bills.
What do you receive?
a) Cost $12.77   Payment $20.00
b) Cost $176.98   Payment $200.00
c) Cost $80.48   Payment $100.00

5
6

6. Explain how you would measure the surface area and
volume of a cereal box.

7. Estimate, then calculate, the surface area and volume
of a rectangular prism with each set of dimensions.
a) length 21 cm, width 19 cm, height 8 cm
b) length 35 cm, width 25 cm, height 5 cm
c) length 4.8 cm, width 3.6 cm, height 1.8 cm

6
8

8. A rectangular prism measures 18.5 cm
by 12.2 cm by 9.0 cm.
Could it hold 2 L of ice cream? Explain.

UNIT

6 Learning Goals

7
8

9. For each measure, would you use a linear,
square, or cubic unit? Explain your choice.
Suggest an appropriate unit.
a) the area of a soccer field
b) the distance between 2 cities
c) the amount of water in a bathtub

✓ use time zone maps
✓ relate 12-h and 24-h clocks
✓ find elapsed times
✓ estimate and count money
   to $10 000
✓ estimate, calculate, and
   develop formulas for surface
   area and volume of a
   rectangular prism
✓ relate cubic centimetres and
   cubic metres
✓ relate linear, square, and
   cubic units
✓ estimate, measure, and
   compare volume and capacity
✓ relate units of mass

10. The gas tank of a large car has capacity 70 L.
How many large cars can be filled with
1 m^3 of gasoline?

9

11. Copy and complete.
a) 16 500 g = ☐ kg   b) 54.2 kg = ☐ g
c) 32 156 kg = ☐ t   d) 8.26 t = ☐ kg
e) 5236 mg = ☐ g   f) 9.56 g = ☐ mg

12. A package of 16 cheese sticks has mass 336 g.
What is the mass of one stick?

Travelling Time

Anika is planning a 2-week vacation in Alberta.
She will fly to Edmonton, then rent a car.
Anika will spend two nights in Edmonton, then drive
to Jasper and Banff.
Then she will visit the Royal Tyrrell Museum
in Drumheller.
Finally, Anika will drive to Calgary and fly home.

Part 1

Anika wants to leave Halifax on a Monday.
She has several flights to choose from.
There are no direct flights.

The cost for Option 1 is
$412.40 per person.
The cost for Option 2
is $508.95 per person.
All prices include taxes.

Option 1

Mon, 11 Jul	**07:00**	Depart	Halifax, NS
Flight AW 431	08:15		
	09:00	Through	Toronto, ON
Flight AW 23	11:15	Connect	Calgary, AB
	11:45		
	12:30	Arrive	Edmonton, AB

Option 2

Mon, 11 Jul	**10:55**	Depart	Halifax, NS
Flight AW 432	12:10	Connect	Toronto, ON
	13:45		
Flight AW 352	**15:55**	Arrive	Edmonton, AB

- For each flight, calculate the total travelling time
  and the total flying time.
  Which flight would you recommend Anika takes? Why?

- Anika will return on a Sunday.
  There is only 1 flight available.
  It leaves Calgary at 10:00 and arrives in Toronto at 15:45.
  The flight leaves Toronto at 16:20 and arrives in Halifax at 19:20.
  What is the total travelling time? The total flying time?

Part 2

On most flights, each passenger can check baggage up to a maximum of 32 kg.

- There will be 125 passengers on one of the flights. Suppose each passenger uses the full baggage allowance. What is the mass of all the luggage? Write your answer in two ways.

- The sum of the length, width, and height of a suitcase must be less than 158 cm. Anika's suitcase has volume 67 500 cm³ and is 25 cm wide. What are possible dimensions of her suitcase?

- Suppose every passenger has a suitcase like Anika's. What is the least possible volume for the airplane's baggage compartment?

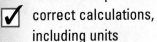

Reflect on the Unit

Write about the different things you measured in this unit, and how you measured them.
How are some of the measures related?

Transformational

Art and Architecture

Learning Goals

- identify and apply transformations
- identify congruent figures
- identify and create similar figures
- construct designs and figures with more than one line of symmetry
- identify the order of rotational symmetry of figures
- relate tiling patterns to transformations

Geometry

Key Words

corresponding sides

corresponding angles

rotational symmetry

The Taj Mahal in India was built in the seventeenth century. The white marble walls are carved with patterns.

- Which figures do you see?
- Which transformations are shown in the photographs?

1

Transformations

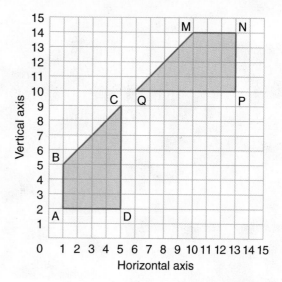

Translations, rotations, and reflections are transformations.

How could you identify a transformation for which Figure ABCD is the image of Figure NMQP?

Which ordered pair describes the location of each vertex?

Explore

Game

You will need:

- scissors
- dry-erase markers
- Figure Cards
- coordinate grid
- blank transparency
- tracing paper
- Transformation Cards
- paper clips

It's a Transforming Experience!

➤ Cut out the Transformation Cards and the Figure Cards. Shuffle each set of cards. Place the cards face down in separate piles. Lay the transparency over the grid. Use paper clips to hold it in place.

➤ Player A selects one card from each pile. On the transparency, Player A:

– draws and labels the figure described on the Figure Card

– draws and labels the image of the figure after the transformation described on the Transformation Card

➤ If you are able to draw the image of the figure, you score 2 points. If you are not able to draw the image, you score no points.

➤ Erase the figure and the image from the transparency. Switch roles. Continue to play until each player has had 4 turns. The player with the most points wins.

Show *and* Share

Share your work with another pair of students.
What strategies did you use to draw the images?

 **Connect** ....

Translation

After a translation, a figure and its image:
• are congruent
• face the same way

Figure ABC was translated
5 squares right and 2 squares down.

The table shows the coordinates of the
vertices of the figure and its translation image.

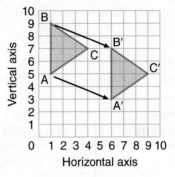

Vertices of Figure ABC	Vertices of Image A′B′C′
A(1, 5)	A′(6, 3)
B(1, 9)	B′(6, 7)
C(4, 7)	C′(9, 5)

Point A′ is the image
of point A.
We write: A′
We say: "A prime"

Reflection

After a reflection, a figure and its image:
• are congruent
• face opposite ways

Figure JKLM was reflected in a vertical
mirror line through the horizontal axis at 5.

The table shows the coordinates of the
vertices of the figure and its reflection image.

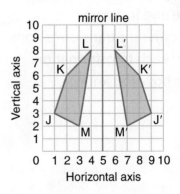

Vertices of Figure JKLM	Vertices of Image J′K′L′M′
J(1, 3)	J′(9, 3)
K(2, 6)	K′(8, 6)
L(4, 8)	L′(6, 8)
M(3, 2)	M′(7, 2)

Any point and its reflection
image are the same distance
from the mirror line.

Rotation

After a rotation, a figure and its image:
• are congruent
• may face different ways

Figure PQRS was rotated
a $\frac{3}{4}$ turn clockwise about R.

> After a $\frac{3}{4}$ turn clockwise, the reflex angle between RS and RS' is 270°.

The table shows the coordinates of the vertices of the figure and its rotation image.

Vertices of Figure PQRS	Vertices of Image P′Q′RS′
P(3, 9)	P′(4, 4)
Q(5, 9)	Q′(4, 6)
R(6, 7)	R(6, 7)
S(2, 7)	S′(6, 3)

> Since R is a vertex on the figure and its image, we do not label the image vertex R′.

Practice

Use tracing paper when it helps.

1. This diagram shows a figure and its image after 3 different transformations. Identify each transformation. Explain how you know.

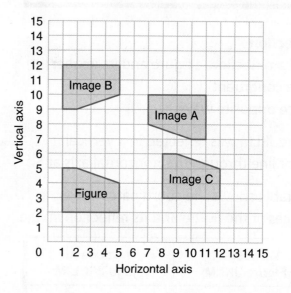

2. Use 1-cm grid paper. Draw a rectangle.
   a) Draw a mirror line.
      Draw the reflection image of the rectangle in the mirror line.
   b) Which different transformation would move the figure onto the image? Explain.

3. Copy the figure and its image onto
   a coordinate grid.
   Describe as many different transformations
   that would move Figure ABCD onto
   the image as you can.
   For each transformation, label the vertices
   of the image.

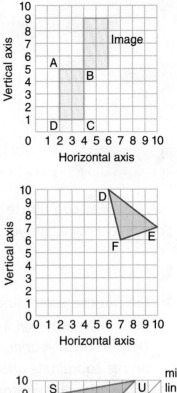

4. a) Find the image of △DEF after the translation
      6 squares left and 1 square down.
   b) Write the coordinates of the vertices
      of the figure and the image.
      How are the coordinates related?
   c) Use your answer to part b to predict the
      coordinates of the image of point G(10, 2)
      after the same translation.

5. a) Find the image of △STU after a reflection
      in the mirror line.
      Write the coordinates of the vertices.
   b) Predict the location of the image of point V(4, 3)
      in the same mirror line.
      How did you make your prediction?

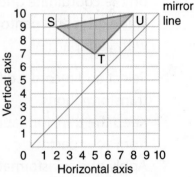

6. a) Draw a figure on a grid.
      Rotate the figure 180° about a point outside
      the figure.
      Can you describe a different transformation
      whose image would coincide with the rotation image?
   b) If your answer to part a is yes, describe the transformation.
      If your answer is no, draw a different figure
      so your answer is yes.

Reflect

When you see a figure and its transformation
image on a coordinate grid, how do you identify
the transformation? Use examples to explain.

Numbers Every Day

Number Strategies

Find the mean of the numbers
in each set.

- 210, 332, 511, 205
- 76, 88, 34, 28, 77
- 7601, 6620, 1774, 3232

Combined Transformations

Explore ·

You will need coordinate grids, scissors, and tracing paper.
Your teacher will give you a large copy of these pentominoes.

What's My Move?

➤ Cut out the pentominoes.
   Each of you chooses 1 pentomino.
   Draw or trace your pentomino
   on the coordinate grid.
   Trade grids and pentominoes
   with your partner.

➤ Select and record 2 different
   transformations.
   Keep the transformations secret
   from your partner.
   Apply one transformation to your
   partner's pentomino.
   Then apply the second transformation
   to the image.
   Draw only the second image.
   Return the grid to your partner.

➤ Identify the combined transformations
   that moved the pentomino onto the final image.
   You score 1 point if you identify the transformations correctly.

➤ Repeat the game as many times as you can.
   The person with more points wins.

Show and Share

Share your grids and transformations with another pair of students.
What strategies did you use to identify your partner's transformations?

➤ To find the final image of rectangle ABCD after a rotation of 180° about C, followed by a reflection in a vertical line through 6 on the horizontal axis:

Trace rectangle ABCD on tracing paper.
Rotate the tracing 180° about C.
Use a sharp pencil to mark
the positions of the vertices of the
rotation image.
Draw the rotation image.
Label the vertices A'B'CD'.

Draw the mirror line through 6 on the horizontal axis. Reflect the rotation image in the mirror line.
Each vertex of the reflection image is the same distance from the mirror line as the corresponding vertex on the rotation image.

Label the vertices of
the final image A"B"C"D".
Read A" as "A double prime."

➤ Triangle X"Y"Z" is the image of △XYZ after a translation, then a reflection in the mirror line.

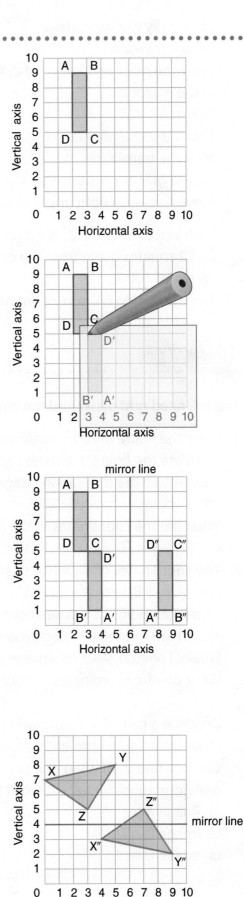

To identify the translation:
Work backward.
Draw the reflection image of △X″Y″Z″
in the mirror line.
This is △X′Y′Z′.
This is the image of △XYZ
after the translation.
On the grid, to go from X to X′,
move 4 squares right and 2 squares down.

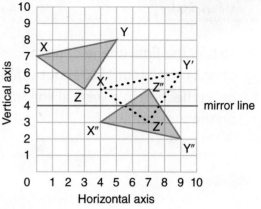

Each vertex of △X′Y′Z′ is 4 squares right of
and 2 squares down from the corresponding
vertex of △XYZ.
The translation is 4 squares right and 2 squares down.

Practice

You will need grid paper and tracing paper.

1. Copy the figure onto a coordinate grid.
   Translate the figure 3 squares right.
   Then rotate the translation image
   90° clockwise about (5, 5).
   What are the coordinates of the final image?

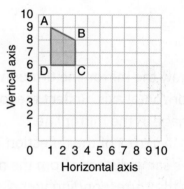

2. The coordinates of my vertices are:
   A(1, 4)   B(1, 9)   C(3, 4)   D(3, 9)
   I am rotated 90° clockwise about (3, 4).
   Then, I am rotated 90° clockwise about (7, 2).
   Finally, I am translated 5 squares left.
   What are the coordinates of my final image?

3. Describe a pair of transformations that
   moves the figure onto each image.
   Can you find more than one pair of
   transformations for each image? Explain.
   a) Image A
   b) Image B
   c) Image C

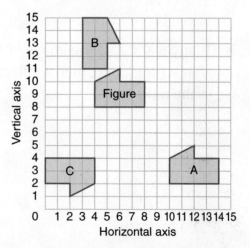

Technology

Computer plugs fit into slots in different ways.
Some plugs are round. They can fit in more
than 1 way. These are coaxial cables and
headphone plugs.
Other plugs can fit only 1 way.
These plugs are serial and parallel port plugs.
They are trapezoidal and cannot be rotated.

4. Draw an irregular quadrilateral on grid paper.
   a) Choose two transformations.
   Apply the first transformation to the quadrilateral.
   Then apply the second transformation to the image.
   b) Use a different colour.
   Apply the transformations from part a in
   the reverse order.
   c) Compare the final images from parts a and b.
   Does the order in which transformations are
   applied matter? Explain.

5. I am an octagon.
   The coordinates of my vertices are:
   P(7, 3)   Q(6, 4)   R(6, 5)   S(7, 6)
   T(8, 6)   U(9, 5)   V(9, 4)   W(8, 3)
   I am translated 5 squares left and 3 squares up.
   Then, I am reflected in a line through (0, 5) and (10, 5).
   Next, I am translated 2 squares right and 2 squares up.
   a) Write the coordinates of my final image.
   b) What do you notice about my final image and me?

Reflect

Suppose you know the location of a figure and
its final image after 2 transformations.
How can you identify the transformations?
Use examples to explain.

Numbers Every Day

Mental Math

Find two 2-digit numbers
with a product of 360.
How many different pairs
can you find?

Congruent Figures

Are these figures congruent?
How could you find out?

Explore

You will need tracing paper, a protractor, and a millimetre ruler.
Your teacher will give you a large copy of these figures.

A B C D E F J

N H K P M L G

➤ Identify pairs of figures that are congruent.
   How do you know they are congruent?
➤ Choose a pair of congruent figures.
   Measure the side lengths.
   Measure the angles.
   Record the side and angle measures.
   Repeat for other pairs of congruent figures.
➤ What do you notice about the side lengths and
   angle measures of congruent figures? Explain.

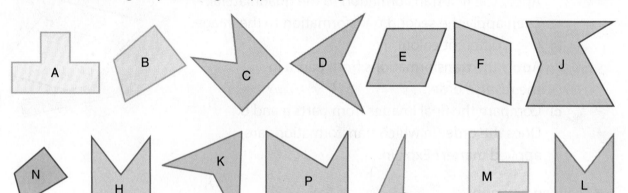

Show and Share

Share your work with another pair of students.
Check that you found the same pairs of figures.
How can you use a ruler and a protractor to tell if two figures are congruent?

A figure and its transformation image are congruent.
If we flip pentagon ABCDE, then rotate it, it appears it would coincide with the other pentagon.

Here is one way to tell if these pentagons are congruent.

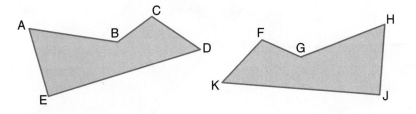

• Measure and record the lengths of all the sides.
  Measure and record all the angle measures.

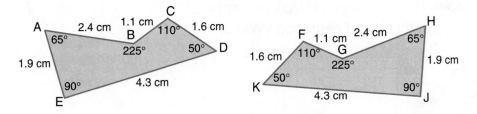

• Compare the measures of **corresponding sides** and of **corresponding angles**.

These pairs of sides have the same length:
AB = HG, BC = GF, CD = FK, DE = KJ, EA = JH

These pairs of angles have the same measure:
∠A = ∠H, ∠B = ∠G, ∠C = ∠F, ∠D = ∠K, ∠E = ∠J

> When congruent polygons coincide, corresponding sides and corresponding angles also coincide.

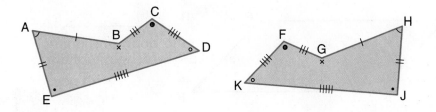

> Use hatch marks and symbols to show which sides and angles are equal.

All the corresponding sides and corresponding angles are equal.
So, the polygons are congruent.

We say: "Pentagon ABCDE is congruent to pentagon HGFKJ."
We write: ABCDE ≅ HGFKJ

The symbol ≅ means "is congruent to."

> Write corresponding vertices in the same order.

1. Quadrilaterals DEFG and JKNM are congruent.
   a) What is the measure of each angle in JKNM?
   b) What is the length of each side in JKNM?

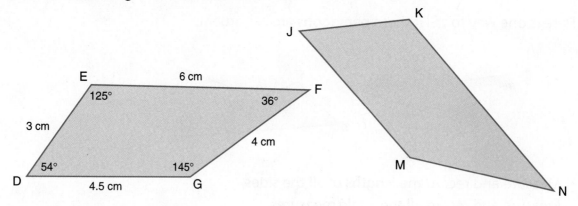

2. **a)** Use tracing paper. Trace pentagon PQRST on paper.
   Label the vertices of the traced pentagon VWXYZ.

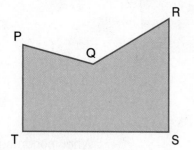

   b) Find the side lengths and angle measures of both pentagons.
   c) Identify the corresponding sides and corresponding angles.

3. Which of these quadrilaterals are congruent?
   How do you know?

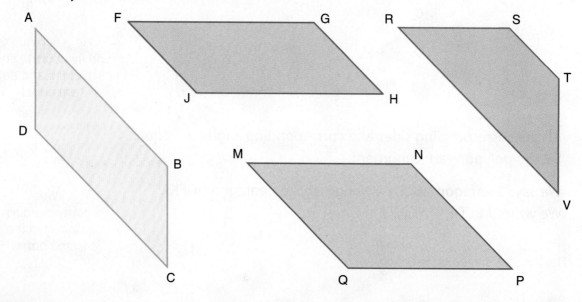

4. Your teacher will give you a large copy of these polygons.
Use a ruler and a protractor.
Which polygons are congruent?
How do you know?

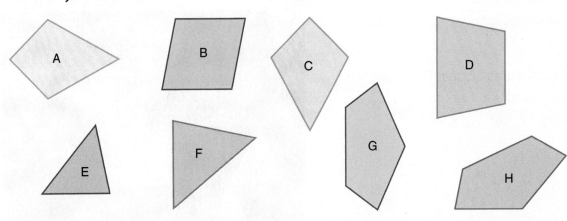

5. Use dot paper.
   a) Draw a quadrilateral with no sides equal.
   Label the quadrilateral MNPQ.
   b) Draw two different quadrilaterals that are not
   congruent to MNPQ.
   Label these quadrilaterals STUV and BCDE.
   Explain why STUV, BCDE, and MNPQ are not congruent.
   c) Draw a quadrilateral that is congruent to MNPQ.
   Label this quadrilateral GHJK.
   How do you know that MNPQ and GHJK are congruent?

6. Copy this figure
onto grid paper.
Draw lines to divide
the figure into
4 congruent polygons.
How do you know the
polygons are congruent?

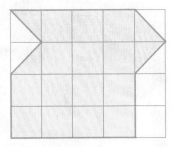

Reflect

When you see two polygons, how can you tell
if they are congruent?
Use a diagram to explain.

4 Similar Figures

Which figures appear to be similar?
How could you find out?

Explore

You will need 4 tangrams, grid paper, scissors, and a protractor.

➤ Share the tans.
Use 1, 2, or more tans to make a quadrilateral.
Each person makes 5 quadrilaterals.
Trace each quadrilateral and label it.
Cut out the quadrilaterals.

➤ Sort the quadrilaterals
into these groups:
  • squares
  • rectangles
  • parallelograms
  • trapezoids
  • other quadrilaterals

➤ Look at the quadrilaterals
in each group.
Which quadrilaterals are
similar? How do you know?

➤ Choose a pair of similar quadrilaterals.
Measure the side lengths and angles in each quadrilateral.
What do you notice?
Repeat for 3 more pairs of similar quadrilaterals.

Show and Share

Share your work with another group.
How did you decide if two quadrilaterals were similar?
How are the angles in similar quadrilaterals related?
How are the side lengths in similar quadrilaterals related?

Connect

These figures are similar.

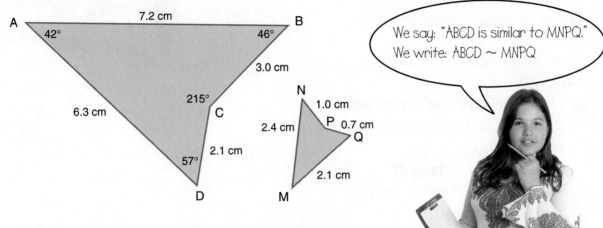

> We say: "ABCD is similar to MNPQ."
> We write: ABCD ~ MNPQ

Each side of quadrilateral ABCD is 3 times the length
of the corresponding side of quadrilateral MNPQ.

3 × MN = AB	3 × 2.4 cm = 7.2 cm
3 × NP = BC	3 × 1.0 cm = 3.0 cm
3 × PQ = CD	3 × 0.7 cm = 2.1 cm
3 × QM = DA	3 × 2.1 cm = 6.3 cm

Each angle in quadrilateral ABCD is equal
to the corresponding angle in quadrilateral MNPQ.

$\angle$A = $\angle$M = 42°
$\angle$B = $\angle$N = 46°
$\angle$C = $\angle$P = 215°
$\angle$D = $\angle$Q = 57°

Similar figures
have the same shape.
They may or may not be
the same size.

Any 2 figures are similar if:
• their corresponding angles are equal *and*
• the side lengths of one figure multiplied by the same number
  are equal to the corresponding side lengths of the other figure

1. Draw a square on grid paper.
   Label it A.
   a) Draw a new square with each side
      2 times as long as each side of square A.
      Label the new square B.
      Are squares A and B similar?
      How do you know?
   b) Try to draw a square that is *not* similar
      to squares A and B.
   c) Are all squares similar? Explain.

2. Draw a rectangle on grid paper.
   Label it D.
   a) Draw a new rectangle with each side
      2 times as long as the corresponding side
      of rectangle D.
      Label the new rectangle E.
      Are rectangles D and E similar?
      How do you know?
   b) Is it possible to draw a rectangle
      that is *not* similar to rectangles D and E?
      If so, draw one.
   c) Are all rectangles similar? Explain.

3. Compare your answers to questions 1c and 2c.
   Explain.

4. Which rectangles are similar? How do you know?

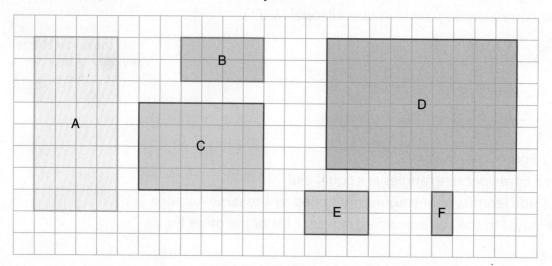

5. Are these figures similar? How do you know?

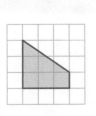 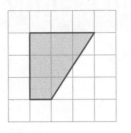

6. Use grid paper.
   a) Draw a right scalene triangle. Label the triangle ABC.
   b) Draw a triangle that is similar to △ABC.
       Label this triangle DEF.
       How do you know the triangles are similar?
   c) Draw a right triangle that is not similar to △ABC.
       Label this triangle GHJ.
       How do you know the triangles are not similar?
   Show your work.

7. Graphic artists use perspective
to make drawings look 3-dimensional.
They draw a vanishing point to show
where the sight lines meet.

   a) Use grid paper.
       •   Draw a vanishing point.
       •   Draw a square away from the
           vanishing point.
       •   Use a ruler to draw a dotted line
           from each vertex of the square
           to the vanishing point.
           Extend these dotted lines to the edge of the paper.
       •   Draw another square with vertices on the dotted lines.
       •   Draw line segments to join the corresponding vertices
           of the two squares. Which solid did you draw?
   b) Explain how drawing with perspective uses similar figures.

Reflect

Are both these statements correct?
All congruent figures are similar. All similar figures are congruent.
Use pictures and words to explain.

Using *The Geometer's Sketchpad* to Explore Similar Figures

Work with a partner.
Use *The Geometer's Sketchpad*.

Follow these steps to draw similar figures.

1. To open a new sketch in *The Geometer's Sketchpad*:

Click: File , then click: New Sketch   Ctrl+N

2. To set your preferences:

Click: Edit , then click: Preferences...

Select the Units tab. Choose these settings:

Preferences

Units | Color | Text

	Units	Precision
Angle:	degrees	units
Distance:	cm	tenths
Other (Slope, Ratio, ...)		hundredths

Apply To: ☑ This Sketch ☑ New Sketches

Help   Cancel   OK

Select the Text tab. Choose these settings:

Preferences

Units | Color | Text

Show Labels Automatically:
☑ For All New Points
☑ As Objects Are Measured

☑ Show Text Palette When Editing Captions

Apply To: ☑ This Sketch ☐ New Sketches

Help   Cancel   OK

Click: OK

3. To **construct a polygon**, choose the Straightedge Tool, .
   Click, hold down the mouse button, and drag
   until the segment is as long as you want it.
   Release the mouse button.
   Place the cursor on one endpoint of the segment, then
   click and drag to construct the next side of the polygon.
   Continue to draw segments until the polygon is complete.

4. To **measure the sides** of a polygon, choose
   the Selection Arrow Tool, .

   Click to select the endpoints of one side of the polygon.
   Click: Measure , then click: Distance
   The length of the side appears in the top left of the screen.
   Click anywhere outside the polygon to deselect the length.

   Repeat to measure each side of the polygon.

5. To **measure the angles** in a polygon, choose the Selection Arrow Tool, .
   Click to select 3 vertices in clockwise order.
   Click: Measure , then click: Angle
   The measure of the angle appears in the top left of the screen.
   Click anywhere outside the polygon to deselect the angle measure.

   Repeat to measure each angle in the polygon.

6. To **change the shape** of the polygon,
   choose the Selection Arrow Tool, .
   Click a line segment.
   Hold down the mouse button.
   Drag the line segment until it is
   where you want it.
   Watch what happens to the
   side and angle measures
   as you move the line segment.
   Release the mouse button.
   Repeat by clicking and moving
   a vertex.

7. To **draw a similar polygon**, select the Point Tool, ◆ .
   Click: Transform , then click: Mark Center   Shift+Ctrl+F

   Click to select each vertex and side of the polygon in clockwise order.
   Click: Transform , then click: Dilate...
   In the dialogue box, click to select Fixed Ratio.
   Type 2.0 in the top box and 1.0 in the bottom box.
   This will double the distance between each vertex and the centre point.
   Click: Dilate

8. Measure the sides and angles of the similar polygon. How do these measures compare to the side and angle measures of the original polygon? Explain.

9. Change the size and shape of the original polygon. What happens to the similar polygon?

   Click and drag the centre point to a new location. What happens? Why?

10. Follow Steps 3 to 9 to draw, measure, and compare other similar polygons.

11. To save your work:
    Click: File , then click: Save As...
    Give your file a name.
    Click: Save

12. To print your work:
    Click: File , then click: Print...

    Click: OK

Reflect

What did you learn about similar figures by using *The Geometer's Sketchpad*?

5 Line Symmetry

How many lines of symmetry does each road sign have?
How can you use reflections to find out?

Explore

· ·

You will need paper, Pattern Blocks, and scissors.

➤ Fold a rectangular piece of paper in half lengthwise and widthwise.
The fold lines divide the paper into 4 congruent sections.
Use Pattern Blocks.
Make a design in one section.
The design must touch both fold lines.
Trace the design.
Remove the Pattern Blocks.

➤ Draw the image of the design after a reflection in a fold line.
Continue to reflect the design in fold lines
until you have drawn the design
in all four sections. Cut out the design.

➤ How many lines of symmetry
does the design have?

Show and Share

Share your design with a classmate.
Compare the numbers of lines of symmetry.
How could you create a figure or design with
8 lines of symmetry?

Numbers Every Day

Calculator Skills

Use the digits 2, 4, 6, 7, 8,
and 9.
Arrange the digits to make:
• the greatest product
• the least product

☐ ☐ ☐ ☐
×   ☐ ☐

Here are ways to make a design with lines of symmetry.

➤ Fold a square of paper in half diagonally.

Fold the paper a second time, along the long side.

Use scissors to cut designs into the edges of the triangle.
Be sure to leave some of the folded sides uncut.

Unfold the paper.
Each fold line is a line of symmetry.

➤ Fold a square of paper edge to edge and along the diagonals.

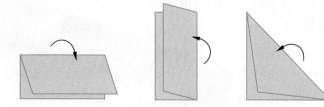  

The paper is now divided into 8 congruent sections.
Draw a broken line along each fold line.
Draw a design in one section.
Reflect the design successively in each broken line.

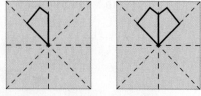 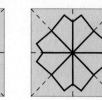

1. Use Pattern Blocks.
   a) Make a design with each number of lines of symmetry: 2, 3, 4
      Trace each design. Show all the lines of symmetry.
   b) Describe how you made each design in part a.

2. This design was made by connecting dots on square dot paper.
   a) Identify the lines of symmetry in this design.
   b) Use dot paper. Create a design with more than one line of symmetry. Identify the lines of symmetry.

3. Copy this design on 1-cm grid paper.
   a) Reflect the design in the broken lines to complete a picture.
   b) How many lines of symmetry does the picture have?

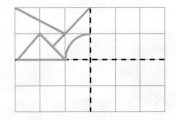

4. Draw a design that has more than 2 lines of symmetry.
   Show all the lines of symmetry.
   How did you draw your design?

5. You will need a square of paper and scissors.
   Fold and cut the paper to make a figure with 4 lines of symmetry.

6. Copy this figure on grid paper.
   Draw squares so the figure has 4 lines of symmetry.
   How did you decide where to draw the squares?

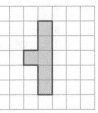

At Home

Reflect

Describe how to draw a figure that has 2 or more lines of symmetry.
Use examples to explain.

Look for designs at home that have more than 1 line of symmetry. Copy each design. Share the designs with your classmates.

Rotational Symmetry

Explore

You will need one of each type of Pattern Block and stickers.
Place a sticker at one vertex of each block.

➤ Trace around the yellow Pattern Block.
The tracing is the frame.
Place the yellow block in the frame.
Record the position of the vertex with the sticker.

➤ Find and record the number of different ways you can place
the yellow block in the frame.
Do not turn the block over.

➤ Repeat the activity for each of the Pattern Blocks.

Show *and* Share

Share your results with another pair of students.
Which block could be placed in its frame the greatest
number of ways? The least number of ways?
Order the blocks from the greatest number
of ways to the least number of ways.

A figure that coincides with itself when rotated
less than a full turn has **rotational symmetry**.

Here is one way to find out if a figure has rotational symmetry.

- Trace the figure.
  Mark one vertex on the tracing and
  the corresponding vertex on the figure.
  Place the tracing to coincide with the figure.

- Turn the tracing on the figure.
  Count the number of times the tracing coincides
  with the figure in one full turn.

In one full turn,
the tracing coincides with
the figure 4 times.
We say the figure has
rotational symmetry of
order 4.

This triangle has no rotational symmetry.
It does not coincide with itself in less than a full turn.

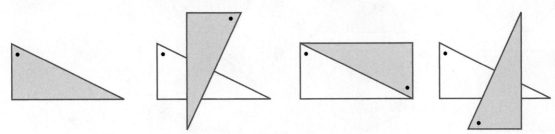

You may use tracing paper.

1. What is the order of rotational symmetry
   for the sails on this windmill?
   How do you know?

2. a) Which figures have rotational symmetry?
      What is the order of rotational symmetry?

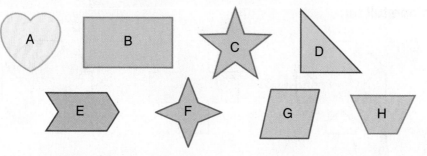

   b) List the figures with rotational symmetry from least to greatest order.

3. Use the figures in question 2.
   a) Which figures have line symmetry?
      List the figures from least to greatest number
      of lines of symmetry.
   b) Compare the lists of the figures in questions 2b and 3a.
      What do you notice?

4. For each regular polygon:
   • List the number of sides.
   • Find the number of lines of symmetry.
   • Find the order of rotational symmetry.

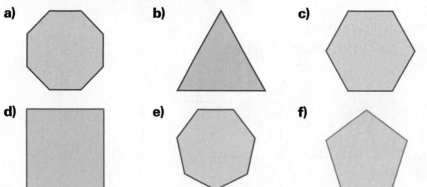

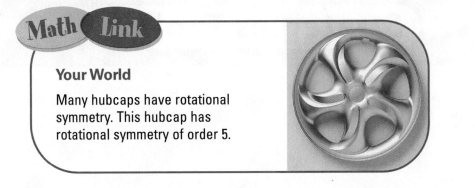

Math Link

Your World

Many hubcaps have rotational symmetry. This hubcap has rotational symmetry of order 5.

5. Copy and complete the table for the polygons in question 4.

Regular Polygon	Number of Sides	Number of Lines of Symmetry	Order of Rotational Symmetry

a) Describe any patterns in the table.
b) Use the patterns to predict the order of rotational symmetry and the number of lines of symmetry for a regular decagon.

> A decagon is a polygon with 10 sides.

6. Choose 2 or more types of Pattern Blocks.
Make a design with each order of rotational symmetry.
Trace each design.

a) 2   b) 3   c) 4   d) 6

7. a) Explain why this figure does not have rotational symmetry.
b) Copy the figure on grid paper.
Draw one or more squares so the figure has rotational symmetry of order 2.
How did you decide where to draw the squares?

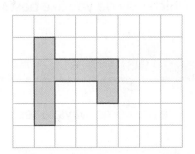

8. Use triangular dot paper. Draw a triangle.
a) How many lines of symmetry does the triangle have?
b) What is the order of rotational symmetry of the triangle? How do you know?
c) Do you think all triangles would give the same results? Explain.

Reflect

How do you know if a figure has rotational symmetry?
Use diagrams and words to explain.

Numbers Every Day

Number Strategies

Use addition, subtraction, multiplication, or division. Find 10 different ways to make 144.

Assessment Focus | Question 7

Strategies Toolkit

Explore

A frog climbed up a tree 20 m tall.
Each day, the frog climbed up 4 m.
Each night, it slid back 2 m.
How many days did it take the frog to climb to the top of the tree?

Solve the problem.
Represent your thinking as many different ways as you can.

Show *and* Share

Share your work with another pair of students.
Compare the ways you represented your thinking.
Which way do you like best? Why?

Connect

Here are some ways to represent your thinking.

Strategies for Success

- **Get unstuck.**
- **Check and reflect.**
- **Focus on the problem.**
- **Represent your thinking.**
- **Select an answer.**
- **Do your best on a test.**
- **Explain your answer.**

With words

A written explanation can give lots of information.
You can use math language to describe the steps you
followed, the patterns you noticed, and your ideas.

With a diagram

You can draw a diagram to show important details.
Your diagram can show how you visualized the
problem, what parts changed, or how they changed.

With numbers

You can use numbers to show your thinking in a formal way.
The numbers may be in a table, in calculations, or in equations.

More than one way

Sometimes, the best way to represent your thinking
is with words, diagrams, and numbers.

When you have completed your answer, ask yourself:

Would someone else be able to understand
my thinking by looking at my answer?
What could I add to make my answer more clear?

Practice

Solve each problem. Each time, show
your thinking at least 2 different ways.

Name	Mass	Equipment	Food
Shawn	60 kg	38 kg	25 kg
Martha	56 kg	42 kg	33 kg
Bubba	75 kg	63 kg	35 kg

1. Three hikers want to cross a river
   to get to a campsite on the other shore.
   The boat holds a maximum of 300 kg.
   Describe how the hikers can cross the river
   making the fewest trips.
   Can they do this more than one way? Explain.

2. Use Pattern Blocks.
   Suppose a yellow block is worth $3.00,
   a red block is worth $1.50, a blue block is worth $1.00,
   and a green block is worth $0.50.
   Make 5 different designs that are each worth $10.00.

Reflect

Describe some ways you can represent your thinking.
Give an example of when you might use each way.

Animator

An animator uses artistic talent and sophisticated graphics software to make movie scenes. But while the software may be sophisticated, basic geometry is at its core.

Every movement of an object within an animated scene involves one or more transformations. The animator chooses direction and speed, and the software performs the transformations to match. Animators continually adjust their instructions to make a scene more realistic or exciting. New "routines" are stored and shared with the other animators working on the project. Although everything appears three-dimensional, calculations are done using two-dimensional transformations with sizing changes.

Computer animators can recreate details that would be impossible to get on film alone. Sometimes, they can make the unbelievable seem real.

Tiling Patterns

Explore

You will need tracing paper and scissors.
Your teacher will give you a large copy of these figures.

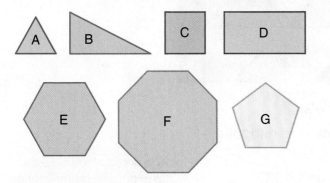

Cut out the figures.

➤ Choose one figure. Make sure it is different
from the figures chosen by others in your group.
Trace copies of the figure to make a design.
Think about translations, rotations, and reflections.
Write to explain how your design can be created
by repeatedly transforming the first figure.

➤ Repeat the activity with a different figure.
Which figures make a tiling pattern? How do you know?
Which figures do not make a tiling pattern?

➤ Select a pair of figures you think will make a tiling pattern together.
Explain why you chose the figures.
Trace copies of the figures to check they can be used
to make a tiling pattern.
How can you use transformations to create the pattern
from the first tracing?

Show and Share

Share your work with another group of students.
Try to think of different transformations to describe your classmates' patterns.

A tiling pattern covers a surface with no gaps or overlaps.

➤ This tiling pattern is made with congruent copies
of a right isosceles triangle.

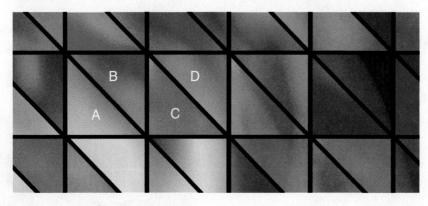

Suppose the first figure is A.
To get figure B, rotate figure A 180° about the midpoint
of the side it shares with figure B.
To get figures C and D, rotate figures A and B 180°
about the midpoint of the side figures B and C share.
We can repeat similar transformations to make the
tiling pattern.

> You could also make the
> tiling pattern by reflecting
> and translating.

➤ This tiling pattern is made with congruent copies
of a regular octagon and a square.

The octagon alone does not tile the plane.
A design made with regular octagons leaves spaces
that are squares.
Suppose the first octagon is figure A.
To get figure B, rotate figure A 180° about the midpoint
of the side it shares with figure B.
Then continue to rotate these octagons to get the design.

> You could
> also make the
> tiling pattern
> by reflecting.

1. Draw and cut out 4 congruent copies of each type of triangle:
   • acute scalene   • equilateral   • obtuse isosceles
   a) Use each type of triangle to make a tiling pattern.
      Which transformations could you use to make your pattern?
   b) Do all triangles make tiling patterns? How do you know?

2. You will need a large copy of these tiling patterns. For each pattern,
   explain how you could use transformations to make the pattern.
   a)   b) 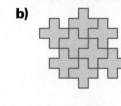   c)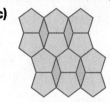

3. You will need triangular dot paper and scissors.
   • Draw a quadrilateral on triangular dot paper.
     Each vertex of the quadrilateral must coincide with a dot.
     Carefully cut out the quadrilateral.
   • Trace and cut out 7 copies of the quadrilateral.
   • Use the 8 quadrilaterals to create a tiling pattern.
   • Record your tiling pattern on another piece of dot paper.
   • Explain how you could use transformations to make your pattern.

4. Which pairs of figures can be used to make a tiling pattern?
   How do you know?
   a) a rectangle and a hexagon   b) a square and a rectangle
   c) a circle and a triangle   d) a kite and a square

5. a) Use triangular dot paper.
      Create a tiling pattern.
   b) Explain how you could use
      transformations to create the pattern.

Reflect

When you see a design with congruent figures,
how do you decide which transformations
could have been used to create it?
Use an example to explain.

Numbers Every Day

Number Strategies

Write each number as a decimal.
• six and seven-tenths
• eighty-five and
  two-hundredths
• five hundred and fifty-five
  thousandths
• one million one hundred
  and nineteen-hundredths

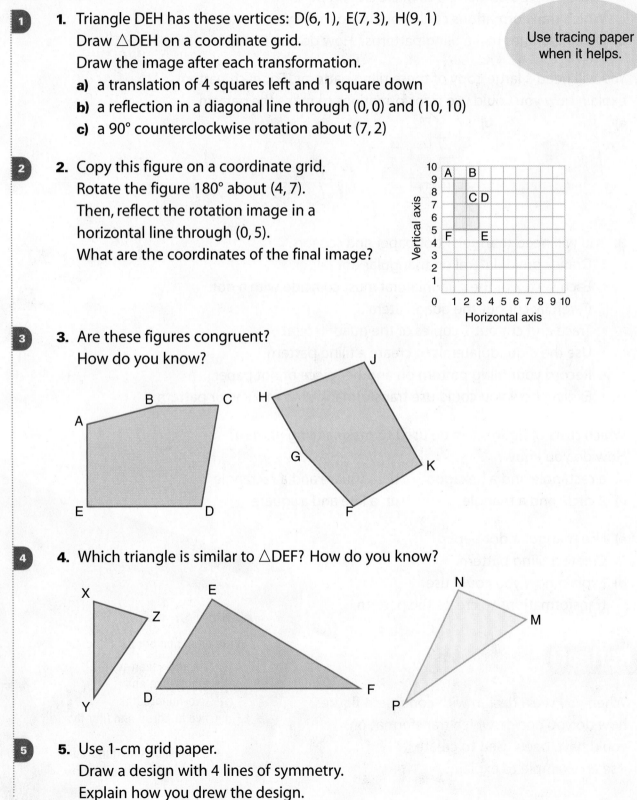

LESSON

1

1. Triangle DEH has these vertices: D(6, 1), E(7, 3), H(9, 1)
   Draw △DEH on a coordinate grid.
   Draw the image after each transformation.
   a) a translation of 4 squares left and 1 square down
   b) a reflection in a diagonal line through (0, 0) and (10, 10)
   c) a 90° counterclockwise rotation about (7, 2)

   Use tracing paper when it helps.

2

2. Copy this figure on a coordinate grid.
   Rotate the figure 180° about (4, 7).
   Then, reflect the rotation image in a
   horizontal line through (0, 5).
   What are the coordinates of the final image?

3

3. Are these figures congruent?
   How do you know?

4

4. Which triangle is similar to △DEF? How do you know?

5

5. Use 1-cm grid paper.
   Draw a design with 4 lines of symmetry.
   Explain how you drew the design.

6

6. What is the order of rotational symmetry for each figure?
How do you know?

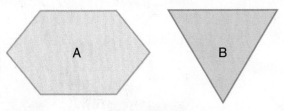

5
6

7. Copy this figure on grid paper.
Draw 2 squares so the figure has line symmetry
and rotational symmetry.
   a) How did you decide where to draw
   the squares?
   b) What is the order of rotational symmetry?
   c) How many lines of symmetry
   does your figure have?

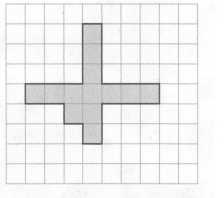

8. You will need Pattern Blocks.
Create a tiling pattern with each group
of blocks.
   a) hexagon, trapezoid, and blue rhombus
   b) square and trapezoid
   c) triangle and square
Record each tiling pattern on square or
triangular dot paper.
Explain how you could use transformations
to make each pattern.

8

9. Use grid paper.
Draw a figure you can use to make
a tiling pattern.
Use transformations to cover the paper
with the design.

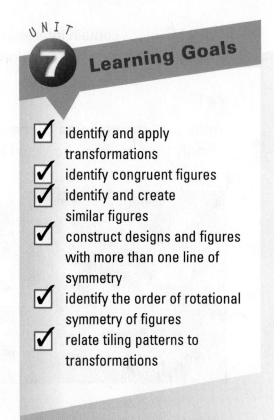

UNIT

7 Learning Goals

- ☑ identify and apply transformations
- ☑ identify congruent figures
- ☑ identify and create similar figures
- ☑ construct designs and figures with more than one line of symmetry
- ☑ identify the order of rotational symmetry of figures
- ☑ relate tiling patterns to transformations

Many buildings contain interesting designs
that show symmetry and transformations.

Part 1

These patterns are found on the Alhambra Palace in Spain.
Identify the transformations and the symmetry in each pattern.

Part 2

Sketch some figures you could use in a mural.
Design a mural on grid paper.
Use the figures you sketched.
Use transformations to create a design
that has line symmetry and rotational symmetry.
Colour your design.

Part 3

Write about your mural.
Describe:
• the transformations you used
• the line symmetry and the rotational symmetry

Check List

Your work should show
☑ accurate identification
  of transformations
  and symmetry
☑ a mural design, using
  transformations, that
  shows both line and
  rotational symmetry
☑ a clear explanation of how
  you constructed your design
☑ correct use of geometric
  language

Reflect on the Unit

How are line symmetry and rotational symmetry
related to transformations?
Use diagrams to explain.

Probably Polyhedra

You will need labels, grid paper, triangular dot paper, a cube, a square pyramid, a triangular prism, and a regular tetrahedron.

> A polyhedron is a solid whose faces are polygons. All prisms and pyramids are polyhedra.

Part 1

➤ Choose a polyhedron.
Use labels.
Number the faces with consecutive numbers beginning at 1.

➤ What is the probability of rolling each number?
Predict how many times the polyhedron will land on each number when you roll it 30 times.

> Record the number the polyhedron lands on.

➤ Roll the polyhedron 30 times.
Record the number the polyhedron lands on in a tally chart.
How do the results compare with your predictions?

Part 2

➤ Repeat Part 1 for each of the polyhedra.
Remember to record your predictions and results.

Predict how many times each polyhedron will land on
each number when you roll it 90 times.

Combine your results with those of 2 other groups.
How do the combined results compare with your predictions?

Predict how many times each polyhedron will land on
each number when you roll it 300 times.

Combine your results for each polyhedron
with those of 9 other groups.
How do the combined results compare with your predictions?

Part 3

➤ Draw a net for
each polyhedron.
Use the nets to
explain your results
for Parts 1 and 2.

Display Your Work

Create a summary of your work.
Use pictures, numbers, and words.

Take It Further

Create a game using one or more of the numbered polyhedra.
Write the rules for your game.
Play your game with another group of students.

Fractions, Percents,

Read the Label!

Learning Goals

- express fractions in simplest form
- relate mixed numbers and improper fractions
- compare and order mixed numbers and fractions
- explore addition and subtraction of fractions
- explore percents
- relate percents to fractions and decimals
- estimate and calculate percents
- solve multistep problems using percents
- use ratios for part-to-part and part-to-whole comparisons
- explore equivalent ratios
- explore rates
- solve problems involving fractions, percents, ratios, and rates

CRANBERRY Cocktail

1.89 L 100% Recommended daily intake of vitamin C

$\frac{2}{3}$ Fl WEI CA RIES

30% LESS SALT THAN OUR REGULAR NO TRANS FAT

CRUNCHOES
100% WHOLE WHEAT CRACKERS
LIGHT
250 g

FAT FREE

OOTIES
RUIT SNACKS

FROOTIES
FRUIT SNACKS
POUCHES
10 WOW! 67% MORE

Food packages provide a lot of information, such as brand name, type of product, quantity, and nutritional data.

Ratios, and Rates

Key Words

• • • • • • • • • • • • • • • • •

simplify

simplest form

percent

terms of a ratio

ratio

equivalent ratios

rate

continuous line graph

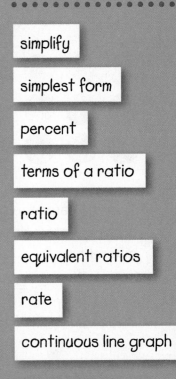

- Choose one product in the shopping basket that has a fraction on its label.
  Copy the fraction.
  Identify the numerator and the denominator.
  Draw a picture to represent the fraction.

- Choose one product in the shopping basket that has 100% on its label.
  What do you think this means?

1 Equivalent Fractions

10 out of 15 counters are red.
$\frac{10}{15}$ are red.

2 out of 3 equal rows are red.
$\frac{2}{3}$ are red.

$\frac{10}{15}$ and $\frac{2}{3}$ name the same fraction of the counters, but say it in a different way.

$$\frac{10}{15} = \frac{2}{3}$$

$\frac{10}{15}$ and $\frac{2}{3}$ are equivalent fractions.

Explore

➤ Use Fraction Circles.
Find as many pairs of equivalent fractions as you can.
Record each pair you find.

➤ Find a way to write an equivalent fraction for each fraction below.
Draw or write to explain what you did.

$\frac{1}{3}$ $\frac{4}{5}$ $\frac{7}{12}$ $\frac{5}{8}$ $\frac{12}{16}$ $\frac{6}{12}$

Show and Share

Share your work with another pair of students.
How did you find each equivalent fraction?
Explain your method.
Does your method work for all fractions? Explain.

➤ To find an equivalent fraction with a greater numerator
and denominator, multiply the numerator and the
denominator by the same number.

Find equivalent fractions for $\frac{5}{12}$.

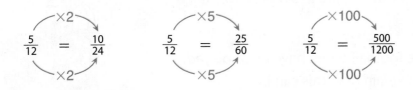

So, $\frac{10}{24}$, $\frac{25}{60}$, and $\frac{500}{1200}$ are equivalent to $\frac{5}{12}$.

> As long as you
> multiply the numerator
> and the denominator
> by the same number, you do
> not change the value of the
> fraction. The same is true
> when you divide.

➤ To find an equivalent fraction with a lesser numerator
and denominator, divide the numerator and the
denominator by the same number.

Find an equivalent fraction for $\frac{24}{60}$.

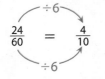

So, $\frac{4}{10}$ is equivalent to $\frac{24}{60}$.

$\frac{4}{10}$ is a simpler form of $\frac{24}{60}$.

> The number
> you multiply or divide by
> cannot be 0.

When you find an equivalent fraction by
dividing, you **simplify** the fraction.

Further,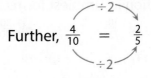

$\frac{2}{5}$ is the **simplest form** of $\frac{24}{60}$.

Use Fraction Circles when they help.

1. Each picture represents 1 whole.
   Write 3 equivalent fractions to represent the shaded part of each picture.

   a)   b)   c) d)

2. Write 3 equivalent fractions to represent the unshaded part
   of each picture in question 1.

3. Find equivalent fractions with a denominator of 15.

  a) $\frac{1}{5}$ **b)** $\frac{2}{3}$ **c)** $\frac{12}{30}$ **d)** $\frac{8}{60}$

4. Write 3 equivalent fractions for each fraction.

  a) $\frac{1}{2}$ **b)** $\frac{5}{6}$ **c)** $\frac{20}{50}$ **d)** $\frac{4}{5}$

  e) $\frac{20}{30}$ **f)** $\frac{25}{35}$ **g)** $\frac{18}{24}$ **h)** $\frac{50}{60}$

5. Which fractions in question 4 are in simplest form?
How do you know?

6. Two-quarters of the football game have been played.
It is now half time. Explain how this can be.

7. Which pairs of fractions are equivalent? How do you know?

  a) $\frac{1}{6}$ and $\frac{6}{36}$ **b)** $\frac{8}{14}$ and $\frac{4}{7}$ **c)** $\frac{32}{40}$ and $\frac{20}{32}$

  d) $\frac{24}{36}$ and $\frac{3}{9}$ **e)** $\frac{12}{15}$ and $\frac{36}{45}$ **f)** $\frac{3}{4}$ and $\frac{9}{16}$

8. Madelaine says she can use a clock to show that
$\frac{5}{60}$ and $\frac{1}{12}$ are equivalent fractions.
Do you think she is correct? Explain.

9. Write each fraction in simplest form.

  a) $\frac{32}{56}$ **b)** $\frac{50}{75}$ **c)** $\frac{300}{900}$ **d)** $\frac{21}{63}$

  e) $\frac{16}{20}$ **f)** $\frac{8}{32}$ **g)** $\frac{100}{175}$ **h)** $\frac{48}{60}$

10. Write a fraction to describe each situation.
Then write each fraction in simplest form.

  a) 45 min as a fraction of one hour **b)** 45¢ as a fraction of one dollar

  c) 10 eggs as a fraction of one dozen **d)** 3 months as a fraction of one year

  e) 8 bottles of water as a fraction of a case of 24 bottles

11. Tuan sold $\frac{2}{3}$ of his raffle tickets on Saturday
and $\frac{2}{9}$ of them on Sunday.
Did Tuan sell more tickets on Sunday than Saturday?
Explain using words or drawings.

Reflect

List two ways you can find equivalent fractions.
Choose one way. Choose a fraction. Write 3 fractions
that are equivalent to the fraction you chose.

Numbers Every Day

Number Strategies

Find each result.

$13 + 4 \times 2 - 1$
$43 \times 2 - 3 \times 15$
$100 - 25 \times 2 + 50$

In what order did you
complete the operations
each time?

Relating Mixed Numbers and Improper Fractions

I have $\frac{5}{3}$ slices of French toast.

I have $1\frac{2}{3}$ slices of French toast.

$\frac{5}{3}$ and $1\frac{2}{3}$ represent the same amount.

The numerator of $\frac{5}{3}$ is greater than the denominator. $\frac{5}{3}$ is an improper fraction.

$1\frac{2}{3}$ has a whole number part and a fraction part. $1\frac{2}{3}$ is a mixed number.

Explore

You will need Cuisenaire rods or strips of coloured paper.

➤ Choose a mixed number. Use Cuisenaire rods to model the mixed number. Write the mixed number as an improper fraction. Repeat for 2 different mixed numbers.

When the dark green rod is one whole, the red rod is one-third.

So, this is $\frac{8}{3}$, or $2\frac{2}{3}$.

➤ Choose an improper fraction. Use Cuisenaire rods to model the improper fraction. Choose an appropriate rod to represent 1 whole. Write the improper fraction as a mixed number. Repeat for 2 different improper fractions.

➤ Without using Cuisenaire rods, how could you:
  • rename a mixed number as an improper fraction?
  • rename an improper fraction as a mixed number?
  Record each method.

LESSON FOCUS | Convert between mixed numbers and improper fractions.

Show *and* Share

Compare your methods with those of another pair of students.
Use Cuisenaire rods to show why your methods make sense.

Connect . . . .

➤ To write $2\frac{3}{4}$ as an improper fraction:
Draw a diagram to represent $2\frac{3}{4}$.

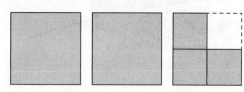

The diagram shows 2 wholes and 3 quarters, or $2\frac{3}{4}$.
Divide each whole to show quarters.

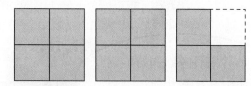

2 wholes is the same as 8 quarters.
8 quarters and 3 quarters is 11 quarters, or $\frac{11}{4}$.
So, $\frac{11}{4}$ is the same as $2\frac{3}{4}$.

To get the same result,
multiply the whole number
by the denominator
and add the numerator.
2 x 4 = 8
8 + 3 = 11
The result is the number of
quarters in $2\frac{3}{4}$.
So, $\frac{11}{4}$ is the same as $2\frac{3}{4}$.

➤ To write $\frac{13}{5}$ as a mixed number:
Draw a diagram showing 13 fifths.

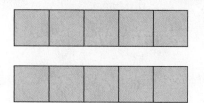

Because a fraction
represents division, I can also
divide the numerator by the denominator.

$$5 \overline{\smash{)}13}$$
$$2 \text{ R3}$$

There are 2 wholes, with 3 fifths left over.
So, $2\frac{3}{5}$ is the same as $\frac{13}{5}$.

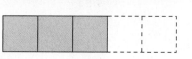

There are 5 fifths in 1 whole and 10 fifths in 2 wholes.
There are 2 wholes, with 3 fifths left over.
So, $2\frac{3}{5}$ is the same as $\frac{13}{5}$.

292

Use Cuisenaire rods or coloured strips when they help.

1. Write an improper fraction and a mixed number to describe each picture.

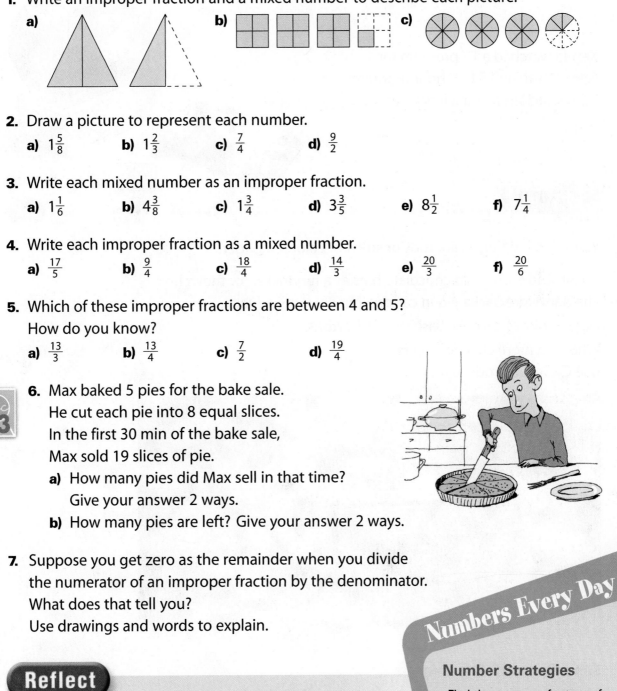

   a)

   b)

   c)

2. Draw a picture to represent each number.

   a) $1\frac{5}{8}$ b) $1\frac{2}{3}$ c) $\frac{7}{4}$ d) $\frac{9}{2}$

3. Write each mixed number as an improper fraction.

   a) $1\frac{1}{6}$ b) $4\frac{3}{8}$ c) $1\frac{3}{4}$ d) $3\frac{3}{5}$ e) $8\frac{1}{2}$ f) $7\frac{1}{4}$

4. Write each improper fraction as a mixed number.

   a) $\frac{17}{5}$ b) $\frac{9}{4}$ c) $\frac{18}{4}$ d) $\frac{14}{3}$ e) $\frac{20}{3}$ f) $\frac{20}{6}$

5. Which of these improper fractions are between 4 and 5?
   How do you know?

   a) $\frac{13}{3}$ b) $\frac{13}{4}$ c) $\frac{7}{2}$ d) $\frac{19}{4}$

6. Max baked 5 pies for the bake sale.
   He cut each pie into 8 equal slices.
   In the first 30 min of the bake sale,
   Max sold 19 slices of pie.
   a) How many pies did Max sell in that time?
      Give your answer 2 ways.
   b) How many pies are left? Give your answer 2 ways.

7. Suppose you get zero as the remainder when you divide
   the numerator of an improper fraction by the denominator.
   What does that tell you?
   Use drawings and words to explain.

Numbers Every Day

Number Strategies

Find the common factors of
the numbers in each set.

   • 6, 12, 30
   • 15, 20, 75
   • 14, 42, 63

Reflect

What is the difference between a mixed number
and an improper fraction?
Describe how to rename an improper fraction
as a mixed number. Use an example to explain.

Comparing and Ordering Mixed Numbers and Fractions

Kenda watched a TV program for $1\frac{1}{2}$ h.
Garnet watched 5 half-hour programs.
Who watched TV for a longer time?

Explore

You will need Cuisenaire rods or strips of coloured paper.

Dusan and Sasha sold chocolate bars as a fundraiser for their choir.
The bars were packaged in cartons, but sold individually.
Dusan sold $2\frac{2}{3}$ cartons. Sasha sold $\frac{5}{2}$ cartons.
Who sold more chocolate bars?
Use Cuisenaire rods to find out.

Show and Share

Share your solution with another pair of students.
How did you decide which rods to use to represent one whole,
one-third, and one-half?
How did you find out which number was greater?
Try to find a way to compare $2\frac{2}{3}$ and $\frac{5}{2}$ without using rods.

Here are some ways to compare and order mixed numbers and improper fractions.

➤ To order $2\frac{1}{4}$, $\frac{11}{6}$, and $\frac{8}{3}$ from least to greatest:
Use number lines.

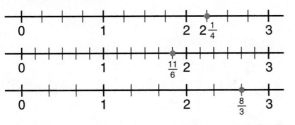

The order from least to greatest is $\frac{11}{6}$, $2\frac{1}{4}$, $\frac{8}{3}$.

➤ To compare $1\frac{2}{3}$ and $\frac{7}{4}$:
Write $1\frac{2}{3}$ as an improper fraction.

Draw a diagram.
Divide the whole to show thirds.

1 whole is the same as 3 thirds.
3 thirds and 2 thirds is 5 thirds, or $\frac{5}{3}$.

Write each improper fraction as
an equivalent fraction with the same denominator.
List the multiples of 3: 3, 6, 9, **12**, …
List the multiples of 4: 4, 8, **12**, …
12 is a common multiple of 3 and 4.

Find an equivalent fraction
for $\frac{5}{3}$ with twelfths:

$$\frac{5}{3} = \frac{20}{12}$$

Find an equivalent fraction
for $\frac{7}{4}$ with twelfths:

$$\frac{7}{4} = \frac{21}{12}$$

Compare $\frac{20}{12}$ and $\frac{21}{12}$:
$\frac{20}{12} < \frac{21}{12}$, so $1\frac{2}{3} < \frac{7}{4}$

> I could write $\frac{7}{4}$ as $1\frac{3}{4}$
> and compare $1\frac{2}{3}$ and $1\frac{3}{4}$.
> The whole number parts are equal.
> So, I need to compare the
> fraction parts.
> Draw and colour circles
> to represent $\frac{2}{3}$ and $\frac{3}{4}$.
>
>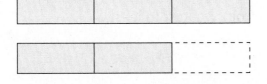
>
> From the drawings, $\frac{2}{3} < \frac{3}{4}$
> This means that $1\frac{2}{3} < 1\frac{3}{4}$.
> So, $1\frac{2}{3} < \frac{7}{4}$

Use materials to help.

1. Find equivalent improper fractions so the fractions in each pair
   have the same denominator.
   Then compare the fractions.
   Use the symbols >, <, or =.

   a) $\frac{8}{3}$ and $\frac{6}{4}$ b) $\frac{12}{5}$ and $\frac{8}{3}$ c) $\frac{14}{6}$ and $\frac{17}{8}$

   d) $\frac{11}{10}$ and $\frac{20}{15}$ e) $\frac{9}{5}$ and $\frac{8}{6}$ f) $\frac{12}{9}$ and $\frac{11}{5}$

2. Use 1-cm grid paper.
   Draw three 12-cm number lines like the one below.

   Show quarters on one line.
   Show halves on another line.
   Show eighths on the third line.
   Use the number lines to order these numbers from greatest to least.
   $\frac{7}{2}$, $\frac{23}{8}$, $1\frac{3}{4}$

3. Use 1-cm grid paper.
   Draw three 12-cm number lines like the one below.

   Use the number lines to order these numbers from greatest to least.
   $2\frac{1}{2}$, $\frac{11}{3}$, $1\frac{5}{6}$

4. Copy and complete. Write >, <, or =.

   a) $\frac{5}{8} \square \frac{7}{16}$ b) $\frac{3}{4} \square \frac{9}{12}$ c) $2\frac{1}{2} \square \frac{9}{2}$

   d) $\frac{13}{10} \square 1\frac{1}{5}$ e) $\frac{29}{5} \square 6\frac{2}{10}$ f) $3\frac{5}{6} \square 3\frac{8}{12}$

5. Order the numbers in each set from least to greatest.
   Show how you did it.

   a) $\frac{7}{6}$, $\frac{15}{12}$, $1\frac{2}{9}$ b) $1\frac{3}{4}$, $\frac{7}{3}$, $\frac{7}{6}$ c) $\frac{7}{4}$, $\frac{15}{10}$, $\frac{11}{5}$ d) $\frac{10}{4}$, $2\frac{1}{3}$, $\frac{9}{2}$

6. Hisa says that $\frac{17}{3}$ is greater than $5\frac{3}{4}$. Is she correct?
   Use pictures, numbers, and words to explain.

7. Hosea has $\frac{7}{2}$ cups of flour.
   Does he have enough flour for a recipe that calls for $4\frac{1}{3}$ cups of flour?
   How do you know?

8. Adriel watched a $1\frac{3}{4}$-h movie on TV.
   Nadir watched 3 half-hour sitcoms.
   Who watched more TV?

9. After a basketball game, the teams had a pizza party.
   The Jets ate $3\frac{1}{2}$ pizzas. The Barracudas ate $\frac{37}{12}$.
   Which team ate more pizza?

10. Amrita, Pan, and Cora baked pies for the fund-raising sale.
    Amrita cut her pies into sixths.
    Pan cut his pies into eighths.
    Cora cut her pies into quarters.
    Amrita sold $\frac{11}{6}$ pies, Pan sold $1\frac{7}{8}$ pies, and Cora sold $\frac{9}{4}$ pies.
    Who sold the most pies? The fewest pies?
    Show how you know.

11. Florence and her friend Rafael build and race model cars.
    Florence's car completed $2\frac{1}{4}$ laps of a track in 1 min.
    Rafael's car completed $\frac{8}{3}$ laps of the track in the same time.
    Whose car was faster? How do you know?

Reflect

Describe 3 ways to compare improper
fractions and mixed numbers.
Use examples to explain.
Which way do you prefer? Why?

Numbers Every Day

Mental Math

Find 5 multiples of each number.
- 4
- 7
- 9
- 11
- 12

Machinist

Think about all the parts used to build something, such as a car or a bicycle. Each part must be produced. Then all the parts are assembled to build the finished product.

A machinist uses tools, such as lathes, milling machines, and machining centres. He produces metal parts with precise dimensions. The machinist reviews drawings or written specifications to calculate the dimensions. Then he carefully plans where to cut or drill to make the part. The dimensions of the parts must be very precise. Sometimes the dimensions of the parts must be accurate to the nearest $\frac{1}{2500}$ mm!

The machinist monitors the temperature of the part as it is produced. Changes in temperature cause metal to expand or contract. This can affect the dimensions of the finished part. The machinist also listens for sounds that indicate there may be a problem, such as a dull cutting tool or too much vibration.

After the part has been made, the machinist carefully measures it and checks his work against the specifications.

Mixed Numbers and Decimals on a Calculator

TECHNOLOGY

You can use a calculator to write a fraction or a mixed number as a decimal.

➤ Write $\frac{9}{8}$ as a decimal.

Recall that a fraction represents division.

Press: 9 ÷ 8 = to display 1.125

➤ Write $1\frac{7}{8}$ as a decimal.

Here are 2 ways to write $1\frac{7}{8}$ as a decimal.

- $1\frac{7}{8}$ means $1 + \frac{7}{8}$.

  First change $\frac{7}{8}$ to a decimal. Press: 7 ÷ 8 = to display 0.875

  Then add 1.

  Press: + 1 = to display 1.875

  $1\frac{7}{8} = 1.875$

- First, change $1\frac{7}{8}$ to an improper fraction.

  One whole is the same as 8 eighths.

  8 eighths + 7 eighths = 15 eighths, or $\frac{15}{8}$

  Then, change $\frac{15}{8}$ to a decimal.

  Press: 15 ÷ 8 = to display 1.875

  $1\frac{7}{8} = 1.875$

Practice

1. Predict what $2\frac{7}{8}$, $3\frac{7}{8}$, and $15\frac{7}{8}$ would be when written as decimals. Check your predictions.

2. a) Write each fraction as a decimal: $\frac{1}{8}$, $\frac{2}{8}$, $\frac{3}{8}$, $\frac{4}{8}$
   b) Look at your answers to part a.
      How much greater is each decimal than the preceding one?
      Use the pattern to predict what $\frac{5}{8}$ and $\frac{6}{8}$ would be
      when written as decimals. Check your predictions.

3. Write each mixed number as a decimal.
   a) $4\frac{1}{5}$ b) $1\frac{3}{4}$ c) $1\frac{17}{20}$ d) $12\frac{1}{2}$ e) $2\frac{9}{10}$

Adding Fractions

Mary and John each ate
2 pieces of pie.
How much did they eat
between them?

Explore

You will need Pattern Blocks and
triangular grid paper.
The yellow hexagon represents one whole.

➤ Estimate the sum of the fractions
in each pair.
Use Pattern Blocks to find each sum.

$$\frac{1}{6} + \frac{2}{6} \qquad\qquad \frac{2}{3} + \frac{2}{3}$$

$$\frac{1}{2} + \frac{3}{6} \qquad\qquad \frac{1}{3} + \frac{1}{2}$$

$$\frac{1}{3} + \frac{4}{6} \qquad\qquad \frac{1}{2} + \frac{4}{6}$$

➤ Use triangular grid paper.
Sketch the blocks you used to find each sum.
Write the sum under each sketch.

Show *and* Share

Share your estimates and solutions with
another pair of students.
What strategies did you use to estimate each sum?
How did you use Pattern Blocks to find each sum?
Which sums can be written in more than one way?
How did you decide which way to write these sums?

Zack and Ronny each bought a small pizza at the Pizzaway Shop.

Zack ate $\frac{3}{4}$ of his pizza and Ronny ate $\frac{7}{8}$ of his.

How much pizza did Zack and Ronny eat together?

Add: $\frac{3}{4} + \frac{7}{8}$

Here is one way to add $\frac{3}{4}$ and $\frac{7}{8}$.

First estimate: $\frac{7}{8}$ is close to 1.

So, $\frac{3}{4} + \frac{7}{8}$ is about $\frac{3}{4} + 1 = 1\frac{3}{4}$.

Since $\frac{7}{8} < 1$, then $\frac{3}{4} + \frac{7}{8}$ is a little less than $1\frac{3}{4}$.

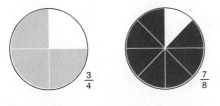

Use Fraction Circles to model $\frac{3}{4}$ and $\frac{7}{8}$.

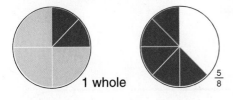

Use eigths to fill the fraction circle for $\frac{3}{4}$.

Take 2 eighths from $\frac{7}{8}$.

Put them with the $\frac{3}{4}$ to make 1 whole.

That leaves 5 eighths.

1 whole

$\frac{5}{8}$

1 whole and 5 eighths equals 1 and 5 eighths.

So, $\frac{3}{4} + \frac{7}{8} = 1\frac{5}{8}$

This is an addition sentence.

$1\frac{5}{8}$ is close to $1\frac{3}{4}$.

So, the answer is reasonable.

Together, Zack and Ronny ate $1\frac{5}{8}$ pizzas.

You may use Pattern Blocks or Fraction Circles.

1. Write an addition sentence for the shaded part of each picture.

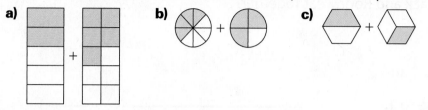

a)   **b)**   **c)**

2. Estimate. Use a number line.
   Is each sum greater than 1 or less than 1?
   How do you know?

   a) $\frac{1}{4} + \frac{2}{4}$ **b)** $\frac{2}{5} + \frac{7}{5}$ **c)** $\frac{3}{4} + \frac{1}{2}$ **d)** $\frac{1}{10} + \frac{3}{4}$

3. Add.

   a) $\frac{2}{3} + \frac{1}{3}$ **b)** $\frac{3}{4} + \frac{2}{4}$ **c)** $\frac{1}{2} + \frac{2}{3}$ **d)** $\frac{5}{6} + \frac{1}{3}$

   e) $\frac{2}{8} + \frac{1}{4}$ **f)** $\frac{2}{3} + \frac{4}{6}$ **g)** $\frac{5}{8} + \frac{3}{4}$ **h)** $\frac{1}{3} + \frac{3}{4}$

Where possible, give your answers in simplest form for questions 4 to 9.

4. Parker eats $\frac{3}{4}$ of a sandwich for lunch
   and $\frac{3}{4}$ of a sandwich after school.
   How many sandwiches does Parker eat in all?
   Use pictures, words, or symbols to explain your answer.

Math Link

Music

Musical notes are named for fractions.
The type of note shows a musician
how long to play the note. In math
two halves make a whole — in music
two half notes make a whole note!

whole note   half note   quarter note   eighth note   sixteenth note

5. Nimmi spends $\frac{1}{2}$ h practising the bassoon each day.
She also spends $\frac{3}{4}$ h practising the guitar.
How much time does Nimmi spend each day
practising her instruments?

6. Leroy's parrot loves oranges.
It eats $\frac{1}{4}$ of an orange with breakfast
and $\frac{3}{4}$ of an orange for lunch.
How much orange does the parrot eat in all?

7. On Saturday, Roberta swam for $\frac{5}{6}$ h in the morning
and for $\frac{1}{2}$ h in the afternoon.
How many hours did Roberta swim that day?

8. How many different ways can you add
$\frac{2}{3} + \frac{5}{6}$?
Draw diagrams to help you explain each way.

9. Each guest at Tai's birthday party brought one gift.
The graph shows the gifts that Tai received.

Tai's Birthday Gifts

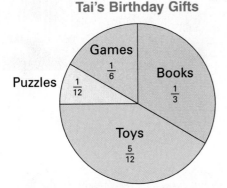

a) What fraction of the gifts were:
  • toys or books?   • puzzles or toys?
  • games or puzzles?   • books or games?

b) Which 2 types of gifts represent $\frac{1}{4}$ of all the gifts?
Explain how you know.

Reflect

Before you add 2 fractions, how can you tell
if their sum is greater than or less than 1?
Use examples in your explanation.

Numbers Every Day

Calculator Skills

Describe 3 ways to find
the quotient of 196 ÷ 4
without using the ÷ key.

Subtracting Fractions

Explore

You will need Fraction Circles.

Use the Fraction Circle pieces to explore ways to subtract the fractions in each pair. Record your work.

$$\frac{5}{8} - \frac{2}{8} \qquad \frac{3}{4} - \frac{1}{4}$$

$$\frac{1}{2} - \frac{1}{4} \qquad \frac{3}{4} - \frac{1}{8}$$

$$\frac{5}{6} - \frac{2}{3} \qquad \frac{2}{3} - \frac{1}{4}$$

Show and Share

Share your solutions with another pair of students.
Show how you used the Fraction Circle pieces
to find the differences.

Connect

Zena and Beth each coloured a spinner.
Zena coloured $\frac{2}{3}$ of her spinner and Beth coloured $\frac{1}{2}$ of hers.
How much more of her spinner did Zena colour than Beth?
Subtract: $\frac{2}{3} - \frac{1}{2}$

Here is one way to find $\frac{2}{3} - \frac{1}{2}$.

- First estimate: $\frac{2}{3}$ is between $\frac{1}{2}$ and 1.
  So, $\frac{2}{3} - \frac{1}{2}$ is less than $\frac{1}{2}$.

```
 +————————————————+————+————————+
 0                1/2  2/3       1
```

Model $\frac{2}{3}$ with
Fraction Circle pieces.

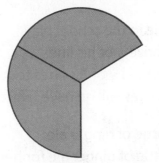

Place the $\frac{1}{2}$ piece over
the $\frac{2}{3}$ piece.

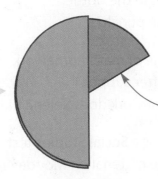

This sector
represents
the difference
of $\frac{2}{3}$ and $\frac{1}{2}$.

Find a Fraction Circle piece
equal to the difference.

The difference is $\frac{1}{6}$.

So, $\frac{2}{3} - \frac{1}{2} = \frac{1}{6}$

Zena coloured $\frac{1}{6}$ more of her spinner than Beth coloured of hers.

Practice

Use Fraction Circles.

1. Estimate. Use a number line.
   Is each difference less than $\frac{1}{2}$ or greater than $\frac{1}{2}$?
   How do you know?
   a) $\frac{5}{6} - \frac{1}{2}$ b) $\frac{7}{8} - \frac{1}{8}$ c) $\frac{4}{6} - \frac{1}{3}$ d) $1 - \frac{5}{6}$

2. Subtract.
   a) $\frac{3}{4} - \frac{2}{4}$ b) $\frac{5}{8} - \frac{3}{8}$ c) $\frac{5}{6} - \frac{1}{3}$ d) $\frac{7}{8} - \frac{3}{4}$
   e) $\frac{3}{4} - \frac{1}{3}$ f) $1 - \frac{1}{3}$ g) $\frac{3}{4} - \frac{2}{3}$ h) $\frac{3}{6} - \frac{1}{3}$

3. Sam has the lead role in the school play.
   He still has to memorize $\frac{1}{2}$ of his lines.
   Suppose Sam memorizes $\frac{1}{3}$ of his lines today.
   What fraction of his lines will he have left to memorize?

4. Freida had $\frac{3}{4}$ of a bottle of ginger ale.
   She needs $\frac{1}{2}$ of a bottle of ginger ale for her fruit punch.
   How much will be left in the bottle
   after Freida makes the punch?

5. Selena had $\frac{3}{4}$ of a page of math homework to do.
   She did $\frac{1}{3}$ of a page after supper.
   How much math homework does Selena have left to do?

6. Ayal is preparing for a Social Studies test.
   He studied $\frac{1}{6}$ of the material on Monday
   and $\frac{1}{2}$ of the material on Tuesday.
   Ayal says he has just $\frac{1}{3}$ of the material left to study.
   Is Ayal correct? How do you know?

7. Suppose Hector practised the violin for $\frac{3}{4}$ h
   and Joanna practised for $\frac{5}{6}$ h.
   a) Who practised more?
   b) What fraction of an hour more?
   Explain how you know.

8. The difference of two fractions is $\frac{1}{3}$.
   a) What might the fractions be?
   b) How many pairs of fractions can you find?

9. The sum of two fractions is $\frac{5}{6}$.
   One of the fractions is $\frac{1}{2}$.
   What is the other fraction?

Numbers Every Day

Numbers Every Day

Find each product.

24×9

12×18

6×36

3×72

Describe any patterns you see.

Reflect

How is subtracting two fractions
the same as adding two fractions?
How is it different?

Fraction Match Up

Your teacher will give you a set of game cards.

The object of the game is to find the most pairs of game cards with equivalent expressions.

➤ Shuffle the game cards.
   Arrange cards, face down, in 4 rows of 5 cards.

➤ Player 1 turns over two cards.
   If the expressions are equivalent, Player 1 keeps the cards.
   If the expressions are not equivalent, turn both cards face down again.

➤ Player 2 has a turn.

➤ Continue to play until all the cards have gone.
   The player with more cards wins.

6 Exploring Percents

What does "9 out of 10 dogs" mean?

Explore

A group of students was planning a trip to Gros Morne National Park in Newfoundland.

The students were surveyed to find out which attraction they would most like to visit.

The table shows the results of the survey.

Attraction	Number of Students
Lobster Cove Head Lighthouse	21
Tablelands Hiking Trail	24
Western Brook Pond Boat Tour	33
Broom Point Fishing Station	22

How many students are in the group? What fraction of the students chose each attraction?

Show and Share

Share your results with another pair of classmates.
How did you find the number of students in the group?
How else could you name each fraction?
What fraction of the students did not choose the boat tour?
Explain.

This hundredths grid has 100 small squares.
The grid represents 1 whole.

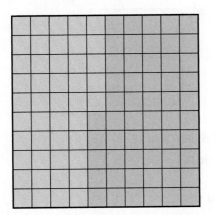

Each square represents $\frac{1}{100}$ of the grid.
Forty-five squares are green.
Fifty-five squares are blue.

Here are 4 ways to describe the green part of the grid.

➤ Compare the number of green squares to the
   total number of squares:
   45 out of 100 squares are green.

➤ Write a fraction.
   $\frac{45}{100}$ of the grid is green.

➤ Write a decimal.
   0.45 of the grid is green.

➤ Write a **percent**. Use the percent symbol, %.
   45% of the grid is green.

Here are 4 ways to describe the blue part
of the grid.

➤ Compare the number of blue squares to the
   total number of squares:
   55 out of 100 squares are blue.

➤ Write a fraction.
   $\frac{55}{100}$ of the grid is blue.

➤ Write a decimal.
   0.55 of the grid is blue.

➤ Write a percent.
   55% of the grid is blue.

You read 45% as 45 percent.
Percent means "per hundred"
or "out of 100."

1. Write a fraction with hundredths, a decimal, and a percent to name the shaded part of each grid.

    a)   **b)**   **c)**

2. Write a fraction with hundredths, a decimal, and a percent to name the unshaded part of each grid in question 1.

3. For each grid in question 1, add the percents you used to name the shaded and unshaded parts.
   What do you notice? Why do you think this happens?

4. Estimate the percent of each grid that is shaded.
   Then count the squares to check.

    a)   **b)**   **c)**

5. Colour a hundredths grid to show each percent.
   Then write each percent as a decimal.

    a) 84%   **b)** 17%   **c)** 25%   **d)** 100%

6. **a)** Use a hundredths grid. Colour 20% red,
       13% blue, 32% green, and 23% yellow.
   b) Write a fraction to describe the part
       of the grid that is each colour.
   c) Write a decimal and a percent to describe
       the part of the grid that is not coloured.

7. **a)** Use a hundredths grid.
       Choose a different colour for each
       attraction in *Explore*.
       Colour a section of the grid to show the
       number of students who chose that attraction.
   b) Write a percent to describe each section
       of the grid in part a.

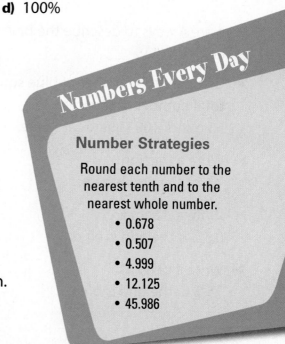

Numbers Every Day

Number Strategies

Round each number to the
nearest tenth and to the
nearest whole number.
   • 0.678
   • 0.507
   • 4.999
   • 12.125
   • 45.986

8. Write as a percent. Then write as a decimal.

    a) 64 out of 100   **b)** $\frac{50}{100}$ **c)** 1 out of 100   **d)** $\frac{17}{100}$

9. Write each percent as a fraction with hundredths. Then write as a decimal.

    a) 13%   **b)** 5%   **c)** 79%   **d)** 64%

10. Ninety-seven percent of Earth's water is salt water.
What percent is fresh water?
How do you know?

11. The graph shows the water contents of some foods.

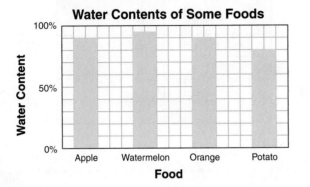

Water Contents of Some Foods

    a) About what percent of each food is water?

    b) About what percent of each food is not water?

    c) Write each percent in the graph as a fraction.

12. Janette bought a portable CD player on sale.
The regular price was $100. She was charged $89.

    a) What percent of the regular price did Janette pay?

    b) What percent of the regular price did she receive as a discount?

13. Salvo said that of the 100 students in the choir,
62% are girls and 48% are boys.
Is this possible?
How do you know?

At Home

Reflect

What does percent mean?
Use words and pictures
to explain.

Percents are often used to describe
discounts. Look through some flyers
your family receives in the mail.
List 3 different percents you see
offered as discounts. Order the
percents from greatest to least.
Which is the best discount?

Relating Fractions, Decimals, and Percents

This is a floor plan for a daycare centre. How can you describe each part of the floor plan?

Quiet Room		Washrooms	Storage
Hallway			Office
		Kitchen	
Play Room			
		Lunch Room	

Explore

You will need a 10-cm by 10-cm grid.

➤ Design a floor plan for an apartment unit. Your plan should include:
  • 2 bedrooms
  • a kitchen and dining area
  • a living room
  • a bathroom
  • a laundry room

The living room should be the largest space.
The kitchen and dining area should be L-shaped.
One bedroom should be larger than the other.
The laundry room should be the smallest space.

➤ Describe each part of your floor plan as a fraction, a decimal, and a percent.

> Because of place value, I know I can write a fraction like $\frac{15}{100}$ as 15 hundredths, or 0.15.

Show *and* Share

Share your floor plan with another pair of students.
How are your floor plans alike? How are they different?
Compare the strategies you used to describe each part of the plan 3 ways.

➤ Fractions, decimals, and percents are 3 ways to describe parts of one whole.

A fraction can be written as a decimal or a percent.
A decimal can be written as a fraction or a percent.
A percent can be written as a fraction or a decimal.

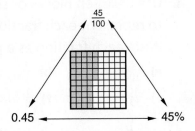

$\frac{45}{100}$

0.45 ⟷ 45%

You can use a percent to describe any part of one whole.

➤ What percent of this figure is shaded?

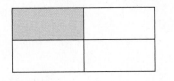

$\frac{1}{4}$ of the figure is shaded.

Think: Percent means "out of 100," so we need to write an equivalent fraction with hundredths.

$$\overset{\times 25}{\frac{1}{4}} = \underset{\times 25}{\frac{25}{100}} = 25\%$$

$\frac{25}{100}$ is the same as 0.25. So, 0.25 of the figure is shaded.

25% of the figure is shaded.

➤ What percent of these counters are yellow?

$\frac{6}{12}$, or $\frac{1}{2}$ of the counters are yellow.

Write an equivalent fraction with hundredths.

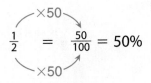

$$\overset{\times 50}{\frac{1}{2}} = \underset{\times 50}{\frac{50}{100}} = 50\%$$

$\frac{50}{100}$ is the same as 0.50. So, 0.50 of the counters are yellow.

50% of the counters are yellow.

1. Use Base Ten Blocks or shade a hundredths grid
    to represent each fraction.
    Write each fraction as a percent and as a decimal.
    a) $\frac{6}{100}$ **b)** $\frac{81}{100}$ **c)** $\frac{17}{50}$ **d)** $\frac{3}{10}$
    e) $\frac{1}{50}$ **f)** $\frac{1}{5}$ **g)** $\frac{7}{20}$ **h)** $\frac{3}{4}$

2. Use Base Ten Blocks or shade a hundredths grid
    to represent each decimal.
    Write each decimal as a fraction and as a percent.
    Write each fraction in simplest form.
    a) 0.97   **b)** 0.03   **c)** 0.16   **d)** 0.5

3. Use Base Ten Blocks or shade a hundredths grid
    to represent each percent.
    Write each percent as a fraction and as a decimal.
    Write each fraction in simplest form.
    a) 14%   **b)** 99%   **c)** 25%   **d)** 40%

4. What percent of each whole is shaded?
    How do you know?
    a)   **b)**   **c)**

5. What percent of each set is shaded?
    How do you know?
    a)   **b)**   **c)**

6. Is each fraction greater than or less than 50%?
    Explain how you know.
    a) $\frac{7}{10}$ **b)** $\frac{3}{4}$ **c)** $\frac{11}{25}$ **d)** $\frac{6}{6}$

7. Luis used a calculator to find a decimal
    and a percent equal to $\frac{1}{4}$.
    How might Luis have done this?

314

8. Use the data in the table.
   Is each statement true or false?
   Explain how you know.
   a) More than 50% of the audience were adults
      or seniors.
   b) Of the audience, $\frac{58}{100}$ were children or teens.
   c) More than $\frac{1}{4}$ of the audience were adults.
   d) Less than 0.5 of the audience were
      teens or adults.

Members of the Audience

Age Group	Percent
Children	13%
Teens	45%
Adults	34%
Seniors	8%

9. Monica made this object from Snap Cubes.
   Monica made 9 more objects just like this one.
   She laid them one next to the other
   to form a square.
   Monica said she could use the square
   to write a percent and a decimal for $\frac{6}{10}$
   and for $\frac{4}{10}$. Is she correct?
   Explain.

10. Ravi got 18 out of 20 on a math quiz.
    Karli got 85% on the quiz.
    Whose mark was greater? Explain.

11. Which is least? Which is greatest?
    How do you know?
    10% $\frac{1}{10}$ 0.01

12. Write a percent that represents:
    a) a very little of something
    b) almost all of something
    c) a little more than $\frac{3}{4}$ of something
    d) between 0.25 and 0.50 of something
    How did you choose each percent?

Reflect

How are fractions, decimals, and percents alike?
How are they different?
Use examples in your explanations.

Numbers Every Day

Number Strategies

List all the prime factors of
each number.

- 1000
- 64
- 72
- 18

Estimating and Finding a Percent

Which number best represents
the shaded part of this figure:
$\frac{1}{4}$, $\frac{3}{10}$, $\frac{2}{5}$, $\frac{1}{2}$, $\frac{3}{5}$, $\frac{3}{4}$, or 1?

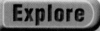

You will need a transparency of a Fraction Circle with tenths.
Your teacher will give you a large copy of these circles.

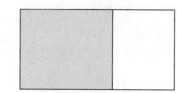

➤ Estimate the percent of each circle that is shaded.
Record your estimates.
Place the transparency over each circle
to check your estimates.

Favourite Sports

➤ Eighty students were surveyed
about their favourite sport to play.
The results are shown in the circle graph.
Estimate the percent of students
who said hockey was their favourite.

Hockey

Baseball

Basketball

Soccer

Show *and* Share

Share your results with another pair of
students. Use the percents to estimate the
number of students who chose each sport.
How do you know your answers
are reasonable?

You can use the relationships among fractions, decimals, and percents to solve percent problems.

➤ Sylvie has a collection of 197 sports bobbleheads. About 25% of them are hockey players. Estimate the number of bobbleheads that are hockey players.

PRONGER

Round 197 to 200.
Find 25% of 200.

$25\% = \frac{25}{100}$

Find an equivalent fraction with denominator 200.

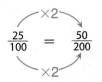

$$\frac{25}{100} = \frac{50}{200}$$

So, 25% of 200 = 50
25% of 197 is about 50.

About 50 of the bobbleheads are hockey players.

➤ Of the 30 students in Larry's class, 14 of them take the school bus. Estimate the percent of the students who take the school bus.

15 is $\frac{1}{2}$ of 30.
So, 14 is almost $\frac{1}{2}$ of 30.

Think: Percent means "out of 100."
So, find an equivalent fraction with denominator 100.

$$\frac{1}{2} = \frac{50}{100}, \text{ or } 50\%$$

Almost 50% of the students take the school bus.

➤ Jacy earned $150 shovelling snow.
He used 40% of his money to buy a CD player.
How much did the CD player cost?

The CD player cost 40% of $150.
Here are 2 ways to find 40% of $150.

$40\% = \frac{40}{100}$, or $\frac{4}{10}$
To find $\frac{4}{10}$ of 150, find an equivalent
fraction with denominator 150.

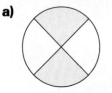

$$\frac{4}{10} = \frac{60}{150}$$

So, 40% of 150 = 60
The CD player cost $60.

$40\% = \frac{40}{100}$, or $\frac{4}{10}$
$\frac{1}{10}$ of $150 = \frac{150}{10} = 15$
So, $\frac{4}{10}$ of $150 = 4 \times 15$
$$= 60$$
The CD player cost $60.

Practice

1. Estimate the percent of each figure that is shaded.
   Show how you did it.

   a) 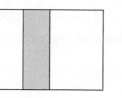   b)   c)

2. a) What percent of the counters are green?
   b) What percent are yellow?

3. Estimate.
   a) 9% of 80   b) 51% of 140   c) 19% of 75
   d) 10% of 62   e) 75% of 104   f) 25% of 47

4. Find each amount.
   a) 50% of 20   b) 25% of 60   c) 10% of 80
   d) 75% of 200   e) 50% of 400   f) 25% of $8

318

5. Tabitha did a survey.
She found that 6 out of her 23 classmates take music lessons.

a) Estimate the percent of Tabitha's classmates
who take music lessons.
Explain your estimation strategy.

b) Estimate the percent who do not take music lessons.

6. Shania wrote a multiple choice test with 24 questions.
How many questions does she need to answer correctly
to score 75%?
Explain how you know.

7. Mayumi had 60 sports cards.
She gave 30% of them to Charlie.
How many cards does Mayumi have left?

8. Ramon's hockey team scored 12 goals.
Ramon scored 25% of the goals.
How many goals did Ramon score?

9. Abeni received $50 for her birthday.
She spent 30% of the money on a CD.
Does she have enough money left to buy a computer game
that costs $30 including tax? How do you know?

10. Ten percent of 300 is 30.
How could you find 90% of 300?

11. **a)** Josef got 45 out of 100 on a math quiz.
What percent is that?

b) Josef got 80% on a true/false science quiz.
He got 20 questions right.
How many questions were on the test?

Numbers Every Day

Mental Math

Use the multiplication fact
25 × 25 = 625 to help you
find each product.

- 26 × 25
- 25 × 27
- 24 × 26
- 25 × 50

Reflect

Create your own problem that involves a percent.
Solve the problem. Show your work.

Exploring Ratios

On her bird-watching expedition, Cassie spotted 6 yellow-bellied sapsuckers and 3 Baltimore orioles sitting on a fence.

Here are some ways Cassie compared the birds she saw.
- The number of sapsuckers compared to the number of orioles:
  6 sapsuckers to 3 orioles
- The number of sapsuckers compared to the number of birds:
  6 sapsuckers to 9 birds

Cassie could also have compared the birds using fractions.
What fraction of the birds were sapsuckers? Orioles?

Explore

You will need twelve 2-colour counters and a paper cup.

➤ Put twelve 2-colour counters in the cup. Shake the cup and spill the counters onto the table.
➤ Compare the counters in as many ways as you can. Record each comparison.

Show *and* Share

Share your results with another pair of students. In which result did you compare one part of the set to another part of the set? In which result did you compare one part of the set to the whole set?

The number of red counters compared to the total number of counters is 7 to 12.

Mahit has 4 brown rabbits and 5 white rabbits.

A **ratio** is a comparison of 2 quantities with the same unit.

➤ You can use ratios to compare the numbers of brown and white rabbits.

The ratio of brown rabbits to white rabbits is 4 to 5.
The ratio 4 to 5 is written as 4:5.

The ratio of white rabbits to brown rabbits is 5 to 4, or 5:4.

white rabbits to brown rabbits:

5 to 4 or 5:4

These are part-to-part ratios.

The numbers 4 and 5 are the **terms of the ratio**.
Order is important in a ratio.
5 to 4 is not the same as 4 to 5.

➤ You can also compare the parts to the whole.
Here are some other ratios you can use to compare the rabbits:

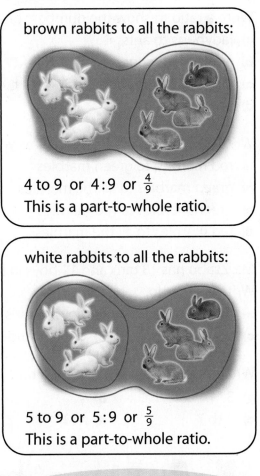

brown rabbits to all the rabbits:

4 to 9 or 4:9 or $\frac{4}{9}$
This is a part-to-whole ratio.

white rabbits to all the rabbits:

5 to 9 or 5:9 or $\frac{5}{9}$
This is a part-to-whole ratio.

A ratio that compares
a part of a set to the whole set is a fraction.
When we read a ratio like $\frac{4}{9}$,
we say "four to nine."

1. Write each ratio 2 ways.
   a) apples to pears

   b) caps to scarves

   c) roses to daisies

2. Write a ratio to show the numbers of:
   a) ladybugs to ants
   b) ants to ladybugs
   c) ladybugs to insects
   d) ants to insects

3. Write each ratio in as many ways as you can.
   a) red marbles to green marbles
   b) green marbles to all the marbles
   c) green marbles to red marbles
   d) red marbles to all the marbles

4. Ms. Zsabo has 13 girls and 11 boys in her class. Write each ratio.
   a) girls to boys   b) boys to girls
   c) boys to students   d) girls to students

5. What is being compared in each ratio?
   a) 3 : 4   b) $\frac{4}{7}$
   c) 3 to 7   d) 4 : 3

6. Draw 2 diagrams to illustrate the ratio 3 : 5.
Explain each diagram.

7. Write 4 different ratios for this picture.
Explain what each ratio compares.

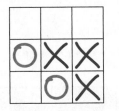

8. Write a ratio to show the numbers of:
   a) triangles to squares
   b) squares to rectangles
   c) triangles to all figures
   d) red figures to yellow figures
   e) yellow triangles to yellow rectangles
   f) red triangles to yellow squares

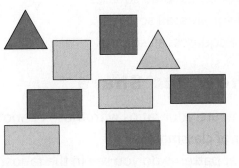

9. Write as many ratios as you can for the trail mix recipe.
Explain what each ratio compares.

TRAIL MIX
1 scoop raisins

3 scoops nuts

2 scoops dried papaya

1 scoop sunflower seeds

10. Describe how you would find the ratio of students
to teachers in your school.

Numbers Every Day

Calculator Skills

Find two numbers with a
sum of 12.2 and a product
of 34.65.

Reflect

Name the two types of ratios.
Give an example of each type.
Draw diagrams to illustrate your examples.

10

Equivalent Ratios

Explore

How many different ways can you write each ratio?

red squares : blue squares
red squares : all squares
blue squares : all squares

Show *and* Share

Compare your ratios with those of another
pair of classmates.
What patterns do you see in the ratios?
Try to write more ratios that extend each pattern.

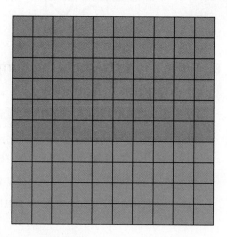

Connect

Kim is planting a border in her garden.
She plants 5 marigolds for every 3 geraniums.
The ratio of marigolds to geraniums is 5 : 3.

How many geraniums would Kim plant for each number of marigolds?

    10   15   20

In each case, what is the ratio of marigolds to geraniums?

Here are 2 ways to solve the problem.

➤ You can use Colour Tiles to represent the plants.
  Use yellow tiles to represent marigolds.
  Use red tiles to represent geraniums.

  • Start with 10 yellow tiles.

  Think: For every 5 yellow tiles, you need 3 red tiles.
          Arrange your yellow tiles into groups of 5 tiles.
          You can make 2 groups.
          So, you need 2 groups of 3 red tiles.

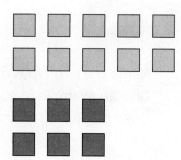

That makes a total of 6 red tiles.
These represent 6 geraniums.
The ratio of marigolds to geraniums is 10:6.

- Add a group of 5 yellow tiles.
  You now have 15 yellow tiles.
  Add another group of 3 red tiles.
  You now have 9 red tiles.
  These represent 9 geraniums.
  The ratio of marigolds to geraniums is 15:9.

- Add a group of 5 yellow tiles.
  You now have 20 yellow tiles.
  Add another group of 3 red tiles.
  You now have 12 red tiles.
  These represent 12 geraniums.
  The ratio of marigolds to geraniums is 20:12.

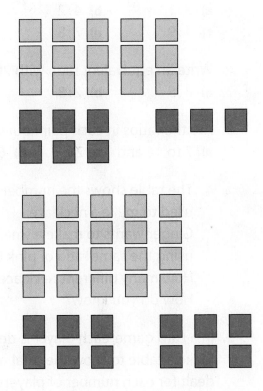

➤ You can use a table and patterns to find the ratios.

There are 5 marigolds for every 3 geraniums.

To get 10 marigolds, multiply 5 marigolds by 2.
So, multiply 3 geraniums by 2 to get 6 geraniums.

To get 15 marigolds, multiply 5 marigolds by 3.
So, multiply 3 geraniums by 3 to get 9 geraniums.

To get 20 marigolds, multiply 5 marigolds by 4.
So, multiply 3 geraniums by 4 to get 12 geraniums.

Kim plants: 10 marigolds with 6 geraniums
15 marigolds with 9 geraniums
20 marigolds with 12 geraniums

The ratios of marigolds to geraniums are:
10:6, 15:9, and 20:12
Each ratio is equal to 5:3.
Because the ratios are equal, we say that
5:3, 10:6, 15:9, and 20:12 are **equivalent ratios**.

Marigolds	Geraniums	Ratio
5	3	5:3
10	6	10:6
15	9	15:9
20	12	20:12

The numbers in the Marigolds column are multiples of 5. The numbers in the Geraniums column are multiples of 3.

1. Write 2 equivalent ratios for each ratio.
   a) 3:1   b) 4:2   c) 1:2   d) 5:6   e) 3:5
   f) 4:9   g) 7:8   h) 10:6   i) 1:1   j) 2:5

2. Write an equivalent ratio with 20 as one of the terms.
   a) 4:5   b) 2:8   c) 7:4   d) 10:3

3. Are the ratios in each pair equivalent? Explain how you know.
   a) 7 to 14 and 1 to 2   b) 6:9 and 3:2   c) 1 to 10 and 4 to 40

4. The table shows the number of beads
   used to make a necklace.
   Ginger wants to make a smaller necklace
   using the same ratio of pink to white beads.
   How many different necklaces could Ginger make?
   How do you know?

Colour	Number
Pink	30
White	35

5. In a card game, each player is dealt 5 cards.
   Make a table to show the total number of cards
   dealt for each number of players from 3 to 6.
   Write each ratio of players to cards dealt.

Total Number of Cards Dealt	Number of Players

6. The ratio of players to soccer balls at practice sessions is 5:2.
   How many soccer balls are needed for 20 players?

7. Ms. Olivieri's class plays a game in teams.
   Each team has the same number of students.
   The ratio of teams to players is 8:32.
   a) How many students are in Ms. Olivieri's class?
   b) How many students are on each team?

8. The word "fun" has a vowel to consonant ratio of 1:2.
   a) Find 3 words with a vowel to consonant ratio of 2:3.
   b) Choose a vowel to consonant ratio and find 3 words for it.

9. Chef Blanc uses 4 parts of oil for every 3 parts of vinegar
   to make a salad dressing.
   Suppose he uses 12 parts of oil.
   How many parts of vinegar will he use?

10. Su Mei's recipe for bean salad calls for 3 cans of lima beans,
    2 cans of pinto beans, and 1 can of kidney beans.
    Su Mei is making bean salad for her family reunion.
    Suppose she uses 9 cans of lima beans.
    a) How many cans of pinto beans will she use?
    b) How many cans of kidney beans will she use?

11. Katherine has diabetes.
    At each meal, she must estimate the mass in grams
    of carbohydrates she plans to eat and inject
    the appropriate amount of insulin.
    Katherine needs 1 unit of insulin for
    15 g of carbohydrates.
    Katherine's lunch has 60 g of carbohydrates.
    How many units of insulin should Katherine inject?

12. To make a jug of instant iced tea, Malaika uses
    6 cups of water and 3 scoops of iced tea powder.
    Bart uses 8 cups of water and 5 scoops of powder.
    Will Malaika's and Bart's iced tea have the same strength?
    Explain.

13. List all the ratios that are equivalent to 2 : 3
    and have a second term that is less than 40.
    Explain how you did it.

Reflect

Write two ratios that are equivalent.
Explain how you know they are equivalent.
Write two ratios that are not equivalent.
Explain how you know they are not equivalent.

Exploring Rates

How fast is the car travelling?
At this speed, how far will
the car travel in half an hour?
In 2 h?
What does the highway sign mean?

Explore

You will need a clock or a watch with a second hand.

How many triangles do you think
you can draw in 1 min?
Have your partner time 1 min as you
draw as many triangles as you can.
Count the triangles.
Switch roles. Time 1 min as
your partner draws triangles.
Compare your results.

Based on your results, about
how many triangles could
you draw in 2 min? In 3 min?
In 30 s?

Show and Share

Share your results with another pair of students.
How did you estimate how many triangles
you could draw in 2 min? In 3 min? In 30 s?
What assumptions did you make?
How many triangles could you draw in 1 h? Explain.

Ramona drew 52 stars in 1 min.
We say that Ramona's rate of drawing stars is
52 stars per minute.
We write this as *52 stars/min.*

Here are some other rates.
- A tortoise travels 0.2 km/h.
- The pretzel-making machine
  makes 8 bags of pretzels/min.
- Todd paid $0.87/L for gas.
- My cactus grows 1.5 cm/year.

> The word "per"
> means "for every"
> or "in every."

> A **rate** is a ratio that compares
> two items measured in different units.
> The speed of the tortoise compares
> a distance in kilometres to
> a time in hours.

You can use pictures, tables, and graphs
to solve rate problems.

➤ Juan typed 9 pages in 3 h.
At this rate, how many pages could Juan type in 5 h?

Draw a picture.
Juan types 9 pages in 3 h.
In 1 h, he types $\frac{9}{3}$, or 3 pages.
His rate of typing is 3 pages/h.

1 h   1 h   1 h

So, in 5 h, Juan types 5 × 3, or 15 pages.

➤ A killer whale travels at an average speed of 50 km/h.
How far does it travel in 5 h?

Draw a graph.
Plot points to represent the distance
travelled in each time.
100 km in 2 h, 200 km in 4 h, 300 km in 6 h
Then, draw a line from the origin
through the points.

On the graph, draw a vertical line through 5 h.
Then draw a horizontal line from the graph
to the *Distance* axis.
This line meets the axis at 250 km.

So, the whale travels 250 km in 5 h.

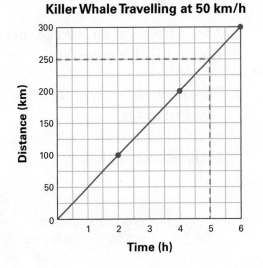

Killer Whale Travelling at 50 km/h

➤ Ainsley paid $0.95/min to make a long distance telephone call to her aunt in Scotland.
Ainsley's bill was $11.40. How long did they talk?

 Make a table.
Each minute cost $0.95.
Keep adding $0.95 for every minute.
Extend the table until you get to $11.40.

Time (min)	1	2	3	4	5	6	7	8	9	10	11	12
Cost	$0.95	$1.90	$2.85	$3.80	$4.75	$5.70	$6.65	$7.60	$8.55	$9.50	$10.45	$11.40

Ainsley and her aunt talked for 12 min.

 **Practice**

1. Write each amount as a rate.
   a) A fast reader can read 500 words every minute.
   b) Min did 13 chin-ups in 1 min.
   c) A cheetah can run 70 km in 1 h.
   d) When fighting a fire, a fire truck uses about 200 L of water every minute.

2. Mira rode her bicycle 20 km in 2 h.
   At that rate, how far did Mira ride each hour? Each half hour?

3. Jasper made 4 bracelets in 1 h.
   At this rate, how long would it take him to make 20 bracelets?

4. A train travels at an average speed of 80 km/h.
   How long will it take the train to travel 320 km?

5. This graph shows how far a hurricane travelled in 4 h.
   What was the hurricane's average speed in kilometres per hour?

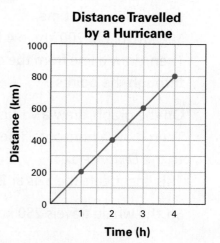

Distance Travelled by a Hurricane

This graph and the graph on page 329 are **continuous line graphs**.

330

6. Naja was paid $40 for 5 h of work.
How much would she earn if she worked for 8 h?

7. Gas costs $0.89/L.
Ali pays $18.69 to fill his gas tank.
Use a table.
How many litres of gas did Ali buy?

8. Kari checked her pulse and counted 21 beats in 15 s.
Draw a graph. At that rate, how many beats would
Kari have counted in each time?

a) 30 s   **b)** 45 s   **c)** 1 min

9. A snail travels 12 m in 2 h.
At that rate, how long will it take the snail to travel 18 m?

10. Ken has 90 min of basketball practice every 3 days.
  a) How many minutes of practice would
  Ken have in 6 days?
  b) How many days would it take for Ken to put in
  6 h of practice?
  c) Can you assume that Ken has 30 min of practice
  every day? Explain.

11. Jacinthe does 60 chin-ups in 5 min.
Jamar does 20 chin-ups in 2 min.
Which person does more chin-ups every minute?
How do you know?

12. Express each bird's average speed in kilometres per hour.
  a) An eagle flies 90 km in 2 h.
  b) An owl flies 19 km in half an hour.
  c) A spur-winged goose flies 9 km in 10 min.

Reflect

Give 3 examples of rates.
Explain what each rate means and tell
when it would be used.

Numbers Every Day

Number Strategies

Replace □ with a number so
the sum is divisible by 5 and
by 11.

3 + 7 + 17 + 10 + □

How did you choose
the number?

Strategies Toolkit

Explore

Take turns to choose the answer for one question.
Think aloud as you decide on the answer
so your partner hears your thinking.

> Andrea has these coins:
> 15 pennies, 12 dimes, and 8 nickels
>
> 1. What fraction of the coins are dimes?
>   a) $\frac{12}{20}$ b) $\frac{12}{35}$
>   c) $\frac{6}{17}$ d) $\frac{12}{27}$
>
> 2. What is the ratio of pennies to dimes?
>   a) $15:8$ b) $5:4$
>   c) $12:15$ d) $3:7$

Show and Share

Share your work with another pair of students.
What strategies did you use to choose your answer?

Connect

Here are some strategies you can use to select
the answer for a multiple-choice question.

Before you start

☑ Make sure you understand
what you are supposed to do.
Is it okay to guess?
Is there only one correct answer?
Where should you record your answer?

**Strategies
for Success**

- Get unstuck.
- Check and reflect.
- Focus on the problem.
- Represent your thinking.
- Select an answer.
- Do your best on a test.
- Explain your answer.

For each question

☑ Read the question carefully.
Underline the key words.

☑ Draw a sketch or make a calculation
if it helps.

☑ Before you look at the choices,
try to answer the question.

☑ Read *all* the choices.

☑ Which choice is closest to your answer?
That is probably the correct answer.

☑ If you have trouble deciding, go back
and read each choice again.

• Cross out any choices you know
are not correct.

• If two choices appear to be the same,
identify any differences.

Organizing your time and checking

☑ Leave questions that you
cannot figure out until the end.

☑ If it is okay to guess,
make your best guess.

☑ Read all the questions
and your choices.
Check you have
not missed
any questions.

Practice

1. Where would you place the fraction $\frac{3}{5}$ on this number line?

```
|----+----+----+----+----+----|
0    a    b   1/2   c    d    1
```

2. Write a multiple-choice question about fractions, ratios, or percents
on one side of an index card. Write the answer on the other side.
Trade questions with a classmate. Answer your classmate's question.

Reflect

What is your favourite strategy for answering multiple-choice
questions? Explain how you would answer the questions.

LESSON

1

1. Write 3 equivalent fractions for each fraction.

   a) $\frac{3}{4}$ **b)** $\frac{3}{7}$ **c)** $\frac{18}{27}$ **d)** $\frac{20}{80}$

2. Write each fraction in simplest form.

   a) $\frac{16}{32}$ **b)** $\frac{15}{20}$ **c)** $\frac{18}{45}$ **d)** $\frac{15}{50}$

2

3. Write each mixed number as an improper fraction.

   a) $3\frac{1}{4}$ **b)** $7\frac{2}{3}$ **c)** $4\frac{1}{2}$ **d)** $2\frac{7}{8}$

4. Write each improper fraction as a mixed number.

   a) $\frac{14}{5}$ **b)** $\frac{17}{8}$ **c)** $\frac{11}{3}$ **d)** $\frac{15}{6}$

1
2

5. A class ordered four 12-slice pizzas for lunch.
   The students ate 40 slices.
   a) Write an improper fraction and a mixed number
   for the number of pizzas the students ate.
   b) Write a fraction in simplest form for how many pizzas
   were left over.

3

6. Copy and complete. Use >, <, or =.

   a) $\frac{3}{2} \square 1\frac{1}{2}$ **b)** $\frac{8}{5} \square 1\frac{7}{10}$ **c)** $\frac{25}{8} \square 2\frac{3}{4}$

7. Order from least to greatest.
   Show your work.

   a) $\frac{9}{2}, 2\frac{1}{6}, \frac{7}{3}$ **b)** $\frac{7}{2}, 3\frac{1}{4}, \frac{15}{4}$ **c)** $\frac{35}{20}, 1\frac{1}{4}, \frac{15}{10}$

4
5

8. Use Pattern Blocks.
   Hanu mixed $\frac{1}{2}$ cup of pineapple juice and $\frac{1}{3}$ cup of soda water
   to make a fruit drink.
   a) How much drink did Hanu make?
   b) Hanu wants to add some orange juice so that he will have 1 cup.
   How much orange juice should Hanu add?

5

9. Use Pattern Blocks.
   The sum of two fractions is $\frac{2}{3}$.
   One fraction is $\frac{1}{2}$.
   What is the other fraction?

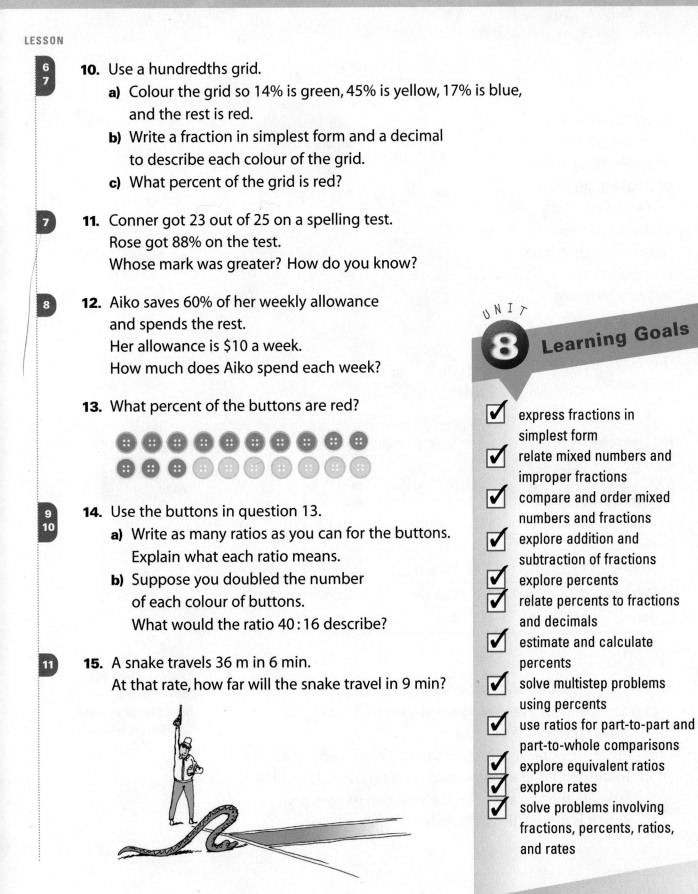

6
7

10. Use a hundredths grid.

a) Colour the grid so 14% is green, 45% is yellow, 17% is blue, and the rest is red.

b) Write a fraction in simplest form and a decimal to describe each colour of the grid.

c) What percent of the grid is red?

7

11. Conner got 23 out of 25 on a spelling test.
Rose got 88% on the test.
Whose mark was greater? How do you know?

8

12. Aiko saves 60% of her weekly allowance and spends the rest.
Her allowance is $10 a week.
How much does Aiko spend each week?

13. What percent of the buttons are red?

9
10

14. Use the buttons in question 13.

a) Write as many ratios as you can for the buttons. Explain what each ratio means.

b) Suppose you doubled the number of each colour of buttons.
What would the ratio 40 : 16 describe?

11

15. A snake travels 36 m in 6 min.
At that rate, how far will the snake travel in 9 min?

UNIT

8 Learning Goals

☑ express fractions in simplest form
☑ relate mixed numbers and improper fractions
☑ compare and order mixed numbers and fractions
☑ explore addition and subtraction of fractions
☑ explore percents
☑ relate percents to fractions and decimals
☑ estimate and calculate percents
☑ solve multistep problems using percents
☑ use ratios for part-to-part and part-to-whole comparisons
☑ explore equivalent ratios
☑ explore rates
☑ solve problems involving fractions, percents, ratios, and rates

Robert's favourite breakfast is a scrambled egg, a slice of whole-grain toast, and a 250-mL glass of chocolate milk. Here is some nutrition information about Robert's breakfast. The percents are the percents of the recommended daily values.

Eggs Nutrition facts Per 1 large egg (50 g)
Calories 70
Fat.........................5 g
Protein....................6 g
Calcium 2%
Iron 2%

Bread Nutrition facts Per 2 slices (90 g)
Calories 210
Fat ....2.5 g
Protein....................8 g
Calcium 0%
Iron 15%

Chocolate Milk Nutrition facts Per 250 mL
Calories 160
Fat ....2.8 g
Protein ....8.6 g
Calcium 27%

1. Every day, children and teens need to eat about 1 g of protein for every kilogram of their body mass.
   a) Robert has a mass of 45 kg.
      How many grams of protein should he eat each day?
   b) To the nearest gram, how much protein is in this breakfast?
      Estimate the percent of his daily protein requirement
      Robert is getting in this breakfast.

> Notice that the information about the bread is for 2 slices, but Robert eats only 1 slice.

2. **a)** Find the total number of calories in Robert's breakfast.

   b) To the nearest gram, how much fat is in Robert's favourite breakfast?

   c) Each gram of fat contains about 9 calories. About how many calories in this breakfast come from fat?

   d) Nutritionists recommend that no more than $\frac{1}{3}$ of the calories we eat should come from fat. Does Robert's breakfast fall within this healthy limit?

3. The daily calcium requirement used to calculate the percents on labels is 1100 mg.

   a) What is the total percent of calcium in Robert's breakfast?

   b) About how much calcium is in his breakfast?

4. The daily iron requirement used to calculate the percents on labels is 14 mg.

   a) What is the total percent of iron in Robert's breakfast?

   b) About how much iron is in his breakfast?

5. Choose a typical breakfast you enjoy eating. Describe it, remembering to include your serving sizes. Copy the information about calories, fat, protein, calcium, and iron in each serving from the nutrition labels for each product. Complete questions 1 to 4 for your breakfast. Do you think your breakfast is healthy? Explain.

Reflect on the Unit

How are fractions, decimals, and percents related? Use examples in your explanation.

Unit

1. A recursive pattern has 2 and 5 as the first 2 terms.
What might the pattern be? Give three different answers.

2. Solve each expression. Explain why the answers are different.
   a) $15 + 6 \div 3$ **b)** $(15 + 6) \div 3$

3. Magazines are packed into cartons for distribution.
Each hour one person can pack 45 cartons.
How many people are needed to pack 1200 cartons each hour?

4. a) Use linking cubes to build the object shown in this net.
   b) Draw the object on triangular dot paper.
   c) Draw the front, top, and side views of the object.

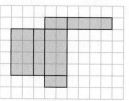

5. Find each product or quotient.
Round each answer to the nearest thousandth if necessary.
   a) $7.5 \div 5$ **b)** 48×0.001 **c)** $24.31 \div 10$
   d) 5.603×3 **e)** 29×0.01 **f)** $0.078 \div 4$

6. The table shows Canadian trout production in 2002.

Province	ON	NL	SK	QC	NB	NS	BC	MB
Mass (t)	4650	1600	914	850	550	434	100	16

   a) Find the mean, the median, and the mode masses of trout produced.
   b) Which average best represents these numbers? Explain.

7. Nishaant recorded the forecast high temperature and
the actual high temperature in degrees Celsius on
the first day of each month for 8 months.
   a) Draw a scatter plot of the data.
   b) Is there a trend in the graph? Explain.

Forecast High (°C)	10	9	13	15	17	17	22	23
Actual High (°C)	8	12	10	14	17	20	21	25

8. A rectangular box has length 25 cm, width 22 cm, and height 16 cm.
   a) What is the volume of the box?
   b) What is the surface area of the box?

338

9. Use 1-cm grid paper.
Draw a quadrilateral. Label it ABCD.
Draw a quadrilateral similar to ABCD.
Label this quadrilateral MNPQ.
How do you know ABCD and MNPQ are similar?

10. Identify the order of rotational symmetry
of the design on this tile.

11. Which figures can be used to make a tiling pattern?
How do you know?

a) **b)** **c)**

12. Choose a figure from question 11.
Use the figure and transformations to make a design.
Explain how you did this.

13. Rename each fraction in simplest form.
   a) $\frac{25}{30}$ **b)** $\frac{12}{16}$ **c)** $\frac{8}{12}$ **d)** $\frac{21}{24}$

14. Add or subtract.
   a) $\frac{3}{5} + \frac{7}{10}$ **b)** $\frac{7}{8} - \frac{1}{4}$ **c)** $\frac{3}{4} + \frac{1}{2}$ **d)** $\frac{1}{4} + \frac{2}{3}$

15. Julie has $64. She spends 25% and saves the rest.
How much does Julie spend?

16. Write two equivalent ratios for each ratio.
   a) $6:5$ **b)** $4:10$ **c)** $2:6$ **d)** $5:3$

17. Ingrid is training for a marathon.
To avoid dehydration, she drinks 200 mL of water
every 15 min. Today she plans to run for 90 min.
How much water should she take with her?

Perimeter, Area,

Stationery Design

Greeting cards
come in a variety of
shapes and sizes.

You can buy a greeting
card for just about
any occasion!

Learning Goals

- measure and calculate perimeter
- estimate, measure, and
  calculate area
- explore how the areas of
  rectangles, parallelograms, and
  triangles are related
- develop formulas for the area
  of a parallelogram and the area
  of a triangle
- develop formulas for the
  volume and surface area of a
  triangular prism
- sketch polygons, given perimeter
  and area measurements

and Volume

Key Words

variable

base

height

- What measurements are needed to make the envelope for a greeting card?

- Why is the area of paper used important when calculating costs?

Perimeter

How can you find the perimeter of
this square?
Remember, a formula is a shortcut
to state a rule.

3 cm

 Explore

You will need square dot paper and triangular dot paper.
Share the work.

Draw 15 different polygons.
Make sure there are at least two of
each of these types of polygons:

- square
- rectangle
- parallelogram
- rhombus
- triangle

Find the perimeter of each polygon.
For which types of polygons
can you find a shortcut to calculate the perimeter?
Write the shortcut as a formula.

Show *and* Share

Share your formulas with another group of students.
Compare your formulas.
Discuss any differences.
For which types of polygons is it possible to write
more than one formula? Explain.

For any polygon, we can find its perimeter by adding the side lengths.
For this hexagon:

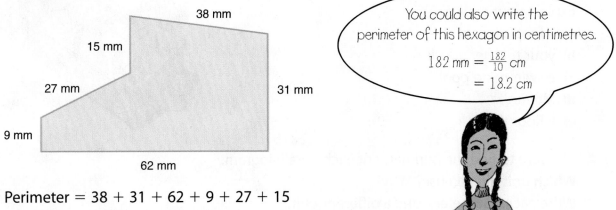

38 mm

15 mm

27 mm

31 mm

9 mm

62 mm

You could also write the perimeter of this hexagon in centimetres.

$182 \text{ mm} = \frac{182}{10} \text{ cm}$

$= 18.2 \text{ cm}$

Perimeter $= 38 + 31 + 62 + 9 + 27 + 15$

$= 182$

The perimeter of this hexagon is 182 mm.

We can find shortcuts for calculating the perimeters of some polygons.

➤ A parallelogram has two pairs of equal sides.

Here is one rule for the perimeter of a parallelogram.

Add the measures of a longer side and a shorter side.
Then multiply by 2.

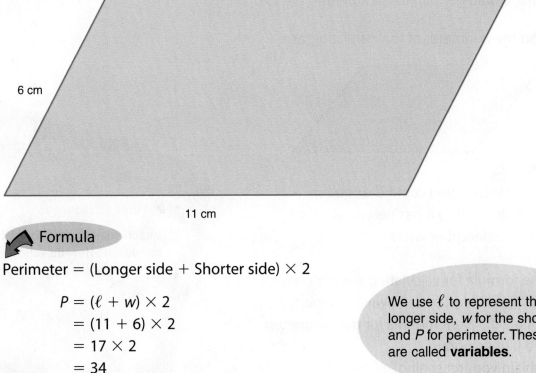

6 cm

11 cm

Formula

Perimeter $=$ (Longer side $+$ Shorter side) $\times 2$

$P = (\ell + w) \times 2$

$= (11 + 6) \times 2$

$= 17 \times 2$

$= 34$

The perimeter of this parallelogram is 34 cm.

We use ℓ to represent the longer side, w for the shorter side, and P for perimeter. These letters are called **variables**.

1. Which unit would you use to measure
   the perimeter of each item?
   Explain your choice.
   a) a football field
   b) your teacher's desk
   c) a swimming pool
   d) Manitoba
   e) a floor tile

2. Measure to find the perimeter of each parallelogram.
   Which unit did you use? Why?
   Write each perimeter using a different unit.
   a)

   b)

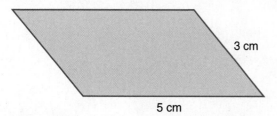

3. Refer to question 2.
   Suppose the lengths of the longer sides of each parallelogram
   increase by 2 cm.
   What would happen to each perimeter? Explain.

4. Find the perimeter of this parallelogram.

   3 cm

   5 cm

   Describe how you could change the
   parallelogram so it has perimeter 20 cm.
   Give 2 different answers.

5. One formula for calculating the perimeter
   of a parallelogram is shown in *Connect*.
   Write a different formula for the perimeter
   of a parallelogram.
   Explain your reasoning.

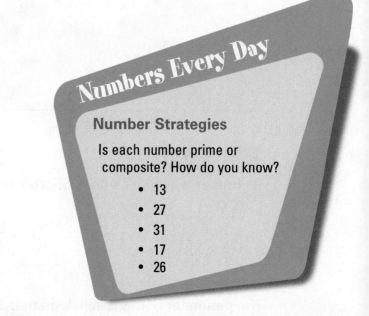

Numbers Every Day

Number Strategies

Is each number prime or
composite? How do you know?

- 13
- 27
- 31
- 17
- 26

6. a) Find the perimeter of each polygon.

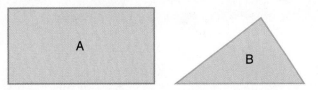

b) Suppose the side lengths of each polygon are doubled.
What would happen to each perimeter? Explain.

7. The perimeter of a triangular field is 1.4 km.
How long might each side be?

8. Your teacher will give you a large copy of these regular polygons.

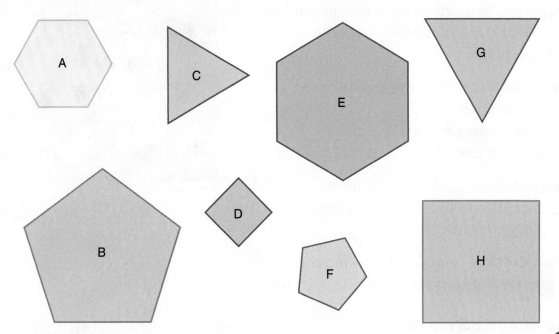

a) Find and record the perimeter of each polygon.
b) How is the perimeter of a regular polygon related
to the number of its sides?
Write a formula to find the perimeter of a
regular polygon.

At Home

Reflect

How are the side lengths of a figure
and its perimeter related?
Use examples to explain.

Choose one room in your home.
Find the perimeter of the floor.
Which units did you use to measure?

Exploring Rectangles

Explore

You will need 1-cm grid paper.

➤ Draw a 2-cm by 3-cm rectangle on grid paper.
Find the area of the rectangle.

➤ Suppose the length of the rectangle doubles.
Predict the area of the new rectangle.
Check your prediction.

➤ Suppose the width of the original
rectangle doubles.
Predict the area of the new rectangle.
Check your prediction.

➤ Suppose both the length and the width double.
Predict the area of the new rectangle.
Check your prediction.

➤ How does the area of each new rectangle
compare to the area of the original rectangle?

Show and Share

Share your work with another pair of students.
Describe any patterns.
What do you think happens to the area of a rectangle when the
length triples? The width triples? Both the length and the width triple?

Connect

Edmond built a crate for his dog.
The dimensions of the floor of the crate
are 0.8 m by 1.2 m.

0.8 m

1.2 m

➤ You can use formulas to find the perimeter and the area of the floor of the crate.

Perimeter = (Longer side + Shorter side) $\times$ 2

$P = (\ell + w) \times 2$

$\quad = (1.2 + 0.8) \times 2$

$\quad = 2 \times 2$

$\quad = 4$

Area = Length $\times$ Width

$A = \ell \times w$

$\quad = 1.2 \times 0.8$

$\quad = 0.96$

The perimeter of the floor of the crate is 4 m and the area is 0.96 m^2.

In the formula for the area of a rectangle, the length and the width are the factors and the area is the product.

➤ You can write the floor area of the crate in square centimetres.

Use: 1 m = 100 cm

$A = (1.2 \times 100) \times (0.8 \times 100)$

$\quad = 120 \times 80$

$\quad = 9600$

The floor area of the crate is 9600 cm^2.

So, 0.96 m^2 and 9600 cm^2 are equal areas.

When you convert a measure of area from square metres to square centimetres, each dimension is multiplied by 100, so the area is multiplied by 100 $\times$ 100, or 10 000.

➤ Edmond doubled the width of the crate. How do the perimeter and the area of the floor of the new crate compare to those of the original crate?

The width of the new crate is: 2 $\times$ 0.8 m = 1.6 m

$P = (\ell + w) \times 2$ $\qquad$ $A = \ell \times w$

$\quad = (1.6 + 1.2) \times 2$ $\qquad$ $\quad = 1.6 \times 1.2$

$\quad = 2.8 \times 2$ $\qquad\qquad$ $\quad = 1.92$

$\quad = 5.6$

The perimeter of the floor of the new crate is 5.6 m and the area is 1.92 m^2.

The perimeter of the new crate is 5.6 m $-$ 4 m, or 1.6 m greater than the original.

The area of the new crate is 1.92 m^2, which is 2 $\times$ 0.96 m^2.

So, the area of the new crate is double the original area.

1. Which unit would you use to express each perimeter and area? Explain your choice.
   a) a park close to your home
   b) the cover of your notebook
   c) the library floor in your school
   d) your bedroom closet ceiling
   e) the top of a chalkbrush

2. Find the perimeter and the area of each rectangle. Write each measure in two different units.

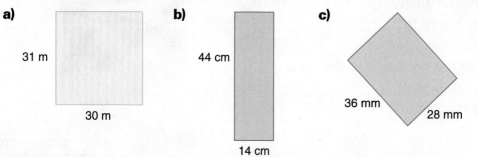

   a) 31 m, 30 m
   b) 44 cm, 14 cm
   c) 36 mm, 28 mm

3. For each area in question 2, which numbers are factors and which are products?

4. Rectangle A has area 40 cm^2 and length 8 cm.
   The area of rectangle B is one-half the area of rectangle A.
   The rectangles have the same length.
   What is the width of rectangle B?

5. Which has the greater area? Explain.
   a) a rectangle with area 0.84 m^2
   b) a rectangle with area 8400 cm^2

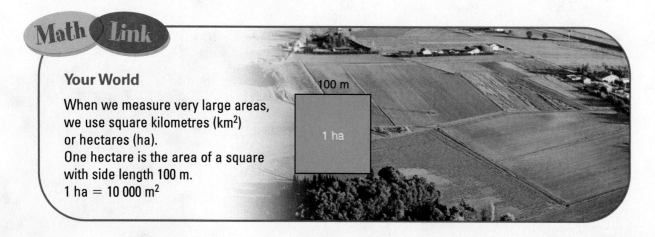

Math Link

Your World

When we measure very large areas, we use square kilometres (km^2) or hectares (ha). One hectare is the area of a square with side length 100 m.
1 ha = 10 000 m^2

100 m

1 ha

6. A rectangle has dimensions 3 cm by 5 cm.
What happens to the perimeter of the rectangle in each case?
   a) The width is doubled.
   b) The length is doubled.
   c) Both the length and the width are doubled.
   Show your work.

7. The perimeter of a square is 20 cm.
What is the area of the square?
How do you know?

8. Lena used 34 m of fencing to enclose a rectangular section
of her backyard.
What might the area of the enclosed section be?
Give 3 different answers.

9. A square room has area 16 m².
What is the perimeter of the room?

10. Pat is making rectangular placemats each with area 1200 cm².
She wants to put braid trim around the edges.
How much trim does Pat need for each placemat?
Is there more than one answer? Explain.

Reflect

What happens to the perimeter and the area
of a rectangle if the length and the width are
multiplied by the same number?
Use diagrams to explain.

Strategies Toolkit

Explore

Christine plans to frame her Grade 4 saxophone certificate with a 5-cm wide mat.
The certificate measures 30 cm by 25 cm.
What is the area of the glass that covers Christine's certificate and the mat?

Conservatory of Music

Grade 4 Certificate

This is to certify that
Christine Lishman
passed the Grade Four Examination
in *Saxophone Playing*
at the Conservatory of Music.

May 4, 2005

Show *and* Share

Share your work with another pair of students.
Describe the strategy you used to solve the problem.

Connect

Best Ride Sports sells snowboard equipment and clothing.
The store measures 15 m by 13 m.
The checkout desk measures 3 m by 1 m.
A display shelf measures 11 m by 2 m.
The floor around the desk and shelf is tiled.
What area of the floor is tiled?

Strategies

- **Make a table.**
- **Use a model.**
- **Draw a diagram.**
- **Solve a simpler problem.**
- **Work backward.**
- **Guess and check.**
- **Make an organized list.**
- **Use a pattern.**
- **Draw a graph.**
- **Use logical reasoning.**

What do you know?
- The store measures 15 m by 13 m.
- The checkout desk is 3 m by 1 m and the shelf is 11 m by 2 m.
- The floor that is not covered by the desk and shelf is tiled.

What strategy will you use to solve the problem?
- You could **draw a diagram**.
- Sketch the store, the desk, and the shelf.
- Mark the dimensions on the sketch.

Find the total area of the store.
Then find the area covered by the desk and the shelf.
Subtract the area covered by the desk and the shelf from the total floor area.

Check your work.
Is the sum of the tiled area and the areas covered by the desk and the shelf equal to the total area?

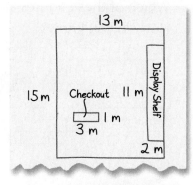

Practice

Choose one of the

Strategies

1. The Wongs are putting a flagstone deck around their pool.
   The pool is rectangular.
   Its dimensions are 8 m by 4 m.
   The deck will surround the pool.
   It will have a width of 2 m.
   a) What is the area of the deck?
   b) How much security fencing is required around the deck?

2. Scalene △ABC has related side lengths.
   Side AB is 7 cm shorter than side BC.
   Side AC is 4 cm longer than side BC.
   The perimeter of △ABC is 48 cm.
   What is the length of each side?

Reflect

Choose one of the problems in this lesson.
Could you have solved the problem *without* drawing a diagram?
Explain.

Area of a Parallelogram

Which of these figures are parallelograms?
How do you know?

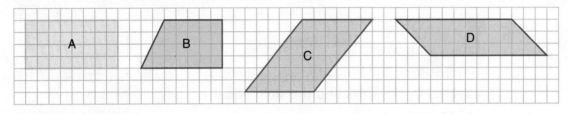

Explore

You will need scissors and 1-cm grid paper.

➤ Copy parallelogram A
on grid paper.
Estimate, then find, the
area of the parallelogram.

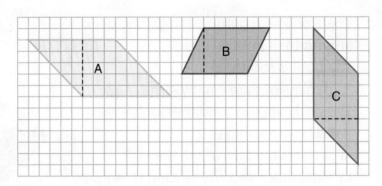

➤ Cut out the parallelogram.
Cut along the broken
line segment.

➤ Arrange the two pieces to form a rectangle.
What is the area of the rectangle?
How does the area of the rectangle compare
to the area of the parallelogram?

➤ Repeat the activity for parallelograms B and C.

Show *and* Share

Share your work with another pair of students.
Can every parallelogram be changed into a rectangle
by cutting and moving one section? Explain.
How is the area of a parallelogram related to the area
of the rectangle? Explain.

Numbers Every Day

Number Strategies

List 5 numbers that are
divisible by both 4 and 6.
What do the numbers
have in common?

To estimate the area of this parallelogram, count the whole squares and the part squares that are one-half or greater.

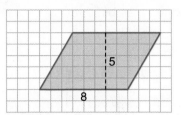

There are:
- 33 whole squares
- 8 part squares that are one-half or greater

The area of this parallelogram is about 41 square units.

Any side of a parallelogram is a **base**.
The **height** of the parallelogram is the length of a line segment that joins parallel sides and is perpendicular to the base.

A rectangle is a parallelogram.
The length is the base. The width is the height.
The area of a parallelogram is the same as the area of a rectangle with the same base and height.

Use b for base.
Use h for height.

Area = Base × Height
$A = b \times h$
$= 8 \times 5$
$= 40$
The area of the rectangle is 40 square units.

Area = Base × Height
$A = b \times h$
$= 8 \times 5$
$= 40$
The area of the parallelogram is 40 square units.

1. Copy each parallelogram onto 1-cm grid paper.
   Draw a rectangle with the same base and height.

a)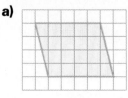

b)

c)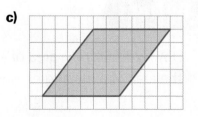

2. Estimate, then find the area of each parallelogram.

a)

b)

c)

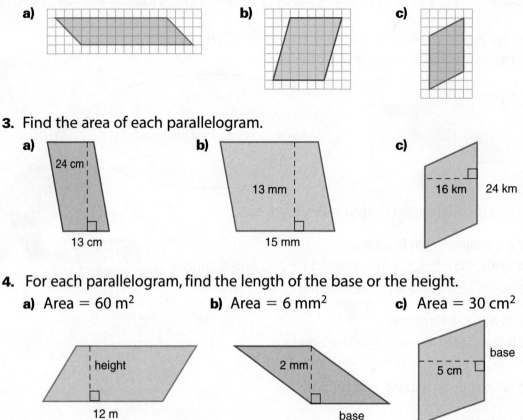

3. Find the area of each parallelogram.

a)

24 cm

13 cm

b)

13 mm

15 mm

c)

16 km 24 km

4. For each parallelogram, find the length of the base or the height.

a) Area = 60 m² 　　 b) Area = 6 mm² 　　 c) Area = 30 cm²

height

12 m

2 mm

base

base

5 cm

5. Which has the greatest area? The least area?
   a) a rectangle with base 10 cm and height 5 cm
   b) a parallelogram with base 7 cm and height 8 cm
   c) a square with sides 7 cm long

6. Sketch a parallelogram with area 24 square units.
   How many different ways can you do this?
   Explain.

7. A student says the area of this parallelogram is 20 cm².
   Explain the student's error.

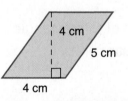

4 cm

5 cm

4 cm

8. Which parallelogram has the greater area? Explain.
   a) a parallelogram with base 15 cm and height 6 cm
   b) a parallelogram with base 15 cm and side length 6 cm

Reflect

How is finding the area of a parallelogram like finding
the area of a rectangle? How is it different?

Exploring Triangles and Rectangles

Explore

You will need scissors and 1-cm grid paper.

➤ Draw a rectangle on grid paper.
Find and record the area of the rectangle.

➤ Draw a triangle inside the rectangle so that:
  • At least one side of the triangle coincides with one side of the rectangle.
  • The third vertex is on the opposite side of the rectangle.
  Shade the triangle.
  Estimate the area of the triangle.

➤ Cut out the rectangle. Then cut out the triangle.
Arrange the unshaded pieces to cover the triangle.
What is the area of the triangle? How do you know?

➤ Repeat the activity 2 more times.
Use a different side of the rectangle for one side of the triangle.
Use different points for the third vertex of the triangle.

Show and Share

Share your work with another student.
Compare the area of the rectangle and the area of the triangle inside it.
What do you notice? Explain.

Connect

Any side of a triangle can be its base.
The height of a triangle is the perpendicular line segment that joins the base to the opposite vertex.

height

base

LESSON FOCUS | Relate the area of a triangle to the area of a rectangle.

355

Here is one way to find the area of this triangle.

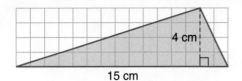

- Draw a rectangle with the same base and height.

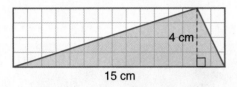

- Find the area of the rectangle.
  Area = 15 cm × 4 cm
       = 60 cm²

- The pieces of the rectangle outside the triangle
  can be rearranged to make a congruent triangle.

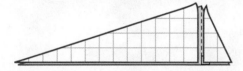

The areas of the congruent triangles are equal.
So, the area of one triangle is one-half the area of the rectangle.
One-half of 60 is 30.
The area of the triangle is 30 cm².

The area of a triangle is one-half the area of the rectangle
with the same base and height.

We can write a formula for the area of a triangle:

Area = (Base × Height) ÷ 2
   $A = (b \times h) \div 2$

> Each square represents 1 cm².
> I estimate the area of the triangle by counting squares and part squares.
> The area of this triangle is about 30 cm².

Practice

1. Estimate, then find, the area of each triangle.

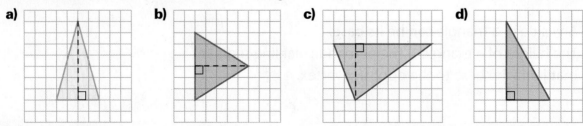

a) b) c) d)

2. What is the area of the sail
on Matthew's windsurfer?

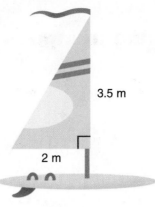

3.5 m

2 m

3. Each triangle has area 12 m².
Find each base or height.

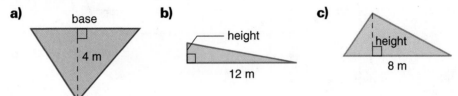

a)

base

4 m

b)

height

12 m

c)

height

8 m

4. Use 0.5-cm grid paper.
   a) Draw as many different triangles as you can with area 16 cm².
   b) How do you know the triangles are different?
   c) Have you drawn all possible triangles? Explain.

5. Which triangle has the greater area? How do you know?
   a) Triangle A has base 13 m and height 5 m.
   b) Triangle B has base 9 m and height 8 m.

6. A rectangle and a triangle have the same area.
   The dimensions of the rectangle are 6 m by 8 m.
   The base of the triangle is 8 m.
   What is the height of the triangle? How do you know?

7. A triangle has area 21 cm².
   Its base is 7 cm long.
   Would all triangles with base 7 cm have
   area 21 cm²? Explain.

Reflect

How are the areas of triangles and rectangles related?
Use examples to explain.

Exploring Triangles and Parallelograms

Explore

You will need scissors, tape, and 1-cm grid paper.

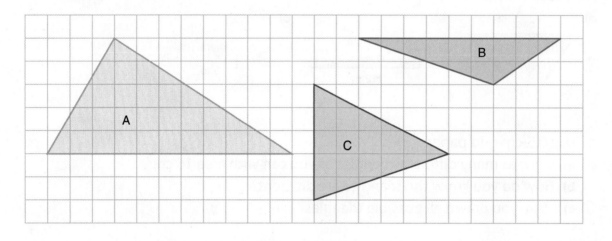

➤ Make 2 copies of triangle A on grid paper.
Cut out the triangles.

➤ Arrange the triangles to make a parallelogram.
Find the area of the parallelogram.
What is the area of triangle A?

➤ Repeat the activity for triangles B and C.

Show *and* Share

Share your work with another pair of students.
Did you make the same parallelogram each time?
Can two congruent triangles always be joined
to make a parallelogram? Explain.
How is the area of a triangle related to the area
of the parallelogram? Explain.

Numbers Every Day

Number Strategies

Write each measure
in metres.

- 344 mm
- 1045 cm
- 1.872 km

Here is one way to find the area of this triangle.

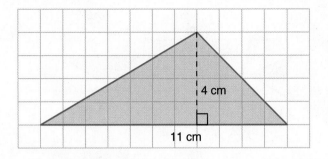

- Draw a congruent triangle.
  Cut out both triangles.
  Arrange the triangles to make a parallelogram.

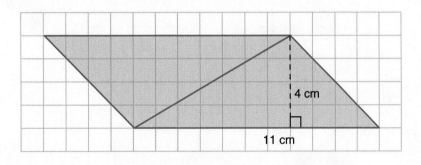

- Find the area of the parallelogram.
  $A = b \times h$
  $\quad = 11 \times 4$
  $\quad = 44$

- Two congruent triangles were used to make
  the parallelogram.
  So, the area of the triangle is one-half the area
  of the parallelogram.
  One-half of 44 is 22.

  The area of the triangle is 22 cm².

  We can use the formula for the area of a triangle:

Area = (Base × Height) ÷ 2
Or, $A = (b \times h) \div 2$

The area of a triangle is one-half the area of the parallelogram with the same base and height.

1. Copy each triangle on 1-cm grid paper.
Draw a related parallelogram.

a)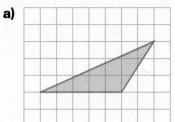

b)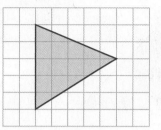

c)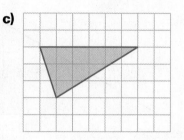

2. Find the area of each triangle.

a)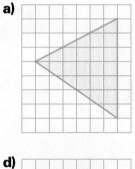

b)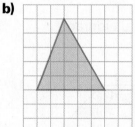

c)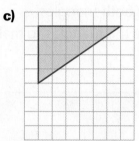

d)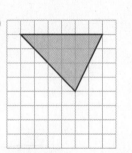

e)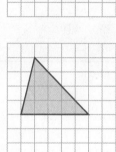

f)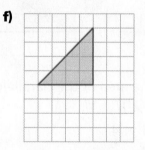

3. Find the base or height of each triangle.

a) Area = 18 cm²

b) Area = 32 m²

c) Area = 480 mm²

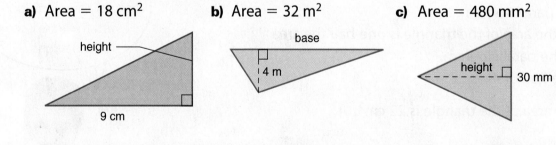

4. Mark is designing a skateboard ramp.
He has sketched the side view.
What is the area of this face of the ramp?

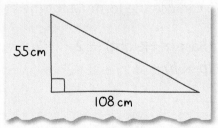

5. Draw a parallelogram on 1-cm grid paper.
   Draw a diagonal to divide the parallelogram into 2 triangles.
   Find the area of each triangle.

6. Use 1-cm grid paper.
   Draw 3 different triangles with base 5 cm and height 6 cm.
   Find the area of each triangle.
   How do the areas compare? Explain.

7. Draw each triangle on 1-cm grid paper.
   Then find the area of the triangle.
   a) base 12 cm and height 4 cm
   b) base 6 cm and height 4 cm
   c) base 12 cm and height 2 cm
   d) base 6 cm and height 2 cm
   Compare the bases, the heights, and the areas of the 4 triangles.

8. Use 1-cm grid paper.
   How many different triangles can you draw
   that have base 5 cm and height 3 cm?
   Sketch each triangle.
   Find the area of each triangle.

9. Find the area of this triangle.
   a) Suppose the base is doubled.
      Explain what happens to the area.
   b) Suppose both the height and the base
      of the original triangle are doubled.
      Explain what happens to the area.
   c) What do you think happens to the area when
      both the height and the base are tripled? Explain.
   Show your work.

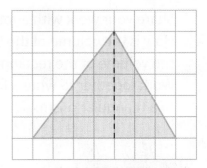

Volume of a Triangular Prism

7

Explore

You will need modelling clay, dental floss, and a ruler.

➤ Use the clay to make a rectangular prism.
Measure its dimensions.
Calculate its volume.

➤ Use dental floss.
Cut the prism along a diagonal of one base
to make two congruent triangular prisms.
What is the volume of each triangular prism?
How do you know?

Show *and* Share

Share your work with another pair of students.
How is the volume of the triangular prism related to
the volume of the rectangular prism?
Work together to write a formula to find the volume
of a triangular prism.

Connect

➤ The volume of a rectangular prism can be found by using a formula:

Volume of a rectangular prism = Base area × Height

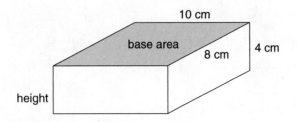

A cut through the diagonal of one base makes
2 congruent triangular prisms.

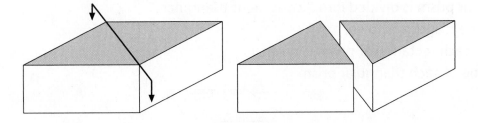

Since the prisms are congruent, their volumes are equal.
So, the volume of one triangular prism is one-half the volume
of the rectangular prism.

The area of the base of each triangular prism is
$\frac{1}{2}$ the base area of the rectangular prism.

We can write this formula for the volume of a triangular prism:

Volume of a triangular prism = Base area × Height

We can use this formula to find the volume of any triangular prism.

This triangular prism is 10 cm high.

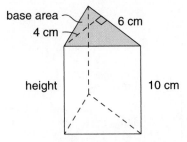

Its triangular face has base 6 cm and height 4 cm.

Area of triangular face = $(b \times h) \div 2$
$\qquad\qquad\qquad\quad = (6 \times 4) \div 2$
$\qquad\qquad\qquad\quad = 24 \div 2$
$\qquad\qquad\qquad\quad = 12$

The base area of the prism is 12 cm².

The volume of the triangular prism = Base area × Height
$\qquad\qquad\qquad\qquad\qquad\qquad\quad = 12 \times 10$
$\qquad\qquad\qquad\qquad\qquad\qquad\quad = 120$

The volume of the prism is 120 cm³.

1. Each rectangular prism is divided into 2 congruent triangular
   prisms along the diagonal shown.
   The volume of each rectangular prism is given.
   Find the volume of each triangular prism.

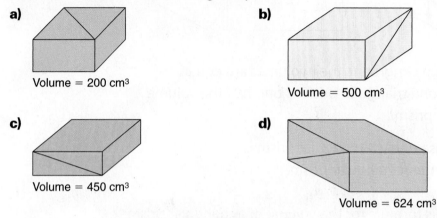

   a)
   Volume = 200 cm³

   b)
   Volume = 500 cm³

   c)
   Volume = 450 cm³

   d)
   Volume = 624 cm³

2. Estimate the volume of each triangular prism.
   Then calculate to check.

   a)
   15 cm
   Base area = 10 cm²

   b)
   Base area = 2 m²
   5 m

3. Find the volume of each triangular prism.

   a)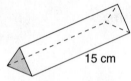
   4 cm
   11 cm
   5 cm

   b)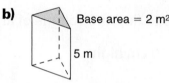
   2 cm
   9 cm
   6 cm

   c)
   3 m
   4 m
   8 m

4. A triangular prism has height 12 cm.
   Each triangular face has base 4 cm and height 7 cm.
   a) Find the volume of the prism.
   b) Double the height of the prism.
      What happens to the volume?
   c) Double the base of the triangular face.
      What happens to the volume?
   d) Double the height of the triangular face.
      What happens to the volume?
   e) What happens to the volume when all 3 dimensions
      in parts b, c, and d are doubled?

5. A triangular prism has a base that is a right triangle.
The volume of the prism is 100 cm³.
   a) Sketch the prism.
   b) What might the dimensions of the prism be?
   List possible values for the height of the prism,
   and the base and height of the triangular face.
   c) How many different sets of dimensions can you find?
   List all those you find.

6. Use grid paper. Draw a net of a prism with a right triangular base.
Label the dimensions. Calculate the volume of your prism.

7. Use Pattern Blocks. One green block has a volume of 1 cubic unit.
Here is a pattern of green blocks.

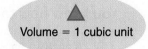

Volume = 1 cubic unit

Frame 1   Frame 2   Frame 3

This pattern continues.
What is the volume of the blocks in Frame 15? How do you know?

8. A triangular prism has a base that is
an equilateral triangle.
The smaller prism has a base that is also
an equilateral triangle.
How many of the smaller prisms will fit inside
the larger prism?

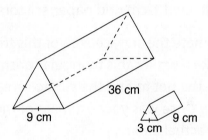

36 cm
9 cm
9 cm
3 cm

9. A chocolate bar has the shape of a triangular prism 10 cm long.
The base of the prism is a right isosceles triangle
with sides 5 cm, 5 cm, and about 7 cm.
Twenty of these chocolate bars are to be packaged
in a box that is a rectangular prism.
What could the dimensions of the box be? Explain your choice.

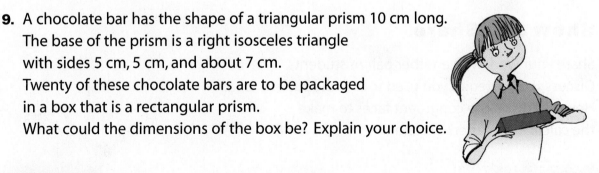

Reflect

How is the volume of a triangular prism related to
the volume of a rectangular prism?
Use diagrams in your explanation.

Surface Area of a Triangular Prism

You know how to find the area of a rectangle.

$A = b \times h$

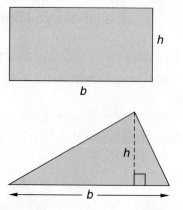

You know how to find the area of a triangle.

$A = (b \times h) \div 2$

You will use these measures to find the surface area
of a triangular prism.

Explore

You will need 1-cm grid paper, scissors, and a ruler.

➤ Estimate the surface area of this triangular prism.
➤ Make a net for this triangular prism.
   Use the net to find the surface area of the prism.
➤ How close was your estimate of the area to
   the actual area?

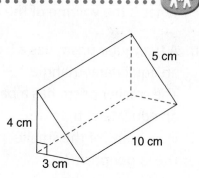

Show *and* Share

Share your work with another pair of students.
Discuss the strategies you used to find the surface area.
How could you use congruent faces to make
the calculation easier? Explain.

Connect

A triangular prism has 5 faces.
To find the surface area, find the area of each of the 5 faces
and then add the areas.

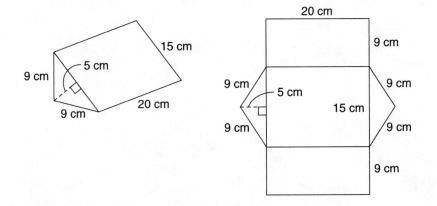

The two triangular faces are congruent.
Each triangle has a base of 15 cm.
The height of each triangle is measured as 5 cm.
So, the area of each triangular face is: $(b \times h) \div 2 = (15 \times 5) \div 2$
$$= 37.5$$

There are 2 triangular faces, so their total area is: $2 \times 37.5 \text{ cm}^2 = 75 \text{ cm}^2$

There are 3 rectangular faces.
Their areas are: $9 \times 20 + 15 \times 20 + 9 \times 20 = 180 + 300 + 180$
$$= 660$$

The total area of all the faces of the triangular prism is:
$75 \text{ cm}^2 + 660 \text{ cm}^2 = 735 \text{ cm}^2$
So, the surface area of the prism is 735 cm^2.

For any triangular prism:
The surface area = The sum of the areas of the 3 rectangular faces +
$\qquad$ $2 \times$ The area of the triangular base

Practice

Use a calculator when you need to.

1. Estimate the surface area of each prism.
   Calculate each surface area.
   Order the prisms from greatest to least surface area.

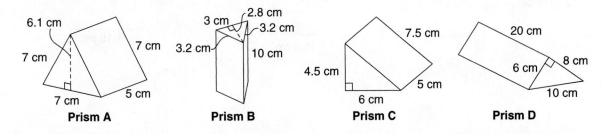

Prism A   Prism B   Prism C   Prism D

2. Find the surface area of each triangular prism.

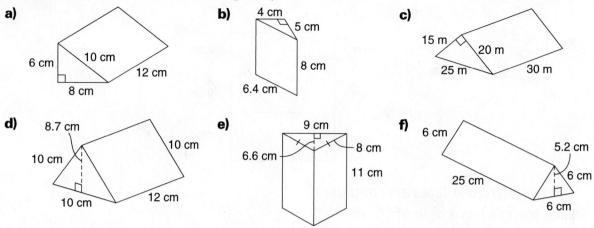

a)

b)

c)

d)

e)

f)

3. In *Connect*, you saw one word formula for the surface area
of a triangular prism.
Think of a different way to calculate the areas of the 3 rectangular faces.
Use your ideas to write a different word formula for the surface area.

4. A triangular prism has length 8 cm.
What would be the surface area of the prism if it had triangular faces
with these dimensions?

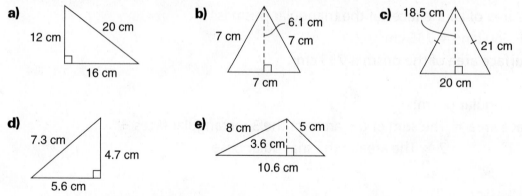

a)

b)

c)

d)

e)

5. Suppose you want to construct a triangular prism 15 cm long
with the greatest surface area.
Which of these triangles should you choose for its base?
Explain your choice.

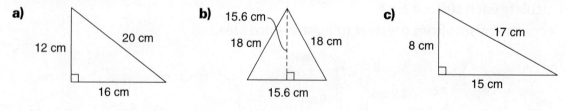

a)

b)

c)

6. A student said if you double all the dimensions of a triangular prism you will double its surface area.
Is the student correct?
Use words, numbers, and pictures to explain your answer.

7. This triangle is one of the bases of a triangular prism. What should the length of the prism be so its surface area is between 100 cm² and 150 cm²?

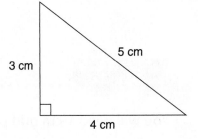

8. The 3 rectangular faces of a triangular prism have areas of 30 cm², 40 cm², and 50 cm².
The 2 triangular faces have a combined area of 12 cm².
What are the dimensions of the triangular prism?
Explain your thinking using pictures, numbers, and words.

9. A triangular prism has a surface area of about 84 cm² and a length greater than 4.5 cm.
Select the most likely triangular face for the prism.
Give reasons for your choice.

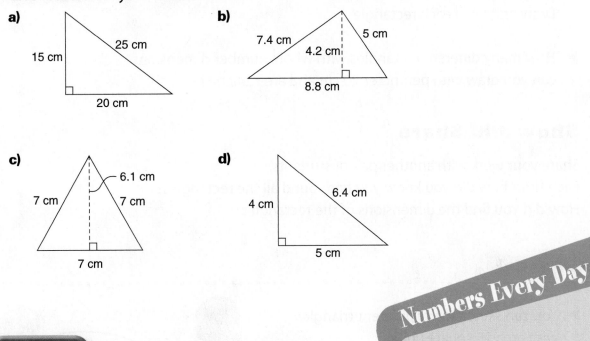

Reflect

How is the strategy for finding the surface area of a triangular prism similar to the strategy for finding the surface area of a rectangular prism?
How is it different?

Numbers Every Day

Number Strategies

Find the common factors of the numbers in each pair.
- 40, 72
- 45, 63
- 50, 80
- 55, 132

Sketching Polygons

Explore

You will need 1-cm grid paper.

➤ How many different rectangles with whole number dimensions can you draw with perimeter 14 cm? Draw and label each rectangle.

➤ How many different rectangles with whole number dimensions can you draw with area 16 cm²? Draw and label each rectangle.

➤ How many different rectangles with whole number dimensions can you draw with perimeter 20 cm and area 24 cm²?

Show and Share

Share your work with another pair of students.
Each time, how did you know you had found all the rectangles?
How did you find the dimensions of the rectangles?

Connect

➤ You can sketch many different triangles with area 25 square units.

> I know a triangle with area 25 square units has the same base and height as a rectangle with area 50 square units.

The table shows some possible measurements of base and height with product 50.

Base (units)	Height (units)
1	50
2	25
5	10
10	5
25	2
50	1

Each of these triangles has area 25 square units.

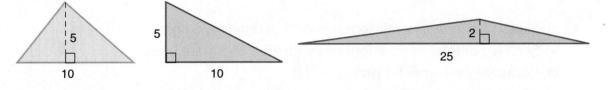

➤ You can sketch many different parallelograms with perimeter 12 units.

One formula for the perimeter of a parallelogram is:

Perimeter = (Shorter side + Longer side) × 2

When the perimeter is 12 units, the sum of a shorter side and a longer side is 6 units. The table shows some possible lengths of the sides.

Shorter Side (units)	Longer Side (units)
1	5
2	4
3	3

Each of these parallelograms has perimeter 12 units.

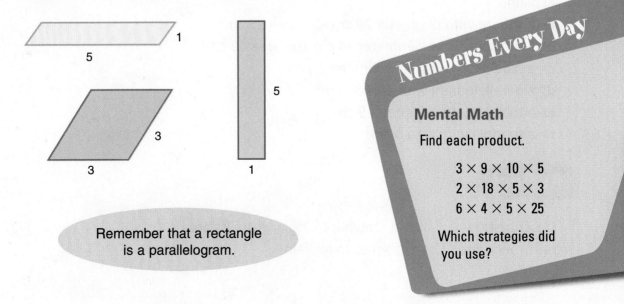

Remember that a rectangle is a parallelogram.

1. Match each area measurement
   with an appropriate figure.
   Explain your thinking.
   a) 32 square units
   b) 36 square units
   c) 20 square units

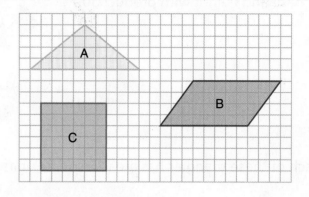

2. a) Sketch 2 different parallelograms with perimeter 26 units.
   b) Sketch 2 different parallelograms with area 26 square units.
   c) Compare your work for parts a and b.
      What did you do differently?

3. Use a compass and a ruler.
   Construct 2 different triangles with perimeter 22 cm.
   a) How did you find the side lengths?
   b) How did you know which side lengths were not possible?

4. Madhu is designing an unusual workshop.
   She plans to make it triangular.
   The floor will have area 7.4 m^2.
   a) Sketch some possible layouts for Madhu's workshop.
   b) Which layout is most likely? Why?

5. You need 1-cm grid paper. Sketch each figure.
   For which parts is it possible to sketch more than one figure?
   Explain.
   a) a square with perimeter 20 cm and area 25 cm^2
   b) a rectangle with perimeter 14 cm and area 10 cm^2
   c) a parallelogram with perimeter 24 cm
   d) a parallelogram with area 36 cm^2
   e) a triangle with perimeter 9 cm
   f) a triangle with area 6 cm^2

Reflect

Describe how you would sketch a triangle, given its area
or its perimeter. Use examples to explain.

Plumber

A plumber installs and repairs pipes that carry water, natural gas, and steam. She reads and interprets technical drawings to plan the layout of a job. Fitting the piping to match the drawings with the least pipe wasted is like solving a puzzle!

The plumber chooses the type and size of pipe for the job. Then she figures out how much pipe is needed. She uses hand and power tools to measure, cut, bend, and join pipes. Once the piping is installed, the plumber tests for leaks.

A plumber is a licenced tradesperson. She may work for a plumbing company or for a business that requires a full-time plumber. Plumbers can also be self-employed (own their own plumbing business) and employ and train other plumbers.

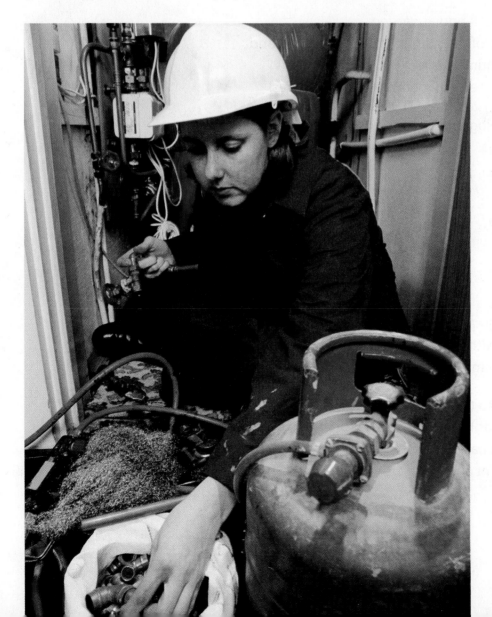

LESSON

1

1. Measure to find the perimeter of each polygon.
   Which unit did you use? Why?

   a)
   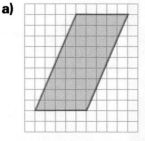
   A

   b)
   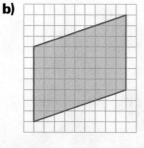
   B

2. Calculate the perimeter of a regular hexagon with
   side length 4.8 cm. Show your work.

2

3. Tania dug this rectangular garden.
   a) Find the area of the garden in square metres and
   in square centimetres.
   b) Find the perimeter in metres and centimetres.

   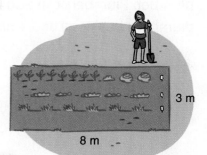
   3 m
   8 m

4

4. For each parallelogram, identify a base and a height.
   Then find its area.

   a)
   b)
   c)

   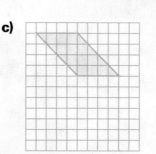

5. Which has the greater area?
   a) a rectangle with base 7 cm and height 3 cm
   b) a parallelogram with base 6 cm and height 4 cm

5

6. A rectangle and a triangle have the same area.
   The rectangle has base 5 cm and height 4 cm.
   What might the base and height of the triangle be?
   Give two different answers.

7. Find the area of each triangle.

a) 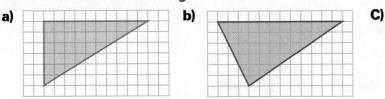   b)   C)

8. Sketch 3 different triangles with area 32 cm².

9. Some oil spilled on the ground during the loading of an oil truck.
The clean-up crew marked a triangular section on the ground
that contained the spill.
The base of the triangular section is 12 m. The height is 5 m.
What area of the ground was covered by the spill?

10. A triangular prism has a base that is a right triangle.
The triangle has base 5 cm and height 12 cm.
The third side of the triangle is 13 cm.
The prism is 25 cm long.
   a) Sketch a net of the prism.
   Calculate its surface area.
   b) Sketch the prism. Calculate its volume.
   c) What would you do to the prism to double
   its volume? Explain.

11. Sketch a rectangle with perimeter 18 cm that has
the least area possible. The length and width
are whole numbers of centimetres.
What is the area of the rectangle?

12. Sketch each figure.
For which parts is it possible to draw more
than one figure? Explain.
   a) a parallelogram with area 12 cm²
   b) a triangle with area 3 cm²
   c) a rectangle with perimeter 28 cm
   d) a triangle with perimeter 46 cm
   e) a rectangle with perimeter 36 cm and
   area 77 cm²

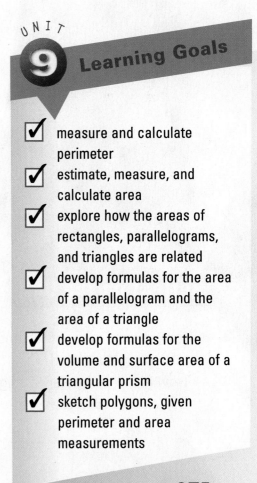

UNIT

9 **Learning Goals**

✓ measure and calculate
perimeter

✓ estimate, measure, and
calculate area

✓ explore how the areas of
rectangles, parallelograms,
and triangles are related

✓ develop formulas for the area
of a parallelogram and the
area of a triangle

✓ develop formulas for the
volume and surface area of a
triangular prism

✓ sketch polygons, given
perimeter and area
measurements

Stationery Design

You will need a ruler, coloured pencils or markers,
1-cm grid paper, scissors, and tape.

1. Design and create a greeting card and its envelope.
   On grid paper, record a pattern for the card and for the envelope.

2. What is the area of the card? The envelope?
   What is the perimeter of the card? The envelope?

Reflect on the Unit

How are the areas of rectangles, parallelograms,
and triangles related?
How is the perimeter of a figure related to its side lengths?
Use examples to explain.

3. Suppose you have a rectangular piece of paper that measures 28 cm by 43 cm.
How many cards could you cut from one piece of paper? How many envelopes?

4. Write about your design.
- How did you choose the shape of your card? The envelope?
- How did you choose the dimensions of the card and figure out the dimensions of the envelope?

10

Camping in Treetops!

Patterns in Number

Learning Goals

- represent patterns in different ways
- relate number patterns to patterns on graphs
- explore patterns in geometry
- relate distance, average speed, and time
- use a computer to explore patterns
- pose and solve problems involving patterns

and Geometry

Key Words

Euler's Formula

non-adjacent

Francine is planning a treetop camping expedition. Campers will enjoy a day of tree climbing.
At night they will sleep in treeboat hammocks high up in a tree!

The table shows the cost of the expedition.

Number of Campers	Cost ($)
1	225
2	375
3	525
4	675

- Describe the patterns in the table.
- How could you represent the patterns a different way?
- Suppose 12 people went on the expedition. How could you find the total cost?

1 Representing Patterns

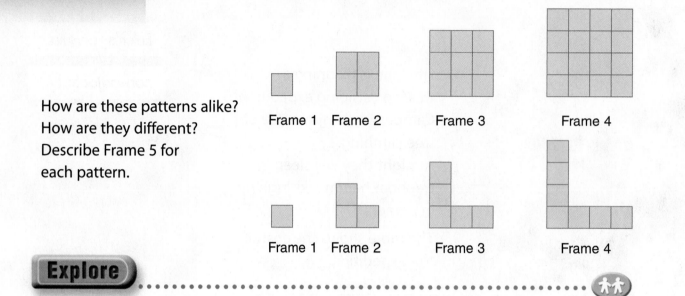

Frame 1 Frame 2   Frame 3   Frame 4

Frame 1 Frame 2   Frame 3   Frame 4

How are these patterns alike?
How are they different?
Describe Frame 5 for
each pattern.

Explore

You will need Colour Tiles or congruent squares, and grid paper.

➤ Use Colour Tiles.
   Build the first 4 frames of a growing pattern.
   Record your pattern on grid paper.
➤ Make a table.
   Record each frame number and
   the number of tiles in a frame.
   Write these numbers as an ordered pair.
➤ Write a pattern rule for the number
   of tiles in a frame.
➤ Graph the data. How are the graph and
   the growing pattern related?
➤ Use your graph to predict the number
   of tiles needed for Frame 10.

Frame Number	Number of Tiles in a Frame	Ordered Pair
1		

Show and Share

Share your work with another pair of students.
How could you use your table or graph to find out
if any frame in the pattern has 100 tiles?

Here are some different ways to represent a growing pattern.

➤ Model the pattern on a grid.

Frame 1   Frame 2   Frame 3   Frame 4   Frame 5

➤ Make a table.

Frame Number	Number of Tiles in a Frame	Ordered Pair
1	2	(1, 2)
2	4	(2, 4)
3	6	(3, 6)
4	8	(4, 8)
5	10	(5, 10)

The frame number is the first coordinate. The number of tiles in a frame is the second coordinate.

➤ Write a pattern rule.
From the table, 2 tiles are added each time.

The pattern rule for the number of tiles in a frame is:

Start at 2. Add 2 each time.

Here is another way to state the pattern rule: The number of tiles in a frame is double the frame number.

➤ Draw a graph. Use the numbers in the table.
Draw and label coordinate axes.
Mark points at (1, 2), (2, 4), (3, 6), (4, 8), and (5, 10).

To find the number of tiles in Frame 7,
extend the graph.
From (5, 10), move 1 square right and
2 squares up to reach (6, 12).
Repeat this translation to reach (7, 14).
Frame 7 has 14 tiles.

The graph is too small to find the number
of tiles in Frame 100.
We use a pattern rule instead.
The number of tiles in a frame is
double the frame number.
So, the number of tiles in
Frame 100 is: $2 \times 100 = 200$

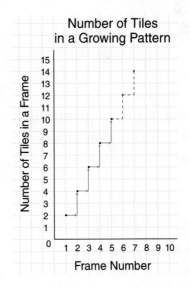

Number of Tiles
in a Growing Pattern

To get from one point to the next,
move 1 square right and 2 squares up.

1. Use grid paper.
   For each table:
   • Write a pattern rule.
   • Shade squares on grid paper to model the pattern.
   • Graph the pattern.

   a)

Frame Number	Number of Squares in a Frame
1	3
2	6
3	9
4	12
5	15

   b)

Frame Number	Number of Squares in a Frame
1	5
2	6
3	7
4	8
5	9

2. Record each growing pattern in a table.
   Then represent the pattern on a graph.

   a)

   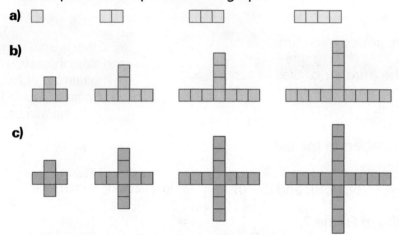

   b)

   c)

3. Use your tables or graphs from question 2.
   a) Find the number of tiles needed for Frame 10.
   b) Write a pattern rule.

4. For each pattern in question 2:
   a) Which frame has 25 tiles?
      How do you know?
   b) Which frame has 37 tiles?
      How do you know?
   c) Does any frame have 40 tiles? Explain.

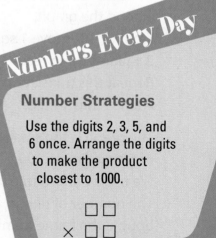

Numbers Every Day

Number Strategies

Use the digits 2, 3, 5, and 6 once. Arrange the digits to make the product closest to 1000.

$$\begin{array}{r} \square\,\square \\ \times\ \square\,\square \\ \hline \end{array}$$

5. Here are the first 4 frames of a growing pattern.

a) Draw the next 3 frames on grid paper.

b) Make a table.
Record the frame number and the number
of squares in a frame for each of the first 7 frames.

c) Graph the data in the table.
When can you use the graph to find the number
of squares in a frame you have not drawn?

6. Use grid paper.
a) Draw a growing pattern to model
the data in the table.
Extend the pattern to Frame 7.
b) How did you decide how to draw
the pattern?

Frame Number	Number of Squares in a Frame
1	4
2	8
3	12
4	16
5	20

7. Use grid paper.
a) Draw a growing pattern to model this graph.
b) Make a table.
Record the frame number and the
number of squares in a frame.
c) How many squares are in Frame 10? Frame 100?
How do you know?
d) Which frame has 31 squares? 57 squares?
How do you know?
e) Does any frame have 50 squares? Explain.

**Number of Squares
in a Growing Pattern**

Number of Squares in a Frame (y-axis: 0–15)

Frame Number (x-axis: 1 2 3 4 5 6 7 8 9 10)

Reflect

Describe some of the different ways you can represent
a pattern. Use examples to explain.

Relating Graphs and Input/Output Machines

This table shows the input and output from an Input/Output machine with one operation.

Input	Output
2	8
3	12
4	16
5	20

How could you find the operation and the number in the machine?

Explore

You will need grid paper.

➤ Each of you chooses a different Input/Output machine.

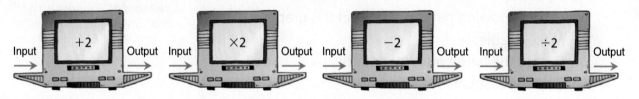

➤ Use these input numbers: 2, 4, 6, 8
Find the output for each input number.
Record the input and output in a table.

➤ Use grid paper. Each of you must use the same scale.
Draw a graph of the data in your Input/Output table.
Start at the left. Describe how to move from one point to the next.
Compare your graph with those of other students in your group.

Show *and* Share

Share your work with another group of students.
How are the graphs for the Input/Output machines the same?
How are they different? How are the points on each graph
related to the numbers in the Input/Output table?

➤ To draw a graph for this Input/Output machine:

Make an Input/Output table. Choose 5 different input numbers.

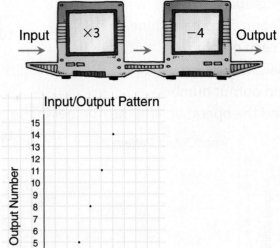

Input	Output
2	2
3	5
4	8
5	11
6	14

Draw and label a coordinate grid. Mark points at (2, 2), (3, 5), (4, 8), (5, 11), and (6, 14).

Input/Output Pattern

➤ To draw an Input/Output machine that will produce the graph to the right:

Record the input and output numbers in a table.

Input	Output
1	3
2	5
3	7
4	9
5	11

The output numbers increase by 2 each time.
So, the input numbers are multiplied by 2:
$1 \times 2 = 2$
But the output for 1 is 3. To get 3, we add 1 to 2.
The Input/Output machine doubles each input, then adds 1.

Input/Output Pattern

This Input/Output machine will produce the graph.

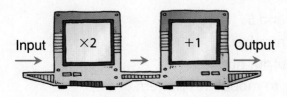

Practice

1. Each graph shows the numbers for an Input/Output machine.
   For each graph:
   - Make a table for the input and output numbers.
   - Find the operation and the number in the machine.

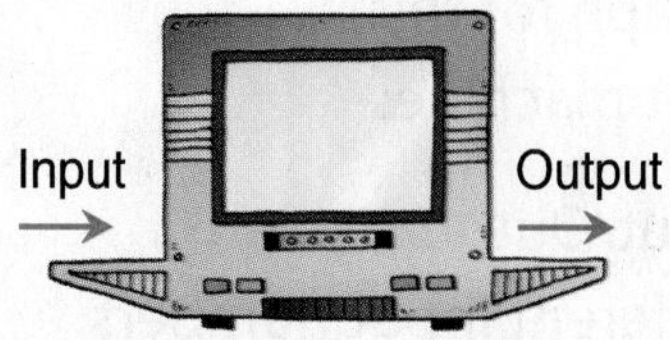

a)

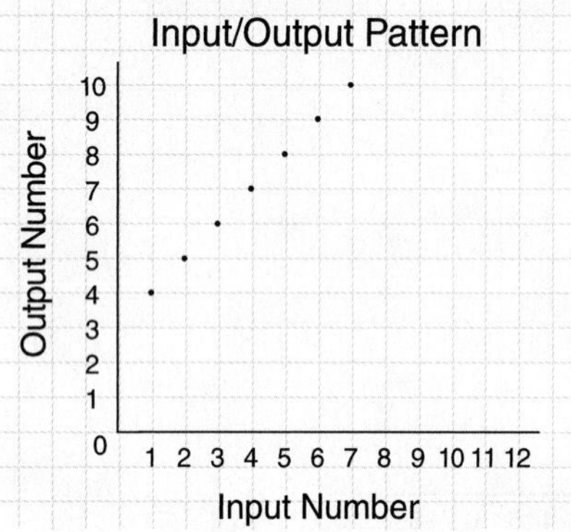

b)

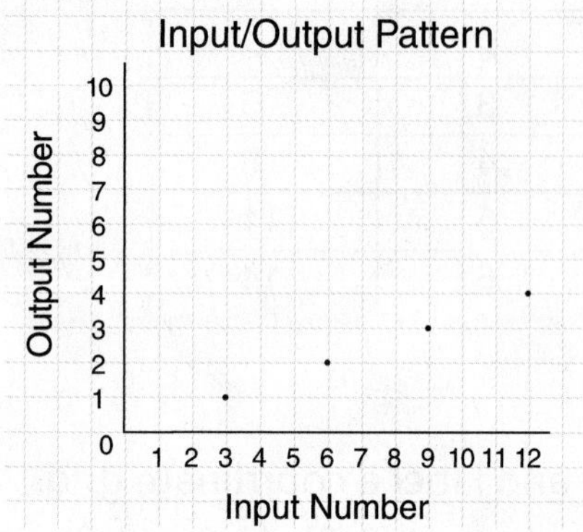

2. Draw a graph to compare the input and output numbers for each machine.
   Each time, use these input numbers: 3, 4, 5, 6, 7
   Use the graphs to find the output when the input is 10.

a)

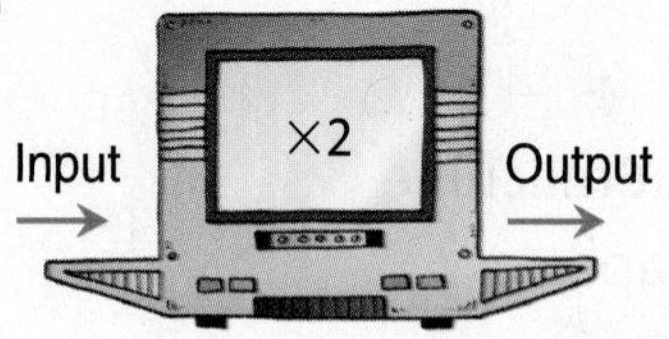

b)

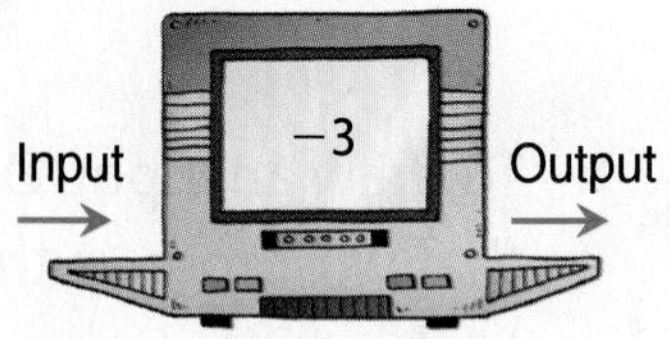

3. Draw a graph to compare the input and output numbers for this machine.
   Use these input numbers: 3, 4, 5, 6, 7
   Compare this graph to your graphs from question 2.
   How are the graphs the same? How are they different?

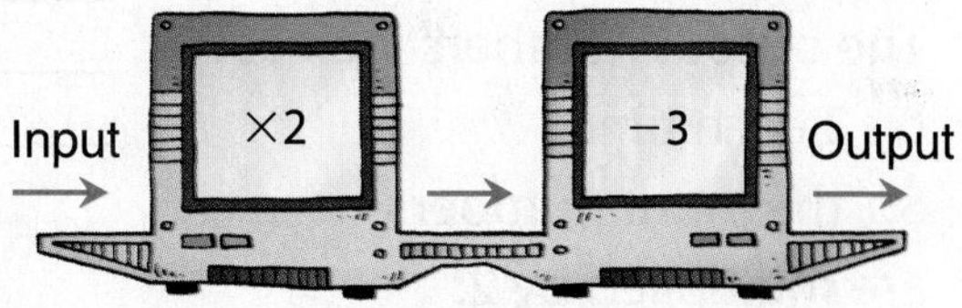

4. Here are 3 frames of a growing pattern.

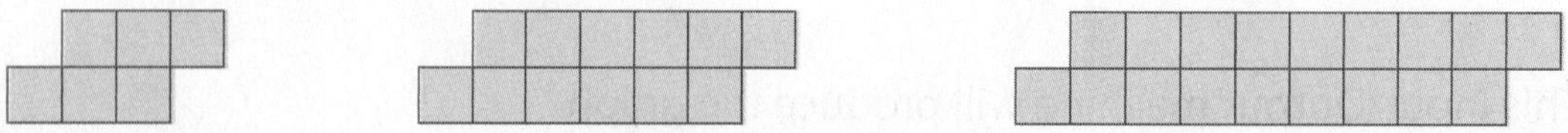

   a) Use grid paper. Draw Frames 4 and 5.
   b) The frame number is the input number.
   The number of squares is the output number.
   Draw an Input/Output machine to model this pattern.

5. Use grid paper.
Draw the first 5 frames of a growing pattern.
  a) Record the pattern in a table.
  b) Draw a graph to represent your pattern.
  c) Suppose the frame number is the input number and
    the number of squares in a frame is the output number.
    Draw an Input/Output machine that will produce
    the graph in part b.

6. The graph shows how the mass of a carton of books
is related to the number of books in the carton.

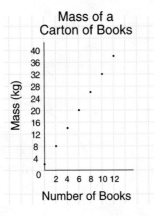

  a) Make a table to display the data.
  b) Draw an Input/Output machine that will give
    the numbers in the table.

7. A candle is 300 mm tall.
Every minute it burns, it gets 5 mm shorter.
  a) Make a table to show the height of the candle
    every minute for the first 10 min.
  b) Graph the data in the table.
  c) How tall will the candle be after 30 min?

Reflect

Suppose you look at a graph of input and
output numbers.
How can you tell which numbers and operations
were used in the Input/Output machine?
Use examples to explain.

Numbers Every Day

Mental Math

Use these numbers.

343 225 111 156 267 419

• Which two numbers have
  the least difference?

• Find two numbers whose
  sum has 0 ones.

Patterns in Geometry

Explore •••

Your teacher will give you a large copy of these polygons.

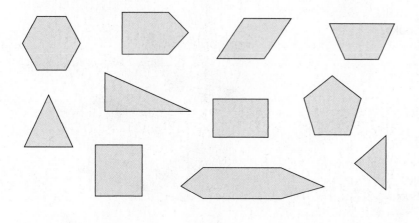

> A diagonal is a line segment that joins vertices that are not next to each other. These vertices are **non-adjacent**.

➤ Draw all the diagonals in each polygon.

➤ Record your work in a table like this:

Number of Sides	Number of Diagonals
3	

➤ What patterns do you see in the table?
Use patterns to predict the number of diagonals in an octagon.
Check your prediction.

Show *and* Share

Share your patterns with another pair of students.
In a polygon, how is the number of sides related to the number of diagonals?
How did you predict the number of diagonals in an octagon?

We can use patterns to find other relationships in geometry.

The table shows the numbers of faces, vertices, and edges for different prisms.

Prism		Faces	Vertices	Edges
Triangular Prism		5	6	9
Rectangular Prism		6	8	12
Pentagonal Prism		7	10	15
Hexagonal Prism		8	12	18

➤ The number of faces plus the number of vertices
   is 2 more than the number of edges.
   A rectangular prism has 6 faces, 8 vertices, and 12 edges.
   $6 + 8 = 2 + 12$

   Here are some more patterns for prisms.

➤ The number of faces of a prism is 2 more than
   the number of sides on the base.
   A hexagon has 6 sides.
   A hexagonal prism has $6 + 2$, or 8 faces.

➤ The number of vertices of a prism is double
   the number of sides on the base.
   A triangle has 3 sides.
   A triangular prism has 3×2, or 6 vertices.

➤ The number of edges of a prism is triple
   the number of sides on the base.
   A pentagon has 5 sides.
   A pentagonal prism has 5×3, or 15 edges.

This relationship
is called
Euler's Formula.
It is named for
Leonhard Euler,
who discovered it.

1. You will need pyramids.

Pyramid	Number of Faces	Number of Vertices	Number of Edges
Triangular			
Rectangular			
Pentagonal			
Hexagonal			

a) Copy and complete the table.

b) Describe the patterns you see.

c) How do the patterns for pyramids compare to the patterns for prisms?

2. Here is a growing pattern.

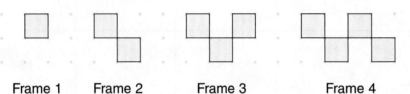

Frame 1   Frame 2   Frame 3   Frame 4

a) Draw the next 3 frames on square dot paper.

b) Copy and complete the table for 7 frames.

c) How is the number of vertices related to the frame number?

d) How is the number of sides related to the frame number?

Frame Number	Number of Vertices	Number of Sides
1		

3. This pattern was made with toothpicks.

a) How is the number of triangles related to the number of toothpicks?

b) How is the number of triangles related to the perimeter?

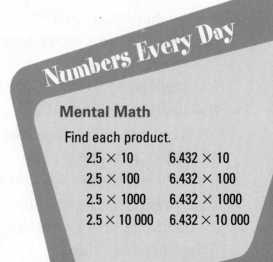

Numbers Every Day

Mental Math

Find each product.

2.5×10	6.432×10
2.5×100	6.432×100
2.5×1000	6.432×1000
$2.5 \times 10\ 000$	$6.432 \times 10\ 000$

4. Each polygon has all the diagonals drawn from one vertex.

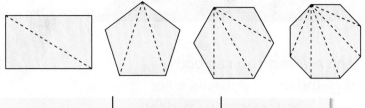

Number of Sides	Number of Diagonals	Number of Triangles

a) Copy and complete the table.

b) How is the number of sides related to the number of triangles formed by drawing diagonals from one vertex?

c) Predict the number of triangles formed for a 10-sided polygon. A 20-sided polygon.

5. Use 0.5-cm grid paper.
   a) Sketch different rectangles, each with area 36 cm². Record the lengths and widths in a table.
   b) Graph the data in a table. Describe the graph.

Math Link

Your World

Ethnomath is the study of the math related to the culture of a people.

Gloria Gilmer studies math patterns in African-American hairstyles. She is interested in the geometric designs, tessellations, and patterns that are commonly used in hair braiding and weaving.

Reflect

How does identifying patterns help us describe relationships in geometry?

Biometric Engineer

Biometrics involve measuring and analyzing human body characteristics. These include fingerprints, iris patterns, voice patterns, facial patterns, and hand measurements. Even identical twins have different fingerprints and iris patterns. Biometric devices are often seen in science-fiction and action movies.

A biometric engineer develops scanning devices and software to convert and store the scanned information in digital form. Biometric technology is used for airport security and for entrance to some theme parks, such as Walt Disney World. It will likely soon replace passwords and pass cards.

Relating Distance, Average Speed, and Time

Explore ··· 👫

You will need a stopwatch, a measuring tape or a metre stick, masking tape, and grid paper.

Measure and mark distances of 5, 10, 15, and 20 m on the floor or ground.

➤ Walk 5 m at a slow steady pace.
Your partner measures the time
to the nearest second.
Repeat for 10, 15, and 20 m.
Each time, walk at the same pace.
Record the times and distances
in a table.

➤ Switch roles.
Repeat the activity.
This time, walk at a fast steady pace.

➤ Graph the data in each table
on separate graphs.
Plot time on the horizontal axis and
distance on the vertical axis.
Use the same scales on both graphs.
How are the two graphs the same?
How are they different?

Show *and* Share

Share your work with another pair of students.
Describe any patterns in the tables.
How does changing pace affect the appearance
of a graph that compares distance and time? Explain.

Numbers Every Day

Mental Math

Which number does not belong in
this number pattern? Why?

6, 12, 18, 24, 48, 96

LESSON FOCUS | Explore the relationships among distance, average speed, and time.

393

Shelby travelled 90 km each hour.
The table shows the total distances she travelled in different times.

Time (h)	Distance (km)
0	0
1	90
2	180
3	270
4	360
5	450

➤ We can display these data on a continuous line graph.

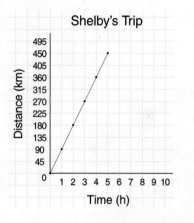

Smaller distances are also possible.
So, adjacent points are joined with a line segment.
Times that are a fraction of an hour are possible.

➤ The times are input numbers
and the distances are output numbers.

The input numbers increase by 1 each time.
The output numbers increase by 90 each time.
Each output number is the product of 90 and the input number.

An Input/Output machine with × 90 will produce
the numbers in the table.

Every hour Shelby travels 90 km.
She is travelling at an average speed of 90 km/h.

There is a relationship among distance,
average speed, and time.
The distance travelled is the product
of the average speed and the time:

Distance = Average speed × Time

For example, 360 = 90 × 4

You will need grid paper.

1. For each table:
   • Draw a continuous line graph.
   • Draw an Input/Output machine.
   • Find the average speed.

a)

Time (s)	Distance (m)
0	0
1	4
2	8
3	12
4	16
5	20

b)

Time (s)	Distance (m)
0	0
1	50
2	100
3	150
4	200
5	250

2. Students are raising money by walking 5 km in a charity walk-a-thon.
Zachary walks at an average speed of 1 m/s.
Yasmin walks at an average speed of 1.5 m/s.
Faiz walks at an average speed of 2 m/s.

Time (s)	Distance (m)

   a) Copy and complete this table for each student for the first 10 s.
   b) Draw a continuous line graph for each student. Use the same scale each time.
   c) Compare the graphs in part b.

3. John went for a hike.
He walked at an average speed of 5 km/h.

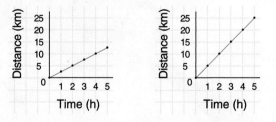

   a) Which graph represents John's trip? How do you know?
   b) What is the average speed in the other graph? How did you find out?

4. Casey plans to visit a friend who lives 320 km away.
He expects to travel at an average speed of 80 km/h.
How long will it take Casey to get to his friend's house?

5. Skylar jogs at an average speed of 2 m/s.
Rylee jogs at an average speed of 3 m/s.
The girls have a race.
Rylee gives Skylar a 10-m head start.
a) Copy and complete the table for the first 10 s.

Time (s)	Rylee's Distance (m)	Skylar's Distance (m)
0	0	10
1	3	12

b) Graph the data on the same grid.
c) When does Rylee pass Skylar?
How do you know?

6. Here are 3 ways to charge for a taxi ride.
- $2.50 per ride + $2.00 per km
- $15.00 per ride + $0.10 per km
- $0.25 per km

a) Copy and complete the table up to 5 km
for each way.

Distance (km)	Cost ($)

b) Draw a graph to display each way.
c) Suppose you were a taxi driver.
How would you charge your customers? Explain.

At Home

Reflect

What is meant by the term
average speed?
Use examples to explain.

The next time you travel in a car,
measure the time it takes to travel 2 km
at different speeds. Compare the time
it takes to travel 2 km in town to the
time it takes to travel 2 km on the highway.

Using *AppleWorks* to Explore Patterns

Work with a partner.

Use *AppleWorks*.
Follow these steps to explore how
changing average speed affects the
distance travelled in a given time.

1. Open a new spreadsheet in *AppleWorks*.

   Click:
   Spreadsheet

2. To **enter the data**:
   Click cell A1 to select it. Type: Time (h)
   Press Enter.
   Enter hours 0 to 5 in cells A2 to A7.
   Click cell B1 to select it. Type: Distance (km)
   Press Enter.
   Click cell B3 to select it.
   Distance is the product of average speed and time.
   Type the formula: =A3*55
   Press Enter.

   You have entered a formula to find a product.
   The time in cell A2 is multiplied by the average speed 55 km/h.
   The product is displayed in cell B2.

   To **copy the formula**:
   Click cell B2 to select it.

   Click: Edit , then click: Copy   Ctrl+C

   Click cell B3 to select it.

   Click: Edit , then click: Paste   Ctrl+V

   Repeat for cells B3 to B6.

3. To **format the spreadsheet**:
   Click cell A1 to select it.

   Click: Format , then click: Style   ▶

   Click: Bold   Ctrl+B

   Repeat for cell B1.

4. To **change the width of the columns**:
   Click cell A1.
   Hold down the mouse button and drag to cell B1.
   Release the mouse button.
   Click: Format , then click: Column Width...
   Enter 85 pt for the column width.
   Click: OK

   Column Width

   Column Width: | 85 pt
   ☐ Use default
   ⑦ | OK | Cancel

5. To **select cells A2 to B6**:
   Click to select cell A2.
   Hold down the mouse button and drag to cell B6.

6. To **create a continuous line graph**:
   Click: Options , then click: Make Chart...   Ctrl+M

   Click the Gallery tab, then click: [X-Y Line]

   No options should be selected.

   Options
   ☐ Color   ☐ Shadow
                    ☐ Square grid

   To **give the graph a title**:
   Click the Labels tab.
   Select Show Title.
   Make sure Show Legend
   is not selected.
   Type: Distance Travelled

   Chart Options

   Gallery | Axes | Series | Labels | General
   ☑ Show Title
   Title: Distance Travelled
   ☑ Horizontal
   ☐ Shadow
   ☐ Show Legend

   To **label the axes**:
   Click the Axes tab.

   Click: ⦿ X axis

   Type the Axis label: Time (h)
   Enter these settings.

   Minimum: | Maximum: | Step size: | ☐ Log:
   0 | 6 | 1 |

Click: ⊙ Y axis

Type the Axis label: Distance (km)

Enter these settings:

Minimum:	Maximum:	Step size:	☐ Log:
0	500	50	

Click: OK

7. To **move the graph**:

Click the graph to select it.

Click and hold down the mouse button.

Drag the graph until it is where you want it.

Release the mouse button.

8. To **print the graph**:

Click: File , then click: Print...   Ctrl+P

Click: OK

9. To **save your spreadsheet**:

Click: File , then click: Save As...   Shft+Ctrl+S

Name your file.

Then click: Save

10. Explore what happens to the distance travelled
as the average speed changes.

Click to select cell B2.

Change 55 to 100.

Copy cell B2 and paste the new formula into cells B3 to B6.

How does the graph change?

11. Repeat Step 10 for different average speeds.

Reflect

How does using a spreadsheet help you to explore
the relationships among distance, average speed, and time?

Strategies Toolkit

Explore

When you take a test, how do you make sure you do your best?

- Brainstorm tips for taking a test.
- Think about what you can do before a test, as well as when you are writing the test.
- Record your ideas on a chart.

Show and Share

Share your chart with another group of students. Discuss your test-taking strategies.

Connect

Here are some things you can do to help yourself do well on tests.

Getting Ready

☑ Find out what will be covered on the test.

☑ Review your notes and the textbook. Try sample questions.

☑ Think about what worked well for you on previous tests.

☑ Think about what you are good at. That will help you be calm and confident.

☑ Practise difficult questions with a friend or family member.

☑ Get a good night's sleep. Eat a nutritious breakfast.

☑ Gather all the equipment you need.

Strategies for Success

- **Get unstuck.**
- **Check and reflect.**
- **Focus on the problem.**
- **Represent your thinking.**
- **Select an answer.**
- **Do your best on a test.**
- **Explain your answer.**

When you first get the test

- ✓ Listen to the instructions carefully.
- ✓ Find out how much time you will have.
- ✓ Read the instructions. Ask about anything that is not clear.
- ✓ Look over the whole test.
- ✓ Be calm and confident.

Answer the questions

- ✓ Read the questions carefully.
- ✓ Start by answering the questions you find easy.
- ✓ Leave any that you are stuck on for later.
- ✓ Work steadily. Don't get stuck in one place.
- ✓ Remember strategies for answering different kinds of questions.

When you have finished the questions

- ✓ Use any time you have left to check your work. For each question, ask yourself:
  - Did I answer the question?
  - Did I leave anything out?
  - Is my answer reasonable? (Does it make sense?)

Practice

1. Look at the strategies in *Connect*.
   a) Which strategies do you already use?
   b) Which strategies do you often forget or have trouble with?

2. Choose one or two of the strategies to practise. Make an action plan to help you work on the strategies. Here is an example.

To improve my test taking skills, I am working on: _____

What I will do to reach my goal	Who will help me	How I will know I am getting better

Reflect

Describe some things you can do to help you do better on tests.

LESSON

1

1. Use triangular dot paper.
   Draw 5 frames of a growing pattern.
   a) In a table, record the frame number and the number
      of triangles in the frame.
   b) Draw a graph to represent your pattern.
   c) Use the graph to find the number of triangles in Frame 10.
   d) Does any frame have 20 triangles? 30 triangles?
      How do you know?

2. Use grid paper.
   a) Draw a growing pattern to match this graph.
      How did you decide how to draw the pattern?
   b) Make a table.
      Record the frame number and the number
      of squares in a frame.
   c) Which frame has 48 squares? 88 squares?
      How do you know?
   d) Does any frame have 60 squares? 100 squares?
      How do you know?

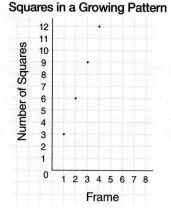

Squares in a Growing Pattern

2

3. a) Make a table for this Input/Output machine.

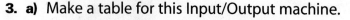
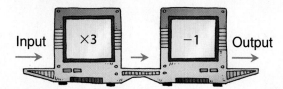

Input   ×3   −1   Output

   b) Graph the data in the table.
   c) Use the graph to find the output when the input is 12.

4. The graph shows the input and output numbers
   for an Input/Output machine.
   a) Draw the Input/Output machine.
   b) Which input number has output 30?
   c) Which output number has input 10?

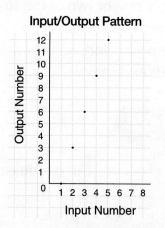

Input/Output Pattern

402

3

5. Use 0.5-cm grid paper.
Draw as many different rectangles as you can
that have perimeter 20 cm.
   a) Find the area of each rectangle.
   Record the width and area of each rectangle in a table.
   b) Graph the data in the table. Did you join the points? Explain.
   c) Describe the graph.
   How can you use the graph to find the width and area
   of a rectangle with perimeter 20 cm that you did not draw?

4

6. For the table:
   a) Draw a graph.
   b) Draw an Input/Output machine.
   c) Find the average speed.

Time (s)	Distance (m)
1	22
2	44
3	66
4	88
5	110

7. James jogged 27 km in 3 h.
What was his average speed?

8. Kelly plans to visit her cousin.
The distance from Kelly's house to
her cousin's house is 540 km.
Kelly thinks she will be able to drive
an average speed of 90 km/h.
How long will it take Kelly to make the trip?

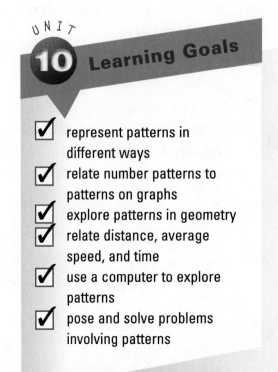

UNIT
10 Learning Goals

☑ represent patterns in
different ways
☑ relate number patterns to
patterns on graphs
☑ explore patterns in geometry
☑ relate distance, average
speed, and time
☑ use a computer to explore
patterns
☑ pose and solve problems
involving patterns

You will need:
- a length of rope
- a metre stick or measuring tape
- grid paper

Tree climbers use many different knots and hitches.
A stop knot is always tied at the end of the rope.
The stop knot will keep the climber from falling off the rope.
Here are some of the knots that can be used as a stop knot:

Overhand Knot

Double Overhand

Figure Eight

Part 1

➤ Measure and record the length of the rope.

➤ Choose one of the stop knots.
Tie one knot in the rope.
Measure and record the new length of the rope.

➤ Continue until you have tied 5 knots in the rope.
Tie the same kind of knot each time.
Measure and record the length of the rope after
tying each knot.

Part 2

➤ Draw a graph to compare the number of knots to
the length of the rope.
Describe any patterns you see.

➤ Use your graph to make predictions.
Check each prediction.
Explain any differences between your predictions
and the actual results.

Part 3

➤ Choose a different stop knot or use a thicker
or thinner rope.
Investigate the relationship between the number
of knots and the length of the rope.

➤ Write about what you find out.

Check List

Your work should show
- ☑ a precise record of your measurements
- ☑ a correctly constructed and labelled graph
- ☑ a clear description of the patterns and relationships you discover
- ☑ a logical explanation of your findings

Reflect on the Unit

Write about different ways you can represent patterns.
Use examples to explain.

Probability

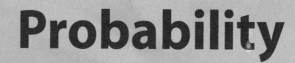

Alien Encounters!

Learning Goals

- use the language of probability
- use fractions and percents to describe probability
- count possible outcomes using tree diagrams
- conduct probability experiments
- compare experimental results to predictions
- use probability to solve problems

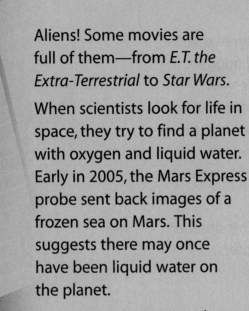

Aliens! Some movies are full of them—from *E.T. the Extra-Terrestrial* to *Star Wars*.

When scientists look for life in space, they try to find a planet with oxygen and liquid water. Early in 2005, the Mars Express probe sent back images of a frozen sea on Mars. This suggests there may once have been liquid water on the planet.

Scientists are one step closer to finding life on Mars!

Use the words *certain, likely, unlikely, possible,* or *impossible* to describe each statement.

- There is life on Mars.
- Earth's atmosphere contains oxygen.
- If a planet has oxygen and liquid water, there will be life on the planet.
- If aliens exist, they will look like humans.

1

Describing Probabilities

In a legend, a knight is given two sacks.
Each sack contains all gold nuggets,
all rocks, or a mixture of the two.
The knight can keep one of the sacks.
Ten times for each sack, the knight may
take an object, look at it, and return it.
How can this help the knight choose the
sack with more gold?

In *Explore*, you will model this situation
using paper bags and counters.

Explore

Your teacher will give you 2 paper bags, marked A and B.
Each bag contains 10 counters.
Each bag may contain all yellow counters, all blue counters,
or some counters of each colour.
The yellow counters represent gold nuggets.
The blue counters represent rocks.

➤ Draw a counter from bag A.
Record its colour and replace it.
Do this a total of 10 times.
Based on your results, use a word and a fraction to describe
how likely you are to draw a yellow counter from bag A.

➤ Repeat these steps for bag B.

➤ Based on your experiment, which bag would you choose? Why?

➤ Open the bags.
Did you make the correct choice? Explain.

Show *and* Share

Share your results with other pairs of students.
How did the experiment help you choose a bag?
Why might groups have had different fractions for bags that
contained the same combination of yellow and blue counters?

Connect . . . .

A probability tells us the likelihood of an event.
The fractions you wrote in *Explore* were **experimental probabilities**.
They were based on the results of an experiment.

$$\text{Experimental probability} = \frac{\text{Number of times an outcome occurs}}{\text{Number of times the experiment is conducted}}$$

We can also write probabilities without conducting experiments.
These are called **theoretical probabilities**.
When all the outcomes are equally likely,

$$\text{Theoretical probability} = \frac{\text{Number of favourable outcomes}}{\text{Number of possible outcomes}}$$

The students in Sergio's class make
a graph of their favourite sports.
Then they put their names in a hat.

Sergio draws a name without looking.

From the graph, there are 30 students in the class.

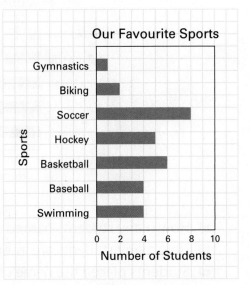

Our Favourite Sports

- It is very unlikely that the person drawn
  prefers gymnastics.
  Only 1 of the 30 people chose gymnastics.
  The probability of choosing a person
  whose favourite sport is gymnastics is $\frac{1}{30}$.

- It is very likely that the person drawn prefers a team sport.
  Eight people chose soccer, 5 chose hockey, 6 chose basketball, and 4 chose baseball.
  $8 + 5 + 6 + 4 = 23$
  Twenty-three of 30 people chose team sports.
  The probability of choosing a person whose favourite sport is a team sport is $\frac{23}{30}$.

- It is certain that the person drawn is in Sergio's class.
  All 30 people are in his class.
  The probability of choosing a person in Sergio's class is $\frac{30}{30}$, or 1.

- It is impossible that the person drawn prefers golf.
  No one in the class chose golf as her or his favourite sport.
  The probability of choosing a person whose favourite sport is golf is $\frac{0}{30}$, or 0.

All probabilities are between 0 and 1.

Practice

1. The students in Ann's class made a graph of their favourite animated movies.

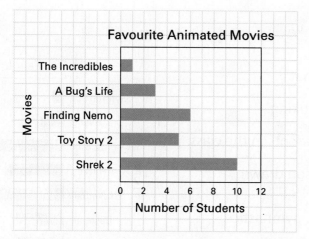

Favourite Animated Movies

Movies: The Incredibles, A Bug's Life, Finding Nemo, Toy Story 2, Shrek 2

Number of Students

   a) How many students named each movie as their favourite?
   b) How many students are in Ann's class?
   c) Students placed the name of their movie in a bag.
      Ann drew one name without looking.
      What is the probability that Ann will draw *Shrek 2*?
      The Incredibles? *Mulan*?

2. Jamar and Yvonne are playing a game with this spinner. Jamar wins a point if the pointer lands on green or blue. Yvonne wins a point if the pointer lands on red or yellow. Is this a fair game? Explain how you know.

A fair game is one where all players are equally likely to win.

3. Suppose you put counters in a bag. Someone will draw 1 counter from it. Describe, with pictures or words, the counters you would put in the bag for each situation. Explain how you decided how many counters of each colour to use.

a) Red is certain to be drawn.

b) Red and blue are equally likely to be drawn.

c) Green is more likely than red to be drawn, but less likely than yellow.

d) Blue is likely, but not certain, to be drawn.

4. A standard deck of playing cards has 52 cards in 4 suits: hearts, diamonds, clubs, and spades. The deck is shuffled and you pull out 1 card at random. Use words and fractions to describe the probability of each event. Then, order the events from most likely to least likely.

a) The card is a heart.

b) The card is black.

c) The card is the Jack of spades.

d) The card is an 8.

e) The card is a red face card.

Reflect

What does it mean to say that an event is "possible, but highly improbable"? Use examples to explain.

Numbers Every Day

Number Strategies

Write each fraction as a percent.

- $\frac{1}{5}$
- $\frac{13}{100}$
- $\frac{3}{10}$
- $\frac{7}{20}$

Probability and Percent

You have described probabilities using words
such as *likely* and *unlikely*.
You have also used fractions.
Another way to describe a probability is to use a percent.

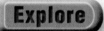 Explore

At the pet store, Guan-yin buys 100 biscuits
for her dog, Ping-Ping.
She buys 75 beef-flavoured biscuits, 15 cheese-flavoured,
and 10 chicken-flavoured.
When she gets home, Guan-yin shakes the bag
and pulls out one biscuit.

• What is the probability that Guan-yin draws
  a cheese-flavoured biscuit from the bag?
• How many ways could you state this probability?
• What is the probability of drawing a
  beef-flavoured biscuit?
  Write the probability at least 3 different ways.

Show *and* Share

Compare your probability statements with
those of other students.
How many different ways have you found
to state probabilities?
Are all of them equivalent? How do you know?
Work together to write the probability
of other possible events related to the dog biscuits.

Numbers Every Day

Mental Math

Find each sum. Describe the
strategies you used.

14 + 25 + 36
39 + 17 + 33
75 + 48 + 25

Sam buys different flavours of canned food for his cat.
On a shelf, he has 14 tins of fish, 2 tins of chicken, and 4 tins of beef.

Sam pulls a tin off the shelf without looking.

➤ What is the probability that he picks a tin of chicken-flavoured cat food?

There are 20 tins of cat food on the shelf.

- Using words:
  Only 2 of the 20 tins are chicken.
  So, picking chicken is unlikely.

- Using a fraction:
  Two of the 20 tins are chicken.
  The probability of picking chicken is $\frac{2}{20}$, or $\frac{1}{10}$.

- Using a decimal:
  The probability of picking chicken is $\frac{1}{10}$, or 0.1.

- Using a percent:
  To express $\frac{2}{20}$ as a percent, find an equivalent fraction
  with a denominator of 100.

$$\frac{2}{20} = \frac{10}{100}, \text{ or } 10\%$$

$\times 5$

$\times 5$

When we express a
probability as a percent,
we often use the word
chance to describe it.

  The chance of picking chicken is 10%.

➤ What is the probability that Sam picks a tin of fish-flavoured cat food?

There are 14 tins of fish.
This is greater than one-half the total number of cans.
So, Sam is likely to pick fish.
The probability of picking fish is $\frac{14}{20}$, or $\frac{7}{10}$, or 0.7.

To express this fraction as a percent, find an
equivalent fraction with denominator 100.

$$\frac{14}{20} = \frac{70}{100}, \text{ or } 70\%$$

$\times 5$

$\times 5$

Sam has a 70% chance of picking fish.

1. Look at this spinner.
   Some sectors are striped, some are spotted,
   and some are solid colours. The pointer is spun.
   Use a fraction, a decimal, and a percent to describe the probability
   of each event.

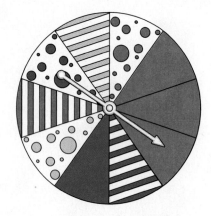

   a) The pointer will land on a blue spotted sector.
   b) The pointer will land on a striped sector.
   c) The pointer will land on a solid yellow sector.
   d) The pointer will land on a red sector.

2. Jenna and Vijay place 50 coloured tiles in a bag.
   They use 25 green tiles, 10 red tiles, 5 yellow tiles, and 10 blue tiles.
   One tile is picked without looking.
   Jenna says,   Vijay says,

   The probability of picking a green tile is $\frac{1}{2}$.

   I think the chance of picking red is 50%.

   Who is right? Explain your thinking.

3. Draw a spinner.
   Colour it so that the probability of spinning blue
   is 40%, red is 30%, green is 20%, and yellow is 10%.
   Describe how you divided the spinner into sectors
   and decided how to colour the sectors.

4. Alima is running a game at her school carnival.
   She floats 20 plastic fish in a small pool.
   One fish has a mark that can only be seen
   once it is caught.
   Each person plays until a fish is caught.
   Then, the fish is returned to the pool.
   If you catch an unmarked fish, you win a small prize.
   If you catch the marked fish, you win a large prize.
   a) Use words, fractions, a decimal, and a percent
      to describe each probability.
      • You win a small prize.
      • You win a large prize.
      • You win something.
      • You do not win anything.
   b) Would you play the game if it cost $2? Explain.

5. Thanh has 20 felt pens in a pencil case.
   He has 6 blue pens, 5 red pens, 2 yellow pens, 3 green pens,
   2 brown pens, 1 purple pen, and 1 black pen.
   Thanh reaches into the case without looking and pulls out one pen.
   Write a percent to describe the probability of each event.
   a) Thanh picks either a yellow or a green pen.
   b) Thanh picks either a blue or a red pen.
   c) Thanh picks a coloured pen.
   d) Thanh picks a grey pen.
   e) Thanh picks a purple pen.

6. Tomas has a bag of 200 hard candies.
   Suppose he chooses a candy without looking.
   There is a 25% chance he will get a cherry candy.
   How many cherry candies are in the bag?
   Explain your thinking.

Reflect

Your friend tells you, "There's a 90%
chance I'll be able to come to
the movie tomorrow."
What does "90% chance" mean?

At Home

Each night for a week, find a
weather forecast for the next day.
Record the probability of precipitation.
Record if there is any precipitation
the next day.
Would you say the forecasts that week
were accurate? Explain.

Tree Diagrams

The events you have explored so far have involved one action,
such as drawing a card or spinning a pointer.
Some events involve two or more actions.

For his party, Jordan buys juice boxes and
slices of pizza.
He buys equal amounts of apple, orange,
cherry, grape, and cranberry juice.
He also buys equal numbers of pepperoni,
vegetarian, and plain pizza slices.

• How many different combinations
  of one juice and one pizza slice
  can Jordan's guests have?

• Carla is the first guest to arrive.
  She chooses her juice and pizza slice
  without looking.
  What is the probability she will get
  an orange juice and a vegetarian pizza slice?

Show *and* Share

Compare your method for finding all the
possible combinations of juice and pizza with
those of other pairs of students.
Was one method more efficient than another?
Explain.
How did you find the probability that Carla
got orange juice and a vegetarian pizza slice?

Numbers Every Day

Number Strategies

Write each percent as a
fraction and as a decimal.

75%

20%

3%

95%

When an event involves two or more actions, a tree diagram can help us find and count all the possible outcomes.

➤ Ramon's class is preparing for an all-day hike.
Each student will make a small bag of trail mix for the hike.
To make the mix, students must choose one ingredient from each of three lists.
How many different kinds of trail mix can Ramon make?

List A	*List B*	*List C*
coconut	raisins	chocolate chips
oat flakes	dried apricots	sunflower seeds
puffed rice		

Ramon uses a tree diagram to list all the possible combinations he can make:

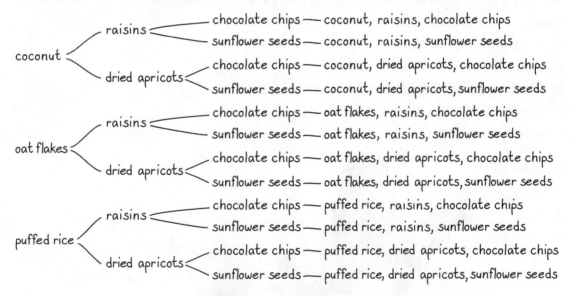

coconut
  raisins
    chocolate chips — coconut, raisins, chocolate chips
    sunflower seeds — coconut, raisins, sunflower seeds
  dried apricots
    chocolate chips — coconut, dried apricots, chocolate chips
    sunflower seeds — coconut, dried apricots, sunflower seeds

oat flakes
  raisins
    chocolate chips — oat flakes, raisins, chocolate chips
    sunflower seeds — oat flakes, raisins, sunflower seeds
  dried apricots
    chocolate chips — oat flakes, dried apricots, chocolate chips
    sunflower seeds — oat flakes, dried apricots, sunflower seeds

puffed rice
  raisins
    chocolate chips — puffed rice, raisins, chocolate chips
    sunflower seeds — puffed rice, raisins, sunflower seeds
  dried apricots
    chocolate chips — puffed rice, dried apricots, chocolate chips
    sunflower seeds — puffed rice, dried apricots, sunflower seeds

Ramon can make 12 different types of trail mix.

➤ Ramon chooses the ingredients by pointing at the list without looking.
What is the probability his trail mix will have raisins and chocolate chips?

All 12 combinations are equally likely.
Three combinations have raisins and chocolate chips.
The probability Ramon's trail mix will have raisins and chocolate chips is $\frac{3}{12}$, or $\frac{1}{4}$.
As a percent, there is a 25% chance that Ramon's trail mix will have raisins and chocolate chips.

Practice

Draw a tree diagram to help you answer each question.

1. Aisha is making earrings for her friends.
   She has a basket full of yellow, orange, and pink glass beads.
   There is the same number of beads of each colour.
   Each earring uses 2 beads.
   a) Describe the earrings Aisha can make.
   b) Aisha picks the beads from her basket without looking.
      What is the probability she will create an earring with 2 pink beads?

2. Steven and Mansa toss a penny, a nickel, then a dime.
   a) What are all the possible outcomes?
   b) Steven gets a point if he tosses 2 or 3 heads.
      Mansa gets a point if he tosses 1 or 2 tails.
      Is this game fair?
      If not, how could you change it to be fair?

3. Shauna is getting ready for a "crazy costumes" party.
   She will wear either her clown suit or her ballet tutu.
   On her head, Shauna can wear a hockey helmet,
   a punk wig, or a Mexican sombrero.
   On her feet, she can wear swimming flippers,
   furry monster slippers, or a pair of sparkly high heels.
   a) How many different 3-part costumes can Shauna create?
   b) Suppose all the costume choices are equally likely.
      What is the probability Shauna's costume will include a ballet tutu?

4. Hyo Jin is buying a new car.
   She can choose from 5 paint colours—black, blue, red, silver,
   or gold—and 2 upholstery colours—grey or black.
   a) List all the possible combinations of paint and
      upholstery colours.
   b) Suppose Hyo Jin were to choose colours
      by pointing at lists without looking.
      What is the probability she would end up
      with a silver or black car with grey upholstery?

5. To play a carnival game, you spin 2 large spinners
   like these.
   If the pointers land on a star and a happy face
   in the same turn, you win a prize.
   What is the probability you will win a prize
   on your first turn?

Reflect

How do you know when you have found all the possible
outcomes in an event involving two or more actions?

Strategies Toolkit

Explore

You will need a copy of this spinner.
Suppose you spin the pointer on this spinner 24 times.
Predict how many times the pointer will land
on each colour. Explain your thinking.
Spin the pointer and record what happens.
Explain what you found out.

Show *and* Share

Share your explanation with a classmate.
Which part of your explanation helped to make it clear?

Connect

Here are some ways to explain your thinking.

Describe your idea:

Think about explaining the problem to someone
who has never seen it before. Include details.
Use the language of the problem. Use thinking words
such as *I noticed, I was surprised, I think/thought, I wondered.*

Strategies for Success

- **Get unstuck.**
- **Check and reflect.**
- **Focus on the problem.**
- **Represent your thinking.**
- **Select an answer.**
- **Do your best on a test.**
- **Explain your answer.**

Justify your thinking:

Tell **how** you know something is true.
Defend your idea.
Give proof for your statements.
Use thinking words and cause and effect phrases like:
because …, so that means …, as a result, if you … then …

Include examples:

Use examples to make your idea clear.
Include labelled sketches or diagrams.
If you have made tables or done calculations,
put those in, too.

Practice

1. Make a three-part spinner that is different
   from that used in *Explore*.
   Colour the sectors red, blue, and yellow.
   Repeat the activity from *Explore* using your spinner.

2. Compare your spinner to a classmate's spinner.
   Predict what will happen if you both spin
   your pointers once.
   Explain your prediction. Spin the pointer to check it.

Reflect

Describe two things that are important when you are explaining
an answer to someone who has not done the question.

Conducting Experiments

Suppose you drop a spoon.
Do you think it is more likely to land rightside up
or upside down, or are both ways equally likely?
You will conduct an experiment to find out.

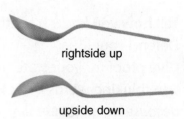

rightside up

upside down

Explore

You will need a bag and 10 plastic spoons.

➤ Place 10 plastic spoons in a bag.
Shake them up and drop them on the floor.
Count how many spoons land rightside up
and how many land upside down.
Record your results.

Suppose you dropped 100 spoons.
Use the results of your first trial.
Predict how many spoons would
land rightside up.

➤ Repeat the experiment 9 more times.
This is the same as dropping 100 spoons.
Record your results each time.
Total the results.

Compare your prediction with your results. What do you notice?
Use your results from 10 trials. Predict the number of spoons
that would land rightside up if you dropped 1000 spoons.

Show and Share

Combine your results with those of other groups of students.
What is the total number of spoons dropped?
If necessary, drop more spoons so the total is 1000.
How many spoons landed rightside up?
How do these results compare with your prediction? What do you notice?

We did not know if the outcomes of the spoon experiment
are equally likely.
We cannot calculate the theoretical probability.
We can calculate the experimental probability.

In some situations, we can find both
theoretical and experimental probabilities.

Kelsey and Max toss a coin and spin the
pointer on a spinner with congruent sections
numbered 1 to 5.
What is the probability of getting "heads and 3?"

➤ Find the theoretical probability.
Kelsey and Max used a tree diagram
to count all the possible outcomes.

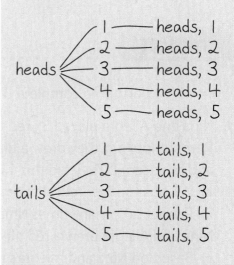

There are 10 possible outcomes
for this experiment.
All the outcomes are equally likely.
Only 1 of the outcomes is
"heads and 3."
The theoretical probability for
"heads and 3" is $\frac{1}{10}$, or 10%.

➤ Find the experimental probability
of "heads and 3."
Kelsey and Max spun the pointer
and tossed the coin 100 times.
"Heads and 3" came up 8 times.
The experimental probability of
"heads and 3" in 100 trials was $\frac{8}{100}$, or 8%.

➤ Kelsey predicted that, in 1000 trials, she would get "heads and 3":
$\frac{1}{10} \times 1000 = \frac{1000}{10}$, or 100 times

Kelsey and Max combined their results with those of other students. In 1000 trials, they found that "heads and 3" came up 110 times.
This is an experimental probability of $\frac{110}{1000}$, or 11%.

The experimental probability is close to the theoretical probability of 10%.

The predicted result is close to the actual result.

> *The more trials we conduct, the closer the experimental probability may come to the theoretical probability.*

Practice •

Work with a partner to complete these experiments.

1. Nina and Allegra placed 35 red tiles and 15 yellow tiles in a bag. Without looking, they drew a tile from the bag, recorded its colour, and replaced it. They did this 100 times.
   a) What is the theoretical probability of drawing a red tile?
   b) Predict how many times Nina and Allegra should get a red tile.
   Nina and Allegra drew a red tile from the bag 58 times.
   c) Based on Nina and Allegra's results, what is the experimental probability of drawing a red tile?
   d) Nina said, "I think we did something wrong." Do you agree? Why?
   e) Try the experiment. Record your results.
      What is your experimental probability of drawing a red tile?

2. Your teacher will give you a large copy of a blank 5-part spinner and a paperclip. Colour the spinner using red and blue.
   a) What is the theoretical probability of the pointer landing on red? On blue?
   b) Predict how many times the spinner should land on each colour in 100 spins.
   c) Spin the pointer 100 times. Record the results.
      Calculate the experimental probabilities.
   d) Predict the number of times the pointer lands on each colour in 200 trials.
   e) Find another pair who coloured the spinner the same way you did.
      Combine your results so you have 200 trials.
      How do the predicted and actual results compare?

424

3. Use an octahedron numbered 1 to 8.
   When you roll the octahedron, the result is the number
   on the bottom face.

   a) What is the theoretical probability of rolling
      a 2? An odd number?
   b) Roll the octahedron 100 times. Record the results.
   c) What was the experimental probability of rolling a 2?
      An odd number?
   d) Combine your experimental results with those
      of other students so you have 400 trials.
      What are the experimental probabilities?

4. Zeroun and Ammon are playing a game.
   They spin the pointers on these spinners.
   If both pointers land on odd numbers,
   Zeroun wins; otherwise Ammon wins.

   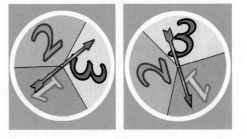

   a) Who is more likely to win?
      How do you know?
   b) Use two spinners like these.
      Play the game at least 30 times.
      Were the results what you expected?
      Explain.
   c) How could you change the game to make it fair?
      Try playing the game again using your new rules.
      Is the new game fair? Explain.

5. Imagine you toss a coin several times.
   You get 5 heads in a row.
   a) Does this mean something is wrong with
      your experiment?
   b) What is the probability of getting tails on
      your next toss? Explain your thinking.

Reflect

What is the difference between experimental
and theoretical probability?
Are they ever equal? Never equal?
Use examples to explain.

Numbers Every Day

Number Strategies

In a Grade 6 class, there are
11 boys and 15 girls.
Write a ratio to compare:
  • boys to girls
  • girls to the whole class
  • the whole class
    to boys

LESSON

1

1. Ayesha, Laurel, Gemma, Reid, Emma, Gita, and Maas write
   their names on small pieces of paper and put them into a hat.
   A name is pulled from the hat without looking.
   Use a fraction to describe the theoretical probability
   of each event.
   Then order the events from most likely to least likely.
   a) The name drawn starts with a "G."
   b) The name drawn does not start with a vowel.
   c) The name drawn ends with an "a."
   d) The name drawn contains an "e."
   e) The name drawn contains a "z."

2. Two hundred fifty-five thousand tickets were sold for the
   Heart & Stroke Foundation's Spring 2005 lottery.
   The probability of winning a prize was about 1 in 5.
   a) What was the probability of not winning?
   b) Your friend says, "If I buy 5 tickets, I'm certain to win a prize!"
      Do you think your friend is correct? Explain.

2
3

3. A soccer club is holding a draw for a gift basket.
   Club members have sold 300 tickets.
   The first ticket drawn wins the basket.
   State each probability as a fraction and a percent.
   a) Afna bought 3 tickets.
      What is the probability she will win?
   b) Ayub's father bought 12 tickets.
      What is the probability he will win?
   c) Alexa's mother bought 30 tickets.
      What is the probability she will win?

3

4. Nkiru is choosing a track suit.
   The sweatshirts come in navy, red, white, and grey.
   The track pants come in white, grey, and navy.
   a) Use a tree diagram to show all the different suits Nkiru can buy.
   b) What fraction of the suits have matching tops and pants?

5. Nalren and Chris made up a game with these spinners.
Each player chooses a number.
Players take turns to spin both pointers.
If the sum of the two numbers matches
your number, you win a point.

a) What are the possible sums?

b) What is the theoretical probability that
the sum will be 10? 6?

c) Suppose you played this game.
Which number would you choose? Why?

d) Use a pair of spinners like these.
Play the game at least 20 times.
Use the number you suggested in part c each time.
What was the experimental probability of that sum?

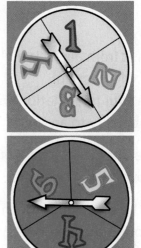

6. Jessica and Saima are rolling a regular decahedron.
It has 10 faces labelled 0 to 9.

a) What is the theoretical probability
of rolling 3?

b) What is the theoretical probability of
rolling an odd number?

c) In 100 rolls, how many times would
you expect to get a 3? An odd number?
Explain your reasoning.

d) Saima rolled the decahedron 100 times.
She rolled 3 sixteen times.
What is Saima's experimental probability
of rolling 3?
Explain how this compares to the
theoretical probability.

7. Hassan and Eric tossed a coin.
They got heads 6 times in a row.
Eric said, "I don't think this is a fair coin."

a) What do you think Eric meant by a "fair coin?"

b) Do you agree with Eric?
Explain your thinking.

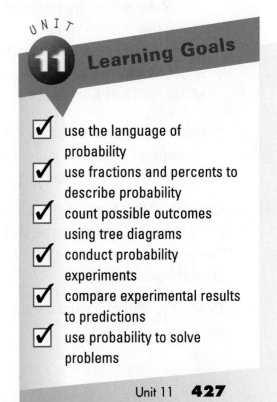

UNIT

11 Learning Goals

- ✓ use the language of probability
- ✓ use fractions and percents to describe probability
- ✓ count possible outcomes using tree diagrams
- ✓ conduct probability experiments
- ✓ compare experimental results to predictions
- ✓ use probability to solve problems

A visit from aliens is highly unlikely—but it could happen!
Use your imagination and your knowledge of probability to answer these questions.

One afternoon, a fleet of spaceships is hovering above your schoolyard.

As the spaceships touch down, small faces peer out through the windows. Each face is green or purple, has 3, 5, or 8 eyes, and is shaped like a triangle or a hexagon.

1. How many different face types might you see? Use a table or a tree diagram to explain your thinking.

2. You are one of 40 students and 10 teachers who rush out to greet the aliens. Who will approach the spaceships? To decide, names are put in a hat. One name will be drawn. What is the probability of each outcome?
   a) A student will be chosen.
   b) You will be chosen.

The aliens are playing a game with a spinner and a number cube. The cube is numbered 1 to 6. The spinner has 4 equal sectors, labelled 1 to 4.

Each player writes down a number between 0 and 5. He or she then rolls the cube and spins the pointer. The lesser number is subtracted from the greater number.

To win, the difference must equal the number the player wrote.

3. Play the game many times.
   Each time, record the numbers and their difference.
   Calculate the experimental probability
   of getting each difference.

4. a) List all the possible differences.
   b) Find the theoretical probability
      of getting each difference.

5. The aliens invite you to have a turn.
   The prize is a trip to their planet!
   a) Suppose you want to win the trip.
      What number would you pick? Why?
   b) Suppose you do not want to win the trip.
      What number would you pick? Why?

Reflect on the Unit

Think of two games you like to play that involve probability.
Describe some ways that probability affects the outcome of
the games. What other factors affect who wins?

Flight School

You will need grid paper, scissors, paper clips, tape, a measuring tape, and a stopwatch.

Part 1

➤ Each of you builds 2 different paper airplanes. For each airplane, use only 1 piece of grid paper. You may use scissors, paper clips, and tape.

Part 2

➤ Number your airplanes from 1 to 4. Mark a start line. Take turns to throw each airplane while your partner times the flight. Measure the distance travelled. Complete 4 trials for each airplane. Record your results in a table.

Airplane Number	Distance (cm)				Time (s)			
	Trial 1	Trial 2	Trial 3	Trial 4	Trial 1	Trial 2	Trial 3	Trial 4
1								
2								

Part 3

➤ Find the mean distance travelled by each airplane.
Find the mean time for each airplane.
Graph the data on the same grid.
Which airplane had the greatest average speed? How do you know?

➤ Find the average speed of each airplane.
Is the fastest airplane different from the other airplanes? Explain.
Is the airplane that flew the greatest distance
different from the other airplanes? Explain.

Display Your Work

Create a summary of your work.
Use pictures, numbers, and words.

Take It Further

Use your observations to create the "ultimate paper airplane."
Test your new airplane for distance and speed.
Compare this airplane to the other airplanes.
Write down any conclusions.

Unit

1

1. Which numbers are divisible by 3? By 6?
   How do you know?
   a) 2682   b) 1001   c) 741   d) 4260

2. Identify each pattern rule.
   Write the next 2 terms. Find the 12th term.
   a) 3, 9, 21, 45, 93, …
   b) 500, 483, 466, 449, 432, …

2

3. Is 63 a prime number? Is 101?
   How can you tell without finding the factors?

4. Jenna earns $15 a driveway to shovel snow.
   Last week she shovelled 7 driveways.
   Then she bought 3 posters for $6 each.
   Which expression shows how much money Jenna has left? Explain.
   a) $7 \times (15 - 3) \times 6$ b) $7 \times 15 + 3 \times 6$ c) $7 \times 15 - 3 \times 6$

5. The table shows the population of
   downtown Brampton by age in 2001.
   a) What was the total population of
      downtown Brampton in 2001?
   b) How many more people aged 20 to 39 lived
      in downtown Brampton in 2001 than people
      aged 40 to 59?

Population of Downtown Brampton, 2001

Age Group	Population
0 to 19	1065
20 to 39	1605
40 to 59	1455
60+	1105

3

6. Use a ruler, a protractor, and a compass.
   Construct quadrilateral ABCD with these measures:
   AB = 90 mm   AC = 45 mm   BD = 40 mm   CD = 50 mm $\angle$CAB = 65°

7. Which diagrams are nets? For each net, identify the solid.
   For each diagram that is not a net, explain how to change it so it is a net.
   a)   b)   c)

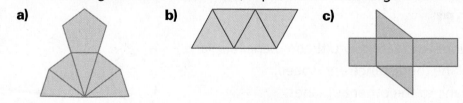

4

8. Use decimals.
Round each number to the nearest tenth of a million.
a) 678 537 299   b) 4 009 682   c) 20 099 879

9. Copy each statement.
Write a decimal with thousandths to make each statement true.
a) 5.38 < ☐   b) ☐ > 0.019   c) ☐ < 3.04

10. A regular hexagon has sides 0.01 m long.
What is the perimeter of the hexagon?
Write your answer using 2 different units.

5

11. The graph shows the causes of deforestation
of the tropical rainforest.
a) Which is the main cause of deforestation?
How do you know?
b) Which cause results in about twice as much
deforestation as commercial farming?

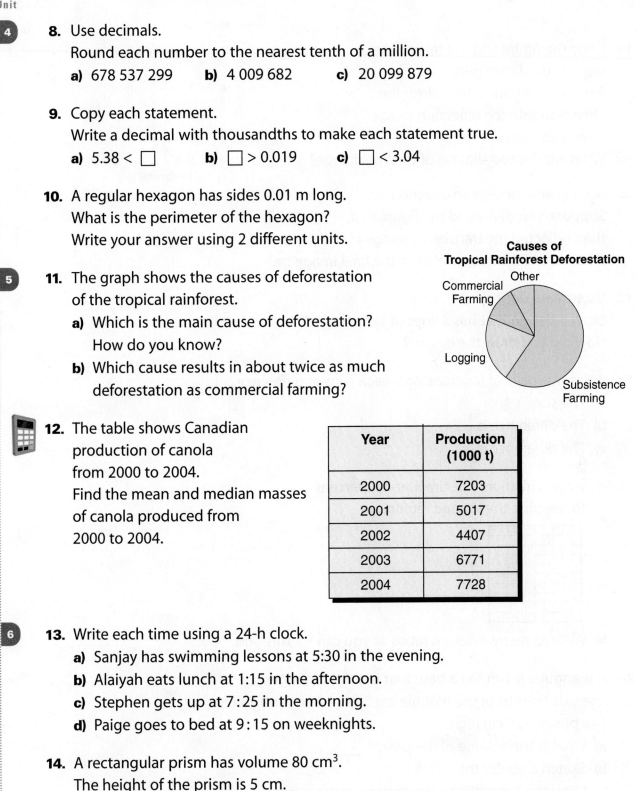

**Causes of
Tropical Rainforest Deforestation**

12. The table shows Canadian
production of canola
from 2000 to 2004.
Find the mean and median masses
of canola produced from
2000 to 2004.

Year	Production (1000 t)
2000	7203
2001	5017
2002	4407
2003	6771
2004	7728

6

13. Write each time using a 24-h clock.
a) Sanjay has swimming lessons at 5:30 in the evening.
b) Alaiyah eats lunch at 1:15 in the afternoon.
c) Stephen gets up at 7:25 in the morning.
d) Paige goes to bed at 9:15 on weeknights.

14. A rectangular prism has volume 80 cm³.
The height of the prism is 5 cm.
What might the dimensions of the base be?
Give 2 different answers.

7

15. Copy the figure and the mirror line
onto a coordinate grid.
Reflect the figure in the mirror line.
Then translate the reflection image
5 squares down.
What are the coordinates of the final image?

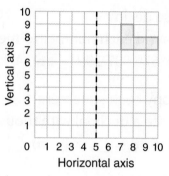

16. Look at your answer to question 15.
Suppose you translated the figure first,
then reflected the translation image in the mirror line.
What would the coordinates of the final image be?

17. Use square dot paper.
Draw a design that has 4 lines of symmetry.
How did you draw the design?

8

18. Write two pairs of fractions with each sum or difference.
 a) The sum is $\frac{2}{3}$.
 b) The difference is $\frac{1}{8}$.
 c) The difference is $\frac{3}{5}$.

19. a) Write a fraction, a decimal, and a percent
to describe the shaded region.

 b) Write as many different ratios as you can for this grid.

9

20. A triangular prism has a base that is a right triangle.
The side lengths of the triangle are 5 cm, 12 cm, and 13 cm.
The prism is 20 cm high.
 a) What is the volume of the prism?
 b) Sketch a net for the prism.
  Label the net with the dimensions of the prism.
 c) What is the surface area of the prism?

9

21. Find the area of each figure.
   a) a parallelogram with base 12 cm and height 7 cm
   b) a triangle with base 16 cm and height 9 cm

22. Use 1-cm grid paper.
   Sketch each figure.
   a) a rectangle with perimeter 40 cm and area 91 cm^2
   b) a parallelogram with area 45 cm^2

10

23. Here is a growing pattern made with regular hexagons.

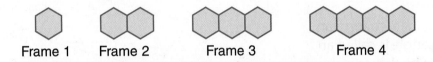

Frame 1   Frame 2   Frame 3   Frame 4

   a) Record the frame numbers and the perimeters in a table.
   b) Draw a graph to display the data in the table.
   c) Which frame has perimeter 30 units? 42 units?
   d) Does any frame have perimeter 60 units? 70 units? Explain.

11

24. Suppose you put coloured tiles in a paper bag.
   How many tiles of each colour would you put in the bag
   so the probability of drawing blue is 25%, red is 40%,
   green is 15%, and yellow is 20%?
   Give three different answers.

25. Shawna rolled a number cube
   labelled 1 to 6 one hundred times.
   She recorded her results in a tally chart.
   A classmate looked at Shawna's results
   and said, "In the next roll of the number cube,
   it is unlikely the result will be 1.
   It is probable the result will be 4."
   Do you agree with Shawna's classmate?
   Explain.

Number	Tally
1	II
2	HHT HHT HHT III
3	HHT HHT HHT
4	HHT HHT HHT HHT HHT HHT I
5	HHT HHT HHT I
6	HHT HHT HHT III

Illustrated Glossary

acute angle: an angle that measures less than 90°; ∠ABC is acute

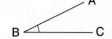

acute triangle: a triangle with all angles less than 90°; all angles are acute; △DEF is acute

a.m.: a time between midnight and just before noon

angle: two straight lines meet to form an angle; each side of an angle is called an arm; we show an angle by drawing an arc

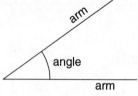

area: the amount of surface a figure or region covers; we measure area in square units, such as square centimetres or square metres

average: a single number that represents a set of numbers; see *mean*, *median*, and *mode*

average speed: a measure of how fast an object is moving on average

axis (plural: axes): a number line along the edge of a graph; we label each axis of a graph to tell what data it displays

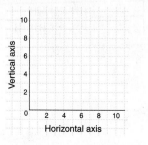

bar graph: a graph that displays data by using vertical or horizontal bars

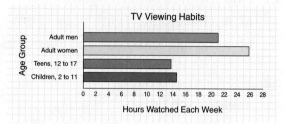

base: the face of a solid or the side of a polygon from which the height is measured

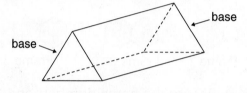

bias:

1. a graph with bias shows data in a way that someone else wants you to see them

2. a sample with bias does not truly represent the population

billion: one thousand million

broken line graph: a graph showing data points joined by line segments to show trend; for example, radio listening increased from 1998 to 1999 and decreased from 1999 to 2003

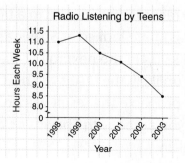

436

capacity: a measure of how much a container can hold

Cartesian plane: see *coordinate grid*

centimetre: a unit used to measure length; 1 cm = 0.01 m

circle graph: displays data using a circle divided into sectors; shows how data represent portions of one whole or one group

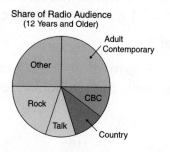

Share of Radio Audience
(12 Years and Older)

circumference: the distance around a circular object

clockwise: the direction the hands on a clock turn

 Clockwise

combination: a selection of items from different groups to make a smaller group; for example, if you have green shorts and white shorts and a green top and a white top, you get these combinations:

Shorts	Tops	Combinations
green	green / white	green, green / green, white
white	green / white	white, green / white, white

common multiple: a number that is a multiple of two or more numbers; 6 is a common multiple of 2 and 3

compatible numbers: pairs of numbers that are easy to compute

composite number: a number with three or more factors; 8 is a composite number because its factors are 1, 2, 4, and 8

concave polygon: a polygon with at least one angle greater than 180°

congruent: figures that have the same size and shape, but not necessarily the same orientation

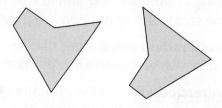

continuous line graph: a graph in which points on the line between the plotted points also have meaning; for example, in 1.5 h the hurricane travelled 300 km

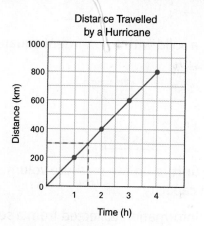

Distance Travelled
by a Hurricane

convex polygon: a polygon with all angles less than 180°

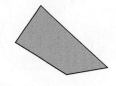

coordinate grid: a vertical number line and a horizontal number line that intersect at right angles at 0

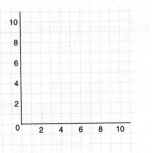

coordinates: the numbers in an ordered pair that locate a point on a grid

corresponding angles: angles that have the same relative position in a polygon

corresponding sides: sides that have the same relative position in a polygon

counterclockwise: in the opposite direction to the direction the hands on a clock turn

Counterclockwise

cube: a solid with 6 congruent square faces

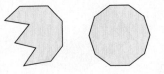

cubic unit: a unit to measure volume and capacity

data: information collected from a survey or experiment

decagon: a polygon with 10 sides

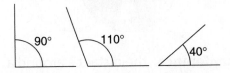

decahedron: a solid with 10 faces

decimal: a way to write a fraction or mixed number; the mixed number $3\frac{2}{10}$ can be written as the decimal 3.2

decimal point: separates the whole number part and the fraction part in a decimal; we read the decimal point as "and"; we say 3.2 as "three *and* two-tenths"

decimetre: a unit to measure length; 1 dm = 0.1 m and 1 dm = 10 cm

degree:

1. a unit to measure the size of an angle; the symbol for degrees is °

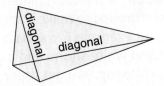

2. a unit to measure temperature; we write one degree Celsius as 1°C

denominator: the part of a fraction that tells how many equal parts are in one whole; the bottom number in a fraction

diagonal: a line that joins 2 vertices of a figure, but is not a side

difference: the result of a subtraction

dimensions:

1. the measurements of a figure or an object; a rectangle has 2 dimensions, length and width; a cube has 3 dimensions, length, width, and height

2. for an array, the number of rows and the number of columns

displacement: the volume of water moved, or displaced, by an object put in the water; the displacement of this cube is 50 mL

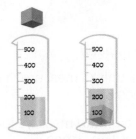

dividend: the number to be divided

divisor: the number by which another number is divided

dodecahedron: a solid with 12 faces

edge: where 2 faces of a solid meet

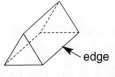
edge

elapsed time: the amount of time that passes from the start to the end of an event

equally likely: the outcomes of an event that are equally probable; for example, if you toss a coin, it is equally likely that the coin will land heads up as tails up

equally probable: see *equally likely*

equation: uses the = symbol to show two things that represent the same amount; for example, $5 + 2 = 7$

equilateral triangle: a triangle with all sides equal

equivalent: Having the same value;
$\frac{2}{3}$ and $\frac{6}{9}$ are equivalent fractions;
2 : 3 and 6 : 9 are equivalent ratios;
4.5 and 4.50 are equivalent decimals

estimate: close to an amount or value, but not exact

Euler's formula: in a polygon, the number of faces plus the number of vertices is 2 more than the number of edges

experiment: in probability, a test or trial used to investigate an idea

experimental probability: the probability of an event calculated from experimental results

expression: a mathematical statement with numbers and operations

face: see *edge*

factors: numbers that are multiplied to get a product

fair game: a game where all players have the same chance of winning

Fibonacci number: any number in the Fibonacci sequence

Fibonacci sequence: 1, 1, 2, 3, 5, 8, 13, …; each number after the first pair is the sum of the two numbers before it

formula: a short way to state a rule

gram: a unit to measure mass; 1000 g = 1 kg

grid: see *coordinate grid*

growing pattern: a pattern where each term or frame is greater than the previous term or frame

Frame 1   Frame 2   Frame 3

1, 3, 8, 10, 15, 17, 23, …

height: the perpendicular distance from the base to the opposite side or vertex

hexagon: a polygon with 6 sides

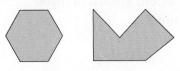

439

hundredth: a fraction that is one part of a whole when it is divided into 100 equal parts; we write one-hundredth as $\frac{1}{100}$, or 0.01

image: the figure that is the result of a transformation

improbable: an event that is unlikely to happen, but not impossible

icosahedron: a solid with 20 faces

improper fraction: a fraction that shows an amount greater than one whole; $\frac{3}{2}$ is an improper fraction

infer (verb): draw a conclusion by reasoning

inference (noun): a conclusion drawn by reasoning

Input/Output machine: performs operations on a number (the input) to produce another number (the output)

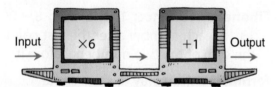

integers: the numbers . . . −3, −2, −1, 0, 1, 2, 3, . . .

inverse operation: an operation that undoes another operation; addition and subtraction are inverse operations

irregular polygon: a polygon that does not have all sides equal or all angles equal; here are two irregular hexagons

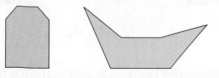

isometric drawing: a drawing of an object on triangular dot paper as the object would appear in three dimensions

isosceles triangle: a triangle with 2 sides equal

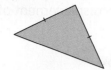

key: see *pictograph*

kilogram: a unit to measure mass; 1 kg = 1000 g

kilometre: a unit to measure long distances; 1 km = 1000 m

kite: a quadrilateral where two pairs of adjacent sides are equal

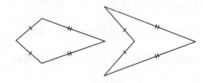

line graph: see *broken line graph* and *continuous line graph*

line symmetry: a figure has line symmetry when it can be divided into two congruent parts; if we fold the figure along its line of symmetry, the parts coincide

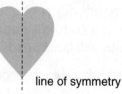

line of symmetry

linear dimension: length, width, depth, height, thickness

linear unit: a unit to measure a linear dimension

litre: a unit to measure the capacity of a container; 1 L = 1000 mL

mass: how much matter is in an object; measured in milligrams, grams, kilograms, or tonnes

mean: a number that represents the centre of a set of numbers; to find the mean, add the numbers in the set, then divide by the number of numbers; for example, for the number set 12, 15, 10, 11, the sum is 48; there are 4 numbers in the set; the mean is $48 \div 4 = 12$

median: the middle number when the data are arranged in numerical order; for an even number of data, the median is the mean of the two middle numbers; for example, for the number set 11, 12, 14, 15, the two middle numbers are 12 and 14, the median is 13

metre: a unit to measure length; 1 m = 100 cm

milligram: a unit to measure mass; 1000 mg = 1 g

millilitre: a unit to measure capacity; 1000 mL = 1 L; 1 mL = 1 cm^3

millimetre: a unit to measure length; 1 mm = 0.1 cm; 10 mm = 1 cm

million: one thousand thousand

mirror line: a line in which a figure is reflected; see *reflection*

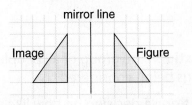

mixed number: has a whole number part and a fraction part; $3\frac{1}{2}$ is a mixed number

mode: the number that occurs most often in a set of numbers; for example, in the number set 8, 6, 10, 4, 7, 6, 9, 6, the mode is 6

multiple: a multiple of a number has that number as a factor; 10, 15, and 20 are multiples of 5

multiplication fact: a sentence that relates factors to a product

net: an arrangement that shows all the faces of a solid, joined in one piece; it can be folded to form the solid

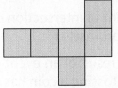

number line: has numbers in order from least to greatest; the spaces between pairs of consecutive numbers are equal

numerator: the part of a fraction that tells how many equal parts to count; the top number in a fraction; in the fraction $\frac{2}{3}$, the numerator is 2

obtuse angle: an angle measuring between 90° and 180°

obtuse triangle: a triangle with one angle greater than 90° and less than 180°

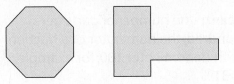

octagon: a polygon with 8 sides

operation: something done to a number or quantity; addition, subtraction, multiplication, and division are operations

ordered pair: a pair of numbers that describe a location on a coordinate grid; the first number tells the horizontal distance from the origin; the second number tells the vertical distance from the origin; for example (6, 3)

origin: the point of intersection of the axes on a coordinate grid

outcome: one result of an event or experiment; tossing a coin has two possible outcomes: heads or tails

p.m.: a time between noon and just before midnight

palindrome: a word, a phrase, or a number that reads the same from both directions; noon and 636 are palindromes

parallel: lines that are always the same distance apart

parallelogram: a quadrilateral with both pairs of opposite sides parallel

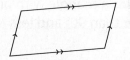

pattern rule: describes how to make a pattern; for the pattern 1, 2, 4, 8, 16, …, the pattern rule is: start at 1; multiply by 2 each time

percent: the number of parts per hundred; the numerator of a fraction with denominator 100; for example, $\frac{31}{100}$ is 31%

perimeter: the distance around a closed figure; the sum of the side lengths

period: in a large whole number, each group of 3 place values from right to left

perpendicular: two lines that intersect at a right angle

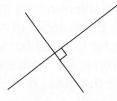

pictograph: uses pictures and symbols to display data; each picture or symbol can represent more than one object; a key tells what each picture represents

Drive	🚶🚶
Cycle	🚶🚶🚶
Walk	🚶🚶🚶🚶
Bus	🚶🚶🚶🚶🚶🚶🚶🚶🚶🚶

🚶 = 1 student

plot: use an ordered pair to locate and mark a point on a coordinate grid

polygon: a closed figure with three or more straight sides; named by the number of its sides; for example, a five-sided polygon is a pentagon

population: the group of all people or things being considered

prediction: a decision on how likely or unlikely it is that an event will happen

prime number: a whole number with exactly two factors, itself and 1; for example, 7, 13, 19, and 23 are prime numbers

prism: a solid with 2 bases

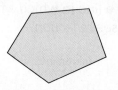

Rectangular prism

Triangular prism

442

probability: the likelihood of a particular outcome; the number of times a particular outcome occurs written as a fraction of the total number of outcomes

probable: an event that is likely, but not certain, to happen

product: the result of a multiplication

proper fraction: describes an amount less than one; a proper fraction has a numerator that is less than its denominator

protractor: an instrument that measures the number of degrees in an angle

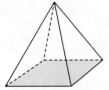

pyramid: a solid with 1 base

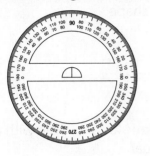

Rectangular pyramid   Triangular pyramid

quotient: the number obtained by dividing one number into another

quadrilateral: a figure with 4 sides

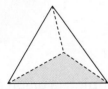

range: tells how spread out the numbers in a set of data are; found by subtracting the least value from the greatest value

rate: a comparison of quantities measured in different units; for example, 50 km/h

ratio: a comparison of quantities measured in the same unit

rectangle: a quadrilateral, with 2 pairs of equal opposite sides and 4 right angles

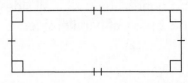

recursive pattern: a pattern in which each term can be found by applying the pattern rule to the previous term

reflection: reflects a figure in a mirror line to create a congruent image

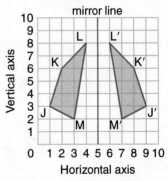

reflex angle: an angle between 180° and 360°

regular figure: see *regular polygon*

regular polygon: has all sides equal and all angles equal; here is a regular hexagon

remainder: what is left over when one number does not divide exactly into another number

repeating decimal: a decimal with a repeating pattern in the digits that follow the decimal point; for example, 0.3333...

repeating pattern: a pattern with a core that repeats; the core is the smallest part of the pattern that repeats

rhombus: a quadrilateral with all sides equal and 2 pairs of parallel sides

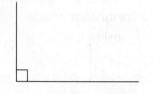

right angle: a 90° angle

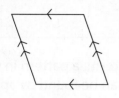

right triangle: a triangle with one 90° angle

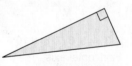

rotation: a transformation in which a figure is turned about a fixed point, called the turn centre

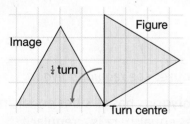

rotational symmetry: a figure that coincides with itself in less than one full turn has rotational symmetry; for example, a square has rotational symmetry of order 4

round: to estimate a number to a certain place value; for example, 397 482 rounded to the nearest thousand is 397 000

sample: a small group chosen from the population; samples are often used for surveys

scale:

1. the numbers on the axis of a graph that show the scale

2. the drawing of an object is to scale if the drawing and the object are similar; the drawing is larger or smaller than the object but has the same shape

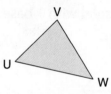

scalene triangle: a triangle with no sides equal

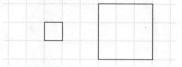

scatter plot: a graph of data that is a set of points

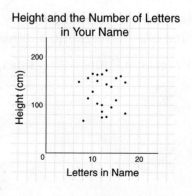

Height and the Number of Letters in Your Name

second: a small unit of time; there are 60 seconds in 1 minute; 60 s = 1 min

sector: a portion of a circle bounded by 2 radii and part of the circumference

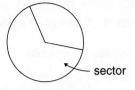
sector

SI (International System of Units) notation: a standard way to give measures for time, date, mass, volume, and other quantities

similar figures: figures that have the same shape, though they may not be the same size; these hexagons are similar

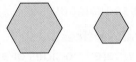

simplest form:

1. a ratio with terms that have no common factors other than 1

2. a fraction with numerator and denominator with no common factors other than 1

solid: has length, width, and height; solids have faces, edges, vertices, and bases; we name some solids by the number and shape of their bases

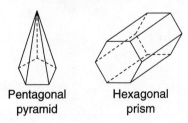

Pentagonal pyramid   Hexagonal prism

speed: a measure of how fast an object is moving

square: a quadrilateral with equal sides and angles; each angle is a right angle, or 90°

square unit: a unit to measure area

standard units: metres, square metres, cubic metres, kilograms, and seconds are some standard units

straight angle: an angle that measures 180°

sum: the result of addition; the sum of 5 and 2 is 7, or $5 + 2 = 7$

surface area: the sum of the areas of the faces of a prism

survey: used to collect data; you can survey your classmates by asking them which is their favourite ice cream flavour; see also *bias*

tenth: a fraction that is one part of a whole when it is divided into ten equal parts; we write one-tenth as $\frac{1}{10}$, or 0.1

term:

1. one number in a number pattern; for example, the number 4 is the third term in the pattern 1, 2, 4, 8, 16

2. one of the numbers being compared in a ratio

theoretical probability: the number of favourable outcomes written as a fraction of the total number of possible outcomes

thousandth: a fraction that is part of a whole when it is divided into 1000 equal parts; we write one-thousandth as $\frac{1}{1000}$, or 0.001

tiling pattern: a pattern made with congruent copies of one or more figures that covers a surface with no gaps or overlaps

tonne: a unit used to measure a very large mass; 1 t = 1000 kg

transformation: a translation (slide), a reflection (flip), and a rotation (turn) are transformations

translation: slides a figure from one location to another; a translation arrow joins matching points on the figure and its image; this figure has been translated 6 squares left and 2 squares up

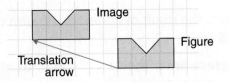

translation arrow: see *translation*

trapezoid: a quadrilateral with 1 pair of parallel sides

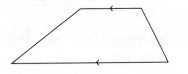

tree diagram: a visual representation of all outcomes when there is more than one choice to be made; flipping a coin twice leads to 4 possible outcomes

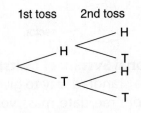

triangular prism: see *prism*

triangular pyramid: see *pyramid*

trillion: one thousand billion, or one million million

turn centre: see *rotation*

vertex (plural: vertices):
1. a point where two sides of a figure meet
2. a point where two or more edges of a solid meet

volume: the amount of space occupied by an object; volume can be measured in cubic centimetres (cm^3); $1\ cm^3 = 1\ mL$

Index

Acknowledgments

Pearson Education would like to thank the Bank of Canada and the Royal Canadian Mint for the illustrative use of Canadian bills and coins in this textbook. In addition, the publisher wishes to thank the following sources for photographs, illustrations, and other materials used in this book. Care has been taken to determine and locate ownership of copyright material in this text. We will gladly receive information enabling us to rectify any errors or omissions in credits.

Photography

Cover: Thomas Kitchin and Victoria Hurst/firstlight.ca; p. 2 Ian Crysler; p. 3 Ian Crysler; p. 4 Topical Press Agency/Getty Images; p. 7 Ian Crysler; p. 8 Ian Crysler; p. 10 Courtesy of Eric Hancock; p. 13 Ian Crysler; p. 16 Ian Crysler; p. 17 Ian Crysler; p. 20 Philip and Karen Smith/Photodisc/Getty Images; p. 21 Corel Collections *Divers and Diving*; p. 22 (top) Courtesy of www.alpenregion.ch; p. 22 (bottom) Ian Crysler; p. 23 Ian Crysler; p. 24 Ian Crysler; p. 25 Ian Crysler; p. 28 Volker Steger/ Photo Researchers Inc.; p. 29 (top) Rob Rowan/Progressive Image.CORBIS; p. 29 (bottom) Ian Crysler; p. 30 (background) Photos.com select/Index Stock Imagery; p. 30 (inset) Lynn M. Stone/Nature Picture Library; p. 31 AbleStock/Index Stock Imagery; p. 33 Ian Crysler; p. 35 Ian Crysler; p. 36 Ian Crysler; p. 37 CAMR/A.B. Dowsett/Photo Researchers, Inc.; p. 38 (top) John Cancalosi/Nature Picture Library; p. 38 (bottom) Ian Crysler; p. 40 Sexto Sol/Photodisc/Getty Images; p. 41 (top) Japan Age fotostock/firstlight.ca; p. 41 (bottom) Michael Freeman/CORBIS; p. 42 Photodisc/Getty Images; p. 43 design pics/firstlight.ca; p. 44 (left) Digital Vision Ltd.; p. 44 (right) Valerie Giles/Photo Researchers Inc.; p. 45 Ian Crysler; p. 50 Frank Siteman/Photo Edit, Inc.; p. 52 Courtesy of Canadian Stamp Auctions Ltd., Montreal, Quebec, Canada; p. 53 Ian Crysler; p. 55 Ian Crysler; p. 57 Michelle D. Bridwell/Photo Edit, Inc.; p. 58 Ian Crysler; p. 59 (top) Canadian Press/Charles Dharapak; p. 59 (bottom) Michael S. Yamashita/CORBIS; p. 59 (banner) creatas/firstlight.ca; p. 59 (inset) Photodisc/Getty Images; p. 61 Ian Crysler; p. 62 Paul Beard/Photodisc/Getty Images; p. 63 Canadian Press/Boris Spremo; p. 65 Ian Crysler; p. 68 Ian Crysler; p. 72 Wolfgang Kaehler; p. 73 Ian Crysler; p. 75 CORBIS; p. 78 Bach/zefa/CORBIS; p. 78 (inset) M. Jepp/zefa/ Masterfile Corporation; p. 79 Ian Crysler; p. 85 Ian Crysler; p. 88 Cen Lu/Maxx Images; p. 90 Ian Crysler; p. 91 Ian Crysler; p. 92 Ian Crysler; p. 93 Ian Crysler; p. 100 Corel Collections *Lighthouses*; p. 102 Ian Crysler; p. 105 Photodisc/Getty Images; p. 108 Ian Crysler; p. 109 Ian Crysler; p. 110 (top) Chris Lisle/CORBIS; p. 110 (bottom) Ian Crysler; p. 111 Ian Crysler; p. 112–113 Janet Foster/ Masterfile; p. 113 (inset) Steve Watts/Canadian Geographic. Used by permission of William Big Bull; p. 114 (left) Courtesy of Yann Pindeler; p. 114 (right) Steven E. Wilson, MDEQ OGS specimen (specimen from MDEQ Office of Geological Survey collection); p. 115 Ian Crysler; p. 116 Getty Images; p. 117 Ian Crysler; p. 120 Robinson, James/ Animals Animals/Earth Scenes; p. 121 Panstock/firstlight.ca; p. 125 Reuters/CORBIS; p. 125 (inset) AFP/Getty Images; p. 125 (banner) Canadian Press/ Associated Press AP/Koji Sasahara; p. 131 (top) Kindra Clineff/ Index Stock Imagery; p. 131 (bottom) Ian Crysler; p. 132 (top) David Young-Wolff/Photo Edit, Inc.; p. 132 (bottom) Canadian Press/Dreamworks/Courtesy of Everett Strevt; p. 133 Ian Crysler;

p. 134 Ian Crysler; p. 136 Courtesy of Manurewa High School New Zealand in partnership with RNZFB Guide Dog Services; p. 138 Bettman/ CORBIS; p. 139 Corel Collection Caves; p. 140 Ian Crysler; p. 142 (top) Corel Collection *American National Parks*; p. 142 (bottom) Canadian Press/Ron Poling; p. 143 Ian Crysler; p. 144 Ian Crysler; p. 146 Ian Crysler; p. 147 Courtesy of Joe McIver, www.joesworld.ca; p. 148 Ian Crysler; p. 150 Merlin D. Tuttle, Bat Conservation International; p. 151 (top) Canadian Press STRPA/ Gareth Coplay; p. 151 (bottom) Canadian Press STRCOC/Jean-Baptiste Benavent; p. 153 Ian Crysler; p. 155 Canadian Press/ Jonathan Hayward Strjoh; p. 156 Ian Crysler; p. 158 Ian Crysler; p. 159 Ian Crysler; p. 161 Eric Hosking/Photo Researchers, Inc.; p. 162 Canadian Press/Adrian Wyld; p. 163 Digital Vision Ltd.; pp. 166–167 Ian Crysler; p. 172 Ian Crysler; p. 173 Ian Crysler; p. 175 Canadian Press/Brantford Expositor/ Brian Thompson; p. 176 Ian Crysler; p. 178 Ian Crysler; p. 180 Corel Collection; p. 181 Canadian Press/Andre Forget/COC; p. 185 Courtesy of North of Superior Tourism; p. 186 (top) Brian Summers/ firstlight.ca; p. 186 (bottom) Ian Crysler; p. 187 Leonard de Selva/CORBIS; p. 188 (background) Canadian Press/Edmonton Sun/Darryl Dyck; p. 188 (inset) Michael Newman/Photo Edit Inc.; p. 189 Ian Crysler; p. 190 Ian Crysler; p. 192 Ian Crysler; p. 196 Ian Crysler; p. 198 Ian Crysler; p. 201 Minden Pictures/ firstlight.ca; p. 202 Ian Crysler; p. 203 Photodisc/Getty Images; pp. 204–205 (background) James Lauritz/Digital Vision Ltd.; p. 204 (inset top) Mike Randolph/ Masterfile Corporation; p. 204 (inset bottom) Photo Link/ Photodisc/Getty Images; p. 205 (inset top) Lawrence Manning/ CORBIS; p. 205 (bottom) James Lauritz/Digital Vision Ltd.; p. 207 Ian Crysler; p. 208 Canadian Press/Ryan Remiorz; p. 209 Ian Crysler; p. 210 Ian Crysler; p. 212 Corel Collection *Cruise Ships*; p. 213 Ian Crysler; p. 215 Ian Crysler; p. 220 Ian Crysler; p. 224 Ian Crysler; p. 225 Ian Crysler; p. 226 Plain Pictures/firstlight.ca; p. 228 Ian Crysler; p. 230 Brand X/firstlight.ca; p. 232 Ian Crysler; p. 235 Photocanada.com; p. 236 Bayne Stanley/firstlight.ca; p. 236 (inset) Royalty-Free CORBIS; p. 236 (banner) Digital Vision Ltd.; p. 237 Ian Crysler; p. 238 Robert Holmes/CORBIS; p. 238 (inset) Canadian Press WFP/Ken Gigliotti; p. 239 Corel Collection Bears; p. 240 Corel Collection *Nesting Birds*; p. 241 Ian Crysler; p. 244 Royalty-Free CORBIS; pp 244–245 Tyrell Museum/Buddy Mays/CORBIS; p. 245 (centre) Corel Collection *Wilderness*; p. 245 (right) Photodisc/Getty Images; pp. 246–247 (background) Corel Collection *World Landmarks*; p. 247 (inset left) fotos and photos/Index Stock, Inc.; p. 247 (inset right) Photodisc/Getty Images; p. 248 Ian Crysler; p. 250 Ian Crysler; p. 255 Photodisc/ Getty Images; p. 256 Ian Crysler; p. 260 (top) Superstock/Maxx Images; p. 260 (bottom) Ian Crysler; p. 261 Ian Crysler; p. 265 Jose Luis Pelaez Inc./ CORBIS; p. 267 (left to right) Aspen Stock/ Maxx Images; Aspen Stock/Maxx Images; Aspen Stock/Maxx Images; S. Solum/ PhotoLink/Photodisc/Getty Images; Aspen Stock/ Maxx Images; p. 268 Ian Crysler; p. 269 Ian Crysler; p. 270 Ian Crysler; p. 271 Ian Crysler; p. 272 Photodisc/Getty Images; p. 273 Dave Starrett; p. 275 Ian Crysler; p. 276 Tom Wagner/ CORBIS SABA; p. 276 (inset) Fred Prouser/Reuters/CORBIS; p. 276 (banner and inset) Douglas Kirkland/CORBIS; p. 277 Ian Crysler; p. 282 (top) Kevin Welsh/Maxx Images; p. 282 (bottom left) Kevin Welsh/Maxx Images; p. 282 (bottom centre) Kevin Welsh/ Maxx Images; p. 282 (bottom right) Barry Winker/Maxx Images; p. 283 Ian Crysler; p. 284 Ian Crysler; p. 285 Ian Crysler; p. 288 Ian

Crysler; p. 291 Ian Crysler; p. 292 Ian Crysler; p. 294 Ian Crysler; p. 295 Ian Crysler; p. 298 (left) Mitch Kezar/Stone/ Getty Images; p. 298 (centre) William Taufic/CORBIS; p. 298 (right) Spencer Grant/Photo Edit, Inc.; p. 300 Ian Crysler; p. 301 Ian Crysler; p. 303 Melaine Acevedo/Botanica/Picture Arts; p. 304 Ian Crysler; p. 307 Ian Crysler; p. 308 Mary Ellen McQuay/ firstlight.ca; p. 309 Ian Crysler; p. 311 (top) Mike Agliolo/Photo Researchers, Inc.; p. 311 (bottom) Ian Crysler; p. 312 Ian Crysler; p. 316 Canadian Press/Tom Hanson; p. 317 Ian Crysler; p. 320 Ian Crysler; p. 325 Ian Crysler; p. 327 Ian Crysler; p. 328 Ian Crysler; p. 331 Ian Crysler; p. 332 Ian Crysler; p. 333 Ian Crysler; p. 336 Ian Crysler; pp. 340–341 Ian Crysler; p. 342 Ian Crysler; p. 345 Ian Crysler; p. 346 Ian Crysler; p. 347 (top) Ian Crysler; p. 347 (bottom) Photodisc/Getty Images; p. 348 Photodisc/ Getty Images; p. 353 Ian Crysler; p. 355 Ian Crysler; p. 356 Ian Crysler; p. 359 Ian Crysler; p. 362 Ian Crysler; p. 370 Ian Crysler; p. 373 Dave Thompson/Life File/ Getty Images; p. 373 (banner) Photodisc/ firstlight.ca; pp. 376–377 Ian Crysler; pp. 378–379 Genevieve Summers www.dancingwithtrees.com; p. 378 (inset) TCJ – John Gathright; p. 379 (inset) www.dancingwithtrees.com; p. 380 Ian Crysler; p. 381 Ian Crysler; p. 388 Ian Crysler; p. 389 Bettman/CORBIS; p. 391 (left) Courtesy of Gloria F. Gilmer, Ph.D.; p. 391 (right) Photodisc/ Getty Images; p. 392 (background) Canadian Press/Chuck Stoody; p. 392 (inset left) Ramin Talaie/CORBIS; p. 392 (inset right) Peter MacDiarmid/ Reuters/CORBIS; p. 393 Ian Crysler; p. 396 (top) CORBIS.firstlight.ca; p. 396 (bottom) Ian Crysler; p. 397 Canadian Press/Ryan Remiorz; p. 400 Ian Crysler; p. 401 Ian Crysler; p. 404 Ian Crysler; p. 405 Genevieve Summers www.dancingwithtrees.com; pp. 406–407 European Space Agency/Science Photo Library; p. 410 Ian Crysler; p. 411 Ian Crysler; p. 415 Ian Crysler; p. 417 Ian Crysler; p. 419 Digital Vision Ltd.; p. 420 Ian Crysler; p. 421 Ian Crysler; p. 422 Ian Crysler; p. 423 Ian Crysler; p. 424 Ian Crysler; p. 425 Ian Crysler; p. 427 Ian Crysler; p. 430 Ian Crysler; p. 431 Ian Crysler

Illustrations

Steve Attoe
Francois Escalmel
Philippe Germain
Stephen MacEachern
Steve Mack
Dave Mazierski
Paul McCusker
Allan Moon
NSV Productions
Dusan Petriçic
Michel Rabagliati
Paul Rivoche
Carl Wiens

The Geometers Sketchpad, Key Curriculum Press, 1150 65th Street, Emeryville, CA 94608, 1-800-995-MATH, www.keypress.com/sketchpad.

AppleWorks is a trade-mark of Apple Computer, Inc. registered in the U.S. and other countries